Nazism, the Holocaust, and the Middle East

## Vermont Studies on Nazi Germany and the Holocaust

General Editor:
**Alan E. Steinweis,** Miller Distinguished Professor of Holocaust Studies and Director of the Carolyn and Leonard Miller Center for Holocaust Studies, University of Vermont

Editorial Committee:
**Jonathan D. Huener,** University of Vermont
**Francis R. Nicosia,** University of Vermont
**Susanna Schrafstetter,** University of Vermont

The University of Vermont has been an important venue for research on the Holocaust since Raul Hilberg began his work there in 1956. These volumes reflect the scholarly activity of UVM's Miller Center for Holocaust Studies. They combine original research with interpretive synthesis, and address research questions of interdisciplinary and international interest.

*Medicine and Medical Ethics in Nazi Germany: Origins, Practices, Legacies*
Edited by Francis R. Nicosia and Jonathan Huener

*Business and Industry in Nazi Germany*
Edited by Francis R. Nicosia and Jonathan Huener

*The Arts in Nazi Germany: Continuity, Conformity, Change*
Edited by Jonathan Huener and Francis R. Nicosia

*Jewish Life in Nazi Germany: Dilemmas and Responses*
Edited by Francis R. Nicosia and David Scrase

*The Law in Nazi Germany: Ideology, Opportunism, and the Perversion of Justice*
Edited by Alan E. Steinweis and Robert D. Rachlin

*The Germans and the Holocaust: Popular Responses to the Persecution and Murder of the Jews*
Edited by Susanna Schraftetter and Alan E. Steinweis

*Nazism, the Holocaust, and the Middle East: Arab and Turkish Responses*
Edited by Francis R. Nicosia and Boğaç A. Ergene

# Nazism, the Holocaust, and the Middle East

## Arab and Turkish Responses

*Edited by*
Francis R. Nicosia
*and*
Boğaç A. Ergene

Published in 2018 by
Berghahn Books
www.berghahnbooks.com

© 2018, 2019 Carolyn and Leonard Miller Center for Holocaust Studies,
University of Vermont
First paperback edition published in 2019

All rights reserved. Except for the quotation of short passages
for the purposes of criticism and review, no part of this book
may be reproduced in any form or by any means, electronic or
mechanical, including photocopying, recording, or any information
storage and retrieval system now known or to be invented,
without written permission of the publisher.

**Library of Congress Cataloging-in-Publication Data**

Names: Nicosia, Francis R., editor. | Ergene, Boğaç A., editor.
Title: Nazism, the Holocaust, and the Middle East : Arab and Turkish responses
 / edited by Francis R. Nicosia and Boğaç Ergene.
Description: Oxford ; New York : Berghahn Books, 2018. | Series: Vermont
 studies on Nazi Germany and the Holocaust | Includes bibliographical
 references and index.
Identifiers: LCCN 2017050574 (print) | LCCN 2017056443 (ebook) | ISBN
 9781785337857 (eBook) | ISBN 9781785337840 | ISBN 9781785337840
 (hardback : alk. paper)
Subjects: LCSH: Holocaust, Jewish (1939-1945)—Public opinion. | Public
 opinion—Middle East. | Public opinion—Africa, North. | Arabs—Attitudes.
 | Turks—Attitudes. | Antisemitism—Public opinion. | Antisemitism—
 Germany—Public opinion. | Antisemitism—Middle East. | Antisemitism—
 Africa, North. | National socialism—Public opinion.
Classification: LCC D804.45.M628 (ebook) | LCC D804.45.M628 N39 2018
 (print) | DDC 940.53/180956—dc23
LC record available at https://lccn.loc.gov/2017050574

**British Library Cataloguing in Publication Data**

A catalogue record for this book is available from the British Library

ISBN 978-1-78533-784-0 hardback
ISBN 978-1-78920-503-9 paperback
ISBN 978-1-78533-785-7 ebook

*Today the Arabs' belief in England is not what it was . . . If England does not take up the cause of the Arabs, other Powers will. From India, Mesopotamia, the Hedjaz, and Palestine the cry goes up to England now. If she does not listen then perhaps Russia will take up their call someday, or perhaps even Germany.*

> — Memorandum of the Arab Delegation presented to Winston Churchill at a meeting with him in Haifa, March 1921

*Als völkischer Mann, der den Wert des Menschentums nach rassischen Grundlagen abschätzt, darf ich schon aus der Erkenntnis der rassischen Minderwertigkeit dieser sogenannten "unterdrückten Nationen" nicht das Schicksal des eigenen Volkes mit dem ihren verketten.*

(*As a folkish man who estimates the value of humanity on racial bases, I may not, simply because of my knowledge of their racial inferiority, link my own people's fate with that of these so-called "oppressed nations."*)

> — Adolf Hitler, *Mein Kampf*

# Contents

| | |
|---|---|
| List of Illustrations | x |
| Preface | xii |
| Abbreviations | xv |
| Introduction: Responses to Nazism and the Holocaust in the Middle East and North Africa<br>*Francis R. Nicosia and Boğaç A. Ergene* | 1 |
| 1. Arab Reactions to Nazism and the Holocaust: Scholarship and the "War of Narratives"<br>*Gilbert Achcar* | 23 |
| 2. Turkish Responses to the Holocaust: Ankara's Policy toward the Jews, 1933–1945<br>*Corry Guttstadt* | 42 |
| 3. Demon and Infidel: Egyptian Intellectuals Confronting Hitler and Nazism during World War II<br>*Israel Gershoni* | 77 |
| 4. The Persecution of the Jews in Germany in Egyptian and Palestinian Public Discourses, 1933–1939<br>*Esther Webman* | 105 |
| 5. Defining the Nation: Discussing Nazi Ideology in Syria and Lebanon during the 1930s<br>*Götz Nordbruch* | 128 |

6. Mosul as Paradise: Nazis, Angels, Jewish Soldiers, and
   the Jewish Community in Northern Iraq, 1941–1943      153
   *Orit Bashkin*

7. Philo-Sephardism, Anti-Semitism, and Arab Nationalism:
   Muslims and Jews in the Spanish Protectorate of Morocco
   during the Third Reich                                 179
   *Daniel J. Schroeter*

Appendixes

    A. "The Jewish Question"                                216
        Article by Hüseyin Cahit Yalçın, in the Turkish
        Newspaper *Yeni Sabah*, 24 January 1939

    B. German–Turkish Non-Aggression Pact Signed at Ankara,
       18 June 1941                                         219

    C. "Immigration to the United States is Best!!
       The Supporters of Immigration to Palestine Are Few!!"    221
       Article in the Palestinian Newspaper *Filastin*,
       15 July 1938

    D. "The Policy of Force and Violence in the World"         223
       Article in the Egyptian Newspaper *Al-Ahram*,
       15 November 1938

    E. Memorandum on the Arab Question by the Director
       of the Political Department of the German Foreign
       Office, 7 March 1941                                  226

    F. Telegram from German Foreign Minister Joachim
       von Ribbentrop on Axis Policy and Arab Independence,
       20 July 1941                                          236

    G. The High Commissioner of Spain in Morocco [Luis Orgaz]
       to His Excellency, the Minister of Foreign Affairs [Ramón
       Serrano Súñer], Madrid, 25 October 1941               237

    H. Ambassador of France in Spain [François Piétri] to
       Mr. Admiral of the Fleet, Minister Secretary of State
       for Foreign Affairs [François Darlan], 15 December 1941   240

I. Letter from Amin al-Husayni and Raschid Ali al-Gailani
   to the German Foreign Minister Joachim von Ribbentrop,
   28 April 1942 — 242

J. Memorandum from Amin al-Husayni, Berlin, to
   an Unknown Recipient, 20 October 1943 — 243

K. Letter from Amin al-Husayni to German Foreign
   Minister Joachim von Ribbentrop, Regarding the
   Movement of Jews to Palestine, 25 July 1944 — 246

Index — 248

# Illustrations

## Figures

2.1. A cartoon from the front page of the Turkish magazine *Karikatür* with an image of a German soldier "drunk from victory," August 1940.    47

2.2. An anti-Semitic cartoon from the Nazi newspaper *Der Stürmer* reprinted in the Turkish newspaper *Millî İnkılâp*, July 1934.    51

2.3. An anti-Semitic cartoon that appeared in the Turkish publication *Akbaba* depicting a Jew counting his money, 1934.    52

2.4. An anti-Semitic cartoon that appeared in the Turkish publication *Akbaba* depicting a Jew talking to his son, 1939.    53

3.1. An anti-Nazi cartoon that appeared in the Egyptian journal *Ruz al-Yusuf*, 9 September 1939.    78

4.1. Photograph of the visit of the Palestine Symphony Orchestra in Egypt, January 1937.    109

4.2. Photograph of a gathering of Muslim, Christian, and Jewish employees of the newspaper *La Bourse Egyptiene*, late 1930s.    118

5.1. Photograph of Constantin Zurayq (no date).    142

*Illustrations*

6.1. Photograph of members of the Polish II Corps (Anders' Army) attending an outdoor class at their military base in Iraq, 1942–1943   166

6.2. Watercolor landscape of a wooded grove, by Edward Henryk Herzbaum.   170

6.3. Pencil portrait of a young man, by Edward Henryk Herzbaum.   171

6.4. Pencil drawing of a young Dorcas gazelle, by Edward Henryk Herzbaum.   172

7.1. Photograph of Moroccan Khalifa Mulay El Hassan Ben el Mehdi with Spanish High Commissioner Luis Orgaz Yoldi, 1936.   204

# Maps

0.1. Map of European-controlled states of North Africa, 1914.   9

0.2. Map of the Anglo-French Mandates in the Fertile Crescent, 1922.   10

6.1. Map of Iraq during World War II, with religious and ethnic concentrations.   154

7.1. Map of Spanish Protectorate in Morocco during World War II.   180

# Preface

THE SEVEN CHAPTERS IN THIS book are based on lectures delivered at the symposium "Responses in the Middle East to Nazi Germany and the Holocaust," which took place at the University of Vermont in April 2015. The symposium was organized and sponsored by the Carolyn and Leonard Miller Center for Holocaust Studies at the University of Vermont, with support from the university's Middle East Studies Program. This was the seventh symposium bearing the names of the late Carolyn and Leonard Miller, generous supporters of the Center's work over the years and great friends of the University of Vermont.

Established to honor the work of Professor Raul Hilberg, who served on the faculty of the University of Vermont for more than three decades, the Center for Holocaust Studies is committed to furthering the cause of Holocaust education and to serving as a forum for the presentation and discussion of new perspectives on the history of Nazi Germany and the Holocaust. Professor Hilberg's pioneering scholarship on the history of the Holocaust remains a model and a standard for scholars, and it is his work in the field that has served as an inspiration for the Center's programming and for publications such as this. The Miller Symposia have contributed significantly to the Center's efforts to explore insufficiently charted areas in the history of the Third Reich and the Holocaust. Our goal in organizing them has been to address topical as well as controversial themes in that history, relying on the expertise of some of the most accomplished scholars and other authorities in the field.

The first Miller Symposium, held in April 2000, addressed the question of eugenics and the German medical establishment during the Third Reich. It resulted in the anthology *Medicine and Medical Ethics in Nazi Germany: Origins, Practices, Legacies,* published by Berghahn Books in 2002. The second Miller Symposium, with its focus on German business and industry under National Socialism, took place in April 2002. It dealt with the topic of German business, industry, and finance in the years of the Third Reich. The resulting volume, *Business and Industry in Nazi Germany*, was published by Berghahn Books in 2004. The third Miller Symposium in April 2004 considered the history of the arts in Germany under National Socialism. The volume *The Arts in Nazi Germany: Continuity, Conformity, Change*, published by Berghahn Books in 2006, addresses the roles of artists, writers, musicians, filmmakers, Jewish cultural institutions, American cultural influence, and German youth in the life of the Nazi state. The fourth Miller Symposium in April 2006 brought to the University of Vermont scholars of the history of Jews and Jewish life in Nazi Germany. Their presentations focused on the everyday lives of ordinary German Jews under the steadily increasing persecution by the Nazi state after 1933 and through the beginning of the genocide in 1941. The proceedings from that symposium were published by Berghahn Books in 2010 with the title *Jewish Life in Nazi Germany: Dilemmas and Responses*. In April 2009, the fifth Miller Symposium took place at the University of Vermont and addressed the question of the law and the legal profession in Nazi Germany. From that symposium, Berghahn Books published the book *The Law in Nazi Germany: Ideology, Opportunism, and the Perversion of Justice* in 2013. Finally, the sixth Miller symposium in April 2012 dealt with the question of "ordinary" Germans during the Third Reich, how much they knew about the persecution and mass murder of the Jews, and how they responded as individuals and collectively. The proceedings were published by Berghahn Books in 2015 under the title *Germans and the Holocaust: Popular Responses to the Persecution and Murder of the Jews*.

This volume and the seventh Miller Symposium that produced it represent a slight departure from the previous six Miller Symposia and subsequent Berghahn volumes. Their focus is on people, organizations, and institutions in the Arabic-speaking lands of the Middle East and North Africa and in Turkey, and not on Germany and Europe, during the years of the Third Reich and the Holocaust. Therefore, while leading scholars of the history of modern Europe, modern Germany, and the Holocaust naturally participated in the previous six symposia and conference volumes, the participants in the seventh Miller Symposium and contributors to this volume are scholars of the Middle East and North Africa who study the history, societies, and cultures of the region. Moreover, they are able to do research in the languages of the region, including Arabic, Hebrew, and Turkish. They have published extensively on this particular aspect of that region's recent history, which is the focus this volume. In brief, they possess the scholarly qualifications and focus to help us understand this very important but, until recently, somewhat neglected part of the larger history of Nazi Germany and the Holocaust in Europe.

Once again, we wish to thank the late Carolyn and Leonard Miller and their family for their continued support over the years, as well as our colleagues and staff at the Miller Center for Holocaust Studies at the University of Vermont. The editors—one a historian of Nazi Germany and the Holocaust, the other a historian of the Middle East—hope that this volume will be useful for scholars and students in a variety of educational and institutional settings, in the fields of both the history of Nazi Germany and the Holocaust and the history of the modern Middle East and North Africa.

# Abbreviations

| | |
|---|---|
| ADAP | Akten zur deutschen auswärtigen Politik |
| BCA | Başbakanlık Cumhuriyet Arşivi (Prime Ministry's Republican Archive), Ankara |
| BNR | Bibliothèque Nationale du Royaume du Maroc (National Library of the Kingdom of Morocco), Rabat |
| CDJC | Centre de Documentation Juive Contemporaine (Documentation Center for Contemporary Jewry), Paris |
| CGQJ | Commissariat Général aux Questions Juives (General Commissariat for Jewish Questions) |
| CHP | Cumhuriyet Halk Partisi (Republican People's Party) |
| CZA | Central Zionist Archives, Jerusalem |
| DGFP | Documents on German Foreign Policy 1918–1945 |
| EU | European Union |
| FO | Foreign Office, London |
| MHP | Milliyetçi Hareket Partisi (Nationalist Action Party) |
| NSDAP | Nationalsozialistische Deutsche Arbeiterpartei (National Socialist German Workers' Party) |
| PAAA | Politisches Archiv des Auswärtigen Amts (Political Archive of the Federal Foreign Office), Berlin |
| TNA | The National Archives, London |
| USHMM | United States Holocaust Memorial Museum, Washington, DC |
| VAM | Verein Aktives Museum, Berlin |
| WJC | World Jewish Congress, New York |
| WZO | World Zionist Organization |
| ZMO | Zentrum Moderner Orient (Center for Modern Oriental Studies), Berlin |

*Introduction*

# RESPONSES TO NAZISM AND THE HOLOCAUST IN THE MIDDLE EAST AND NORTH AFRICA

*Francis R. Nicosia and Boğaç A. Ergene*

THE CLOSE GEOGRAPHICAL PROXIMITY OF the Middle East and North Africa (MENA) to Europe is a significant factor in the modern history of Europe, Germany, World War II, and the Holocaust. This large, ethnically, culturally, religiously, and politically diverse region once again became an important theater of war for European and other great powers in 1940. It was also home to ancient Jewish communities in the Arab world, Turkey, and Iran, communities with a combined population of about one million Jews. The fate of these Jewish communities during World War II and the Holocaust in Europe hung in the balance, pending the outcome of the war. In a region so close to German-occupied Europe during World War II, Hitler's regime, in anticipation of victory in the war, intended to extend the "final solution" to the Jews of the Middle East and North Africa. Logistically, this would not have been difficult for the Nazi government given the close proximity of those communities to Europe, their much smaller numbers in comparison to the Jewish population in Europe, and the existence of some degree of animosity or indifference toward Jews among the populations of the MENA region.

This volume considers how some of those diverse populations in the MENA—predominantly, but not exclusively, Arab and Turkish, and predominantly, but not exclusively, Muslim—responded to the possibility of a German victory in the war and to the prospect of Axis domination in some form in those regions. How did they respond to the political philosophy of Fascism in general, particularly to German National Socialism, in Europe? How did they view the second struggle within a generation among the world's existing great powers, in Europe and beyond? How did they react to Nazi anti-Semitism and propaganda, to Nazi persecution of Jews in Germany, and, ultimately, to the systematic mass murder of the Jews in Europe? How much did they know about what was happening to the Jews in Germany and Europe, just some hundreds of kilometers away? And how did they connect these issues with their own interests, within the context of existing and expanding European strategic interests and ambitions in their part of the world?

In recent years, events in the Middle East and beyond have generated a renewed interest among scholars and others in the relationship between Hitler's Germany, Arab states, and the nationalist government of the new Turkish state that emerged after World War I. This is especially true with regard to World War II, within the context of the Nazi persecution and mass murder of the Jews in Europe. Before this, a few scholarly studies appeared beginning in the 1960s, studies that focused on the aims and policies of Nazi Germany in the Middle East. Few if any provided much detail on the reactions of Arab, Turkish, and other leaders, intellectuals, and general populations to German National Socialism, Nazi Jewish policy, and the Holocaust.[1] However, much of the more recent literature has provided more substantive examinations of the responses of the Arab, Turkish, and other populations in the MENA to Nazism, German and European anti-Semitism, and the persecution and destruction of the Jews in Europe. Moreover, with regard to the Arab populations of the MENA region, some consider these responses during World War II and in the turbulent decades in that part of the world after 1945.

Some of the recent literature addresses those responses in the large, complex, and highly diverse Arab world, a region that stretches from the Atlantic coast of Morocco in the west to the Persian Gulf and Iraq's border with Iran in the east, and from the Syrian and Iraqi borders with Turkey in the north to the southern coast of the Arabian Peninsula. It includes the works of authors who are not specifically scholars of the history, societies, and cultures of the Middle East or North Africa.[2] In his analysis of Nazi propaganda in the Middle East during the World War II, Jeffrey Herf observes that the Nazi state, party and the German military "made strenuous efforts with the resources at their disposal to export the regime's ideology in ways that they hoped would strike a nerve among

Arabs and Muslims."[3] He also points out that Allied and German intelligence services "all found evidence that there were individuals and groups from which the Axis might have expected strong support."[4] Scholars of the history of the Third Reich and World War II would certainly agree with Herf's first point, while most scholars of modern Middle Eastern history would concur with the second. Klaus-Michael Mallmann and Martin Cüppers present significant information about Nazi plans and activities with regard to the Middle East during the World War II. This would include efforts to intensify hatred of the Jews among the Arab populations and evidence for Nazi plans to extend the mass murder of the Jews in Europe to the ancient Jewish communities in the Arab lands of the Middle East and North Africa.[5] Their focus on the handful of Arab exiles in wartime Berlin and Rome is indeed important for understanding German and Axis policy toward the Arab world during the war. However, a focus on those Arab exiles in wartime Berlin alone is not an adequate lens for understanding how the diverse populations, organizations, and institutions in the Arab world responded to National Socialism and the Holocaust in Europe.

Much of this recent literature has tended to attribute Arab violence against the Jews in Palestine and elsewhere in the region during those years to a historically rooted, religiously and culturally based hatred of Jews. Klaus Gensicke links the Mufti's particular hatred of the Jews to Arabs in general: "This fanatical extremism has become a tradition that remains as virulent as it was at the time of the 'great uprising' (1936–1939) and represents a failed policy of refusal to compromise, of irreconcilability, and of 'all or nothing.'"[6] Mallmann and Cüppers speculate that the anti-Semitic potential of the Arabs as a whole in 1942, as Rommel seemed poised to achieve victory over Great Britain in Egypt and eventually Palestine, was the same as that among those Europeans who collaborated with the Germans in the genocide against the Jews: "There is no reason, therefore, why the anti-Semitic potential of the Lithuanian, Latvian, or Ukrainian nationalists should have been greater than that of the Arabs as they awaited the German army."[7] In drawing conclusions about Nazi wartime propaganda to the Arab world, a joint effort of the Nazi regime and Arab exiles in Berlin, Herf concludes: "Nazi Germany's Arabic-language propaganda during World War II was the product of a remarkable political and ideological synthesis that took place in wartime Berlin . . . These materials displayed a synthesis of Nazism, Arab nationalism, and fundamentalist Islam."[8] While each of these three points may indeed possess some element of truth for some

Arabs, they also infer general truths about Arabs, Arab history, Arab nationalism, Islam, and Arab responses to National Socialism. As such, they exist without a necessary non-European, non-Western or Middle Eastern historical context.

These historians, along with historians and other scholars of the Middle East and Islam, have taken up the issue of Nazi hopes that Arabs might help them against the Jewish populations of the MENA. As a result, a rapidly growing body of scholarly work has appeared, one that includes monographs, collections of essays, and individual journal articles by scholars of Europe, North Africa, the Middle East, and Islam, including the contributors to this volume, scholars who have examined the complexities and varieties of both Arab and Turkish responses to Hitler's Germany.[9]

The chapters in this volume are authored by regional specialists familiar with local sources and languages of the region, who are able to produce scholarship informed by contextual nuances and variables. In this sense, these chapters are not derivatives of European-centered scholarship on the Holocaust. They exhibit a general recognition of the considerable size, diversity, and complexity of the Middle East and North Africa, and of the consequent multiplicity and range of attitudes and responses to these questions. These varied responses, the natural consequence of such a diverse region, preclude generalizations about the Arab world and Turkey in the 1930s and 1940s. Their knowledge and understanding of the modern history of the region, as well as their research in Arabic, Turkish, Hebrew, and other sources, provide a necessary context for the debates that arise from this very sensitive topic.

The chapters in this collection reflect the "state of the art" in Holocaust Studies that focuses on peoples in the Middle East and North Africa. The volume begins with Gilbert Achcar's reflections on how the Holocaust has shaped the conflicting discourses of the Zionist and non-/anti-Zionist parties in the Arab-Israeli conflict and how, in return, its memory came to be shaped by them. There is evidence for the latter in the attempts to characterize contemporary Palestinians and Arabs in general as supporters of the Nazi policies of Jewish eradication and of the relative popularity of Holocaust denial in the Arab world and beyond. Against such politically motivated and often ahistorical inclinations to redefine the past, Achcar invites all parties to the conflict to acknowledge and dispel their personal biases and prejudices, without which a peaceful engagement among them might be impossible.

The remaining six chapters provide rare and region-specific information about how various communities responded to Hitler's rise to power and to Nazi policies toward European Jews. With this in mind, it is not surprising that the primary task of a number of the chapters is to challenge some prevalent assumptions by providing nuanced and source-based counterarguments. For example, Israel Gershoni's chapter demonstrates that British-controlled Egypt before the war was home to many anti-Fascist, anti-Nazi, and anti-Hitler intellectuals and writers, a fact that is not well known or acknowledged among students of the Holocaust. By focusing on the writings of three popular Egyptian intellectuals during World War II, Tawfiq al-Hakim, 'Abbas Mahmud al 'Aqqad, and Ahmad Hasan al-Zayyat, Gershoni demonstrates that a significant stream in the Egyptian public discourse condemned and rejected the Nazi policies and racism.

Esther Webman further complicates the question of Arab perceptions of the Holocaust in her chapter on two very important Arab newspapers, the Egyptian *al-Ahram,* and the Palestinian *Filastin,* in the 1930s. The chapter surveys how these publications represented the Nazis' rise to power in Germany, their persecution of the Jews, and how these reflections changed over time. It also reveals that the newspapers' coverage of the persecution of the Jews was complex and not entirely consistent. While the consequences of Jewish immigration and settlement in Palestine generated anti-Jewish feelings among Palestinian Arabs, this tendency was much less noticeable in the Egyptian paper, a finding consistent with Israel Gershoni's arguments.

Webman's observations regarding Egypt and Palestine find an echo in Götz Nordbruch's chapter on four major Syrian and Lebanese intellectual figures in the 1930s, Antun Sa'ada, Edmond Rabbath, Constantin Zurayq and Raif Khuri. Nordbruch's research on the writings of these individuals has identified diverging attitudes toward the Nazis and the fate of the European Jews at the time, a finding that must be understood within the context of a wide variety of local and historical factors that influenced the intellectuals' thinking. After the disintegration of the Ottoman Empire following World War I, the peoples of the Levant were busy building their political structures, defining their collective identities, and reimagining intercommunal relationships. Discrepancies in the opinions about these issues translated into a wide spectrum of views on the Jewish question in Europe.

Other chapters in this volume take the reader to the margins of the Middle East and North Africa: Turkey, Northern Iraq, and Morocco.

Corry Guttstadt's chapter looks into Turkey's relationship with Nazi Germany and Fascist Italy, and surveys that country's treatment of European Jewish refugees from Nazi persecution and its own Jewish minority during and after World War II. Although Turkey officially pursued a neutral foreign policy during the war, and many Turkish public voices rejected the persecution of European Jews, Guttstadt argues in her chapter that the Holocaust was largely unnoticed in public life. Furthermore, anti-Jewish and anti-Christian sentiments, related to various forms of Turkish nationalism, became increasingly prevalent in the country during the war. Orit Bashkin, on the other hand, demonstrates in her chapter that the Jewish communities in Northern Iraq possessed the ability and resources to defend themselves against regional and national threats. According to Bashkin, these threats, instead of being consequences of the popularization of Nazi ideology in the country, were connected to regional tensions and opportunistic inclinations on the part of government functionaries who desired to take advantage of a minority group in difficult times. Nevertheless, the Jews of northern Iraq managed to utilize the ethnic diversity in the region, which also included Kurdish, Turkoman, Sunni Arab, and Christian communities, and devised strategic alliances with other groups to shield themselves and their possessions during a very difficult period.

In his chapter, Daniel Schroeter surveys how various political movements and ideologies had an impact on the peoples of northern Africa, Jews, and others, specifically in the Spanish protectorate of Morocco during the 1930s and World War II. The main contribution of the chapter, consistent with the overall argument of this volume, is that the social, political, and legal circumstances of local Jewish communities in the region—in this case, Morocco and northwest Africa—can only be understood in the context of the imperialist rivalry between Spain and France. Additional contextual considerations include the popularity of various forms of nationalism and Pan-Islamic movements, and the intensification of Jewish settlement in Palestine, as well as the influence of European anti-Semitism. Without a nuanced appreciation of all these factors in relation to each other, it would be impossible to explain, for example, why the Spanish government defended Sephardi Jews in Morocco while it simultaneously promoted anti-Semitic ideas at home.

Cutting-edge research, such as that contained in the present volume, also provides insight into some of the potential and much-needed avenues of future development in the subfield. Although some regions in the MENA, particularly Egypt and Palestine, and to some extent Syria,

Lebanon, and Turkey, have received scholarly attention in recent years, there seems to be a dearth of scholarly research in European languages on others, including Iran, the Arabian Peninsula, and much of North Africa. Also, there is still a lack of *comparative* scholarship on Nazism and the Holocaust *within* the context of the Middle East and North Africa. Historical studies that focus on a particular region often remain confined to that setting and do not make concerted attempts to consider parallel trends in other parts of the Middle East or North Africa. When comparisons are made in scholarly works on this topic, they are often done within the context of European settings and events. Thus, Esther Webman's, Götz Nordbruch's and Daniel Schroeter's chapters, which seek to make explicit interregional comparisons, require our recognition and appreciation.

Moreover, this subfield has been developed for the most part by European, American, and Israeli scholars. With the exception of two, none of the contributors to this volume is indigenous to the regions on which they focus: Egypt, Syria, Palestine, Lebanon, Iraq, Morocco, and Turkey. While the contributors do make serious efforts to engage regional scholarship, indigenous historians and their viewpoints are generally underrepresented in the subfield. However, certain methodological choices are well represented in the collection. They include research based on systematic readings of contemporary newspapers, journals, and literary materials, as well as some focus on the lives, works, and actions of specific intellectuals in order to make broader generalizations about public opinion and societal attitudes toward Nazi Germany and the fate of Europe's Jews in the Holocaust. Political history also receives attention in the volume, as multiple contributors make use of government documents from official archives. Moreover, Orit Bashkin uses an exemplary ethnographic methodology. Beyond the confines of this volume, however, relatively little research exists on the lives and circumstances of indigenous Jewish communities all over the region, research that focuses on how these communities were uniquely affected by the rise of Hitler and Nazism in Germany. Besides Orit Bashkin's chapter on Jews in Iraq, Corry Guttstadt covers the relatively limited literature on the Jews of Turkey in the early and mid-twentieth century, thereby providing nuanced and contextually based understandings of these communities and their struggles at the time of the Holocaust and thereafter.

Finally, there is still a need to connect these discussions to broader historical trends and developments in the region. The history of modernization in the Middle East and North Africa begins in the mid-nineteenth century, and there now exists a growing literature on how this process influenced the lives of minorities, including Jewish communities in various parts of the Ottoman Empire, Qajar Iran, and Egypt.[10] This literature not only provides valuable information on how modern regional administrations governed their minorities but also reflects on intercommunal relationships involving different ethnic and confessional groups. To what extent can we understand the history of Jewish experience in the MENA before and during World War II without this background? It is within the contexts of broader historical trends that connected the nineteenth century to the twentieth century that the peoples of the region reacted to Nazism and the Holocaust. For example, it is difficult to separate the anti-Jewish sentiment and policies in modern Middle East from the Ottoman legacy pertaining to Muslim–non-Muslim relations. Thus, any consideration of the modern Turkish and Iraqi governments' policies toward their Jewish minorities should be based on this historical context in order to identify how intra-communal tensions and state-society relations in the Ottoman Empire influenced the historical processes related in the following pages. Similarly, should we not understand the attitudes toward Jewish peoples in Lebanon, Syria, Palestine, and Egypt in the broader context of the rising, regionally specific, nationalist movements, which again find their roots in the political and intellectual trends of the late nineteenth and early twentieth centuries?

Before we proceed to the chapters, it might be useful to present a summary of the actual intent and policies of Hitler's regime toward the region between 1933 and 1945. That some Arabs sought to make common cause with both Weimar and Nazi Germany in the decades following World War I is both clear and not surprising. It was a logical and inevitable outcome of a post–World War I settlement in the Middle East that clearly did not satisfy the goal of most Arabs for immediate national self-determination and independence from foreign rule. Winston Churchill met with a delegation of Muslim and Christian Arabs in Haifa during his visit to Palestine in March 1921, following Arab unrest and violence there in the immediate postwar years. With a postwar settlement that ignored the expectations and demands of Arabs throughout the region already in place, the atmosphere for this meeting was one of confrontation and recrimination. The Arabs expressed anger over what they perceived as broken promises and betrayal by the Allies during and immediately following World War I. By the time of Churchill's meeting with Arab leaders in Haifa, it had become clear that British and French control over the former Ottoman-Arab territories in the Fertile Crescent would be formalized with League of Nations Mandates. These included a British Mandate for Palestine, with a Jewish National Home that was to be incorporated into that Mandate. This major expansion of Anglo-French imperial control in the region, along with the continuation of European rule in all of North Africa and continuing British control over significant parts of the Arabian Peninsula, would preclude the attainment of Arab national self-determination and independence.

The Arab delegation issued the following warning to Churchill that would be of significance in the decades that followed: "Today the Arabs' belief in England is not what it was . . . If England does not take up the cause of the Arabs, other powers will. From India, Mesopotamia, the Hedjaz and Palestine the cry goes up to England now. If she does not listen, then perhaps Russia will take up their call someday, or perhaps even Germany."[11]

Germany's alliance with the Ottoman Empire during World War I did not preclude a continuation of friendly relations between the new Weimar government in Germany and the new nationalist Turkish Republic that emerged in Anatolia by 1923.[12] Moreover, a defeated Germany continued to enjoy a general sympathy among many Arab na-

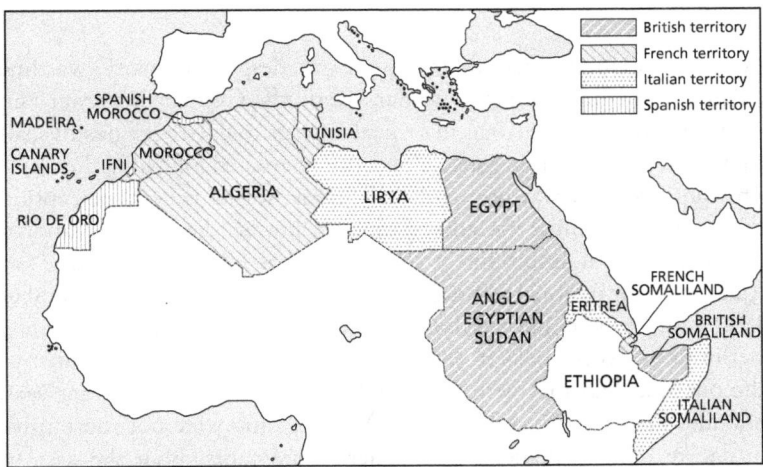

**Map 0.1.** Map of European-controlled states of North Africa, 1914. *Courtesy:* Cambridge University Press and Cox Cartographic Ltd.

*Introduction*

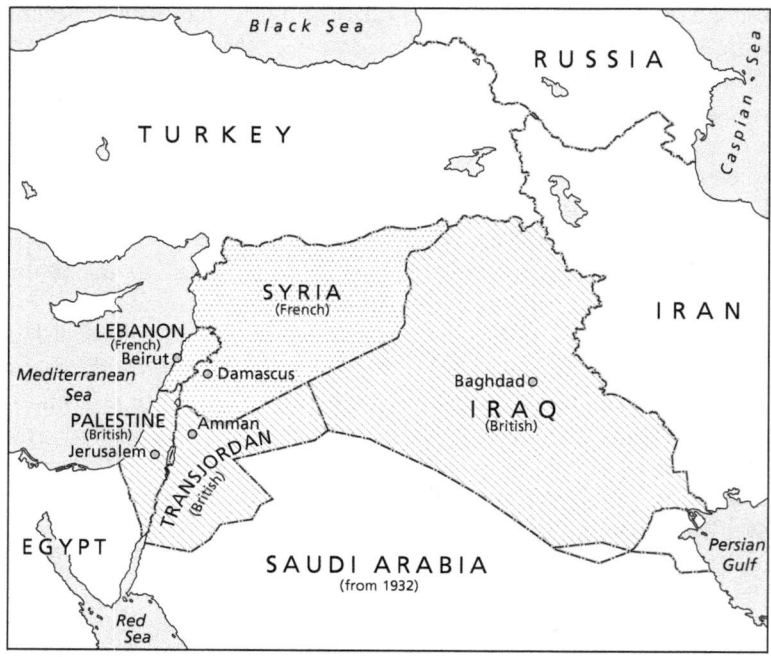

**Map 0.2.** Map of the Anglo-French Mandate states (Iraq, Syria, Lebanon, Transjordan, and Palestine), 1922. *Courtesy:* Cambridge University Press and Cox Cartographic Ltd.

tionalists and intellectuals following the war, despite Germany's wartime alliance with their former Ottoman overlords. Germany's prewar and wartime status among Arabs in general appears to have been positive, although not entirely above suspicion, and it persisted following the war.[13] This positive view was probably due in part to the general perception that Germany, unlike the other European powers, had never harbored tangible imperial ambitions in the region that might compromise the Arab quest for national self-determination in some form. In September 1921, the German ambassador in London, Friedrich Stahmer, notified Berlin of his recent talks in London with an Arab delegation similar to the one that had met with Churchill in Haifa in March of that year. Stahmer's conversations with the Arab delegation were not substantive in nature. They concluded with general statements about the wish of the "Arab people" and Germany to maintain friendly relations in the coming years. In his report to Berlin, Stahmer described the Arab view of past Arab-German relations in the following manner: "They have never had hostile feelings for Germany, having instead trusted Germany more than the other Great Powers because of their impression that, in the pursuit of its interests, Germany has never acted in a purely selfish manner, having instead respected the interests of the indigenous inhabitants."[14] Stahmer's meeting in London with the Arab delegation was the beginning of a succession of initiatives by various Arab nationalist leaders to enlist German diplomatic and later material support for ending the post–World War I status quo in the Middle East, based as it was on Anglo-French and Italian dominance in, and control over, most of the Arabic-speaking world. Some of these initiatives also demanded an end to the Jewish National Home in Palestine. These attempts to secure German support for Arab independence in whatever form are evident during the years of the Weimar Republic, and they continued with greater intensity through the 1930s and World War II.

This general sympathy for Germany following World War I also produced an important constant in German policy toward the Arab world, namely the consistent refusal of both the Weimar and Nazi governments to materially support Arab efforts to achieve real independence from de facto European control. Moreover, both consistently supported the security and territorial integrity of the Turkish state, with the Nazis, of course, supporting Turkish neutrality in World War II. The substance of Nazi Germany's ideological and strategic interests and policies in the Middle East and North Africa, beyond the platitudes about Arab independence and Arab-German-Islamic friendship contained in Nazi propaganda during World War II, was the maintenance of European dominance in some form in the Arab lands, along with the maintenance of an independent and neutral Turkey.[15]

Hitler's policy toward the Arab world reflected a degree of continuity from the Wilhelminian period through the Weimar years and the Third Reich. The Kaiser's government had generally accommodated itself to a status quo that included shared control among the Ottoman, British, French, Italian, and Spanish Empires over the lands of the southern and eastern Mediterranean Sea. It remained generally content with its expanding economic and cultural presence within the existing political structures as it pursued its own colonial ambitions in areas of the world beyond the Middle East and North Africa. Its alliance with the Ottomans in World War I and subsequent defeat precluded any role in the establishment of a postwar order in the region, one that would be based on an expansion of British and French control over the remaining

Ottoman-Arab territories of the Fertile Crescent. The end of World War I more or less completed a process begun almost a century earlier, namely the expansion of European imperial control over the Arab lands of the Fertile Crescent, the Arabian Peninsula, and North Africa. In general, the prewar status quo in the Arab world was retained, albeit without the Ottoman Empire, with an expanded Anglo-French presence in its place, and with the new Jewish National Home in Palestine under British authority, as mandated by the new League of Nations.

The primary foreign policy focus of the new German republic beginning in 1919 was the peaceful revision of much of the postwar settlement in Europe, as contained in the Versailles Treaty. As such, Arabs, particularly in the new Mandates in the Fertile Crescent, viewed Germany as a fellow victim of imposed peace settlements. Given its military and political weakness and diplomatic isolation after the war, Weimar Germany was in no position to contest the new postwar order in the Middle East, even if it had wanted to. Indeed, the governments of the Weimar Republic did not inherit any compelling reasons to challenge the settlement in the Fertile Crescent and Arabia, while the states in North Africa simply remained under the control of their respective prewar European rulers. Therefore, Weimar Germany quietly pursued its rather modest interests in the southern and eastern Mediterranean regions, interests that more or less mirrored those of its Wilhelminian predecessor. It too defined Germany's interests in the Middle East primarily as economic and cultural; as was the case before 1914, the government in Berlin set out to promote those interests within the context of adhering to the political status quo in the region. With its primary focus on Europe, Weimar Germany accepted Anglo-French-Italian-Spanish imperial positions in the Middle East and North Africa, the emergence by 1923 of a modern Turkish national state, and the establishment and future development of the Jewish National Home in Palestine. Moreover, in its acceptance of the postwar settlement in the region, Weimar Germany's response to Arab efforts to reverse the settlement and to achieve Arab national self-determination and independence and an end to the Jewish National Home in Palestine ranged from indifference to outright rejection.[16]

Much like the governments of the Weimar Republic, Hitler's policy regarding Arab demands for independence also ranged from indifference to rejection, notwithstanding Nazi propaganda during the war.[17] Nazi racial ideology and geopolitical ambitions in Europe necessitated a general continuation of the status quo in the Middle East and North Africa, especially Turkish neutrality in the event of a European war. Hitler's quest for German "living space" in central and eastern Europe and his racial world view presumed the maintenance of European colonial rule over much of Africa, Asia, and the Middle East as part of a natural world order in which there was no place for the self-determination of "colonial peoples." Moreover, policies to end Jewish life in Germany between 1933 and 1941 required the dispossession and rapid emigration/deportation of the German Jews, preferably to destinations outside of Europe, including to the Jewish National Home in Palestine.[18] The reliance of Nazi Jewish policy on the continued existence of the Jewish National Home, albeit under British control, meant the rejection, at least before 1938, of Arab initiatives for German diplomatic and material support in their quest to end British colonial rule and the Jewish National Home in Palestine. Thus, Hitler's Germany during the prewar years, as was the case with previous German governments since the late nineteenth century, generally accepted the post–World War I status quo in the Middle East. This strategy changed somewhat in 1938 and 1939 as tensions in Europe increased with Hitler's pursuit of the annexation of Austria, the breakup of Czechoslovakia, and the looming war with Poland. However, Hitler soon realized that growing anti-colonial unrest in the British and French empires around the world was not enough to pressure London and Paris into accepting entirely his plans for central and Eastern Europe. By the summer of 1939, it was clear that Hitler would have to seek his goals in Europe through war. His altered policy of some encouragement and relatively insignificant material support for Arab unrest in Palestine and elsewhere in 1938 and 1939, meant primarily to distract Anglo-French attention from Central Europe rather than actually threaten the existence of the British and French empires, was ultimately unsuccessful.

Germany's victory over France in June 1940, coupled with Italy's entry into the war on Germany's side and the unsuccessful Italian invasions of Greece and Egypt in the fall, directly extended Germany's political and military involvement into the region. It also brought Hitler face to face with the conflicting French, Italian, and Spanish imperial interests in the Mediterranean region, with potential conflicts of interest in the Balkans and Syria between Italy and Turkey, and with Arab demands that a seemingly invincible and victorious Germany formally commit itself to support Arab independence. However, Hitler took the very clear position from the start that Italian interests and ambitions in the entire Mediterranean were paramount in Axis relations and policy, albeit in avoidance of conflict with Turkey. Moreover, France's colonial position in the region would have to be more or less preserved, in the interest of enlisting the support of Vichy France and French civilian and military officials in the colonies against Great Britain and the United States.[19] In the end, Arab hopes for a genuine Axis commitment to Arab independence were brushed aside by Hitler and, of course, by Mussolini, the French government in Vichy, and Franco's government in Spain. Yet, Nazi propaganda broadcasts to the region continued to preach Axis solidarity with Arabs and Muslims everywhere against their common "Anglo-American and Jewish enemies." Even as British forces easily defeated the brief pro-Axis coup of Rashid Ali al-Gaylani in Iraq and, with the assistance of French Gaullist troops, seized control of Syria and Lebanon from the Vichy French in May and June 1941, an explicit German commitment to Arab independence was never forthcoming. Repeated attempts by the increasingly frustrated Mufti of Jerusalem from his prewar and wartime exiles in Lebanon, Iraq, and, beginning in November 1941, Berlin, respectively, to secure such a commitment from Germany, remained unfulfilled.[20] Indeed, the only firm commitment for change in the Arab world that Nazi Germany hoped to undertake was the destruction of the Jewish National Home in Palestine and, with that, of the Jewish communities throughout the Middle East and North Africa.

Germany's primary focus on Europe and its military campaign in the Soviet Union meant that the resources necessary for a victory in the Middle East and North Africa would be limited. This problem was compounded by the infusion of American resources into the war and by the landing of Anglo-American forces in Northwest Africa on 8 November 1942. Moreover, Germany's continuing deference to the interests and ambitions of its Italian ally in North Africa and the Fertile Crescent, coupled with the perceived strategic requirements of protecting the imperial interests of Vichy France and Franco's Spain in North Africa, generally precluded an Axis commitment to Arab independence.[21] In the end, this policy produced no political or strategic advantages for the Axis war effort in the region. The arguments of Arab exiles in Berlin and Rome to Hitler and Mussolini that an Axis military victory in the Mediterranean region was possible only with a clear and active Axis commitment to Arab independence seemed to fall on deaf ears. Indeed, it is not at all certain that an Arab revolt would have occurred even if Hitler had made such an open and clear commitment in 1941 and 1942. With the possible exception of the short-lived pro-Axis coup in Iraq in April and May of 1941, the Arab world remained relatively quiet during the war years.

By the end of 1942, the tide of battle had turned decidedly against the Germans and their Italian allies in North Africa and especially in the Soviet Union. This made Germany's hitherto murky policy toward the Arabs increasingly irrelevant. The New Year 1943 would see the massive defeat of German forces at Stalingrad in February, followed by the final Axis defeat in Tunis and expulsion from North Africa in May. This end of an Axis presence anywhere in the Arab world relegated the Middle East and North Africa further to the periphery of Germany's strategic interests and policy for the remainder of the war. This in turn produced a new and very different imperative for Hitler's government, namely the immediate need to defend its rapidly shrinking position in Europe against Allied offensives from the Soviet Union in the East, from Italy in the South, and from an anticipated Allied invasion of France in the West.

By the fall of 1943, following Italy's surrender in early September, conflicting Italian, French, and Spanish imperial interests, along with Arab nationalism and independence and the elimination of the Jewish National Home in Palestine had for the most part ceased to have any relevance in German policy. Through late 1943 and 1944, the Mufti in Berlin concluded that Germany had never been in a position to help secure Arab independence after all and had in fact never really intended to do so.[22] Indeed, between 1942 and 1944, he found himself unable to reverse Germany's decision to send relatively small numbers of Jewish refugees from German-occupied Europe to Palestine in exchange for German nationals who had been in British custody since the beginning of the war.[23] The Mufti's role in the formation of the Muslim Waffen-SS (Handschar) division in Bosnia in 1943 had little if anything to do with Arab independence, the Middle East, and North Africa. That project was a German idea and a European creation, meant to support Germany's war effort in Europe. It consisted mostly of European Muslims and had little if anything to do with any interests the Nazi regime might still have had in the Middle East and North Africa during the final two years of the war.

**Francis R. Nicosia** is Professor of History Emeritus and Raul Hilberg Distinguished Professor of Holocaust Studies Emeritus at the University of Vermont. His fields of research are the history of the Third Reich, the Holocaust, German-Jewish history, and Nazi policy in the Middle East. His publications include *The Third Reich and the Palestine Question* (1985, 2000); *Zionism and Anti-Semitism in Nazi Germany* (2008, 2010); and *Nazi Germany and the Arab World* (2015, 2017). He is the coauthor (with

Donald Niewyk) of *The Columbia Guide to the Holocaust* (2000). He is also the editor of *Dokumente zur Geschichte des deutschen Zionismus 1933–1941* (2018), volume 77 of the "Schriftenreihe wissenschaftlicher Abhandlungen des Leo Baeck Instituts" series.

**Boğaç A. Ergene** is Professor of History at the University of Vermont. His main fields of research are Ottoman history and the history of Islamic law and legal practice. He is the author of *Local Court, Provincial Society and Justice in the Ottoman Empire: Legal Practice and Dispute Resolution in Çankırı and Kastamonu (1652–1744)* (2003), editor of *Judicial Practice: Institutions and Agents in the Islamic World* (2009), and coauthor (with Metin Coşgel) of *The Economics of Ottoman Justice: Trial and Settlement in a Sharia Court* (2016).

## Notes

Epigraphs: Doreen Ingrams, ed., *Palestine Papers, 1917–1922: Seeds of Conflict* (London, 1972), 118; Adolf Hitler, *Mein Kampf,* Jubiläumsausgabe anläßlich der Vollendung des 50. Lebensjahres des Führers (Munich, 1939), 655.
1. On the question of Nazi Germany's Middle East policy, there was some interest in the mid-1960s with the appearance of the following: Lukasz Hirszowicz, *The Third Reich and the Arab East* (London, 1966); Heinz Tillmann, *Deutschlands Araberpolitik im Zweiten Weltkrieg* (Berlin, 1965); Robert Melka, "The Axis and the Arab Middle East, 1930–1945," PhD diss., University of Minnesota, 1966; Mohamed-Kamal el Dessouki, "Hitler und der Nahe Osten," PhD diss., Free University of Berlin, 1963; Joseph B. Schechtman, *The Mufti and the Führer: The Rise and Fall of Haj Amin el-Husseini* (New York, 1965); and Johannes Glasneck, *Methoden der deutschen Propagandatätigkeit in der Türkei vor und während des Zweiten Weltkrieges* (Halle, 1966). Several additional works on specific aspects of Nazi Middle East policy appeared during the three decades following the 1960s, among them: Bernd Philipp Schröder, *Deutschland und der Mittlere Osten im Zweiten Weltkrieg* (Göttingen, 1975); Yair P. Hirschfeld, *Deutschland und Iran im Spielfeld der Mächte: Internationale Beziehungen unter Reza Schach, 1921–1941* (Düsseldorf, 1980); Francis R. Nicosia, *The Third Reich and the Palestine Question* (Austin, TX, 1985); Uriel Dann, ed., *The Great Powers and the Middle East, 1919–1939* (New York, 1988); and Stanford J. Shaw, *Turkey and the Holocaust: Turkey's Role in Rescuing Turkish and European Jewry from Nazi Persecution, 1933–1945* (New York, 1993).
2. Much of this literature focuses on the life and politics of the Grand Mufti of Jerusalem, Haj Amin al-Husayni, his opposition to Zionism and Jewish settlement in Palestine following World War I, and, in particular, his relationship with Nazi Germany and his exile in Berlin during World War II. They also

tend to emphasize Germany's propaganda campaign during the war. See, e.g., Klaus-Michael Mallmann and Martin Cüppers, *Halbmond und Hakenkreuz: Das Dritte Reich, die Araber und Palästina* (Darmstadt, 2006), published in English as *Nazi Palestine: The Plan for the Extermination of the Jews in Palestine,* trans. Krista Smith (New York, 2010); Klaus Gensicke, *Der Mufti von Jerusalem und die Nationalsozialisten: Eine politische Biographie Amin el-Husseinis* (Darmstadt, 2007), published in English as *The Mufti of Jerusalem and the Nazis: The Berlin Years,* trans. Alexander Fraser Gunn (London, 2011); Jeffrey Herf, *Nazi Propaganda for the Arab World* (New Haven, CT, 2009); Barry Rubin and Wolfgang G. Schwanitz, *Nazis, Islamists, and the Making of the Modern Middle East* (New Haven, CT, 2014); and Matthias Küntzel, *Djihad und Judenhaß: Über den neuen antijüdischen Krieg* (Freiburg, 2002), published in English as *Jihad and Jew-Hatred: Islamism, Nazism and the Roots of 9/11* trans. Colin Meade (New York, 2007). For the Mufti, see the useful collection of his essays in *Through the Eyes of the Mufti: The Essays of Haj Amin, Translated and Annotated,* ed. Zvi Elpeleg (London and Portland, OR, 2015).
3. Herf, *Nazi Propaganda,* 263
4. Ibid.
5. Mallmann and Cüppers, *Halbmond und Hakenkreuz,* 137.
6. Gensicke, *Der Mufti von Jerusalem,* 192.
7. Mallmann and Cüppers, *Halbmond und Hakenkreuz,* 164.
8. Herf, *Nazi Propaganda,* 261.
9. See, most recently, David Motadel, *Islam and Nazi Germany's War* (Cambridge, MA, 2014); Stefan Wild, ed., "Islamofascism?" special issue, *Die Welt des Islams: International Journal for the Study of Modern Islam,* 52, nos. 3–4 (2012); and Omar Kamil, *Der Holocaust im arabischen Gedächtnis: Eine Diskursgeschichte 1945–1967* (Göttingen, 2012). See also Corry Guttstadt, *Die Türkei, die Juden und der Holocaust* (Berlin, 2008), published in English as *Turkey, the Jews and the Holocaust,* trans. Kathleen M. Dell'Orto, Sabine Bartel, and Michelle Miles (New York, 2013); Götz Nordbruch, *Nazism in Syria and Lebanon: The Ambivalence of the German Option, 1933–1945* (New York, 2009); Gilbert Achcar, *The Arabs and the Holocaust: The Arab-Israeli War of Narratives* (New York, 2009); Meir Litvak and Esther Webman, *From Empathy to Denial: Arab Responses to the Holocaust* (New York, 2009); Peter Wien, *Iraqi Arab Nationalism: Authoritarian, Totalitarian, and Pro-Fascist Inclinations, 1932–1941* (New York, 2006); Israel Gershoni and Götz Nordbruch, *Sympathie und Schrecken: Begegnungen mit Faschismus und Nationalsozialismus in Ägypten 1922–1937* (Berlin, 2011); Gerhard Höpp, Peter Wien, and René Wildangel, eds., *Blind für die Geschichte? Arabische Begegnungen mit dem Nationalsozialismus* (Berlin, 2004); and Stanford J. Shaw, *Turkey and the Holocaust.* See also the articles in Ulrike Freitag and Israel Gershoni, eds., "Arab Encounters with Fascist Propaganda, 1933–1945," special issue, *Geschichte und Gesellschaft* 37, no. 3 (2011). These articles are from the international workshop "Arab Responses to Fascism and Nazism, 1933–1945: Reappraisals and New Directions," which took place at Tel Aviv University and the Open University in Israel in May 2010. An older but still very useful source on this question is Stefan Wild, "National Socialism in the Arab Near East Between 1933 and 1939," *Die Welt des Islams* 25 (1985).

10. See, e.g., Feroz Ahmed, *The Young Turks and the Ottoman Nationalities: Armenians, Greeks, Albanians, Jews, and Arabs, 1908–1918* (Salt Lake City, 2014); Michelle Campos, *Ottoman Brothers: Muslims, Christians, and Jews in Early Twentieth-century Palestine* (Stanford, CA, 2010); Julia P. Cohen, *Becoming Ottomans: Sephardi Jews and Imperial Citizenship in the Modern Era* (Oxford, 2014); Will Hanley, *Identifying with Nationality: Europeans, Ottomans, and Egyptians in Alexandria* (New York, 2017); Ussama Makdisi, *The Culture of Sectarianism: Community, History, and Violence in Nineteenth-Century Ottoman Lebanon* (Berkeley, CA, 2000); Bruce A. Masters, *Christians and Jews in the Ottoman Arab World: The Roots of Sectarianism* (New York, 2001); Devin E. Naar, *Jewish Salonica: Between the Ottoman Empire and Modern Greece* (Stanford, CA, 2016); Christine M. Philliou, *Biography of an Empire: Governing Ottomans in an Age of Revolution* (Berkeley, CA, 2011); and Daniel Tsadik, *Between Foreigners and Shi'is: Nineteenth-century Iran and Its Jewish Minority* (Stanford, CA, 2007).
11. Doreen Ingrams, ed., *Palestine Papers, 1917–1922: Seeds of Conflict* (London, 1972), 118.
12. For Turkey, see, e.g., Stefan Ihrig, *Atatürk in the Nazi Imagination* (Cambridge, MA, 2014), chaps. 1–3. See also Corry Guttstadt, *Turkey, the Jews and the Holocaust*; and Stanford J. Shaw, *Turkey and the Holocaust*.
13. See Götz Nordbruch, *Nazism in Syria and Lebanon*, 2–3.
14. Politisches Archiv des Auswärtigen Amts (hereinafter PAAA), Berlin: Pol.Abt. III, Politik 6-Palästina, Bd. I, DB-London an AA-Berlin, K.Nr. 69, 1 September 1921.
15. See Francis R. Nicosia, *Nazi Germany and the Arab World* (New York, 2015), 132–134.
16. This view is referred to often in the correspondence within the German Foreign Office in Berlin, and between it and German diplomatic missions in the Arab world and Turkey during the Weimar and Nazi periods. For the Weimar period, see, e.g., *Gustav Stresemann: His Diaries, Letters, and Papers*, vol. 1, ed. and trans. Eric Sutton (London, 1935), 317. See also PAAA: Botschaft Ankara, Pol.3-Palästina, 1924–1938, "Bericht über meine Reise nach Palästina im März und April 1925," III O 1269, and Pol.Abt. III, Politik 5, Bd. I, Aufzeichnung von Sobernheim an V.L.R. von Richthofen, 8 December 1924. See also Akten zur Deutschen Auswärtigen Politik (hereinafter ADAP), Serie B, Bd. II-1, 363–371.
17. For the Nazi period, see, e.g, Institut für Zeigeschichte (hereinafter IfZ): Nachlaß Werner-Otto von Hentig, ED 113/34, "Großarabien und die Lage in Syrien," Aufzeichnung Werner-Otto von Hentig, 26 February 1941; and ED 113/6, "Der Orient in seiner politischen Entwicklung seit dem Weltkrieg" (no date). See also Zentrum Moderner Orient (hereinafter ZMO): Nachlaß Höpp, 1.26, Aufzeichnung über Fragen des Vorderen Orients, Politische Abteilung, U.St.S. Pol.Nr. 959, 6 November 1941; ADAP: Serie D, Bd. XIII/2, Nr. 515. See more generally Francis R. Nicosia, *Nazi Germany and the Arab World*, chaps. 3–7.
18. See Francis R. Nicosia, *Zionism and Anti-Semitism in Nazi Germany* (New York, 2010).
19. See, e.g., Galeazzo Ciano, *Ciano's Diplomatic Papers*, ed. Malcolm Muggeridge, trans. Stuart Hood (London, 1948), 44, 246, 250–251, 258, 278; and Ga-

leazzo Ciano, *Ciano's Hidden Diary, 1937–1938*, ed. Malcolm Muggeridge, trans. Andreas Mayor (New York, 1953), 116, 191. See also Nir Arielli, *Fascist Italy and the Middle East, 1933–1940* (Basingstoke, 2010), 144–162; and Nicosia, *Nazi Germany and the Arab World*, 116–127, 154–179.
20. See, e.g., Amin al-Husayni *Mufti-Papiere: Briefe, Memoranden, Reden und Aufrufe Amin al-Husainis aus dem Exil, 1940–1945*, ed. Gerhard Höpp (Berlin, 2004), 20–23, 39–40, 67–71, 77–78, 91–92, 98–103, 107–112, 116–117, 137–141, 156–159, 183–189, 192–201, 226–228.
21. For France, see, e.g., ADAP: Serie D, Bd. IX, Nr. 479; and the memoirs of two German diplomats at the time, Rudolf Rahn, *Ruheloses Leben: Aufzeichnungen und Erinnerungen* (Düsseldorf, 1949), 145–146; and Otto Abetz, *Das offene Problem: Ein Rückblick auf zwei Jahrzehnte deutscher Frankreichpolitik* (Cologne, 1951), 130–131. See also Roland Ray, *Annäherung an Frankreich im Dienste Hitlers? Otto Abetz und die deutsche Frankreichpolitik 1930–1942* (Munich, 2000). For Spain, see, e.g., ADAP: Serie D, Bd. IX, Nr. 488; Galeazzo Ciano, *The Ciano Diaries 1939–1943*, ed. Hugh Gibson (Safety Harbor, FL, 2001), 312; Stanley Payne, *Franco and Hitler: Spain, Germany and World War II* (New Haven, CT, 2008), 72, 76–77; and Norman J. W. Goda, *Tomorrow the World: Hitler, Northwest Africa, and the Path toward America* (College Station, TX, 1998), chap. 2.
22. See Husayni, *Mufti-Papiere*, 160–162, 189, 215–216; PAAA: R2732, Handakten Ettel, Erlaß des RAM, Arbeitsexemplar, Bd.-, Gesandter Ettel, Aufzeichnung, 16 April 1943; IfZ: Nachlaß Werner-Otto von Hentig, ED 113/6, Aufzeichnung von Hentig, 27 April 1943, and ED 113/2, Abschrift Hamburg, 20 June 1957.
23. For more on the wartime exchange of Jews for German nationals, see Shlomo Aronson, *Hitler, the Allies, and the Jews* (New York, 2004), 330–331; Christopher Browning, *The Final Solution and the German Foreign Office* (New York, 1978), 102–108, 134–141, 164–170; Tuvia Friling, "Istanbul 1942–1945: The Kollek-Avriel and Berman-Ofner Networks," in *Secret Intelligence and the Holocaust: Collected Essays from the Colloquium at the City University of New York Graduate Center*, ed. David Bankier, (New York, 2006), 105–156; Francis R. Nicosia, *Nazi Germany and the Arab World*, 241–257; Dalia Ofer, *Escaping the Holocaust: Illegal Immigration to the Land of Israel, 1939–1944* (New York, 1990), 164, 189–198, 320; and Stanford J. Shaw, *Turkey and the Holocaust*, 256–258, 261–264, 268–269.

# Bibliography

## Archival Source

Politisches Archiv des Auswärtigen Amts. Pol.Abt.III, Politik 6-Palästina, Bd. I.

## Published Sources

Abetz, Otto. *Das offene Problem: Ein Rückblick auf zwei Jahrzehnte deutscher Frankreichpolitik.* Cologne, 1951.

Achcar, Gilbert. *The Arabs and the Holocaust: The Arab-Israeli War of Narratives.* New York, 2009.
Ahmed, Feroz. *The Young Turks and the Ottoman Nationalities: Armenians, Greeks, Albanians, Jews, and Arabs, 1908–1918.* Salt Lake City, 2014.
Arielli, Nir. *Fascist Italy and the Middle East, 1933–1940.* Basingstoke, 2010.
Aronson, Shlomo. *Hitler, the Allies, and the Jews.* New York, 2004.
Browning, Christopher. *The Final Solution and the German Foreign Office.* New York, 1978.
Campos, Michelle. *Ottoman Brothers: Muslims, Christians, and Jews in Early Twentieth-century Palestine.* Stanford, CA, 2010.
Ciano, Galeazzo. *Ciano's Diplomatic Papers.* Edited by Malcolm Muggeridge. Translated by Stuart Hood. London, 1948.
———. *Ciano's Hidden Diary, 1937–1938.* Edited by Malcolm Muggeridge. Translated by Andreas Mayor. New York, 1953.
———. *The Ciano Diaries, 1939–1943.* Edited by Hugh Gibson. Safety Harbor, FL, 2001
Cohen, Julia P. *Becoming Ottomans: Sephardi Jews and Imperial Citizenship in the Modern Era.* Oxford, 2014.
Dann, Uriel, ed. *The Great Powers and the Middle East, 1919–1939.* New York, 1988.
Dessouki, Mohamed-Kamal El. "Hitler und der Nahe Osten." PhD dissertation. Free University of Berlin, 1963.
Freitag, Ulrike, and Israel Gershoni, eds. "Arab Encounters with Fascist Propaganda, 1933–1945." Special issue, *Geschichte und Gesellschaft* 37, no. 3 (2011).
Friling, Tuvia. "Istanbul 1942–1945: The Kollek-Avriel and Berman-Ofner Networks." In *Secret Intelligence and the Holocaust: Collected Essays from the Colloquium at the City University of New York Graduate Center,* edited by David Bankier, 105–156. New York, 2006.
Gensicke, Klaus. *The Mufti of Jerusalem and the Nazis: The Berlin Years.* Translated by Alexander Fraser Gunn. London, 2011. Originally published as *Der Mufti von Jerusalem und die Nationalsozialisten: Eine politische Biographie Amin el-Husseinis* (Darmstadt, 2007).
Gershoni, Israel, and Götz Nordbruch. *Sympathie und Schrecken: Begegnungen mit Faschismus und Nationalsozialismus in Ägypten, 1922–1937.* Berlin, 2011.
Glasneck, Johannes. *Methoden der deutschen Propagandatätigkeit in der Türkei vor und während des Zweiten Weltkrieges.* Halle, 1966.
Goda, Norman J. W. *Tomorrow the World: Hitler, Northwest Africa, and the Path toward America.* College Station, TX, 1998.
Guttstadt, Corry. *Turkey, the Jews and the Holocaust.* Translated by Kathleen M. Dell'Orto, Sabine Bartel, and Michelle Miles. New York, 2013. Originally published as *Die Türkei, die Juden und der Holocaust* (Berlin, 2008).
Hanley, Will. *Identifying with Nationality: Europeans, Ottomans, and Egyptians in Alexandria.* New York, 2017.
Herf, Jeffrey. *Nazi Propaganda for the Arab World.* New Haven, CT, 2009.
Hirschfeld, Yair P. *Deutschland und Iran im Spielfeld der Mächte: Internationale Beziehungen unter Reza Schach, 1921–1941.* Düsseldorf, 1980.
Hirszowicz, Lukasz. *The Third Reich and the Arab East.* London, 1966.

Hitler, Adolf. *Mein Kampf.* Jubiläumsausgabe anläßlich der Vollendung des 50. Lebensjahres des Führers. Munich, 1939.

Höpp, Gerhard, Peter Wien, and René Wildangel, eds. *Blind für die Geschichte? Arabische Begegnungen mit dem Nationalsozialismus.* Berlin, 2004.

Husayni, Amin al-. *Mufti-Papiere: Briefe, Memoranden, Reden und Aufrufe Amin al-Husainis aus dem Exil, 1940–1945.* Edited by Gerhard Höpp. Berlin, 2004.

———. *Through the Eyes of the Mufti: The Essays of Haj Amin, Translated and Annotated.* Edited by Zvi Elpeleg. Translated by Rachel Kessel. London and Portland OR, 2015.

Ihrig, Stefan. *Atatürk in the Nazi Imagination.* Cambridge, MA, 2014.

Ingrams, Doreen, ed. *Palestine Papers, 1917–1922: Seeds of Conflict.* London, 1972.

Kamil, Omar. *Der Holocaust im arabischen Gedächtnis: Eine Diskursgeschichte 1945–1967.* Göttingen, 2012.

Küntzel, Matthias. *Jihad and Jew-Hatred: Islamism, Nazism and the Roots of 9/11.* Translated by Colin Meade. New York, 2007. Originally published as *Djihad und Judenhaß: Über den neuen antijüdischen Krieg.* Freiburg, 2002.

Litvak, Meir, and Esther Webman. *From Empathy to Denial: Arab Responses to the Holocaust.* New York, 2009.

Makdisi, Ussama. *The Culture of Sectarianism: Community, History, and Violence in Nineteenth-century Ottoman Lebanon.* Berkeley, 2000.

Mallmann, Klaus-Michael, and Martin Cüppers. *Nazi Palestine: The Plan for the Extermination of the Jews in Palestine.* Translated by Krista Smith. New York, 2010. Originally published as *Halbmond und Hakenkreuz. Das Dritte Reich, die Araber und Palästina* (Darmstadt, 2006).

Masters, Bruce A. *Christians and Jews in the Ottoman Arab World: The Roots of Sectarianism.* New York, 2001.

Melka, Robert. "The Axis and the Arab Middle East, 1930–1945," PhD dissertation. University of Minnesota, 1966.

Motadel, David. *Islam and Nazi Germany's War.* Cambridge, MA, 2014.

Naar, Devin E.. *Jewish Salonica: Between the Ottoman Empire and Modern Greece.* Stanford, CA, 2016.

Nicosia, Francis R. *Nazi Germany and the Arab World.* New York, 2015.

———. *The Third Reich and the Palestine Question.* Austin, TX, 1985.

———. *Zionism and Anti-Semitism in Nazi Germany.* New York, 2010.

Nordbruch, Götz. *Nazism in Syria and Lebanon: The Ambivalence of the German Option, 1933–1945.* New York, 2009.

Ofer, Dalia. *Escaping the Holocaust: Illegal Immigration to the Land of Israel, 1939–1944.* New York, 1990.

Payne, Stanley G. *Franco and Hitler: Spain, Germany and World War II.* New Haven, CT, 2008.

Philliou, Christine M. *Biography of an Empire: Governing Ottomans in an Age of Revolution.* Berkeley, 2011.

Ray, Roland. *Annäherung an Frankreich im Dienste Hitlers? Otto Abetz und die deutsche Frankreichpolitik 1930–1942.* Munich, 2000.

Rubin, Barry, and Wolfgang G. Schwanitz. *Nazis, Islamists, and the Making of the Modern Middle East.* New Haven, CT, 2014.

Rahn, Rudolf. *Ruheloses Leben: Aufzeichnungen und Erinnerungen.* Düsseldorf, 1949.

Schechtman, Joseph B. *The Mufti and the Führer: The Rise and Fall of Haj Amin el-Husseini.* New York, 1965.

Schröder, Bernd Philipp. *Deutschland und der Mittlere Osten im Zweiten Weltkrieg.* Göttingen, 1975.

Shaw, Stanford J. *Turkey and the Holocaust: Turkey's Role in Rescuing Turkish and European Jewry from Nazi Persecution, 1933–1945.* New York, 1993.

Stresemann, Gustav. *Gustav Stresemann: His Diaries, Letters, and Papers.* Vol. 1. Edited and translated by Eric Sutton. London, 1935.

Tillmann, Heinz. *Deutschlands Araberpolitik im Zweiten Weltkrieg.* Berlin, 1965.

Tsadik, Daniel. *Between Foreigners and Shi'is: Nineteenth-century Iran and Its Jewish Minority.* Stanford, CA, 2007.

Wien, Peter. *Iraqi Arab Nationalism: Authoritarian, Totalitarian, and Pro-Fascist Inclinations, 1932–1941.* New York, 2006.

Wild, Stefan, ed. "Islamofascism?" Special issue, *Die Welt des Islams: International Journal for the Study of Modern Islam,* 52, nos. 3–4 (2012).

———. "National Socialism in the Arab Near East Between 1933 and 1939." *Die Welt des Islams* 25 (1985): 126–173.

*Chapter 1*

# ARAB REACTIONS TO NAZISM AND THE HOLOCAUST
Scholarship and the "War of Narratives"

*Gilbert Achcar*

IN STUDYING THE VAST RANGE of attitudes and responses toward Nazism and the genocide of European Jews that the Nazis orchestrated and perpetrated—the unspeakable tragedy that has become common, albeit disputable and arguably unfortunate, to designate as the Holocaust[1]—there is hardly a topic fraught with as much tension and passion and charged with as much topicality as that of the attitudes displayed in the Arab Middle East or by individuals originating from there. This issue continues to generate a lot of heated discussion—more so even than, say, French or Polish reactions to Nazism and the Holocaust. This is despite the fact that France and Poland were countries directly involved in the perpetration of the Holocaust, whereas none of the Arab or other populations of the Middle East were involved in it.

The main reason for this paradox, surely, is to be found in the Arab-Zionist/Arab-Israeli conflict. We know from common experience that the simple association of the words "Arabs" with "Nazism" or "Holocaust" brings immediately to mind this century-old conflict, which has persisted to this day and continues to generate violence. As for why the association of the aforementioned words brings that conflict to mind, it is, of course, because Israel itself is, largely, a consequence of the culmination of European anti-Semitism in Nazism and the Holocaust. It is indeed a state that was brought into being by the settler migration endeavor that lies at the heart of the Zionist project. The latter originated in a Jewish reaction to anti-Semitism and was therefore decisively propelled by the advent of Nazism as the most acute and extreme form of anti-Semitism, going far beyond anything the founders of the Zionist movement might have imagined in their worst nightmares.

From the time of the United Nations debates that preceded the creation of the state of Israel in 1948 until our time, the various advocates of Zionism have consistently referred to the Holocaust as a crucial legitimizing argument. Invoking the Nazi genocide of the Jews has indeed been Zionism's principal answer to the Arab accusation that it has committed territorial usurpation and ethnic cleansing toward the Palestinians. One striking aspect of this confrontation between narratives is that the terms by which each side designates what it sees as its defining tragedy—the Hebrew term Shoah for the Holocaust, and the Arabic term Nakba for the Zionist takeover of most of Palestine, emptied of most of its original inhabitants—both mean "catastrophe." A major argument on the Zionist side has always been that the alternative to what the Palestinians designate as the Nakba would have been a continuation of the Holocaust in Palestine.[2]

Thus, the war of narratives has indeed been a crucial dimension of the Arab-Israeli conflict since 1948. Although one can find a symbolic confrontation of this kind in every conflict, with each side needing a suitable narrative for the mobilization of its partisans, nowhere to my knowledge did the war of narratives acquire an importance such as the one in the Arab-Israeli conflict, and nowhere does it fulfill a function such as the one in that conflict. This is because war-related narratives in the Arab-Israeli conflict serve much more than the internal function of ensuring each side's mobilization, cohesion, and determination. They serve also— as crucially, if not more so—an external function in the mobilization of support from abroad, beyond the sphere of those who are directly involved in the conflict. The Arab-Israeli war of narratives is indeed one that is fought largely overseas, on the battlefield of global public opinion and, principally, Western public opinion. The latter has been the most important historically because, on the one hand, of the European origin of Zionism, the location of the Holocaust in Europe, and Europe's proximity to the Middle East and, on the other hand, of the multifarious connections of the United States with Israel and the Middle East during the Cold War and after.

The primary reason for the particular importance of the war of narratives in the Arab- Israeli conflict is, however, not a matter of historical, ethnic, or cultural ties. It is rather rooted in the constitutive physical—territorial, demographic, and military—asymmetry between the Zionist/Israeli side and the Arab side. The Zionist project is itself originally predicated on a war of narratives within Jewish communities, with Zionism as an ideological current competing with other views, whether liberal assimilationist or Marxist internationalist. Since its crux consisted of a project of mass resettlement on a territory under foreign control, Zionism needed and sought, from its foundation, a sponsor among contemporary imperial powers, especially powers actually or potentially in charge of Palestine. It thus sought the green light of the Ottoman Empire before World War I and most crucially, during the war and thereafter, of the United Kingdom, which coveted Palestine and ended up controlling it under a League of Nations colonial mandate. Before that, in November 1917, London had expressed official support for the Zionist project in the Balfour Declaration, the letter sent by Foreign Secretary Arthur James Balfour to Baron Walter Rothschild declaring that the British government viewed with favor the establishment of a Jewish National Home in Palestine.

After World War II, the Zionist movement needed the support of the victorious powers and the newly created United Nations for the partition of Palestine and the creation there of an independent Jewish state. During the first Arab-Israeli war, support in weapons from the Soviet Bloc proved crucial for the Zionist side.[3] After it came into being, the state of Israel sided with the West in the Cold War, relying on Western support: French, British, West German, and, most decisively since the mid-1960s, American. A small state by territorial and demographic criteria compared to its Arab geopolitical environment, which Israel was officially at war with during the first decades of its existence and was replaced later on by the emergence of the Islamic Republic of Iran as its main enemy, the Zionist state is inherently based on a continuous structural dependence on foreign support. This support is indeed crucial in order to ensure the military preponderance with which Israel compensates for its relatively small size. Hence, the importance for Israel of winning Western hearts and minds: not those of Western rulers alone but the hearts and minds of the general public as well, since Western states are electoral democracies in which public opinion weighs on governmental policy, including foreign policy.

For their part, the Palestinians and Arabs in general were faced with Israeli military superiority as early as 1948. Defeated and scattered, the Palestinians relied on Arab nationalism, especially Nasser's Egypt since the mid-1950s, while Arab nationalism relied in turn on the Soviet Bloc for its armament in the face of Western support for Israel. There was little need for narrative-building efforts in order to convince the Palestinians, or the Arabs in general, of the rightfulness of the Palestinian cause. The creation of the state of Israel and the Arab defeat in the 1948 Arab-Israeli War have consistently been construed as a climax of the Western colonial enterprise and perceived as a national trauma in all Arab countries. It did not take the Palestinians and other Arabs nearly as much ideological effort to reflect as "imagined communities" as it took the global "Jewish nation" postulated by Zionism. During the heyday of Arab left-wing nationalism, the Arab narrative abroad was mainly deployed toward communist states and movements, and therefore developed mostly anti-colonial and anti-imperialist themes.

After the defeat of the two strongholds of Arab left-wing nationalism, Egypt and Syria, in the Six-Day War of June 1967, at a time when it had become clear that Israel had acquired the nuclear bomb, the perspective of a "liberation of Palestine" by military means began to fade. This led liberal and left Palestinian and Arab intellectuals—of whom the most prominent was undoubtedly Edward Said—and, later on, the Palestine Liberation Organization (PLO)—in which such intellectuals came to play an important role—to the conviction that the Palestinians and the Arab side in general needed to devote much greater attention and effort to the ideological battle to win over a significant portion of Western public opinion and even Jewish-Israeli public opinion. This was seen as indispensable in order to pressure Israel into a compromise that would be acceptable for the Palestinians and hence for the Arabs. From the 1970s onward, this perspective was increasingly challenged by the rise of Islamic fundamentalism, which developed its own religious Weltanschauung and had little consideration for non-Muslim public opinion. Its rise was mirrored on the opposite side, in Israel itself, by the rise of Jewish fundamentalism and neo-Zionism, which showed increasing contempt for non-Jewish public opinion.[4]

A fierce "competition of victims" characterizes the Arab-Israeli conflict,[5] with the Holocaust/Shoah invoked by one side and the Nakba by the other, and both sides projecting themselves as victims of continuous oppression. This claim is hardly disputable in the case of the Palestinians, who suffer as second-class citizens in Israel, as a population under direct or indirect occupation in the West Bank and Gaza and as refugees elsewhere, prevented from returning to the land from which they or their forebears were uprooted. The Zionist counterclaim maintains that Israel and the Jews are the target of Nazi-like hatred and genocidal schemes from the Palestinians, the Arabs, and Iran, if not Muslims at large. This counterclaim emphasizes the rise of a "new anti-Semitism," a category that tends to lump together all brands of unfriendly critique of Israel, and for some of its most rabid users, even friendly critiques.[6]

In such a minefield topic as the Arab-Israeli conflict, no one can expect a discussion of Arab reactions to Nazism and the Holocaust to be a serene historical and factual examination, especially if persons holding contrasting views on the conflict itself are in some way involved. In the exploration of a topic in which two human tragedies are mingling—a gigantic one, fortunately terminated in 1945, and another one of obviously lesser scope but whose tragic consequences, such as people living in refugee camps and/or under protracted military occupation, are still with us seventy years after 1948—the traditional requisites of scholarship merge necessarily with politics and the question of ethics. To borrow Max Weber's words, "axiological neutrality" in the discussion of the topic under consideration may be of the realm of the impossible, with the pretense of neutrality in presenting the facts being itself immediately suspected of partisanship in disguise. I would rather contend that, far from an impossible and illusory "axiological neutrality," discussion of our topic requires a firm commitment to higher ethical values—humanistic values, that is—combined with an effort at reaching the scientific standard by way of introspection.

I will start with the last requirement—namely, reaching the scientific standard by way of introspection. This defines a key condition of sound scholarship. Self-critical awareness has been described by the French sociologist Pierre Bourdieu as a key requisite of what he called "scientificity" in social sciences.[7] Researchers must practice self-analytical investigation in order to identify all possible sources of bias in their social and personal condition, in the same way that those who train to become psychoanalysts must undergo a personal analysis before practicing. In other words, if I am to pretend to scholarship on an issue like the one under discussion, I must first be fully aware of the biases that can result from my ethnic and social belonging, as well as from my upbringing and political views. This awareness aims at separating oneself from the partisan attitude of the activist engaged in political struggle, and strives to neutralize as much as possible one's political stance in considering facts. It is intimately connected to intellectual honesty in not concealing any facts that might compromise one's political stance while highlighting only those that serve it.

No one can be requested to abandon her or his political views for the sake of becoming a scholar. However, anyone pretending to be a scholar and to write a work of scholarship should be able to exercise political restraint in her or his scholarly practice. This relates directly to the crucial ethical imperative of departing from every form of self-centrism, be it egocentrism or ethnocentrism. An excellent statement of this ethical imperative is the famous precept from the Gospel of Matthew: "And why do you behold the mote that is in your brother's eye, but do not consider the beam that is in your own eye?" In other words, let us be aware of the wrongs of the side to which we belong or with which we identify, or even merely sympathize, before exploring the wrongs of the opposite side. Let us always ask ourselves whether our own side is not guilty in one way or another of what we blame the other side for.

These are the very rules that I did my best to follow and urged my readers to follow in my work *The Arabs and the Holocaust: The Arab-Israeli War of Narratives*, which is why I used the above-quoted precept as epigraph to the book. Let me then conform with this same precept here again and start this exploration of the pitfalls of scholarship about our topic with a critical exploration of the problems that mar the narrative of the Arab side, the side to which I belong ethnically and culturally.

The major pitfall is, of course, ethnocentrism, which is indeed a universal disease; altruistic humanism and internationalism are indeed very admirable stances precisely because they are so rare. Ethnocentrism manifests itself most perniciously in the "competition of the victims," when one has eyes only for the tragedy of one's own people and fails to see the tragedy of others or acknowledge its importance. Let me illustrate this with an anecdote from a recent experience: I was participating in an international meeting on peace convened by a major trade union confederation in Istanbul with a high proportion of Kurds present among the participants. There, a Palestinian speaker blamed the audience for not paying enough attention to the Palestinian cause. This person did not realize that Kurds could blame the Palestinians much more for not supporting the Kurdish cause, especially against Arab oppression in countries like yesterday's Iraq or today's Syria. In fact, there has been much more Kurdish support for the Palestinian cause over decades than Palestinian support—or for that matter, Arab support in general—for the Kurdish cause. Likewise, ethnocentrism is striking in the attitude of those Arabs who denounce vehemently anti-Arab racism among Israelis or in Western countries while ignoring or, much worse still, denying the existence of anti-Kurdish or anti-Black racism among Arabs.

Another manifestation of the same ethnocentrism, a manifestation that is directly relevant to our topic, is the denial of the existence of anti-

Semitism among Arabs. The phony argument that Arabs themselves are Semites is extensively used in order to refuse to acknowledge the existence of anti-Jewish hatred among them. The denial is not only about the development of such feelings in Palestine/Israel, where arguably they were and are mingled with national resentment against an oppressor state that claims to represent the Jews of the whole world. It is also often about the racist attitudes that targeted Jews in Arab countries, from Iraq to Morocco, and increased considerably after the Israeli state was born in war in 1948. The claim that there is no widespread anti-Jewish hatred among Arabs, including a trend of racial "anti-Semitism" originally imported from Europe, but only principled anti-Zionism is all the less excusable in that the distinction between the two has been increasingly blurred with the rise of religious fundamentalism in Arab countries over the past several decades. But the denial is also one about history as manifested in the claim that there was no persecution of religious minorities in Islamic history, what Mark Cohen called the myth of "interfaith utopia."[8]

Whereas denial of the wrongs of one's side is a most common feature of ethnocentrism—for example, the reluctance in France to acknowledge the barbarism of French colonialism in Algeria—there is a form of denial that is most peculiar to the Arab world as a widespread phenomenon and consists in denying a crime perpetrated by others. Holocaust denial is pervasive indeed in Arab countries, be it straightforward denial of the genocide or belittling its importance while portraying it in both cases as a "Zionist myth" forged for the political purpose of "blackmailing" people in the West. The peculiarity here is that this is a genocide for which the Arabs bear no more responsibility than they bear for the Armenian genocide, and one that was perpetrated by Europeans with whom Arabs have less in common than they have with the Turks. Yet, there is no phenomenon of denial of the Armenian genocide in Arab countries, whereas Holocaust denial is widespread.

The key to this paradox is, to be sure, the anti-Jewish hatred that developed among Arabs because of the Arab-Israeli conflict, leading many to treat the Holocaust as the central ideological argument of the enemy, an argument that must therefore be repudiated. One important consequence of this denial is failing to acknowledge that the rise of Nazism was decisive in the implementation of the Zionist project, as it enhanced tremendously its credibility among Jews and boosted the immigration of large numbers of Jews to Palestine, where they sought refuge from European anti-Semitism and persecution. The corollary of such a stance is that Jewish immigration into Palestine has come to be regarded as solely motivated by colonialist interests and ideology, not as an immigration that involved a high proportion of people fleeing from persecution and oppression and seeking a refuge wherever they managed to find one, albeit at the expense of another people.

These denials are often combined nowadays with a failure to acknowledge the calamitous role of Amin al-Husayni—the infamous "Mufti of Jerusalem," as he is known in Western publications—in his collaboration with Nazi Germany during the war. This is despite the fact that Amin al-Husayni's attitude has granted the Zionist narrative its main anti-Palestinian and anti-Arab argument. It made much more sense, actually, from an Arab standpoint and from a political perspective, to disavow Husayni and stress that he was in no way representing the attitude of the majority of Palestinians and Arabs in his collaboration with the Nazis, as Arab left-wing nationalism argued in its heyday in the 1960s and 1970s. One pernicious form of the banalization of Nazism, and therefore of Husayni's collaboration with the Nazis for the sake of anti-Zionist polemics, consists in putting Zionism on a par with Nazism. This is a usual form of political insult, which can be seen as "normal" since it is predicated on the view that Nazism is the absolute evil. The equation of Zionism with Nazism thus finds its way even into writings purporting to be scholarly.

I was keen on avoiding all these pitfalls and on observing this ethical-scholarly approach in my own work on Arab reactions to Nazism and the Holocaust. Yet, although it was widely reviewed in the Arab world, my book drew surprisingly few hostile reactions among those Arab intellectuals who commented on it or among reviewers from the fields of Jewish Studies or Holocaust Studies. Most reviews in Arab media and publications praised the book from an enlightened liberal or left-wing perspective. The few who criticized it did so from a nationalist standpoint, on three issues. I was blamed, first, for emphasizing that the Nazi genocide of the Jews was a crime surpassing in amplitude other crimes against humanity in the twentieth century, and one of a much greater magnitude that the initial Palestinian tragedy, the Nakba, which I described as an episode of "ethnic cleansing."

Second, I was blamed for acknowledging the dual nature of Zionism, including the fact that it originated from a reaction to the hatred and persecution of Jews in Europe, when I wrote that "Statist Zionism is a Janus, one face turned toward the Holocaust, the other towards the

Nakba, one towards persecution endured, the other towards oppression inflicted."[9] Here is how I explained this assertion in my book:

> Statist Zionism ... has a twofold nature. On the one hand, it is a form of racism born of a defensive reaction that spawned the idea that Jews were incapable of living among Aryans (the anti-Semitic version) or *goyim* (the Zionist version). As such, it is as morally excusable as the reactive racism of blacks to white racism. On the other hand, statist Zionism, once it created a *Judenstaat* in Palestine as "a portion of the rampart of Europe against Asia, an outpost of civilization as opposed to barbarism"—in the words of its founder, Theodor Herzl—became, *ipso facto,* a fundamentally racist colonial movement comparable to the European forms of colonialism with which it had identified. As Maxime Rodinson wrote in 1973, "Wanting to create a purely Jewish, or predominantly Jewish, state in an Arab Palestine in the twentieth century could not help but lead to a colonial-type situation and to the development (completely normal sociologically speaking) of a racist state of mind, and in the final analysis to a military confrontation between the two ethnic groups."[10]

Finally, I was criticized for exposing and condemning the propagation of anti-Jewish hatred, anti-Semitism, and Holocaust denial in Arab countries, especially by Islamic fundamentalist circles, and for denouncing Amin al-Husayni's rabid anti-Semitism and enthusiasm for the Nazi genocide, even though I did so while deconstructing the much overblown representation of Husayni in Zionist propaganda.

Not surprisingly, this last stance for which I was criticized from an Arab nationalist standpoint is the only one that drew some praise from pro-Israel reviewers, who otherwise criticized more or less vehemently what they described as my "anti-Zionist prejudice," ignoring my emphasis on the dual nature of Zionism in perfect symmetry with my Arab nationalist critics who focused on it. Let me here reflect on this rather singular situation. I am a Lebanese author, that is, a person whose country has been invaded and partly occupied for eighteen years by Israel, then submitted again to a devastating onslaught in 2006. And yet, I am required to be "neutral" toward Zionism and blamed for being critical of it. This certainly merits a pause. Would an Algerian historian be required to be neutral on French colonialism? Would anyone but a Turkish nationalist blame a Kurdish historian for being hostile to Turkish oppression of the Kurds? Would anyone demand that an African American historian be neutral on slavery? In fact, I would rather contend that an analysis of any of these forms of oppression would be seriously flawed if it lacked a critical stance toward them and empathy with their victims, combined with a universal empathy with all victims of similar oppression.

This brings me to what I deem the true and universal lesson of the Holocaust, in accordance with countless thinkers much more directly affected by it than I: not the condemnation of anti-Semitism alone and a one-sided empathy with the Jews, but a humanistic rejection of all forms of discrimination, racism, and ethnic oppression. The necessary response to Nazi anti-Semitism is not in some form of narrow Jewish nationalism, but it consists of upholding universalist humanistic values—values in whose development Jewish thinkers or thinkers of Jewish descent have contributed prominently, a fact that was a key reason for the Nazis' anti-Jewish hatred. Thus, the condemnation of Nazism remains flawed if it is not combined with the repudiation of colonialism—that is, if Nazism is not grasped as part of the culmination of a long history of European colonial-imperialist barbarism perpetrated in the name of civilization, as Hannah Arendt explained so well in her famous *The Origins of Totalitarianism*.[11]

Short of this, the repudiation of Nazism remains ethnocentric, that is to say, it does not radically break with the logic of which Nazism is a culmination. It incurs the kind of denunciation expressed by the Antillean writer Aimé Césaire in his *Discourse on Colonialism*, a classic of anti-colonial (or "post-colonial") literature:

> At bottom, what [the very distinguished, very humanistic, very Christian bourgeois of the twentieth century] cannot forgive Hitler for is not *the crime* in itself, *the crime against man*, it is not *the humiliation of man as such*, it is the crime against the white man, the humiliation of the white man, and the fact that he applied to Europe colonialist procedures which until then had been reserved exclusively for the Arabs of Algeria, the "coolies" of India, and the "niggers" of Africa.[12]

Such flawed ethnocentric attitudes affect very widely the body of writings purporting to be scholarly on the topic of Arab reactions to Nazism and the Holocaust—be they Jewish ethnocentric or Western ethnocentric attitudes that regard the Israelis as part of Western civilization. In this regard, a particular form of German ethnocentrism deserves special mention for its way of redeeming the crimes of German Nazism by scourging the Arabs for the alleged continuation of Nazism and by outbidding everyone else in an "idolization of the Jews" which, as Eleonore Sterling rightly observed, has "a good deal in common" with anti-Semitism.[13]

A striking example of how ideology can spoil and distort scholarship is provided by a German author, Klaus Gensicke, who has reconstructed the Mufti's years in Berlin based on German official archives, along with other sources in English and German. His book was published in English in 2011.[14] It is actually a modified and expanded version of a doctoral dissertation that he submitted in 1987 and published the year after.[15] All that is valuable and interesting in the new book comes from the original dissertation, which was written at the Free University of Berlin under the supervision of Abraham Ashkenasi.[16] Whereas the dissertation draws a clear distinction between Amin al-Husayni and the Palestinian movement after him, the 2007 German version and its 2011 English translation—bearing a foreword by Matthias Küntzel, the author of a book that is much-symptomatic of what is discussed here[17]—combine the bulk of the original edition with an anti-Arab and anti-Palestinian narrative. The result is a neoconservative and neo-Zionist discourse on Islamic jihadi terrorism that provides a blatant illustration of how scholarship can be compromised by ideology.[18]

Ethnocentric attitudes translate in a number of features that can be found across the literature. A frequent feature is a one-sided depiction of Zionism as a "Jewish liberation" movement that denies its colonial dimension—the reverse of the Arab nationalist attitude depicted above. More pervasive still is the emphasis on individuals and currents among Arabs who expressed sympathies for Fascism or Nazism while ignoring totally the existence within the Zionist movement of currents such as the Revisionists and the Maximalists, some of whom held similar sympathies for Italian Fascism. Jewish admirers of fascism are disregarded even though their importance within the Yishuv (the Jewish population in Palestine before 1948) was proportionally larger than that of their Arab counterparts among Arabs.

Another feature is the fervent denunciation of Holocaust denial among Arabs and Palestinians, which, foolish as it is, is denial of a crime by people who were not the perpetrators and hence arguably a lesser evil than German denial of the Holocaust. This distinction is often completely disregarded, ethnocentrism consisting here in treating Arab Holocaust denial as equivalent to the European version. This is done, moreover, while ignoring, if not straightforwardly justifying, the very official Israeli denial of the Nakba, for which the founders of the Israeli state were responsible, although Israel's "New Historians" did much to deconstruct their state's official narrative on this issue and establish the facts of the "ethnic cleansing" that took place in Palestine.[19]

Another manifestation of ethnocentric double standard is the equally widespread denunciation of "the Arabs," with the usual tendency to lump them all together in a single category, as if such a huge and highly diverse population could be politically monolithic. "The Arabs" are criticized for lacking empathy with the Jewish victims of Nazism—although there are significant instances of such empathy—while justifying or simply ignoring the general lack of empathy among most Israelis with the Palestinian victims of ongoing occupation and oppression by Israel's army and state, or of what the Israeli writer David Grossman publicly called "the deeply ingrained institutionalized racism against [Israel's] Arab minority."[20] In the case of some US-based authors, ethnocentrism consists likewise in scourging the Arabs for having persecuted Jews in their countries during the Arab-Israeli wars while failing to compare the fate of Arab Jews during those wars with, for instance, the terrible treatment that was inflicted on Japanese Americans in the United States during World War II.[21] This is not to mention anti-Black racism that was institutionalized in the United States until long after the first Arab-Israeli war.

It is likewise ethnocentric to accuse "the Arabs" of having shared with Nazism, when it was in power, a common hostility to the Jews, without acknowledging that, in Arab eyes, most Jews in Palestine were European colonialists, invited by British imperialism to implement a settler-colonial project on Arab land, whereas Jews in Europe were natives who had suffered an age-old oppression and were victims of racist totalitarianism. Moreover, accusing "the Arabs" of Nazi sympathies completely overlooks the fact that certainly far fewer Arabs were involved in Nazi-like movements, whether in absolute figures or as a proportion of the overall Arab population, than what existed in European countries during the same period.

There was indeed comparably much less prejudice and racism toward native Jews in Arab countries during the time of Nazism than there was in most European countries, and arguably in the United States. The only pogrom registered in an Arab country during World War II took place in Baghdad in 1941; its true history actually bears witness to the fact that the fate of Iraqi Jews at that time was overall much better than that of Jews in most countries of Europe.[22] And yet, a whole literature, much of which claims to be scholarly, pretends that virtually all Arab nationalists, as well as the Arab "street," were pro-Nazi, usually contrasting them, in order to appear "objective," with a minority represented by Arab elites closely tied to Britain, such as the Hashemite dynasty or liberal politicians in Egypt. The purpose here is to portray "the Arabs" as belonging to the camp of the losers of World War II. The correlation of this view would naturally be that the Zionist movement and the Israeli state it founded soon after that war were a deserving part of the victors.

The quintessence of ethnocentric arrogance—combined with anti-Arab racism or, increasingly in recent times, Islamophobia—consists of judging the Arabs against the highest standards of humanism to which only a tiny minority of human beings can claim to conform and hence condemning the Arabs for not conforming to these standards. A good illustration by analogy of this way of judging the Arabs can be found in *Selma,* the 2014 motion picture directed by Ava DuVernay. In one of the film's most vivid scenes, a white registrar asks black civil rights activist Annie Lee Cooper (played by Oprah Winfrey) a number of questions about the US electoral system of such a level of detail that he himself would not know their answers by heart. By the standard of the level of knowledge that the white registrar sets as a requisite in order to grant Cooper the right to vote, hardly any person would be authorized to vote in US elections.

How different is it to blame "the Arabs" for not having fully empathized with the Jews by welcoming them without limits in Palestine, when so many Europeans were participating, directly or indirectly, in the persecution of the Jews, and while the United Kingdom, the United States, and others were often slamming their doors in the face of Jewish refugees? Can anyone fairly blame the Palestinians for "responsibility in the genocide" by way of opposing Jewish immigration to their land while ignoring that many more Jewish refugees entered Palestine between 1933 and 1945, compared to its native population or in absolute numbers, than to any other country in the world? Is it acceptable, moreover, to disregard the fact that Jewish refugees in Palestine were enlisted in a settler-colonial project aimed at creating on Palestinian land a Jewish state—that is, one with a Jewish majority—unlike Jewish refugees in all other countries? Finally, can anyone blame the Palestinians for not having accepted the partition of their country with a population composed in its majority of recent migrants, who, moreover, were granted more than half the country while constituting only one-third of its residents? This is indeed exactly what Resolution 181, adopted on 29 November 1947 by thirty-three out of fifty-seven member states of the United Nations, provided for. Would any other population on earth, confronted with the same situation, react differently and happily cede more than half of its country? To ask the question is to answer it. The problem is that the question is never asked by those who are not able to disentangle justice from prejudice and who prefer to attribute the Palestinian and Arab rejection of Resolution 181 to purported anti-Semitism.

For the reasons I mentioned at the beginning of this contribution, much of what pretended to be "scholarship" on Arab reactions to Nazism and the Holocaust were but salvoes in the war of narratives. This has overwhelmingly been the case on one side of that war, the pro-Israeli side, as there has hardly been a purported "scholarly" engagement with that specific topic on the pro-Palestinian side. This imbalance stems in part from a flawed ideological attitude that is pervasive on the Arab side, and leads to brushing away the whole topic as irrelevant.

Publications on this particular topic have increased considerably in recent decades as a result of the conjunction of three factors. The first is the deterioration of Israel's image due to its wars in Lebanon, from the 1982 invasion of the country onward, with subsequent peaks in image degradation that resulted from the 2006 onslaught on Lebanon, and the successive onslaughts on the Gaza Strip, especially those of 2008–2009 and 2014. The second factor is the expansion of Islamic fundamentalism in Arab countries, which has occurred since the late 1970s, initially boosted by the 1979 Iranian Revolution that led to the founding of the Islamic Republic of Iran. The third factor has been the huge impact of the 11 September 2001 attacks on US soil and the subsequent "war on terror" launched by the George W. Bush administration. The conjunction of these three factors led to a sharp exacerbation of the propaganda war, with the pro-Israel side taking advantage of the increased visibility of Islamic fundamentalism in general, the rise of terrorism of Islamic fundamentalist inspiration in particular, and the concomitant rise of Islamophobia in Western countries.

This was the environment I had to face when I started my own investigation of Arab reactions to Nazi Germany and the Holocaust. Consequently, I had to devote a significant part of my work to a critical examination of a whole range of publications on the topic, academic and otherwise, and a refutation of the accumulation of counter-truths in that regard. Fortunately, I was not the only one to react to this accumulation—far from it. Since the turn of the twenty-first century, a number of scholarly books have appeared in English challenging the view that "the Arabs" were massively sympathetic to Italian Fascism and, more so, to German Nazism when both movements were in power. While they do point to significant instances of Arab sympathy and support for Hitler's Germany and its anti-Semitism, they also present considerable evidence of Arab criticism and rejection of German Nazism and its policies. They have shown much of the existing literature to be heavily biased politically, and inconsistent with the facts. Most of these more recent publications have been dedicated to particular Arab countries of the Middle East, such as Egypt, Iraq, Lebanon, Palestine, and Syria.

Several of the authors of these works—historians from Germany, Israel, and the United States—gathered with a few others in a 2010 workshop in Tel Aviv, organized by Middle Eastern and African history professor at Tel Aviv University Israel Gershoni, who edited the proceedings of the workshop.[23] A second key encounter in this endeavor was the 2015 symposium convened at the University of Vermont's Miller Center for Holocaust Studies by Professors Francis Nicosia and Boğaç Ergene, as well as their colleagues there, of which the present volume is the outcome. These workshops and the collective volumes that resulted from them, in addition to their participants' other writings, have been crucial in putting the discussion of Arab reactions to Nazism and the Holocaust on a sounder scholarly footing. In doing so, in contributing to freeing the scholarly investigation of this topic from the biases that stem from the war of narratives, they have laid building blocks for the future development of a consensual historical narrative that fully acknowledges each side's defining tragedy in its historical accuracy. Such a consensual narrative is indeed one of the requisites of peace, and every addition to its buildup helps to prepare a future of peaceful coexistence. It is a task that is indispensable if the present gloomy trend of history is ever to be reversed.

**Gilbert Achcar** is Professor of development studies and international relations at the School of Oriental and African Studies (SOAS), University of London. His main field of research and scholarship is the contemporary Arab world. He is the author of many books, including *The Arabs and the Holocaust: The Arab-Israeli War of Narratives* (2010); *The People Want: A Radical Exploration of the Arab Uprising* (2013); *Marxism, Orientalism, Cosmopolitanism* (2013); and *Morbid Symptoms: Relapse in the Arab Uprising* (2016). He has chaired the Centre for Palestine Studies at SOAS since its creation in 2012.

## Notes

1. See the discussion of this term in the introduction to my book, Gilbert Achcar, *The Arabs and the Holocaust: The Arab-Israeli war of Narratives,* trans. G. M. Goshgarian (New York, 2010), "Words Laden with Pain," 5–9.
2. This argument was expressed in the crudest form by well-known Israeli historian Benny Morris in the scandal-provoking interview he gave to the Israeli newspaper *Haaretz* in 2004: "There are circumstances in history that justify ethnic cleansing. I know that this term is completely negative in the discourse of the twenty-first century, but when the choice is between ethnic cleansing and genocide—the annihilation of your people—I prefer ethnic cleansing" (Ari Shavit, "Survival of the Fittest," *Haaretz,* 8 January 2004).
3. See Benny Morris, *1948: A History of the First Arab- Israeli War* (New Haven, CT, 2008).
4. According to Israeli sociologist Uri Ram, "Neo-Zionism is particularist, tribal, Jewish, ethnic nationalist, fundamentalist, and even fascist on the fringe" (quoted in Dalia Shehori, "Post-Zionism Didn't Die, It's Badly Injured," *Haaretz,* 28 April 2004).
5. Jean-Michel Chaumont, *La Concurrence des victimes: Génocide, identité, reconnaissance* (Paris, 1997).
6. Bernard Lewis first developed the thesis of a "new anti-Semitism" related to the Arab-Israeli conflict in the last chapter of his 1986 book, *Semites and Anti-Semites: An Inquiry into Conflict and Prejudice* (New York, 1986). It was reissued with a new afterword in 1999. However, Lewis clearly warned then against extending this category to all critiques of Israel: "It is unreasonable and unfair to assume that opposition to Zionism or criticism of Israeli policies and actions is, as such and in the absence of other evidence, an expression of anti-Semitic prejudice. The Arab-Israeli conflict is a political one—a clash between states and peoples over real issues, not a matter of prejudice and persecution" (20). He continues: "It would be palpably unjust, even absurd, to assert that all critics or opponents of Zionism or Israel are moved by anti-Semitism; it would be equally mistaken to deny that anti-Zionism can on occasion provide a cloak of respectability for a prejudice which, at the present time and in the free world, is not normally admitted in public by anyone with political ambitions or cultural pretensions" (22–23).
7. This idea is repeated in much of Pierre Bourdieu's writings. His argument is that social sciences deal with "fields of struggle" in which the social scientists themselves hold a certain (social and intellectual) position, which they must keep in mind in order to control what their production owes to their position.
8. According to Cohen, it is against this myth that what he calls "the neo-lachrymose conception of Jewish-Arab history" was developed. See Mark Cohen, *Under Crescent and Cross: The Jews in the Middle Ages* (Princeton, NJ, 1996), 3–14.
9. Achcar, *Arabs and the Holocaust,* 291.
10. Ibid., 290–291.
11. Hannah Arendt, *The Origins of Totalitarianism* (New York, 1976; 1st ed. 1951).

12. Aimé Césaire, *Discourse on Colonialism*, trans. Joan Pinkham (New York, 2000), 36; emphasis in original.
13. Both—said Sterling, whose parents were murdered in a Nazi concentration camp—"are symptomatic of a sort of hypothermia of complex human relationships and derive from a mental incapacity truly to respect the 'other.' Jews remain foreigners for anti-Semites and philosemites alike." See Eleonore Sterling, "Judenfreunde—Judenfeinde: Fragwürdiger Philosemitismus in der Bundesrepublik," *Die Zeit*, 10 December 1965. See also Frank Stern, *The Whitewashing of the Yellow Badge: Antisemitism and Philosemitism in Postwar Germany* (Oxford, 1992).
14. Klaus Gensicke, *The Mufti of Jerusalem and the Nazis: The Berlin Years*, trans. Alexander Fraser Gunn (London, 2011). The German edition is *Der Mufti von Jerusalem und die Nationalsozialisten: Eine politische Biographie Amin el-Husseinis* (Darmstadt, 2007).
15. Klaus Gensicke, *Der Mufti von Jerusalem, Amin el-Husseini, und die Nationalsozialisten* (Frankfurt, 1988). The epigraph to the 1988 book is a quotation from Salah Khalaf (Abu Iyad) stating that Amin al-Husayni's collaboration with Hitler's Germany "was an error that we all condemn in the strongest possible way." The epigraph of the new version is an out-of-context excerpt from a 1974 quotation from Winston Churchill describing Husayni as the "deadliest enemy of the British Empire."
16. In his foreword to Gensicke's 1988 book, Ashkenasi explains that the Mufti always represented the conservative clans among the Palestinians, that his personality was very divisive, and that his politics were characterized by his uncompromising nature, his Pan-Arab ambitions, the fact that he developed them in exile, and his bad choice of allies. He then asserts that Gensicke's research has shown that, because of these elements, "a political struggle was lost and the Palestinians, who were almost the only organized political national movement and people in colonial prewar time, were left stateless after World War II." See Gensicke, *Der Mufti von Jerusalem, Amin el-Husseini, und die Nationalsozialisten*, 7–8.
17. Matthias Küntzel, *Jihad and Jew-Hatred: Islamism, Nazism and the Roots of 9/11*, trans. Colin Meade (New York, 2007). In a review for the *New York Times* ("Seeds of Hate," 6 January 2008), Jeffrey Goldberg wrote that Küntzel "overreaches ... in his effort to blame Germany for Muslim anti-Semitism" and "oversimplifies the Israeli-Arab conflict."
18. For a discussion of Gensicke's book, see my review of it in the *Journal of Palestine Studies* 65, no. 1 (2015): 102–103.
19. On Israel's New Historians, see Eugene Rogan and Avi Shlaim, *The War for Palestine: Rewriting the History of 1948* (Cambridge, 2007); Benny Morris, ed., *Making Israel* (Ann Arbor, MI, 2007); and Ilan Pappé, *The Idea of Israel: A History of Power and Knowledge* (London, 2014). The most radical critique of Israel's responsibility in the Nakba was written by Israeli historian Ilan Pappé, *The Ethnic Cleansing of Palestine* (Oxford, 2006).
20. David Grossman, "Speech at the Rabin Memorial," *Haaretz*, 5 November 2006. The speech was given in Tel Aviv on 4 November 2006, before a crowd

of one hundred thousand gathered to commemorate the eleventh anniversary of the assassination of Israeli Prime Minister Yitzhak Rabin.
21. For a recent account of this tragedy, see Richard Reeves, *Infamy: The Shocking Story of the Japanese American Internment in World War II* (New York, 2015).
22. On the June 1941 pogrom in Baghdad, see Achcar, *The Arabs and the Holocaust*, 99–103. On this and the history of Iraqi Jews during the 1930s and 1940s, see Orit Bashkin, *New Babylonians: A History of Jews in Modern Iraq* (Stanford, CA, 2012). On the Jews in North Africa during World War II, see Robert Satloff, *Among the Righteous: Lost Stories from the Holocaust's Long Reach into Arab Land* (New York, 2006). On relations between North African Jews and Muslims, an interesting new book is Ethan Katz, *The Burdens of Brotherhood: Jews and Muslims from North Africa to France* (Cambridge, MA, 2015).
23. Israel Gershoni, ed., *Arab Responses to Fascism and Nazism: Attraction and Repulsion* (Austin, TX, 2014).

## Bibliography

Achcar, Gilbert. *The Arabs and the Holocaust: The Arab-Israeli War of Narratives.* Translated by G. M. Goshgarian. New York, 2010.

Arendt, Hannah. *The Origins of Totalitarianism.* New York, 1976 (1st ed. 1951).

Bashkin, Orit. *New Babylonians: A History of Jews in Modern Iraq.* Stanford, CA, 2012.

Césaire, Aimé. *Discourse on Colonialism.* Translated by Joan Pinkham. New York, 2000.

Chaumont, Jean-Michel. *La Concurrence des victimes: Génocide, identité, reconnaissance.* Paris, 1997.

Cohen, Mark. *Under Crescent and Cross: The Jews in the Middle Ages.* Princeton, NJ, 1996.

Gensicke, Klaus. *Der Mufti von Jerusalem, Amin el-Husseini, und die Nationalsozialisten.* Frankfurt, 1988.

———. *The Mufti of Jerusalem and the Nazis: The Berlin Years.* Translated by Alexander Faser Gunn. London, 2011. Originally published as *Der Mufti von Jerusalem und die Nationalsozialisten: Eine politische Biographie Amin el-Husseinis* (Darmstadt, 2007).

Gershoni, Israel, ed. *Arab Responses to Fascism and Nazism: Attraction and Repulsion.* Austin, TX, 2014.

Katz, Ethan. *The Burdens of Brotherhood: Jews and Muslims from North Africa to France.* Cambridge, MA, 2015.

Küntzel, Matthias. *Jihad and Jew-Hatred: Islamism, Nazism and the Roots of 9/11.* Translated by Colin Meade. New York, 2007.

Lewis, Bernard. *Semites and Anti-Semites: An Inquiry into Conflict and Prejudice.* New York, 1986.

Morris, Benny. *1948: A History of the First Arab- Israeli War.* New Haven, CT, 2008.

———, ed. *Making Israel.* Ann Arbor, MI, 2007.

Pappé, Ilan. *The Ethnic Cleansing of Palestine*. Oxford, 2006.
———. *The Idea of Israel: A History of Power and Knowledge*. London, 2014.
Reeves, Richard. *Infamy: The Shocking Story of the Japanese American Internment in World War II*. New York, 2015.
Rogan, Eugene, and Avi Shlaim. *The War for Palestine: Rewriting the History of 1948*. Cambridge, 2007.
Satloff, Robert Satloff. *Among the Righteous: Lost Stories from the Holocaust's Long Reach into Arab Land*. New York, 2006.
Stern, Frank. *The Whitewashing of the Yellow Badge: Antisemitism and Philosemitism in Postwar Germany*. Oxford, 1992.

*Chapter 2*

# TURKISH RESPONSES TO THE HOLOCAUST
## Ankara's Policy toward the Jews, 1933–1945

*Corry Guttstadt*

IN CONTRAST TO MOST OTHER countries in the Middle East, Turkey did not become a theater of war in World War II. After heavy losses in the wars at the beginning of the century, the foreign policy of the young Turkish Republic was focused primarily on maintaining peace and consolidating the country. The government in Ankara sought to maintain neutrality[1] and to keep the country out of the war through adroit alliance politics. Nonetheless, Turkey was greatly affected by World War II. The size of its armed forces increased to more than one million, there was food rationing for the general population, and the course of the war and the possible threats it posed for Turkey were the main topics of public concern.

How did Turkey "respond" to the Holocaust? The very question implies that the fate of the Jews was of concern to Turkey's political class. But an analysis of the press coverage and public statements coming from political circles at the time reveals that Ankara, like many cities around the world, hardly took notice of the genocide of the European Jews against the backdrop of the overall developments in the war.[2] In fact, the German persecution of the Jews did affect Turkey: for one, through Jews who were trying to escape from the German sphere of influence and who sought refuge in, or at the least transit through, Turkey; and second, through the fate of the Turkish Jews living in Europe who themselves became victims of Nazi persecution.

For some time now, Turkish politicians have been eager to present Turkey in countless publications as a country that "prevented its Jews being sent to concentration camps during World War II," and as "a safe haven from persecution for Jewish academics and Jews of all social classes."³ As I will argue in this chapter, this was not the case. Turkey was far from welcoming toward Jews. As this chapter will demonstrate, this was primarily a consequence of Turkey's own nationalist domestic policies at the time.

## Turkish Reactions to the Nazi Seizure of Power in Germany

"I notice with pleasure the enthusiasm your great leader Adolf Hitler has sparked everywhere in your great country, and I am convinced that things in your fatherland, which have been tried so severely, will and must begin to get better now."⁴ With these words, the Turkish ambassador to Berlin, General Kemalettin Sami Pasha, expressed his satisfaction with the Nazis' seizure of power in Germany in an interview he gave to the NSDAP's daily Berlin newspaper, *Der Angriff*, in May 1933. Among Turkey's political class, Hitler's ascension to power in 1933 did not cause significant concern. Prominent journalists—many of them leading politicians—described with admiration "the absolute ideological unity of state, party, youth, and the masses,"⁵ the "German awakening,"⁶ Hitler as "the apple of the eye of 66 Million Germans . . . who has united Germany, as one body, and made it beat like one heart,"⁷ and the NSDAP as "a movement of national unity that has embraced all Germans."⁸

The abolition of democracy and persecution of the opposition, too, were commented on positively by many of these politician-journalists, who believed those measures were necessary to put an end to anarchy and would be welcomed by the population.⁹ The chief editor of the newspaper *Milliyet* and MP for Siirt, Mahmut [Soydan], also a confidant of Atatürk, pointed out that Hitler had to silence the opposition for the sake of providing stability: "Nothing can be said against this system. Political unity is necessary above all else, especially for a country like Germany, which is beset by internal and external difficulties. . . . Chancellor Hitler is moving directly toward a one-party system. If he succeeds, there is no doubt it will be of benefit to the German cause."¹⁰ In *Ulus*, the party newspaper of the governing Cumhuriyet Halk Partisi (Republican People's Party—CHP), Neşet Halit Atay confronted critical voices lamenting the suppression of the press in Nazi Germany with the argument that the "free press" from 1928 to 1933 had been partly responsible for Germany's ruin. He reminded his readers of the negative effect that the writings of "liberal Turkish" journalists had had during the Turkish revolution.[11] And *Milliyet* called the intellectuals and journalists who had fled Germany and continued to voice their opposition through their writings from exile as "traitors to their country."[12]

During the same period, Turkey itself pursued authoritarian policies marked by strong corporatist traits, an aggressive nationalism, and a leader cult.[13] In 1935, the unity of party and state was adopted, the freedom of the press and the freedom to organize were largely abolished, and after the death of Atatürk in 1938, İsmet İnönü, who succeeded him as president and party chairman, received the title of *Millî Şef* (national leader).

Numerous authors at the time drew comparisons between the National Socialist movement in Germany and the nationalist movement in Turkey. But in fact, the majority of commentators took a clear position against the adoption of National Socialism or Italian Fascism as "models" for Turkey's "national revolution," and pointed out the differences between them. Nonetheless, there were officials who openly sympathized with the Nazis both in the high ranks of the party and the security apparatus, and in Turkey, too, left-wing and unequivocally anti-Fascist voices were suppressed and persecuted.

In addition, the 1930s saw the emergence of Turkish-Fascist and racist tendencies outside or on the fringes of the single party, the CHP. Some of their protagonists, such as Nihal Atsız and Cevat Rıfat Atilhan, were open Nazi sympathizers; some among them were in direct contact with German agencies.

During the early period of the Turkish Republic, the Kemalist leadership officially distanced itself from the Turanists' aggressive objectives and rhetoric, and several Turanists were forced to leave the country. After İnönü took over leadership of the country in 1938, Turanist and Turkish-racist associations began to operate openly in Turkey, at times with support from the highest levels of the party. Still, an affinity with Nazi Germany or connections with the German authorities were not the most important marks of Fascist and racist tendencies in these movements; anybody convinced of the superiority of the Turkish "race" had to reject the National Socialist ideology, if only because it assigned the Turks a place far below the Germanic peoples.[14] Not until May 1944 did the government dissociate itself from the Turanists. In May 1944, several journals were banned and twenty-three Turanists brought before a military court and sentenced to prison terms.

## Turkish Neutrality: Changing Views on the Nazis' Aggressive Politics

During the first years of the Nazi regime, many Turkish commentators showed considerable sympathy for Germany's revisionist policies. They considered Germany a "victim of the Versailles treaty," just as Turkey perceived itself as a victim of the 1920 Treaty of Sèvres. Within this reasoning, the fight against the "*Diktat* of Versailles" justified many of the Nazi regime's negative aspects.[15] Consequently, Nazi Germany's systematic violation of the Treaty of Versailles (for example, its remilitarization) was met with a great deal of understanding, since it was likened to the Turkish national struggle that had resulted in the revision of the Treaty of Lausanne.

Burhan Belge, the deputy head of the government press office, welcomed the Nazis' victory in the Saar status referendum of January 1935 in the party newspaper, *Ulus,* with the words: "Without a doubt, only nationalist Turkey is capable of fully understanding nationalist Germany's joy at the Saar referendum."[16] Even the annexation of Austria and the Sudetenland were condoned as a "unification of ethnically German living space." In the mid-1930s, Turkey primarily regarded Bulgaria and Italy as potential threats. Especially after Mussolini had openly declared Italy's expansionist ambitions in the Mediterranean with the term *Mare Nostrum,* public sentiment toward Italy, which had initially been positive, turned negative. Italy's brutal war of conquest in Abyssinia that began in October 1935 was covered extensively and critically in the Turkish press.

Public sentiment changed fundamentally with the German invasion of Bohemia and Moravia in March 1939, and the invasion of Poland six months later.[17] Even journalists known for their pro-German leanings strongly condemned Germany's brutal aggression. In keeping with Kemalist doctrine, Turkey saw itself as a victim of the imperialist global powers and consequently tended to be sympathetic toward other "small" countries that found themselves victims of German, Italian, or Soviet aggression: Czechoslovakia, Poland,[18] Albania, and eventually Greece. Although the Greco-Turkish War of 1919–1922 was still relatively recent and had been fought with great brutality on both sides, the Greek resistance against the Italian occupation in 1940 was met in Turkey with unanimous support.[19]

Fears of Italian aggression, reinforced by the German alliance with Italy (the "Pact of Steel") of May 1939, compelled Turkey to seek closer relations with France and England. Turkey later signed a tripartite agreement with both. But the occupation of several Northern and Western European countries in the course of 1940, and above all the swift defeat of France, again changed the mood in Turkey and raised the question of whether Turkey had "once again backed the wrong horse."[20] A number of commentators expressed their disappointment with England and France, which had "abandoned" Czechoslovakia and Poland, and with France in particular for having surrendered so easily.[21]

In the spring of 1941, the entire Balkan region was under the control of the Axis powers in some way, be it through occupation, coercion, or alliance. In Bulgaria and Romania, large German military units stood at the ready not far from the Turkish border. Faced with this pressure, Turkey accepted the German "invitation" to conclude a pact of friendship and nonaggression, which was eventually signed on 18 June 1941. The German attack on the Soviet Union on 22 June, four days after the conclusion of the treaty between Turkey and Germany, was met with enthusiasm among the political class in Turkey: "All hearts began to beat for a German victory," as the MP Faik A. Barutçu described the mood in Ankara.[22] This enthusiasm, brought on first and foremost by relief over the fact that the two powers that Turkey felt threatened by were now fighting each other, was amplified by old fears of the arch enemy, Russia, with anticommunist sentiments—prevalent among the general public and parts of the political leadership—mixed in.

By June 1941, Turkey's neutrality was ensured through treaties with all sides. In practice, this neutrality took the shape of collaboration with both sides. The British intelligence service was able to operate quite freely on the Turkish Aegean coast, while the Turkish military intelligence service passed detailed information about the Soviets on to the Germans. It is not easy to discern anything resembling "public opinion" toward the warring parties during these years. For one, the Turkish press was subject to multiple instances of censorship.[23] Starting in July 1940, a government decree obligated the press to write about foreign affairs only in accordance with the guidelines issued by the government press office. Consequently, published opinion in essence followed the turns of Turkish foreign policy, so any reporting critical of Nazi Germany was limited mainly to the period of Turkey's "unilateral" pacts with Britain and France.

In June 1941, the political climate changed almost overnight: the German-Turkish pact stipulated that the print and broadcasting media of both countries always be "committed to the spirit of German-Turkish

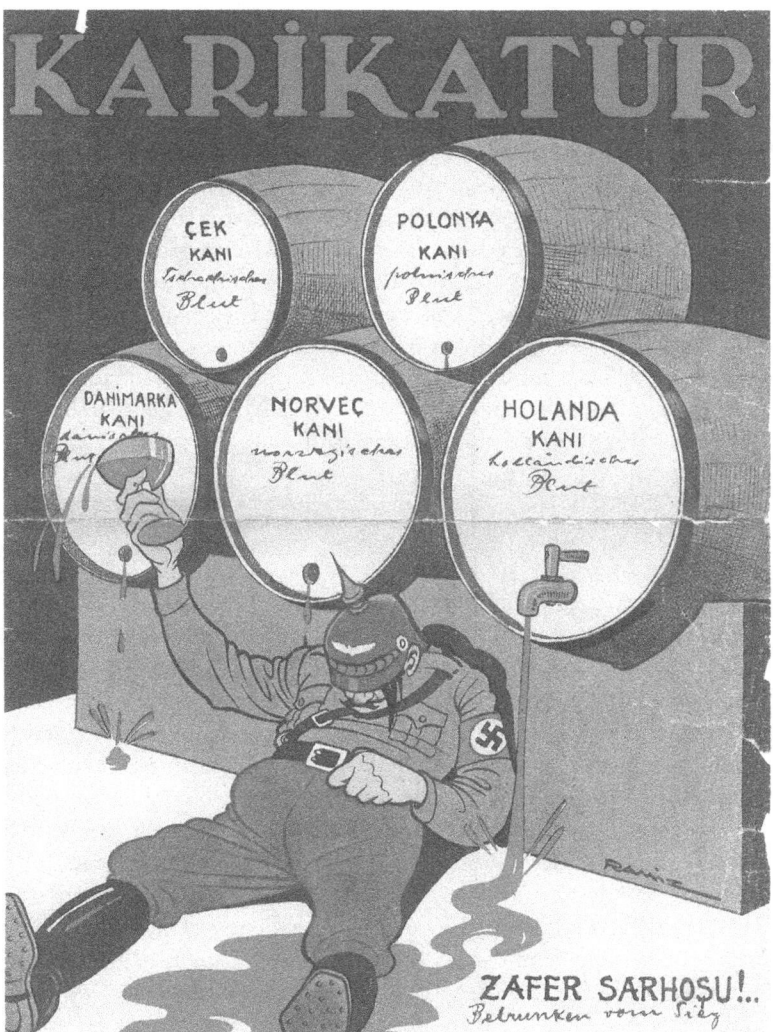

**Figure 2.1.** A cartoon from the front page of the Turkish magazine *Karikatür* with an image of a German soldier "drunk from victory" after the German conquests of Czechoslovakia, Poland, Denmark, Norway, and Holland, August 1940.

friendship." All of Turkey's major newspapers promptly reported that "the harmful propaganda that has sought to destroy the friendship between Germany and Turkey has proved to be unsuccessful."[24] On several occasions, the German embassy put direct pressure on the Turkish leadership to censor any press coverage critical of the Axis powers. In December 1942, the newspaper *Vatan* was banned for three months for putting a picture of Charlie Chaplin from the movie *The Great Dictator* (1940) on its front page. As a rule, there was no need for the Germans to step in: the Turkish government itself was at pains to avoid affronting the German side. In German embassy circles, the head of the government press office, Selim Sarper, was considered "reliable." In addition, quite a few journalists were paid for their pro-German propaganda. German ambassador to Turkey Franz von Papen had a substantial special fund available for this purpose.[25] But the Allies, for their part, ran information agencies as well. A number of newspapers, among them *Yeni Sabah* (published by Hüseyin Cahit Yalçın) and Ahmet Emin Yalman's *Vatan*, were close to the Allies and wrote very critically about Germany's politics and its war effort despite the censorship.

## Turkey's Ambivalent Stance toward Anti-Semitism

It was the Nazi regime's nationalist and authoritarian traits that drew the initial admiration for "Germany's awakening" described above; its policy toward Jews was unequivocally rejected by the majority of commentators. From the outset, the racist, fanatical anti-Semitism prevalent in Germany was dismissed as excessive, uncivilized, absurd, or puerile. According to one commentator, the shape that anti-Semitism had taken in Germany could in no way be condoned from a humanitarian point of view.[26] Even authors known for their philo-Germanism wrote that through these policies, Germany had discredited itself and cut itself off from the community of civilized nations.[27] Still, a certain underlying anti-Semitic attitude comes through even in many of the articles that criticize Nazi anti-Semitism. German anti-Semitism is explained, for instance, as a response to the excessive "influence of the Jews," who had supposedly benefited from the displacement of the aristocracy by, respectively, the French Revolution and the Weimar Republic's "socialist" governments.[28]

In 1935, Falih Rıfkı Atay wrote a series of articles reporting from Germany for *Ulus*. In one of them, written around the time of the NSDAP Nuremberg party convention of 1935, he expressed sympathy for the anti-Jewish policies, repeating the Nazi line that the Jews were "controlling the German press" and the cultural and intellectual life in Germany, and that "for the Germans, the Jewish question [was] a question of national defense." Although the Nazis' demagogic rhetoric, as relayed by Atay, bore obvious similarities to the appeals by Turkish nationalist politicians to finally break the "dominance" of minorities in the Turkish economy, Atay emphasized that "to us Turks . . . racial hostility of this kind is alien." Still, he added, in an allusion to the Armenian genocide and the criticism it had drawn especially among the Western powers, "we were forced to fight a struggle for survival against those who betrayed us."[29]

## Jews in Turkey: Targets of Nationalism and Anti-Semitism

That the majority of Turkey's political class rejected the Nazis' radical anti-Semitism by no means meant that Turkey was free of anti-Semitism.[30] Like other minorities in Turkey, Jews were subjected to forcible assimilation policies and a rigid nationalism. The Kemalist project of Turkification was aimed at ensuring Turkish-Muslim predominance in all areas of society. Occupational bans for non-Muslims were in effect in public service and various professions, and minorities were exposed to a range of restrictive laws regarding freedom of movement, the freedom to organize, and funding for community facilities. The objective of Turkification was the forcible homogenization of the ethnically and religiously heterogeneous population. The settlement law (İskân Kanunu) of June 1934, an important instrument of "population engineering," gave the government the power to relocate populations of entire regions for the sake of their Turkification, and a slew of nationalist holidays and campaigns produced a climate of constant nationalist agitation. These national policies were not specifically anti-Semitic, and affected other non-Muslim and non-Turkish minorities as well. Kurds, for example, faced much more severe repression, both in terms of the number of people affected and the level of violence they encountered.[31]

Nevertheless, nationalist campaigns often targeted Jews. The public campaigns for language Turkification to which Turkey's minorities were subjected, under the slogan *Vatandaş Türkçe Konuş* (Citizen, Speak Turkish), not only repeatedly led to violent assaults against members of minorities but also had a thinly veiled anti-Semitic thrust. Jews who spoke with an "un-Turkish accent" were a favorite topic of Turkish cartoons, and politcians repeatedly referred to the use of other languages (French or Judeo-Spanish) among Jews to accuse them of disloyalty to the state. The nationalist climate, with the atmosphere of threat it generated, along with the occupational bans, were factors that contributed to approximately one-third of Turkey's Jewish population leaving the country between the end of World War I and 1935.[32]

Over the course of the 1930s, anti-Semitic tendencies grew stronger—one of several reasons for this development being the influence of Nazi Germany. Central works of modern anti-Semitism were translated into Turkish and published in Turkey during this period, often bankrolled by Germany. In 1934, Cevat Rıfat Atilhan, who was to become a leading intellectual figure of anti-Semitic political Islam in Turkey, founded the journal *Millî İnkılâp*, which published a translation of *The Protocols of the Elders of Zion* in installments.[33] Articles by the German anti-Semite Theodor Fritsch were also translated into Turkish and published under the title *Yahudilik ve Masonluk*. *Millî İnkılâp* was published with German assistance. While in Germany, Atilhan had most likely met with Julius Streicher, who published *Der Stürmer*, and most of the caricatures appearing in the journal came from *Der Stürmer*, with the German-Jewish names replaced with equally common Turkish-Jewish ones.[34] Several articles by Atilhan appeared, under the pen name "Djev," in *Der Stürmer* and *Weltdienst*, the latter a biweekly anti-Semitic pamphlet published by Ulrich Fleischhauer.[35] However, as recent research shows, Atilhan's connections to Nazi officials have often been exaggerated.[36]

The position of Turkish government agencies was quite ambivalent. In 1936, for example, the Turkish edition of Fritsch's inflammatory pamphlet and the import of postcards depicting anti-Semitic cartoons and several other anti-Semitic publications were banned.[37] On the other hand, Atilhan had the backing of Chief of General Staff Fevzi Çakmak.[38] Within a short period during the 1940s, Hitler's *Mein Kampf* and Henry Ford's *The International Jew* appeared in Turkish. In 1943, *The Protocols of the Elders of Zion* was published in entirety as a book. Some of these titles went through a number of editions. The dissemination of these works was financed by German money.[39] The works translated at the time have been constantly reprinted since then.

Atilhan was an extremist. His poisonous propaganda drew sharp criticism from numerous intellectuals in Turkey, and after the events in Thrace in 1934 (see below), the journal *Millî İnkılâp* was banned. But the Turkish press increasingly used classically anti-Semitic tropes. Diatribes against "Jewish traders" and "stateless, wandering Jews" cropped up in the daily press in connection with economic bottlenecks or Jewish refugees from Eastern Europe. Caricature magazines (which reached a wider audience than many daily newspapers because of the relatively

**Figure 2.2.** An anti-Semitic cartoon copied from the Nazi newspaper *Der Stürmer* and reprinted in the Turkish newspaper *Millî İnkılâp*, July 1934. *Caption:* "For centuries, the Jew has been misleading humanity with death tunes and driving it to catastrophe with a bridle of pearls. The love of race and nation is the best protection against this danger."

low literacy rate) like *Akbaba* and *Karikatür* stigmatized Jews as greedy, deceptive, immoral, and devoid of love for their homeland. These magazines were by no means associated with the extreme right.[40]

As is typical of modern anti-Semitism, Turkish anti-Semitism, too, was often a blend of conspiracy theories, anti-intellectualism, and anti-

**Figure 2.3.** An anti-Semitic cartoon that appeared in the Turkish publication *Akbaba* depicting a Jew counting his money, 1934. *Caption:* "Salomon, they say all nations should reduce their arms. Will they reduce my money as well?"

communism. This expressed itself as incendiary rhetoric against "cosmopolitan freemasons"[41] and progressive and left-wing intellectuals. A variation of anti-Semitism particular to Turkey was directed against the Dönme.[42] Prominent intellectuals from a Dönme background, such as the liberal journalist Ahmet Emin Yalman and the committed anti-

— Oğlum Salamon, hayatta, dayima namuzlu adamlarla aliş viriş et.. Onları aldatmak daha kolaydır!..

**Figure 2.4.** An anti-Semitic cartoon that appeared in the Turkish publication *Akbaba* depicting a Jew talking to his son, 1939. *Caption:* "Salomon, my son, always deal with honest people. It is easier to cheat them."

Fascist female writer and journalist Sabiha Sertel, both publishers of the critical daily *Tan* (Dawn), became particular targets. They were accused of being not Turks but "covert Jews," and *Tan* was compared to a noisy synagogue.[43]

The Turkish government repeatedly denied the very existence of anti-Semitism in Turkey and assured that it would not be tolerated. In the 24 January 1939 issue of *Yeni Sabah,* the journalist and MP Hüseyin Cahit Yalçın published, probably on government assignment, a detailed declaration repudiating any hostility toward Jews in Turkey, which was reprinted in the foreign Jewish press. It must be emphasized here that the National Socialists' racist hatred for Jews, with its eventual policy of extermination, was unambiguously rejected by the majority of the Turkish public. The German consular offices repeatedly reported to Berlin that the anti-Jewish propaganda material sent by German party or government agencies was "unsuitable for Turkey."[44] Nonetheless, 1933 to 1945 constituted the darkest period in the history of Turkey's Jews. Three events from this period had particularly dramatic consequences for them.

## From the Anti-Jewish Riots in Thrace to the Wealth Tax

In late June and early July 1934, the Jews of Thrace (the European part of Turkey) were forced through threats, boycotts, and violent attacks to leave their homes. This took place largely with the tacit agreement of the state security forces, and in several places, government authorities ordered the Jews to leave their places of residence. In Kırklareli, a veritable pogrom took place, with an anti-Semitic mob raiding and plundering Jewish businesses and homes, and committing violent attacks on rabbis and women.[45]

Several thousand Jews fled to Istanbul, and hundreds of Turkish Jews left the country for Palestine or for neighboring Bulgaria and Greece. Only after the international press had reported on the incidents did the Turkish government react, downplaying the events and asserting that anti-Semitism had been imported from outside, since Turks could never be anti-Semites. But the mere fact that the anti-Jewish activities began almost simultaneously all over Thrace indicates an orchestrated plan and gives reason to assume that the state was behind the events. Foreign diplomats reporting on them emphasized the role of the local branches of the CHP (the sole governing political party) and its cultural arm, *Halk Evleri* (People's Houses), in organizing the anti-Jewish boycotts and assumed that the Turkish state had planned the Jews' expulsion.[46] Only a week before the riots began, the above-mentioned İskân Kanunu had been passed into law, which authorized the government to resettle population groups suspected of espionage from border territories and regions of strategic military importance. This applied to Thrace and the Dardanelles. The situation in 1934 was characterized by tensions between Turkey and Bulgaria, and by Turkish fears of Italy's expansionist ambitions. It is quite possible that military and government authorities regarded the Jews living in Thrace as "unreliable."

A few weeks before the pogrom, the region had been placed under special governance, a so-called inspectorate general, with İbrahim Tali [Öngören] as general inspector. Tali had written a report on the region that was replete with anti-Semitic stereotypes and culminated in the call to "finally solve the [Jewish] problem in the most radical way."[47] Not only does the report contradict the government's assertion that there was no anti-Semitism in Turkey, but it also indicates that the state was involved in the expulsion of the Jews. Tali was the highest-ranking government official in the region and had extensive political and military powers.

For the Jewish communities of Thrace, the events spelled the end of an existence that had extended over hundreds of years. Despite the government's promises to protect the Jews and appeals for them to return, no means were provided for them to do so, nor did the government keep its promise to return the possessions stolen during the riots to their owners. During the ensuing period, there were further boycott attempts and incidents of intimidation in Edirne and even in Istanbul.

## Forced Labor Service and the "Wealth Tax"

Another drastic measure that contributed to undermining the trust of many Jews in the Turkish state was the conscription of non-Muslims into forced labor service.[48] In May 1941, during the German advance in the Balkans, non-Muslim men between the ages of twenty-five and forty-five were suddenly drafted into military labor service, in some cases directly from the street. They were shipped to central Anatolia and housed in camps, where they had to work in quarries or build roads, unarmed and guarded by Turkish military personnel. In the memoirs of numerous contemporary witnesses, the fear felt at the time was palpable.[49] The fact alone that the government decrees on the issue used the word *gayrimüslim* (non-Muslim) did not conform to the usual political language of the Republic, which was always at pains to avoid discriminatory language in its official publications. Vitali Hakko, later a well-known businessman in Istanbul, writes in his memoirs: "We were taken from our workplaces like criminals and handed over to the military; many of us were not even able to notify our families . . . There were no Muslim Turks among us. This caused great uncertainty among all of us . . . Why aren't they telling us where we are being taken?"[50] In July 1942, the first "forced labor soldiers" were abruptly discharged—once again without advance notice. However, documents in the Prime Minister's Archives indicate that non-Muslims were still being drafted to perform road construction work in 1943.[51]

The most drastic measure affecting minorities, especially the Jews, in Turkey was the "wealth tax" (Varlık Vergisi), a special tax that the government justified by citing the shortages caused by the war economy. Under the burden of immense military expenditures, the supply situation of the population had grown dramatically worse. The shortage of goods, in part attributable to forced acquisitions by the state, resulted in extreme price increases. Some sources cite an almost 500 percent price increase. The population's dissatisfaction was deliberately directed toward the Jews. The newspapers depicted individual black marketers or suspected "usurers" as "parasites of the Turkish people." Those explicitly named were always non-Muslims. Jews were specifically targeted by articles and caricatures, which employed stereotypical anti-Semitic tropes. This sudden flood of openly anti-Semitic material astonished even the German authorities. Walter Schellenberg, the head of the foreign intelligence service of the SS, sent a collection of Turkish cartoons to the Foreign Office in Berlin with the comment: "All the enclosed cartoons ... show the Jew to be unmistakably a parasite of the people, responsible for all ills ... It has to be all the more remarkable if the Turkish press, known as it is to be very tightly controlled, attacks the Jew as such in such a drastic manner."[52]

On 11 November 1942, the Turkish parliament passed the law that introduced Varlık Vergisi. Although officially the tax was to be levied on all business owners and self-employed people, the taxes for non-Muslims were assessed many times higher than those for Muslims. Turkish politicians declared quite blatantly that the tax was aimed at breaking the "dominance" of foreigners and minorities in the economy.[53] Those incapable of raising the arbitrarily set and often astronomical sums had their property confiscated and auctioned off. In Istanbul, 1,870 people—Jews, Armenians, and Greeks—were arrested and deported for slave labor to a region near the Russian border, where they had to work in the quarry or shovel snow. Twenty-one people died in these camps.

The wealth tax did not exclusively affect Jews. Although the number of Jews living in Turkey was much smaller than that of Christians, the majority of those deported to labor camps was Jewish. In December 1943, the deportees were released; a few months later, the Varlık Vergisi law was finally rescinded. Nevertheless, the confiscated assets were never returned. In effect, Varlık Vergisi was tantamount to state confiscation of the property of non-Muslim minorities, and it served to Turkify most of the companies, real estate, and capital owned by minority members of the bourgeoisie; for the non-Muslim middle classes, Varlık Vergisi spelled instant impoverishment. İshak Alaton, later a well-known businessman in Turkey, recalls in his memoirs that the Turkish officials literally cleared out their home, leaving the family without furniture, the oven, or even light bulbs, while his father was deported to Aşkale.[54]

## Turkey's Policies toward Jewish Refugees

Turkey's nationalist policies were also manifested in its stance toward Jewish refugees. These policies, aimed at the creation of an exclusively "Turkish economy," had already resulted in the dismissal of a large number of non-Muslim Turkish citizens, and from 1932 on, foreigners were generally barred from obtaining work permits for most occupations.[55] Therefore, the information pamphlets published by Jewish organizations in Germany explicitly advised against immigrating to Turkey.[56] Exceptions were made for academics who came to Turkey in the 1930s at the invitation of the Turkish government. Turkey was seeking to modernize its academic institutions, as well as to establish new ones, and was therefore eager to attract renowned scientists. Among the first measures taken by the Nazi regime in Germany in 1933 was the dismissal of Jews and political opponents from universities and cultural institutions. The coincidence of Turkey's search for specialists and scholars with the abrupt expulsion of an entire academic elite from public institutions in Germany facilitated the emigration of numerous academics to Turkey. About 130 academics who were classified by the Nazis as "Jewish" found employment as professors, advisers to Turkish government agencies, lecturers, or academic assistants; a further 100 worked legally in private enterprises or made a living in various occupations. In addition, an estimated 300 to 400 nonprominent refugees in Turkey tried to get by, for the most part, under extremely difficult conditions.

Several publications on "academic exile," memoirs written by some of the former émigrés, and other sources have contributed to the impression that Turkey was an important country of exile for persecuted Jews, a notion that has been readily fostered by Turkish propaganda but is nonetheless inaccurate. The main aim of Turkey's policies on Jewish refugees was to reject them. In May 1937, the Turkish Ministry of Foreign Affairs issued a secret brief aimed at preventing the immigration of Jews. According to the settlement law, Jews were regarded as "unwanted elements," and the right to immigrate was limited to "members of the Turkish race and culture."[57] Numerous nonprominent German-Jewish refugees were expelled.

Over the course of 1938, the number of Jewish refugees increased sharply worldwide as a result of the anti-Semitic incidents and legislation against Jews in Germany, Austria, Romania, and Italy. Against this backdrop, Turkey passed two laws in June 1938 that prohibited the entry or stay of any person without a valid passport or identification card.[58] Although the wording of these laws targeted undesirable refugees in general, the timing indicates that these measures were primarily aimed at Jews. This becomes apparent from a Turkish inquiry to the German Consulate General in Istanbul a few days after the laws' passage. The head of the aliens department of the Turkish police suggested marking the passports of German Jews with a secret mark known only to the police and the Consulate General that would not attract the passport holders' attention.[59] Turkey was not the only country making this kind of request. Switzerland, Sweden, and Portugal also asked the Germans to mark the passports of Jews in order to make their holders distinguishable as Jewish.

During the summer of 1938, country after country issued laws and regulations that would prevent Jews from entering, and in July 1938, at the Évian Conference, almost all participating countries explained why they were not in a position to take in any more persecuted Jews. A few weeks after the conference, on 29 August 1938, the Turkish government issued Decree No. 2/9498, which prohibited the issuing of visas to Jews with German, Hungarian, or Romanian citizenship. The decree stated that, since Jews were increasingly trying to emigrate because of anti-Semitism spreading from Germany to other countries, the measures taken by Turkey in the past had proved insufficient. It is noteworthy that the decree explicitly mentioned that "given the danger of Jewish mass immigration," countries like Switzerland, Italy, France, England, and others had taken measures to prevent Jewish immigration, and it suggested that Turkey follow their lead. The decree was secret; it was not published in either of the two official government publications.[60] Following its issuing, Turkish consulates now demanded proof of "Aryan descent" before granting entry visas to Turkey.

Experts whose work was essential for Turkish institutions or whose stay was considered "useful for . . . economic reasons" could obtain exceptional permission to stay in Turkey. They could also get permission to have their family members join them. But this was a very limited option, since every permit required approval by the entire Council of Ministers. Even some of the German-Jewish academics who had been employed in public positions in Turkey now lost their jobs, and with them, the permission to stay.

The number of people persecuted in Greater Germany for being Jewish who officially found exile in Turkey, including family members, added up to about six hundred people, many of whom spent no more than two years in Turkey.[61] This is just more than one-tenth of 1 percent of the approximately four hundred thousand Jews who had left Germany and Austria before emigration from Greater Germany and German-occupied Europe was halted in October 1941. Turkey is not even mentioned in any of the pertinent statistics on countries providing refuge. In fact, Turkey's anti-minority policies prompted the emigration of several thousand Turkish Jews over the course of the 1930s.

## Transit Refugees

With the German attack on Poland and the beginning of World War II, the question of refuge for Jews took on a completely new dimension. In the German-occupied part of Poland alone, 2 million Jews came under Nazi control and another 1.5 million were living in the part occupied by the Soviets. In addition, several Axis-allied countries in Southeastern Europe enacted anti-Semitic measures: in Romania, the Iron Guard, part of the government since September 1940, launched murderous attacks on Jews, while Bulgaria deported all foreign Jews in 1940. While the number of persecuted Jews trying to find an escape route continued to increase, the conditions of war made escape almost impossible. When the Mediterranean became a theater of war in 1940, the most important sea route to Palestine, leading from French and Italian ports through the Mediterranean, was blocked. With the only remaining escape route to Palestine now leading through Turkey, the country gained immense significance both as a transit country for Jews trying to escape and as a base for organized rescue activities.[62] But the secret decree of August 1938 prevented the transit of Jews through Turkey as well. Given the policies of Britain, which severely curbed Jewish immigration to Palestine beginning in 1936,[63] Turkey had justified fears that Jewish refugees might "get stuck" in Turkey. This was the reason the representative of the Jewish Agency in Istanbul, Haim Barlas, initially focused his efforts on getting transit permits for those Jews who held valid Palestine certificates. He had some success in that the Turkish government permitted two larger groups to pass through in the fall of 1940.

Eventually, in January 1941, the secret decree was somewhat relaxed, and Turkey permitted passage to Jews who had obtained Palestine certificates before the war. Although the revised decree expressly begins with the sentence, "Jews who are subject to restrictions to their life and freedom of movement in their home countries are prohibited from entering Turkey,"[64] and lists only a handful of narrowly defined exceptions, several publications in relation to rescue activities during the Holocaust mistakenly identify it as a decree permitting persecuted Jews entry into—or at least transit through—Turkey. This may be attributable to the fact that the decree was indeed presented in this light in the Turkish press or misinterpreted by readers; after all, it did seem like a breakthrough, given the slight improvement it constituted compared to the previous status quo. In fact, over the course of one year, more than 4,800 Jews who met Turkey's entry requirements were able to reach and transit through the country. But during the crucial years from 1942 to 1944, a multitude of bureaucratic obstacles once again made Turkey a bottleneck with regard to rescue activities.

The best-known incident resulting from these restrictions is the tragic story of the *Struma,* a vessel that reached Istanbul on 15 December 1941, with 765 Jewish refugees on board, most of whom had fled the mass slaughter in Romania. The ship's engine was broken, but the Turkish authorities refused to allow the passengers to disembark, although Jewish relief organizations offered to assume all costs for housing until the passengers would get permission to continue to Palestine. On 24 February 1942, heavy police forces boarded the ship in order to prevent resistance by the passengers, and the *Struma,* without a working engine, was towed into the open sea. Shortly after, the ship was hit by a Soviet torpedo and sank. With the exception of David Stoliar, who managed to save himself by swimming, all the passengers died off the coast of Istanbul.[65]

Even after this tragedy, and even as news about mass killings and the Jews' desperate situation in Romania and other Eastern European countries under Nazi control reached the Turkish authorities, the government upheld its restrictive policies against Jews trying to enter Turkey from Bulgaria or Romania. It must be pointed out, however, that Turkish restrictions constituted merely one of several factors that obstructed the refugees' escape; others included the policies of Great Britain[66] and the Germans' massive efforts to close off escape routes for Jews. Toward Jewish refugees from Greece, however, the stance of the Turkish authorities was somewhat more lenient. In 1943, a collaboration that developed between Jewish activists, the Greek resistance, and the British Secret Intelligence Service on the Aegean coast near Izmir and Çeşme resulted in the rescue of Jews from Greece. More than one thousand Greek Jews were rescued via the Aegean

Sea; the Turkish authorities tacitly tolerated these activities.[67] Essentially, Turkey only changed its position toward Jewish refugees in the summer of 1944, when Germany's eventual defeat was becoming apparent and Romania and other countries had broken their alliance with the Nazi regime.

## Turkish Jews in Europe under Nazi Persecution

On the eve of World War II, twenty thousand to thirty thousand Jews from Turkey were living in Europe.[68] From Paris to Berlin and from Brussels to Milan, Turkish-Jewish communities had their own synagogues and cultural and social associations. Compared with Jewish immigrants from Eastern Europe, they constituted a definite minority. Still, bearing in mind that by 1935, a mere seventy-eight thousand Jews were left in the Turkish Republic, these Turkish exile communities formed a significant group. They were far larger in number than the entire Jewish population of Turkey today. The majority of them lived in France, predominantly in Paris, which developed into a new center of Sephardic life in the interwar period. In Sephardic organizations like the Confédération Universelle des Juifs Sépharadim, which was based in Paris since 1931, Jews from Turkey played a prominent role.

After the occupation of several European countries by Nazi Germany—or, in the case of Germany itself, since 1933—Turkish Jews, too, were subjected to Nazi Germany's measures against Jews. Although the Nazi ideology did not differentiate between Jews of different nationalities, foreign policy considerations continued to force Hitler's regime to act with a certain degree of caution. With the occupation of Western European countries in 1940, the issue of foreign Jews gained particular significance. Tens of thousands of Jews living in these countries were foreigners, citizens of a multitude of countries, thousands of whom were nationals of countries allied with Germany.

Various diplomats protested against the Nazis' discrimination and repressive measures against their Jewish citizens. In the winter of 1940–1941, the representations of several neutral countries (Turkey among them), through concerted protests, managed to exempt businesses owned by their Jewish nationals in France from "Aryanization" and put under the management of administrators affiliated with the respective consulates instead.[69] Likewise, by intervening against the mass arrests of foreign Jews in 1941, numerous diplomats managed to obtain the release of their Jewish fellow citizens. Eventually, the Nazi authorities devised veritable "hierarchies" of persecution for Jews of different groups and nationalities. For a certain time, until 1943, Jews from neutral countries and countries allied with Germany were exempt from several anti-Jewish measures and, temporarily, considered by the Nazis to be "non-deportable."

As a neutral country that played a significant role in the German war effort, Turkey had considerable means to protect its Jewish citizens living in European countries. Turkish diplomats in France, Italy, and Greece repeatedly and successfully intervened on behalf of Turkish Jews. From France, interventions on behalf of about fifty Turkish Jews by Turkish diplomats are documented for the years 1942 and 1943 alone. In most of these cases, the respective Turkish consuls were able to obtain their release, thus saving them from deportation.[70]

## Consequences of Turkey's Population Policies for Its Jewish Citizens Abroad

It proved to be calamitous for the Turkish Jews living in Nazi Germany's sphere of control that Ankara deprived thousands of them of their Turkish citizenship or did not recognize it in the first place. Initially, these measures were not connected with Germany's persecution of the Jews; rather, they were part of Turkey's nationalist population policies. A series of laws and decrees enabled the Turkish government to deprive population groups regarded as undesirable of their Turkish citizenship, among them those who had not taken part in the Turkish "War of Independence" or who were not considered Turkish by culture.[71] Most of these laws and decrees affected people living abroad.[72] The stripping of citizenship came to be used primarily against Jews only after the persecution of Jews by the Nazis had begun, and even more so after 1940, when Jews living in Western European countries occupied by Germany became critically dependent on the protection afforded by their citizenship. This seems to have been no coincidence. A handwritten note from the office of the prime minister's secretary of April 1939 lists three laws (1041, 1312, 2848) under the word *Yahudi* (Jew); these laws would be used in subsequent years for the mass revocation of the citizenship of Jews.[73] What made this legislation even more severe was the fact that the revocation of citizenship entailed a lifelong ban from entering Turkey, even temporarily or as a refugee.[74]

In the winter of 1941–1942, after the various German agencies involved had agreed on the rules of exemption for Jewish citizens of neutral and allied countries, German authorities in France sent the pertinent consulates—Turkish diplomatic representations among them[75]—lists of their imprisoned Jewish nationals, requesting that they confirm their citizenship. On March 24 1942, the Turkish Consulate General in Paris wrote that it could "not acknowledge the twenty-nine people of Jewish religion born in Turkey whose names are on the enclosed list compiled by the camp authorities in Compiègne as regular Turkish citizens," and therefore could not issue them passports or other documents.[76] It is very likely that many of the Turkish Jews interned in the camps of Drancy or Compiègne only found out after their imprisonment that Turkey no longer recognized their citizenship. This is reflected in desperate letters some of them sent in which they implored relatives to send the necessary documents; Jews from other neutral countries had already been released from these camps.[77]

Throughout 1942, the Germans deported hundreds of Jews of Turkish origin from France to the extermination camps, where they were murdered. These were predominantly Jews whose citizenship the Turkish agencies had either revoked or not confirmed, either explicitly or implicitly, by indicating their disinterest to the Germans. At this point, in the summer of 1942, the Turkish agencies could not really foresee the fatal consequences their rejection would have for the Turkish Jews. But the Turkish government continued this policy even after the end of 1942, when the systematic extermination of the Jews was known and it had become abundantly clear what the risk of deportation entailed.

## The German Ultimatum on Repatriation

In contrast to the commitment of several Turkish consuls in the field who tried to protect their Jewish citizens, the main concern of the government in Ankara was to prevent their return to Turkey. One example that makes this evident is Ankara's response to the German ultimatum in October 1942 to repatriate its Jewish citizens from German-controlled areas, or in Nazi parlance, to "return them home" (*Heimschaffung*). Failing that, they would be "included in the general measures regarding Jews"—which meant arrest, deportation and murder, a fact that the Germans took care not to explicitly state. This ultimatum, which was first issued with regard to foreign Jews in France and subsequently extended to all countries under German occupation in Western and Central Europe, was also issued to the other neutral countries and countries allied with Germany.[78] Turkish Jews constituted by far the largest group affected by this measure; the Nazi agencies assumed a figure of four thousand to five thousand Turkish Jews to be repatriated from northern France alone.

Initially, Turkey, like several other countries, did not respond. After all, the ultimatum essentially constituted an act of blackmail: it confronted the respective governments with the alternative of either delivering their Jewish citizens to the Germans and making themselves accomplices, or to approve their forcible expulsion from countries in which they had built new lives for themselves. And, as mentioned, we must assume that in October 1942, the Turkish government was still unaware of the German genocide of the Jews, as were the majority of the Jews to whom the ultimatum applied. But this was about to change. After Polish politicians in exile and Jewish organizations had, in the late fall of 1942, presented extensive evidence of the mass extermination of Jews in German-occupied Poland, the eleven Allied governments issued a joint declaration on 17 December 1942, which stated that German authorities were engaging in the mass murder of European Jews. In January 1943, the Polish government in exile published a pamphlet entitled "The Mass Extermination of Jews in German-Occupied Poland." It was based on a note of the same name from December 1942, which contained several documents that provided evidence for the ongoing extermination of Jews. These documents were conveyed to the governments of the neutral countries.[79]

We know that this information reached Ankara. The December 1942 issue of the government journal *Ayın Tarihi* (History of the month) reported on the declaration and published it verbatim, and the March 1943 issue contained another speech by British Foreign Secretary Anthony Eden about the German annihilation of the Jews.[80] Still, it is noteworthy that the Turkish daily press made absolutely no mention of this or other news about the genocide of the Jews in the winter of 1942–1943, this at a time when Turkey's newspapers generously covered, on a daily basis, Jewish "tax dodgers" and the deportation of individuals "unwilling to pay" to the labor camps in Eastern Turkey.

## "A Mass Immigration of Jews Is to Be Prevented"

At the same time, prompted by the intensification of repressive measures in the German-occupied countries, local Turkish consuls suggested an organized repatriation as well. But the government in Ankara explicitly instructed its diplomatic representations "not to conduct" any group repatriations.[81] By March 1943, only about 120 out of the more than 3,000 Turkish Jews in the northern part of France whose names the Germans had supplied to the Turkish consulate had been repatriated to Turkey.

After the Germans extended the repatriation deadline several times (in the case of Turkey, it was eventually set for the end of September 1943), the secretary of the Turkish Embassy in Berlin, Kemal Koç, announced to the German Foreign Office that Ankara now agreed to repatriate Jews of indisputable Turkish citizenship. This was to happen, however, with the stipulation that "a mass immigration of Jews into Turkey [was] to be prevented," especially of those whose Turkish papers were in order but who had not had any contact with Turkey for decades.[82] Jews who wanted to return to Turkey had to submit an application at the embassy, following which their names were checked first by the consul in charge and then by a government agency in Ankara, a process that could take months. In the winter of 1943–1944, with hundreds of Turkish Jews being shipped to concentration camps by the Germans, several Jewish organizations outside of Turkey, as well as US representatives in Turkey, appealed to the Turkish government to permit these Jews to return and to at least give them shelter until the end of the war. Still Ankara refused.[83] Eventually, between February and the end of May 1944, a further 414 Jews were evacuated to Turkey on six specially designated trains.

Even as late as the spring of 1945, a few weeks before the German surrender, the decision making of Turkish officials was still guided by the policy to hinder the entry of Jews into the country. On 11 April 1945, 137 Jews of Turkish origin, most of whom had been released from the concentration camps at Ravensbrück and Bergen-Belsen as part of a Turkish-German exchange of civilian prisoners, reached Istanbul on board the SS *Drottningholm*. The Turkish authorities denied 119 of them entry into Turkey. Only after arduous negotiations did Jewish aid organizations gain the authorities' consent for the rescued prisoners to leave the ship and to be interned, at the expense of the Jewish Agency, in three boarding houses in Istanbul.

## After the War

The Germans murdered about 2,500 Jews from Turkey living in several European states, mainly in France. After the war, surviving Turkish Jews in France and Belgium voiced their bitter disappointment with Turkey, which, through its passive policy, had delivered the Jews to their German murderers.[84] In Turkey the most committed critics and publicists, who had attempted to provide a counterbalance to the Fascist and pro-German sentiment during the war years, were themselves subjected to persecution as leftists, even after the end of the war. In December 1945, Hüseyin Cahit Yalçın, a steadfast opponent of Germany throughout the war, called in his newspaper, *Tanin,* for a fight against the progressive press. Following his call, nationalist students demonstrated in front of the newsrooms of the anti-Fascist newspapers *Tan* and *Yeni Dünya* and eventually wrecked them. The lecturers Behice Boran, Pertev Boratav, and Niyazi Berkes, who had been vocal in their stance against German and Turkish Fascism, were dismissed from the Faculty of Language, History, and Geography in Ankara.

In 1946, Turkey introduced a multiparty system. In 1947, the decree that had denied persecuted Jews entry into Turkey was revoked. The Varlık Vergisi law had already been abolished in 1944, but while there was public criticism of the tax in Turkey after the war, no property was ever returned to those who had been forced to pay it. Turkey's anti-Jewish policies during the war compelled thirty-five thousand to forty thousand Jews to immigrate to Palestine after 1945, especially after the founding of the State of Israel in 1948.

Anti-Semites and Fascists, inspired by the German example, became a constant in Turkey's political system in the period after World War II. In 1962, Nihal Atsız, along with a group of like-minded people, founded the Türkçülük Derneği, a forerunner of the Fascist Milliyetçi Hareket Partisi (Nationalist Action Party—MHP). Cevat Rıfat Atilhan managed to expand his role as Turkey's leading anti-Semitic writer in Turkey after 1945 and maintained it until his death in 1967. During this period, he was involved in founding several Islamist political parties. New editions of his books continue to be published today and appear on the bestseller lists of Islamist and Fascist newspapers and websites.

## Conclusion

Turkey's policies during World War II were focused on keeping the country out of conflict by way of adroit political maneuvering between the warring parties, a strategy that in the end would allow Turkey to join the winning side. Racist and near-Fascist tendencies were gaining strength during this period, and certain circles were sympathetic to Nazi Germany. Still, official government policy continued to stay the course of an independent Turkish "national revolution." The majority of Turkish commentators rejected the Nazis' radical, racist anti-Semitism. But the persecution of the Jews and its culmination in the Holocaust barely registered in Turkey, although there is incontrovertible evidence that the Turkish government knew about it quite early on. The country continued its restrictive policies vis-à-vis Jewish refugees, regardless of their knowledge of the Jews' persecution, and denied protection to many of its Jewish citizens living in Europe. However, it bears emphasizing that these policies were not prompted by pressure from Germany; they were first and foremost a consequence of Turkey's own nationalist political agenda.

**Corry Guttstadt** is an independent scholar who has taught at the University of Hamburg and has been a research fellow at the United States Holocaust Memorial Museum in Washington, DC, and at Yad Vashem in Jerusalem. Her main field of research is minority policies, especially toward Jews, and anti-Semitism in Turkey. She has also published on topics such as human rights in Turkey, the Kurds, the Armenians, nationalism, and migration. Her book *Die Türkei die Juden und der Holocaust* was published in 2008, in Turkish in 2012, and in English in 2013. She edited the book *Wege ohne Heimkehr* (2014), an anthology of Armenian reports on the deported and the survivors in literature and memory. With Thomas Lutz, Bernd Rother, and Yessica San Roman, she coedited *Bystanders, Rescuers or Perpetrators? The Neutrals and the Shoah* (2016). She is currently working on the Sephardic Jews in France during the Shoah.

## Notes

1. On February 23 1945, Turkey finally declared war on Germany—a condition for joining the founding session of the United Nations. Until 1943, both Germany and the Allies were primarily interested in maintaining Turkish neutrality, the rationale being that the country would be difficult to defend if it were to become involved in the war. See William Hale, *Turkish Foreign Policy since 1774* (Abingdon, 2013), 84. From 1943 onward, the Allies attempted in vain to convince Turkey to enter the war.
2. Corry Guttstadt, *Turkey, the Jews, and the Holocaust* (New York, 2013), 150–151.

3. Statement by the then secretary in charge of EU membership negotiations, Mevlüt Çavuşoğlu, on 27 January 2014 (http://www.ab.gov.tr/index.php?p=49393&l=1). (All translations in this chapter are my own unless otherwise indicated.) There are numerous almost identical statements by Turkish politicians on record. Two films, co-financed by the Turkish Ministry of Foreign Affairs, and a two-volume publication in Turkish by the former diplomat Bilâl N. Şimşir—*Türk Yahudiler: Avrupa Irkçılarına Karşı Türkiye'nin Mücadelesi* [Turkish Jews: Turkey's struggle against the European racists] (Ankara, 2010)—also aim at conveying the impression that Turkey's policy at the time was concerned with the fate of the Jews.
4. *Der Angriff*, 8 May 1933.
5. Falih Rıfkı Atay, chief editor of *Ulus* (the party organ of the single political party) and one of the closest confidants of Atatürk, in *Ulus*, 23 September 1935.
6. Abidin Daver in *Cumhuriyet*, 29 April 1935.
7. Abidin Daver in *Cumhuriyet*, 20 May 1935.
8. E.g., Ahmet Şükrü [Esmer] in *Milliyet*, 30 April 1933. Names in brackets indicate family names adopted in Turkey after 1934.
9. Ahmet Şükrü [Esmer] in *Milliyet*, 25 March 1933.
10. *Milliyet*, 4 July 1933. Mahmut [Soydan] had been appointed chief editor of *Milliyet* on express orders from Atatürk. The article is quoted from Ahmet Asker, "Yeni Türkiye'den Nazi Almanyası'na Karşılaştırmalı Bakışlar ve Algılar, 1929–1939," PhD diss., Mersin University, 2012. I would like to thank Ahmet Asker for making his dissertation available to me, as well as for sending me numerous articles from the Turkish press that form part of the basis of this chapter.
11. *Ulus*, May 20, 1935.
12. *Milliyet*, 20 July 1934, signed "N.A." The author was most likely Nizamettin Ali [Sav], a contributor to *Milliyet* during this period.
13. Hugh Poulton, *Top Hat, the Grey Wolf and the Crescent: Turkish Nationalism and the Turkish Republic* (New York, 1997), 112; Ahmet Yıldız, *"Ne Mutlu Türküm Diyebilene": Türk Ulusal Kimliğinin Etno-Seküler Sınırları (1919–1938)* (Istanbul, 2001), 204–208.
14. Reports of discrimination and violent attacks against non-Jewish Turks in Germany (in some cases because Nazi thugs had mistaken them for Jews) repeatedly triggered vigorous protests among the Turkish public. The Nazis' stance toward Turks and members of other non-European nations was contradictory and contentious among the various Nazi agencies. The classification of Turks, Arabs, and Japanese as "non-Aryans," in keeping with Nazi racial theory, led to foreign policy complications, not least because the Germans considered many of their respective governments as allies. Consequently, the racial theories had to be "modified" to some degree in accordance with foreign policy requirements.
15. See, e.g., a comment titled "Two Fascisms" that is critical of Nazi politics in general but emphasizes that "any change of our stance and political line on the Treaty of Versailles is out of the question, since we, too, were forced to accept this kind of agreement" (*Cumhuriyet*, 1 January 1934).
16. *Ulus*, 16 January 1935.

17. *Yeni Sabah* called the German invasion a "violation" and "a brutal and barbaric act of violence." Quoted in Ahmet Çelik, "İkinci Dünya Savaşı Sürecinde (1939–1945) Muhalif Basın," MA thesis, Süleyman Demirel Üniversitesi, Isparta, 2011, 9.
18. As early as 1830, during the Ottoman era, Polish soldiers who reached Istanbul after their defeat in the revolt of 1830 were granted the founding of a small village (Polonezköy) and military training to produce soldiers who would fight the common Russian enemy. During World War II, Poland's diplomatic representations in Turkey, which had ties with the government in exile in London, published two exile newspapers.
19. Issues 85–87 (December 1940—February 1941) of the Turkish government gazette *Ayın Tarihi* ("History of the Month") provide numerous examples; they also contain quotes from Greek newspapers in which Turkey is thanked for its solidarity and presents received by Greek soldiers.
20. Selim Deringil, "Hasta Adam'ın Dinç Evlatları," *Toplumsal Tarih*, 121 (2004): 78.
21. In 1941, the Turkish daily *Yeni Sabah* published a translation of André Simone's *J'accuse: The Men Who Betrayed France* in installments over several weeks. Apparently, the book's publisher (and translator) Hüseyin Cahit Yalçın, an ardent anticommunist, was most probably unaware that the author (Otto Katz) was a devotee of Stalin.
22. Faik Ahmet Barutçu, *Siyasî Anılar 1939–1954* (Istanbul, 1977), 206.
23. The press was subject to double censorship: first, by the press agency in Ankara, which was subordinate to the government, and second—after the announcement of the state of emergency that was in effect from 1941 to 1945—by the state-of-emergency command office in Istanbul, where almost the entire national press was published.
24. See, e.g., the front page of *Vakit*, 9 October 1941: "Official Announcement: Propaganda Cannot Harm German-Turkish Friendship"—almost identical in *Yeni Sabah,* 10 October 1941, and several other newspapers.
25. Most notable among the German-friendly newspapers were *Cumhuriyet* and *Tasvir-i Efkâr*. On German propaganda and the manipulation of the press in Turkey, see Johannes Glasneck, *Methoden der deutschen Propagandatätigkeit in der Türkei vor und während des Zweiten Weltkrieges* (Halle, 1966); Berna Pekesen, *Zwischen Sympathie und Eigennutz: NS-Propaganda und die türkische Presse im Zweiten Weltkrieg* (Münster, 2014).
26. Mehmet Asım [Us] in *Vakit,* 2 April 1933.
27. Yunus Nadi, "Yahudi Aleyhtarlığının En Şiddetli Şekli," *Cumhuriyet,* 31 March 1933.
28. In almost identical form: Mehmet Asım [Us] in *Vakit,* 2 April 1933; Ahmet Şükrü [Esmer], "Yahudi Aleyhtarlığı," in *Milliyet,* 2 April 1933.
29. *Ulus,* 28 September 1935. The same reasoning can be found in articles by numerous journalists.
30. No thorough study of the origins, spread, and ideological basis of anti-Semitism in Turkey has been written to date. For an overview, see Rıfat N. Bali, *Antisemitism and Conspiracy Theories in Turkey* (Istanbul, 2013).

31. In 1937 and 1938, an insurrection of Alevi Kurds in Dersim, who put up resistance to forced resettlement and Turkification, was put down with much bloodshed in a large military operation. According to Turkish sources, about 10 percent of the local Kurdish population was killed; tens of thousands of Kurdish families were forcibly resettled from this region alone.
32. Guttstadt, *Turkey, the Jews, and the Holocaust*, 22–24.
33. For a biography of Atilhan, see Rıfat N. Bali, *Les relations entre Turcs et Juifs dans la Turquie Moderne* (Istanbul, 2001), 75–106.
34. Bayraktar notes that the signature of the *Stürmer* artist Philip Ruprecht (FIPS) is visible in several of the caricatures published in *Millî İnkılâp*. See Hatice Bayraktar, *Salamon und Rabeka: Judenstereotype in Karikaturen der türkischen Zeitschriften Akbaba, Karikatür und Milli Inkilap 1933–1945* (Berlin, 2006), 36.
35. Fleischhauer's publishing company published Atilhan's book on the Jews' ostensible acts of betrayal on the Palestinian front during World War I in German under the title *Die schöne Simi Simon* (Erfurt, 1934).
36. Atilhan claimed to have personally met with high-ranking Nazi officials in Germany (including Rosenberg and even Hitler himself) and to have secured large amounts of money. No evidence of this can be found in German archives. The German financing of *Millî İnkılâp* also appears to have been wishful thinking on Atilhan's part. See Hatice Bayraktar, *"Zweideutige Individuen in schlechter Absicht": Die antisemitischen Ausschreitungen in Thrakien 1934 und ihre Hintergründe* (Berlin, 2011). My own research has yielded the same result.
37. Başbakanlık Cumhuriyet Arşivi (hereinafter BCA), Decree No. 2/4787 of 8 June 1936, 30.18. 1.2/65.49.11; Decree No. 2/4863 of June 19, 1936, 30.18.1.2/66.53.7.
38. In 1935, the Turkish General Staff had Atilhan's crudely anti-Semitic book *Suzi Liberman'ın Hatıra Defteri* (Istanbul, 1969) distributed to all military units. When Atilhan was charged with attempting to found a Nazi party in Turkey and instigate a military coup in August 1940, Çakmak ordered the case to be dismissed.
39. Report given by Posemann on 3–4 April 1944, at a conference of "officials in charge of Jewish affairs." See Leon Poliakov and Joseph Wulf, *Das Dritte Reich und seine Diener* (Berlin, 1996), 167.
40. In detail in Laurent Mallet, "Karikatür Dergisinde Yahudilerle İlgili Karikatürler (1936–1948)," *Toplumsal Tarih* 34 (1996): 27; and Hatice Bayraktar, "Türkische Karikaturen über Juden (1933–1945)," in *Jahrbuch für Antisemitismusforschung* 13 (2004).
41. Freemasonry was banned (again) in Turkey in 1935.
42. Dönme (literally, "turned around") designates, in a narrower sense, the followers of Sabbatai Twi (Sevi), a "false Messiah" of the seventeenth century, who eventually converted to Islam. Some of his followers founded their own sect whose center was in Salonika. After Salonika had been lost, and once again after the founding of the Republic, almost all Dönme resettled in Turkey. As early as the 1920s and 1930s, the *Dönme* were targeted by a very specific type of anti-Semitism that is particularly virulent in Turkey today. See Marc D. Baer, "An Enemy Old and New: The Dönme, Anti-Semitism, and Conspiracy The-

ories in the Ottoman Empire and Turkish Republic," *Jewish Quarterly Review* 103, no. 4 (2013).
43. On this campaign, see Emin Karaca, *Türk Basınında Kalem Kavgaları* (Istanbul, 1998), 111–125; and Marc D. Baer, *The Dönme: Jewish Converts, Muslim Revolutionaries, and Secular Turks* (Stanford, CA, 2010), 221–223.
44. To give just one example representative of several similar statements, a letter from the German Embassy in Ankara, dated 10 June 1939, to Berlin says, "Distribution of this journal [*Mitteilungen zur Judenfrage*, sent by the propaganda staff in Berlin] to any great extent is out of the question [here] because of the attitude of the Turkish authorities toward the Jewish problem." Politisches Archiv des Auswärtigen Amts, Berlin (hereinafter PAAA), Ankara Embassy, 540, draft.
45. On the events and their political background, see Berna Pekesen, *Nationalismus, Türkisierung und das Ende der jüdischen Gemeinden in Thrakien: 1918–1942* (Munich, 2012). Compilations of accounts by eyewitnesses, diplomats, and the contemporaneous press can be found in Rıfat Bali, *1934 Trakya Olayları* (Istanbul, 2008), as well as in Bayraktar, *"Zweideutige Individuen."*
46. See numerous reports quoted in Bayraktar, *"Zweideutige Individuen."*
47. Tali's report is held in the BCA, 490.01.643.30.1.
48. For a comprehensive description, see Rıfat N. Bali, *Yirmi Kur'a Nafıa Askerleri: II. Dünya Savaşı'nda Gayrimüslimlerin Askerlik Serüveni* (Istanbul, 2008).
49. Contemporary witnesses said Turkish soldiers had threatened that they would never see their families again. Quoted in Rıfat N. Bali, *Cumhuriyet Yıllarında Türkiye Yahudileri: Bir Türkleştirme Serüveni, 1923–1945* (Istanbul, 1999), 417.
50. Vitali Hakko, *Hayatım* (Istanbul, 1997), 88–89.
51. BCA, Resolution No. 2/20507 of 8 September 1943, 30.18.1.2/102.63.12. The Armenian Sarkis Çerkezyan writes in his memoirs that he and the non-Muslims in his unit had to perform four years of forced labor and that this measure even targeted people who had converted to Islam. Sarkis Çerkezyan, *Bu Dünya Hepimize Yeter* (Istanbul, 2003), 113.
52. Letter by Schellenberg, No. 52783/42, dated 12 September 1942, PAAA, R 100889, fiche 2273.
53. E.g., Prime Minister Şükrü Saraçoğlu, quoted in Barutçu, *Siyasî Anılar*, 163.
54. Mehmet Gündem, *Lüzumlu Adam İshak Alaton: Hedefi Belli Olmayan Yelkenliye Hiçbir Rüzgâr Yardım Edemez* (Istanbul, 2012), 36–37.
55. The Law on Activities and Professions in Turkey Reserved for Turkish Citizens starting in 1932, followed by further laws restricting employment opportunities for immigrants.
56. See, e.g., *Jüdische Auswanderung: Korrespondenzblatt für Auswanderungs- und Siedlungswesen*, 1–1934, 16; or Ernst G. Löwenthal, ed., *Philo-Atlas: Handbuch für die jüdische Auswanderung* (Berlin, 1938), 196.
57. Information given by the deputy director general at the Turkish Ministry of Foreign Affairs, Kemal Aziz Payman, to the German Embassy, note from 26 May 1937, regarding a meeting with Payman the previous day, PAAA, German Embassy in Ankara, 681.
58. The "Passport Law" (No. 3519) on 28 June 1938 and the "Law Regarding the Residence and Travel of Foreigners in Turkey" (No. 3529) on 29 June 1938.

59. Letter from the German ambassador August F. W. von Keller to the Foreign Office in Berlin, 2 July 1938, PAAA, R 49005.
60. A facsimile of the decree appears in Bilâl N. Şimşir, *Türk Yahudiler - II* (Ankara, 2010), 592. The publication—supposedly a "document collection"—is a very problematic source. Şimşir is not a historian but a former Turkish diplomat, and the volume contains a striking number of blatant errors (wrong dates, transcription errors, etc.). Moreover, the stated political aim of Şimşir's two-volume collection is to prove "Turkey's struggle against the european racists" (the volume's subtitle). Since this particular document is represented in facsimile and the Turkish archives are still not open to independent researchers, I decided to base my summary on the facsimile printed in Şimşir's book.
61. The figure is based on in-depth analysis of the database of the Verein Aktives Museum (VAM), Berlin, which holds the most comprehensive archive on exile in Turkey, as well as on consultation of a number of additional sources.
62. For an overview of Turkey as a transit country, see Tuvia Friling, "Between Friendly and Hostile Neutrality: Turkey and the Jews during World War II," in *The Last Ottoman Century and Beyond*, vol. 2, ed. Minna Rozen (Tel Aviv, 2002).
63. In response to massive Arab protests against Jewish immigration to Palestine, Britain issued the *White Paper* in May 1939, which limited the number of Jewish immigrants to seventy-five thousand over the following five years. In addition, the British authorities canceled all visas issued to German Jews.
64. Decree No. 2/15132, January 1941. The decree actually constituted a tightening of the existing legislation, since it widened the number of Jews who were prohibited from entering Turkey as follows: "foreign Jews who are subject to restrictions in their home countries . . . regardless of their current religious affiliation"—thus explicitly echoing the definition of people categorized and persecuted as Jewish that Nazi Germany and its allies employed in their anti-Jewish legislation. The decree was not officially published in Turkey. The Central Zionist Archives (CZA) in Jerusalem holds a transcript of the original document, S 25/6308.
65. Douglas Frantz and Catherine Collins, *Death on the Black Sea: The Untold Story of the Struma and World War II's Holocaust at Sea* (New York, 2003), 195–198, 209–211.
66. In July 1943, the British government finally decreed that Jewish refugees who managed to reach Turkey would receive open Palestine Certificates. But this information was not passed on to the Turkish government until months later.
67. Friling, "Between Friendly and Hostile," 407–416. Barbara Spengler-Axiopoulos, "'Wenn ihr den Juden helft, kämpft ihr gegen die Besatzer': Der Untergang der griechischen Juden," in *Solidarität und Hilfe für Juden während der NS-Zeit*, Band 1, ed. Wolfgang Benz and Juliane Wetzel (Berlin, 1996), 159.
68. The exact number is difficult to ascertain. The process of migration extended over several decades and generations, and took place in parallel with the dissolution of the Ottoman Empire. Many of the destination countries—France among them—did not include questions on religion in their censuses.
69. Guttstadt, *Turkey, the Jews, and the Holocaust*, 189–191.

70. Stanford J. Shaw gave copies of some of the files of the Turkish consulates in France to the United States Holocaust Memorial Museum (hereinafter USHMM) in Washington, DC (call no. 1995.A.1202). The few surviving files of the German embassy in Paris, held by the PAAA (Deutsche Botschaft Paris, Paket 2387), also contain evidence of such interventions.
71. Several of these decrees were entirely arbitrary. Decree No. 7559, for example, stipulated the expatriation of women who had not taken part in the "War of Independence"—this although there was no military service for women. See Corry Guttstadt, "Depriving Non-Muslims of Citizenship as Part of the Turkification Policy in the Early Years of the Turkish Republic," in *Turkey beyond Nationalism: Towards Post-nationalist Identities,* ed. Hans-Lukas Kieser (London, 2006).
72. It seems that, initially, one main rationale for the rescinding of citizenship was to prevent the return of Armenians and Greeks and to legalize the appropriation of their assets.
73. BCA, Dosya, 94C45, 30.10.0.0/110/736.5.
74. The Passport Law of June 1938 had reemphasized the ban imposed by the Citizenship Law of 1928 and expanded it to the effect that former Turkish citizens were prohibited from entering Turkey, even if they were in possession of a valid passport or identity papers from other countries. Law No. 3519, Article 4.
75. Centre de Documentation Juive Contemporaine (hereinafter CDJC), Paris: DLIX-12 and 14. Paul Zuckermann, who worked as a clerk in Drancy, mentions in a letter to his wife from 1 January 1942 that at the request of a number of consulates, he was compiling lists of their citizens imprisoned there. See CDJC, Fond 986 (19)-4.
76. USHMM, A-00-2373, call no. 1995, A 1202, folder 1-44.
77. Letters by Lucien Sabah between April 1942 and his deportation on 14 September 1942, in Lucien Sabah, *Drancy, dernier mots* (Paris, 2014). Also letters from Drancy by Rafaél Eskenazi, in the folder Kaurine Eskenazi, *Avoir treize ans sous l'occupation allemande (1941–1945): Lettres de mon père.* Accessible at the Musée d'Art et d'Histoire du Judaïsme, Paris.
78. The dates varied. Turkey was one of the first countries to be issued the ultimatum. For an overview of the responses of the neutral countries, see Rainer Schulze, "Die Heimschaffungsaktion of 1942–43: Turkey, Spain and Portugal and Their Responses to the German Offer of Repatriation of Their Jewish Citizens," *Holocaust Studies: A Journal of Culture and History* 18: nos. 2–3 (2012). See also Corry Guttstadt, Lutz Thomas, Rother Bernd, San Roman Yessica, eds., *Bystanders, Rescuers or Perpetrators? The Neutrals and the Shoah,* vol. 2 (Berlin, 2016), chap. 3.
79. Cláudia Ninhos, "What Was Known in the Neutral Countries about the On-going Genocide of European Jews," in Guttstadt et al., *Bystanders, Rescuers or Perpetrators?* 2:25–137.
80. *Ayın Tarihi* 109: 310–311, 112: 251.
81. Memoir by the then Turkish ambassador in Vichy, Behiç Erkin, Hâtırat 1876–1958 (Ankara, 2010), 567. In a letter from 7 January 1943, Erkin passed this order on to the consulates subordinate to him. See Stanford J. Shaw, *Turkey and*

the *Holocaust: Turkey's Role in Rescuing Turkish and European Jewry from Nazi Persecution 1933–45* (Basingstoke, 1993), 142.
82. Memorandum by von Thadden from 22 September 1943, PAAA, R 99446, fiche 5703.
83. Guttstadt, *Turkey, the Jews, and the Holocaust*, 227–229.
84. "L'attitude des Turcs," *Les cahiers séfardis* nos. 7–9 (1947): 277, or Note by Ezra Natan (undated), a Turkish Jew living in Belgium who was deported to the Buchenwald concentration camp (courtesy of his son, Daniel Natan, who made this letter available to me). The figure of about 2,500 deported Jews of Turkish origin includes former Turkish citizens.

# Bibliography

## Archival Sources

Başbakanlık Cumhuriyet Arşivi (Prime Minister's Republican Archives), Ankara collections of the council of ministers

Politisches Archiv des Auswärtigen Amts (Political Archives of the German Foreign Office), Berlin collections: Ankara Embassy; collections concerning Turkey

Central Zionist Archives, Jerusalem Jewish Agency, Political Department Jerusalem

Centre de Documentation Juive Contemporaine, today part of the Mémorial de la Shoah, Paris

United States Holocaust Memorial Museum Archives, Washington, STANFORD J. SHAW COLLECTION, 1931-1990, (1995.A.1202.)

## Published Sources

Asker, Ahmet. "Yeni Türkiye'den Nazi Almanyası'na Karşılaştırmalı Bakışlar ve Algılar, 1929–1939." PhD dissertation. Mersin University, 2012.
Atilhan, Cevat Rıfat. *Die schöne Simi Simon* (Erfurt, 1934).
———. *Suzi Liberman'ın Hatıra Defteri* (Istanbul, 1969)
Baer, Marc D. *The Dönme: Jewish Converts, Muslim Revolutionaries, and Secular Turks*. Stanford, CA, 2010.
Baer, Marc D. "An Enemy Old and New: The Dönme, Anti-Semitism, and Conspiracy Theories in the Ottoman Empire and Turkish Republic." *Jewish Quarterly Review* 103, no. 4 (2013): 523–555.
Bali, Rıfat N. *Antisemitism and Conspiracy Theories in Turkey*. Istanbul, 2013.
———. *Cumhuriyet Yıllarında Türkiye Yahudileri: Bir Türkleştirme Serüveni, 1923–1945*. Istanbul, 1999.
———. *Les relations entre Turcs et Juifs dans la Turquie Moderne*. Istanbul, 2001.
———. *1934 Trakya Olayları*. Istanbul, 2008.
———. *Yirmi Kur'a Nafıa Askerleri: II. Dünya Savaşında Gayrimüslimlerin Askerlik Serüveni*. Istanbul, 2008.
Barutçu, Faik Ahmet. *Siyasî Anılar 1939–1954*. Istanbul, 1977.

Bayraktar, Hatice. *Salamon und Rabeka: Judenstereotype in Karikaturen der türkischen Zeitschriften Akbaba, Karikatür und Milli Inkilap 1933–1945.* Berlin, 2006.

———. "Türkische Karikaturen über Juden (1933–1945)." *Jahrbuch für Antisemitismusforschung* 13 (2004): 85–108.

———. *"Zweideutige Individuen in schlechter Absicht": Die antisemitischen Ausschreitungen in Thrakien 1934 und ihre Hintergründe.* Berlin, 2011.

Çelik, Ahmet. "İkinci Dünya Savaşı Sürecinde (1939–1945) Muhalif Basın." MA thesis. Süleyman Demirel Üniversitesi, Isparta, 2011.

Çerkezyan, Sarkis. *Bu Dünya Hepimize Yeter.* Istanbul, 2003.

Deringil, Selim. "Hasta Adam'ın Dinç Evlatları." *Toplumsal Tarih* 121 (2004): 76–81.

Erkin, Behiç. *Hâtırat 1876–1958.* Ankara, 2010.

Frantz, Douglas and Catherine Collins. *Death on the Black Sea: The Untold Story of the Struma and World War II's Holocaust at Sea.* New York, N.Y, 2003.

Friling, Tuvia. "Between Friendly and Hostile Neutrality: Turkey and the Jews during World War II." In *The Last Ottoman Century and Beyond,* vol. 2, edited by Minna Rozen, 309–423. Tel Aviv, 2002.

Glasneck, Johannes. *Methoden der deutschen Propagandatätigkeit in der Türkei vor und während des Zweiten Weltkrieges.* Halle, 1966.

Gündem, Mehmet. *Lüzumlu Adam İshak Alaton: Hedefi Belli Olmayan Yelkenliye Hiçbir Rüzgâr Yardım Edemez.* Istanbul, 2012.

Guttstadt, Corry. "Depriving Non-Muslims of Citizenship as Part of the Turkification Policy in the Early Years of the Turkish Republic." In *Turkey beyond Nationalism: Towards Post-nationalist Identities,* edited by Hans-Lukas Kieser, 50–56. London: I.B. Tauris, 2006.

———. *Turkey, the Jews, and the Holocaust.* Translated by Kathleen M. Dell'Orto, Sabine Bartel, and Michelle Miles. New York: Cambridge University Press, 2013.

Guttstadt, Corry, Lutz Thomas, Rother Bernd, and San Roman Yessica, eds. *Bystanders, Rescuers or Perpetrators? The Neutrals and the Shoah.* 2 vols. Berlin, 2016.

Hakko, Vitali. *Hayatım.* Istanbul, 1997.

Hale, William. *Turkish Foreign Policy since 1774.* Abingdon, 2013.

Karaca, Emin. *Türk Basınında Kalem Kavgaları.* Istanbul, 1998.

Löwenthal, Ernst G., ed.. *Philo-Atlas: Handbuch für die jüdische Auswanderung* (Berlin, 1938).

Mallet, Laurent "Karikatür Dergisinde Yahudilerle İlgili Karikatürler (1936–1948)." *Toplumsal Tarih* 34 (1996): 26–33.

Ninhos, Cláudia. "What Was Known in the Neutral Countries about the On-going Genocide of European Jews?" In Guttstadt et al., 2:125–138.

Pekesen, Berna. *Nationalismus, Türkisierung und das Ende der jüdischen Gemeinden in Thrakien: 1918–1942.* Munich, 2012.

———. *Zwischen Sympathie und Eigennutz: NS-Propaganda und die türkische Presse im Zweiten Weltkrieg.* Münster, 2014.

Poliakov, Leon, and Joseph Wulf. *Das Dritte Reich und seine Diener.* Berlin, 1996.

Poulton, Hugh. *Top Hat, the Grey Wolf and the Crescent: Turkish Nationalism and the Turkish Republic.* New York, 1997.

Sabah, Lucien. *Drancy, dernier mots.* Paris, 2014.

Schulze, Rainer. "Die Heimschaffungsaktion of 1942–43: Turkey, Spain and Portugal and Their Responses to the German Offer of Repatriation of Their Jewish Citizens." *Holocaust Studies: A Journal of Culture and History* 18, nos. 2–3 (2012): 49–72.

Shaw, Stanford J. *Turkey and the Holocaust: Turkey's Role in Rescuing Turkish and European Jewry from Nazi Persecution 1933–1945*. Basingstoke, 1993.

Şimşir, Bilâl N. *Türk Yahudiler. Avrupa Irkçılarına Karşı Türkiye'nin Mücadelesi* [Turkish Jews: Turkey's struggle against the European racists]. 2 vols. Ankara, 2010.

Spengler-Axiopoulos, Barbara. "'Wenn ihr den Juden helft, kämpft ihr gegen die Besatzer': Der Untergang der griechischen Juden." In *Solidarität und Hilfe für Juden während der NS-Zeit, Band 1,* edited by Wolfgang Benz and Juliane Wetzel, 125–185. Berlin, 1996.

Yıldız, Ahmet. *Ne Mutlu Türküm Diyebilene": Türk Ulusal Kimliğinin Etno-Seküler Sınırları (1919–1938)*. Istanbul, 2001.

*Chapter 3*

# DEMON AND INFIDEL

Egyptian Intellectuals Confronting Hitler and Nazism
during World War II

*Israel Gershoni*

ADOLF HITLER'S RISE TO POWER and the transformation of Germany into a Nazi state triggered a strong response within the Egyptian intellectual community during 1933 to 1939. On the eve of the war, and throughout the period from 1939 until the defeat of the Axis in North Africa in May 1943, this intellectual interest strengthened, expanded, and solidified. It found expression in hundreds of essays and articles produced by luminary and other intellectuals in local daily, weekly, and monthly newspapers and journals. In addition, dozens of books and publications were devoted to the subject, including books on contemporary history, political and social thought, biographies of Hitler, dramas, fiction, poetry, and memoirs, published during and after the war. Public intellectuals also discussed the war on Egyptian radio broadcasts and were responsible for the production of thousands of cartoons and visual images that appeared in illustrated magazines, a highly popular medium during the war. These intellectuals represented a broad spectrum of public opinion that was not only reflected in their writings but that they also helped to shape.

As I have attempted to show in previous studies on Arab-Egyptian responses to Fascism and Nazism, mainstream intellectuals in Egypt formed and developed an anti-Nazi and anti-Fascist public discourse through the 1930s and 1940s.[1] This discourse consisted of three major negative components: first, Nazi Germany and the Führer were represented as the most terrifying embodiment of a totalitarian police state dictatorship; second, German society was presented as a racist society that did not hesitate to use the most brutal and violent means to purify itself of "inferior" non-Aryan races in order to create a "superior" Aryan "racial" state; third, and perhaps the most widespread of the negative imagery, was the representation of Nazism as a new kind of imperialism.

The Nazi project and Hitler himself were accused of embodying a new Western imperialism, more militaristic, oppressive, and destruc-

**Figure 3.1.** An anti-Nazi cartoon that appeared in the Egyptian journal *Ruz al-Yusuf*, 9 September 1939. *Caption:* "History repeats itself! End of Hitler at the hands of democracy."

tive than any former European imperialist project, including those of Britain and France. Therefore, according to the intellectual producers of this anti-Nazi discourse, the option of "the enemy of my enemy is my ally" (because Germany was waging war against Britain) was inconceivable. In the most realistic and pragmatic outlook of the intellectuals, the old British system of semicolonialism, anchored now on the Anglo-Egyptian Treaty of Alliance of August 1936, was preferred over a new murderous Nazi imperialism. The intellectuals were well aware of the oppressive Nazi elimination of Austria, Czechoslovakia, and Poland, and the wartime occupations of Belgium, Holland, France, and much of Europe, and they knew that the Nazis would never grant independence to Egypt or to any of the other Arab states.[2]

I would like to emphasize that the findings and conclusions of my previous studies have never ignored the specific intellectuals, currents, or opinions in Egypt that sympathized with and supported Nazism and Hitler. Rather, I have attempted to show that these pro-Nazi groups and voices were marginal and sometimes even negligible, particularly in the public sphere, since many of them were underground and subversive. Some of these voices were revealed to the public only after the war. They were certainly overshadowed by the mainstream anti-Nazi sentiments and attitudes dominant in the broad Egyptian print media landscape.[3]

My findings and conclusions have attempted to both problematize and deconstruct a commonly held narrative in the historiography of modern Egypt and the Arab Middle East. This narrative underlines Egyptian and greater Arab sympathy and support for Nazism and Hitler during the 1930s and throughout the war. The popularity of this narrative has created the strong impression that many in Egypt and throughout the Arab world tended to identify with and support Nazi Germany before and during the war. Among the formulators and promoters of this narrative, one can find the most prominent historians and scholars of the Middle East who have written about Egypt in this era, such as Nadav Safran, P. J. Vatikiotis, Afaf Lutfi al-Sayyid Marsot, Elie Khedourie, Sylvia Haim, and Bernard Lewis, as well as Lukasz Hirszowicz and Eliezer Be'eri. In Egypt, they include 'Abd al-Rahman al-Rafi'i, and Muhammad Husayn Haykal.[4] Even today, important historians continue to reproduce and uphold this pro-Nazi (pro-Fascist) narrative.[5]

The extent to which such a narrative is well anchored in Middle Eastern studies can be demonstrated in later historical works produced by more liberal-leftist social historians. In many respects, these revisionist historians deconstruct narratives produced in earlier historiographies in order to present a better understanding of Egypt and the Arab Middle East in that era. Yet, in the context of World War II, these historians simply accepted, almost automatically, the pro-Nazi narrative.[6] Thus, in his excellent study of Salama Musa and the evolution of professional classes in twentieth-century Egypt, Vernon Egger asserts that Musa's short-lived flirtation with Nazism[7] reflects a broader spectrum of positive intellectual attitudes toward Hitler and Nazism. Egger argues:

> Musa's admiration for Nazism came at a time when pro-German sentiment was widespread in Egypt because of its utility as an Egyptian nationalist weapon to be used against the British. During the same period, many intellectuals on the spectrum from fascism to communism were sounding the death knell for liberal democracy.[8]

In the same vein, Joel Beinin and Zachary Lockman, in their important study *Workers on the Nile: Nationalism, Communism, Islam, and the Egyptian Working Class 1882–1954*, a classic in the history of labor in the Middle East, describe the public atmosphere in Egypt on the eve of World War II as follows:

> In the 1930s important sections of the intelligentsia in the colonial and semicolonial countries viewed fascism primarily as a militant form of nationalism. In Egypt some of the *effendiyya* abandoned the secularism and liberalism of the Wafd as a result of their dissatisfaction with the 1936 treaty and the continuing economic and social crisis of the country, and began to embrace more radical nationalist ideologies. Fascism also had a certain appeal, and because it was imported from Italy and Germany, the rivals of Egypt's British over-lords, it seemed to those who despaired of the Wafd's failed liberal parliamentarianism an appropriate ideology to guide a resolute struggle against the British occupation. The relatively small Young Egypt (*Misr al-Fatat*) group led by Ahmad Husayn was the principle Egyptian political organization that attempted to translate fascism into an Egyptian idiom, *but more diffuse pro-German sentiment was widespread at the outbreak of the war.*[9]

This chapter aims to elaborate on my own approach to the subject in an attempt to show that this established narrative, in all its variations, is profoundly misleading. The error made by historians who adhere to this narrative stems, first and foremost, from a lack of scholarly systematic research on intellectuals, intellectual life, intellectual history, and on general public opinion. Those few works that engaged in this research tended to underestimate the resistance of the Egyptian and Arab intellectuals to Nazism while ignoring the rich, multivocal discourse that they developed on the topic.[10] In the broad spectrum of Egyptian print culture, it was primarily the intellectuals who created and disseminated a negative image of Hitler and Nazi Germany.

However, they were not alone. In the political echelon, politicians, ministers, party leaders, and members of Parliament (the Senate and the Chamber of Deputies) participated in portraying Hitler in a similarly negative light. In addition, professionals, journalists, officials, bureaucrats, technocrats, students, and other representatives of the modern urban educated middle class (*effendiyya*), and even segments of the illiterate population, all developed negative images of Hitler and Nazism. In the rich repertoire of images portraying Hitler, two prominent pictures stand out: Hitler as a demon/Satan, and Hitler as the infidel/nonbeliever. The function of the first of these negative portrayals was to present the Führer as a monger of the global war of annihilation, and therefore a profound threat to Europe, the world, and, more specifically, the Arab Middle East. On the other hand, for more popular consumption, the second image of Hitler as an infidel portrayed him as a heretic, undermining the three monotheisms—Islam, Christianity, and Judaism.[11]

In order to demonstrate the negative perceptions of Nazism and Hitler in Egyptian public intellectual discourse, I have chosen to focus on three major public intellectuals: Tawfiq al-Hakim (1898–1987), 'Abbas Mahmud al 'Aqqad (1889–1964), and Ahmad Hasan al-Zayyat (1885–1968). Each of these intellectuals has provided us with a variety of images and representations of Hitler and Nazism. I selected these intellectual luminaries, not because they necessarily reflect the relatively limited intellectual stratum but because their writings, particularly their journalistic productions and popular texts, represented the broader sectors of literate society and the larger public arena. These three fully exploited the new mass culture emerging in Egypt during the 1930s and 1940s by using popular genres appealing to diverse publics beyond the educated elites. This variety of popular genres included journalistic drama, sketches and short plays (Hakim), a popular biography of Hitler, and other anti-Fascist and anti-Nazi essays ('Aqqad), as well as editorials and other essays in the press (Zayyat). In addition, all three appealed to Muslims, Christians, and Jews from both the elite and non-elite Egyptian and Arab communities of readers, thereby representing a mainstream voice in Egypt during the period under discussion. Indeed, tens of thousands of copies of their writings were published and circulated among broader sectors of society, and many of them reappeared in new editions during the war. The editorials of Zayyat, published in *al-Risala*, were distributed at a rate of about thirty thousand to forty thousand copies per week. One-third of these copies circulated in the major Arab capitals. These numbers demonstrate that these three intellectuals enjoyed great popularity and became cultural Gurus of their time.

## Tawfiq al-Hakim

We will begin with Tawfiq al-Hakim's attitude toward Nazi Germany and Hitler and, to some degree, toward Mussolini and Fascism. From 1938 to 1945, Hakim published a series of philosophical and artistic works in which he portrayed Hitler (and more generally, Fascism and Nazism) in a negative and demonic light.[12] One of his most significant collections of essays and short plays on the subject is *Sultan al-Zalam* (The reign of darkness), which was published in Cairo in 1941, amid a war that had already spilled into Egypt. This was a critical year, because at the time it seemed that Hitler was unstoppable in his war in Europe, as well as in the North African campaign, implying that Egypt would soon fall under German and Italian control. The text is a philosophical essay, with three sections of drama, published with the war raging nearby in mind. Hakim felt that a Nazi-Fascist victory would extinguish not only democratic forces but ultimately all of humanity. After learning of the Nazi atrocities, reported in the press and published intelligence sources, and assuming that Nazi Germany would emerge victorious, Hakim was plunged into an apocalyptic mood, lamenting in 1941 that civilization "is not so entrenched in us as we had imagined . . . The dusk descending on man fills me with dread" and "humanity will return to primitive and barbarian ways."[13]

For Hakim, civilization itself was in danger, and the cultural evolution that had begun in Egypt thousands of years before—and continued in Greece (Athens), Italy (Rome), medieval Islam, Renaissance Italy, and France's enlightenment, culminating in transnational modernism—was on the verge of termination. Viewing himself as a "soldier in the service of this human civilization,"[14] Hakim sensed that his cause was close to defeat, since his profound belief in the inexorability of progress and modernity seemed seriously flawed. A new barbaric principle was rising in its stead, "the new law of brute force and the right of the mighty to crush and destroy others and lord it over the planet."[15] Disabused of the notion of a linearly evolving civilization, Hakim concluded that the momentum of enlightenment, rationalism, humanism, scientific discovery, cultural progress, and political liberation would cease as surely as "bombs have been dropping on museums and libraries," and "scientists and intellectuals like Albert Einstein, Sigmund Freud, and Thomas Mann have been forced into exile."[16] Hakim dreaded his own vision of a collective "return to barbarism . . . tribalism, and beastliness."[17] He saw evidence of this in the efforts of Nazism to eradicate monotheistic religions that to him represented divine mercy and were in stark contrast to the police states in which Fascist governments imprisoned entire populations. Thus, according to Hakim, Hitler and Nazism were the "demon" that sought to annihilate the modern enlightenment, and the "infidel" that sought to annihilate the humanistic traditions of monotheism. For Hakim, Hitler blasphemes God, and therefore man and society, which were created in His image.

Hakim's attitude at the time sharply contradicted Anwar al-Sadat's retrospective proclamation that "for England, 1941 was a tragic year. For Egypt, it was a year of hope."[18] Sadat, in exaggerated and vain optimism, envisioned a total defeat for England and a victory for Rommel and Hitler, hoping for the occupation of Egypt by the "liberating" forces of the Axis, in collaboration with the Egyptian militant Free Officers. It can hardly be argued that Sadat had his finger on the pulse of the nation, while Hakim was disconnected from the broader sectors of his society and lived in a remote ivory tower. Hakim was, in fact, the most popular writer in Egypt in that period, selling more books than any of his intellectual peers. His works were often published and then reissued, as the Egyptian public and Arabs in general eagerly consumed the tens of thousands of volumes. The Egyptian youth in particular, including the Young Officers (eventually the Free Officers) themselves, acclaimed Hakim. Jamal 'Abd al-Nasir, who established himself as the *ra'is* (president) of the 1952 July revolution and the new Egyptian republic, recounted that Hakim's writings were a source of inspiration for him, although Hakim's liberal-democratic themes do not seem to have made a lasting impression on Nasir.[19] In this respect, Hakim's writings, unlike Sadat's retrospective revolutionary narrative, appeared as an authentic document of the war. The latter appeared to be an anachronistic political text aimed at legitimizing and justifying the burgeoning revolution and its fierce anticolonial struggle against Britain in the mid-1950s.

Hakim alleged that the most serious crime committed by the Fascist regimes was their campaign against truth. This crusade manifested itself in the persecution of intellectuals and philosophers, the "pursuers of freedom," whom he labeled as sworn enemies of the totalitarian police state. The pursuit of truth, whether via science, philosophy, or religion, was incompatible with chauvinistic nationalism, because "nationalism is collective egoism and egoism is by its very nature blind and irrational, while science is the pure study of truth." For these reasons, Hakim believed that the intellectuals had become "a serious threat to the peoples' tamers/jailers."[20] He referred to the Fascist leaders, Mussolini and particularly Hitler, as "jailers" and "tamers" who totally subdued their people in accordance with their whims and ambitions. He describes the situation in detail:

> The leaders/people tamers detest the learned philosophers who are capable of engaging in objective free study and liberal thought and are committed to the principle of science for the sake of science or science for the sake of the whole of humankind. The leaders/people tamers believe that the philosophers have no right to exist unless they submit totally to the principle of science for the sake of the homeland, namely science at the service of the army and militarism and subservient to the authority of race and blood.[21]

Though he feared for the fate of civilization, Hakim maintained a glimmer of cautious optimism, characteristic of his refusal to concede to anxiety and fear. His worries did not leave him stupefied or impotent but rather strengthened his resolve to combat the "reign of darkness." He saw this conflict as one in which those with material power, the Fascist forces, were conducting an assault on the ranks of the spiritual forces, or enlightened humanity. He depicts the result of this conflict as the victory of light over darkness, and calls for intellectuals in Egypt and the Arab world to unite behind their liberal counterparts in Europe "in the common struggle to defend liberty against dictatorship." He deemed this "a life and death struggle."[22]

Later, in wartime writings such as *Himari Qala Li* (My donkey told me), Hakim continued to wage a fierce campaign against Hitler, *Mein Kampf*, and Nazism. *Himari Qala Li* was first published during the war as a series of dramatic sketches in the most popular dailies in Egypt, including *al-Ahram*. It was eventually published as a collection of articles in Cairo in 1945. In one of his sketches, "My Donkey and Hitler," Hakim made no secret of his allegiance to the Allied cause, or of his antipathy toward the opposing side. By this time, the tide of the war had already begun to swing against Hitler; yet, he was still far from defeat. Hakim portrayed Hitler as a devil whose stated aim was to destroy the world and to end civilization. He accused Hitler of propagating a cult of the Aryan race that included the objective of conquering and enslaving the other races of the world. Hakim viewed him as a militarist and a warmonger whose vision of an ideal world was absolute German domination and the subjugation of all other nations and cultures. Additionally, for Hakim, Hitler was also a pre-monotheistic ("*jahili*") infidel who stood in stark contrast to the prophets who had tried to extricate themselves from specific races or cultures in order to appeal to all of humanity. Hitler worshipped one blood, one land, and one race. In Hakim's accusatory language, "You [Hitler] love only one race, while hating all the other races. You work to raise up only one people, while subjecting all other peoples of the world."[23] Thus, Hakim concludes, unlike the immortal tidings of the monotheistic prophets, Moses, Jesus, and Muhammad, Hitler's career was doomed to failure because humanity would not stand for his diabolical plans.[24]

In this dramatic sketch of Hitler's "monumental failure," Hakim explores the relationship between Hitler's personality, the submissive temperament of the Germanic *Volk*, and their shattering defeat. Indeed, in this later period of the war, it appeared to Hakim as though Hitler and Nazism were on the path to destruction. Hakim places Hitler on trial and concludes that Hitler is responsible for his own downfall; his critical mistake was his assumption that brute force could overpower truth. Prophets, scientists, and great artists have also attempted to bring about a world-historical transformation, but they relied on scientific or moral truth to do so. Though claiming a somewhat prophetic status for himself, Hitler attacked God and religion; in fact, "you [Hitler] attack God and the Church."[25] While trying to enlist art and science into his ranks, he banished many artists and scientists. Prophets courageously pointed to the deficiencies in their societies and suggested a means for improvement in an effort to spread a message that transcended time and nationalistic or ethnic-chauvinist boundaries. For this they were persecuted, and sometimes martyred, but their message was delivered and ultimately it triumphed. Hitler exemplified precisely the opposite traits in his readiness to wage war in order to further his chauvinist, racist agenda. He rebelled against neither his time nor place but rather aspired to satisfy his society's most materialistic and narrowly self-centered urges. Hence, Hitler was a false prophet, who, instead of ameliorating the human condition, returns humans to barbarism, subjecting them to a militarist, racist project that he hoped to realize via the instigation of a world war. In the language of Hakim, projected onto Hitler, "the genius of my [Hitler's] country Germany is a militarist genius (*'abqariyya 'askariyya*) first and foremost."[26] The authentic prophet has the power of a God; the intellectual, the artist, and the scientist have the power of spirit; Hitler had only the materialistic power of militarism and racism.

Several months before Hitler's suicide, Hakim predicted that the fate of anyone who acted obsessively on furthering his "supreme" race, while despising and annihilating other "inferior races," was death. Hakim thus concludes that unlike the immortal tidings and prestige of the prophets, Hitler's career was fated for obscurity, just as all the physical ruin he had left behind him would be rebuilt.[27]

Even in the gloomiest situation, Hakim remains optimistic. "After the possible victory over the reign of darkness,"[28] he anticipates a need for a global de-Nazification program. Since few remained untraumatized by the campaign waged by evil, he predicts that people would have to relearn how to be productive, creative, and happy. Moreover, "the first step on the road to revival after the reign of darkness will be the permanent liquidation of the desire of the strong to use force to rule the weak."[29] In his mind, socialist-oriented liberal democracy, outfitted with a constitution and a parliament, strikes an ideal balance between the appetite for freedom and the social restraints necessary for justice and equality. Though a true socialist democracy had never been established, and thus its feasibility was uncertain, he nevertheless was adamant that postwar man would have to be a new creature, in need of new social and political structures. He hoped that the decline of the "reign of darkness" would be followed by the "era of light": the salvation of mankind from the ravages of war and tyranny through the establishment of a new brand of democratic order, more humane, more socialistic, and more universal. Intellectuals would be tasked with disseminating and institutionalizing socialist democracy. This is the final piece of evidence demonstrating the democratic commitment of many of Egypt's intellectuals. Hakim could not have deemed them suitable for this role had they not shared his passionate antitotalitarian views.[30]

## 'Abbas Mahmud al 'Aqqad

'Abbas Mahmud al 'Aqqad used the genre of popular biography as a means to criticize and attack Hitler's worldview and policies. His major work on the subject, *Hitlar fi al-Mizan* (Hitler in the balance), was a detailed biography of the life of the Führer with special emphasis on the war. It was published in Cairo in early June 1940, when Hitler was at the peak of his power and seemed poised to win the war. 'Aqqad described what he viewed as Hitler's crime against humanity.

He analyzed Hitler's *Mein Kampf* and the application of the theory of race and racial practices in Nazi Germany in the 1930s. According to 'Aqqad, Hitler's commitment to racial persecution and purification eventually led him to develop industries of mass annihilation, the most prominent of which was the Jewish genocide. 'Aqqad warned the Egyptians, as well as the Arabs in general, not to be captivated by the false concept of the Nazis as a friendly force just because they were "the enemy of my enemy," or to view the Nazis as liberators from the British and French imperial yokes. 'Aqqad viewed this concept as a myth that the Arabs would be wise to ignore, because only the Allied powers, by defeating Nazism and Fascism, could give the Arabs the independence and liberation they desired. More specifically, 'Aqqad systematically examined the German historical context of the late 1920s and early 1930s that led to Hitler's rise to power. He described in detail the policies Hitler pursued once in office. However, this alone did not decode the riddle that was Adolf Hitler. An understanding of the psychological profile of the Führer was essential in order to penetrate "the essence of Hitler." Thus, an entire section of *Hitlar fi al-Mizan* is devoted to an extensive quasi-Freudian analysis of what 'Aqqad termed "Hitler's psyche." Although 'Aqqad was not a professional psychiatrist or psychologist, he demonstrated an insightful penetration into Hitler's mind, with a deep understanding of his early background and its impact on his development.[31]

'Aqqad's biographical and psychological account found a definite link between Hitler's family, youth, and upbringing, and the patterns of behavior he subsequently manifested as the all-powerful dictator of Nazi Germany. For 'Aqqad, much of Hitler's distorted personality was attributable to growing up in a broken family. Hitler's father, Alois Schicklgrüber (later Hitler), himself an illegitimate child, was nearly fifty years old when he married Adolf's mother, Klara. Pampered by a loving but weak mother, the young Adolf suffered from the tyranny of a rigid and authoritative father. The instability of Alois's marital life (Klara was his third wife), his repeated moves from town to town, and his restlessness and lack of stability and self-esteem were all projected onto his son and were manifested in the boy's frequent agitation and the insomnia for which he was medicated. Alois's death when Adolf was twelve (according to the book, although in reality, he was thirteen at the time of his father's death) only exacerbated the fragile boy's psychological distress and predicaments. Thus, "Hitler experienced a nasty youth, devoid of the warmth and closeness of family members or close friends."[32] Hitler's poor performance in primary and secondary school was partially attributable to the stress occasioned by his family circumstances. The death of his mother when Hitler was eighteen left him a penniless orphan forced to fend for himself by working odd jobs. He was a lonely and impoverished young man "without the ability to earn a living," yet he maintained an inflated self-image. 'Aqqad notes, "Hitler believed he was Michelangelo's successor in the field of architecture." His early adulthood was one of desperate attempts and repeated failures to become the artist "he believed that by his nature he deserved to be."[33]

'Aqqad's description of Hitler's broken youth and early disappointments and frustrations formed the basis of his psychological profile of the adult Hitler. One indication of Hitler's abnormal personality was his "strange, enigmatic attitude toward women."[34] Because of his father's negative influence, which inhibited his ability to express love for the opposite sex, Hitler never married or entered into a deep relationship with a woman. Rather, all of his emotional energy was channeled into "the National Socialist movement and the German nation." Hitler "invested his soul"[35] in the nation, which served as the compensatory replacement for the wife he never had. Unable to establish intimate and reciprocal personal relationships with others, Hitler completely lacked the positive traits of empathy, compassion, and forgiveness; in their place were manifested the negative characteristics of hostility, aggression, and vengeance toward others.

Another manifestation of Hitler's unique personality was his love for animals, which exceeded the love he demonstrated for humans. Hitler's loyalty to his dog, a large and menacing "watchdog . . . is further proof of his self-love . . . and his isolation from other members of the German race."[36] He compensated for his inability to communicate with humans by communicating with animals. Hitler's love of animals was an indication of his "emotional poverty," an effort to compensate for the warmth and love he had missed in his childhood. In reality, Hitler's "love of dogs and birds derives only from the devilish insinuations of hysteria (*wasaus al-histariya*), from the obstructive mechanisms of egocentrism (*'awarid al-ananiyya*), and the lack of a balanced psychological structure."[37]

According to 'Aqqad, another side of Hitler's distorted personality was a total inability to tell the truth; he was a natural and compulsive liar. In some cases, his lies were so much a part of him that he did not know they were lies. His political performance was based on lies and deception, including self-deception. 'Aqqad writes, "In Hitler's case, a lie is not akin to drinking a hated medicine, but rather like consuming a tasty beverage imbibed in one gulp to quench [one's] thirst."[38] Hitler's self-deception was paralleled by his fundamental difficulty in distinguishing between fact and fantasy. Hitler's world was one of false realities that he himself had created and through which he understood the world in a distorted fashion. He was a man who looked upon the world and acted within it as if it consisted of "fantastic, bewitched castles and the turrets of legends and fairy tales," deceiving both himself and Germany when he promised his people "control over the whole world."[39] The reality of this vision of the future existed only in the Hitler's feverish imagination.

'Aqqad maintained that Hitler's warped character traits were signs of chronic mental illness. Hitler was "sick," a man suffering from schizophrenia, paranoia, hysteria, and hysterical panic, all a direct result of the conditions of his childhood and the complex relationship between him and his parents. 'Aqqad based his clinical diagnosis on psychological studies of Hitler's personality, including the findings and views of German psychiatrists who had examined him when he was in prison in the mid-1920s. As 'Aqqad describes it, Hitler's schizophrenia took the form of "two contradictory personalities," which switched back and forth in his thoughts and actions. Hitler was sometimes logical, sometimes irrational; sometimes sensible, sometimes foolish; sometimes decisive, sometimes hesitant. On some occasions, he acted responsibly; on others, rashly. His schizophrenia was intensified by frequent attacks of hysteria that indicated profound internal anxiety produced by an unbalanced personality suffering from a fundamental lack of confidence. Hitler's hysterical outbursts took the form of uncontrollable agitation and wild screaming at others, both stemming from his obsessive focus on the self and his preoccupation with his own cravings. For 'Aqqad, these episodes of hysteria were the most striking indication of Hitler's sick personality. This psychological background is the explanatory basis for the demonism of Hitler: his insatiable hunger to compensate for early deprivations via conquest and world domination by an exclusive Aryan race, of which Hitler was the supreme leader.[40]

On the somewhat naïve assumption that he had succeeded in deciphering the riddle of Hitler and Nazi Germany, 'Aqqad moves on in the later chapters of *Hitlar fi al-Mizan* to discuss the current war and its potential implications for Europe, the Arabs, and Egypt. As a politically involved public intellectual and member of the Saʿdist Party, a political party whose leadership was from the summer of 1940 onward to argue in favor of Egyptian entry into the war on the Allied side, his position on the war was vehemently pro-Allies and anti-Axis. "The issue today is the war," ʿAqqad declared. In his view, it was a war "between tyranny and human liberty, or between faith in the power of weapons alone versus faith in a life and civilization beyond weapons and devoid of weapons."[41] What "Hitlerism" wanted in the war was "world domination [*al-saytara al-ʿalamiyya*]," the subjugation of other nations, and their total submission to German hegemony. The Nazi war aim was a simple one: "to take everything from everyone and not to give anything to anyone."[42] ʿAqqad repeatedly warned his readers that the victory of Nazi Germany in the war would mean "the victory of power and the rule of power" and the creation of a "new world order," bringing about "the enslavement and exploitation of all other [non-Germanic] peoples and the plundering of all they have."[43] A victory of Hitlerism, with its cult of leadership and submission to the Führer, carried with it the extinction of human liberty: "Freedom will have no existence in a world ruled by an infallible holy man who demands of men what even God the Creator has never demanded of them."[44] Thus, the conflation of demon and infidel depicted Hitler as a vicious monster.

ʿAqqad emphasized that for people everywhere, the choice in the present war was one between two diametrically opposed paths for the future. One was "the Nazi path," which, for ʿAqqad, was "the path of faith in bestial power [*al-quwwa al-hayawaniyya*]," the entrenchment and perpetuation of "the rule of the strong in the world."[45] The other option was "the path of democracy: faith in a life of constitutionalism, which is not a force of bestial constitutionalism [*ghayr shariʿat al-quwwa al-hayawaniyya*], but one of justice, integrity, unbiased fairness, and hope for human progression to a system of norms and laws that will shape the actions of individuals and nations above and beyond the law of the cave and the jungle."[46] Winston Churchill could hardly have phrased the choice confronting humankind in June 1940 in more stentorian terms:

> The issue facing the world is the defeat of Germany and the victory of the democratic states . . . The problem of humanity today is to strike an overwhelming blow at Hitlerian Germany, after which it will have no existence . . . Germany must emerge [from the war] defeated and devoid of any ability to threaten or endanger . . . Any

result that is less than final and total defeat for Germany will not suffice, and any result that is less than absolute victory for democracy will be unsatisfactory.[47]

As he had in his earlier commentaries, and would continue in later ones, 'Aqqad affirmed his complete faith in freedom, democracy, and the "inevitable" victory of the Allies. He vehemently took issue with those who argued that democracy had failed historically and that it was incapable of coping with the complex problems of industrial society and mass politics. "Democracy has not failed nor can it fail,"[48] he stated emphatically. In the modern world, there was no viable alternative to a democratically based order. It was the only social and political path for a progressive enlightened society. Because democracy was the sole basis for human progress, its eventual triumph was assured: "Democracy will not fail but rather will advance and prosper."[49]

When *Hitlar fi al-Mizan* was published in early June 1940, the war was only in its early stages. 'Aqqad, like Hakim and Zayyat, did not know and was not able to know about the systematic genocide of the Jewish people, the Holocaust, which would take place later on in Europe. As liberal intellectuals, they understood their main role in the Egyptian and Arab publics to be one of realistic and cruel exposure of the terrible danger posed by Hitler and Nazi Germany to the Arab world and humanity as a whole. They spared no words on the abomination, blasphemy, and loathing of the "horrors" of Nazi intentions and actions. But similar to other anti-Nazi texts and debates that were popular in Europe, the United States, and other places around the world at the time, they were concentrated primarily on the "crimes of Nazism against humanity." This colossal crime resulted from a totalitarian dictatorship that used intimidation, terror, murder, and brutal and rampant racism, as well as from the oppressive imperialism in its obsessive search for "living space" in which to materialize them. In the most apocalyptic and gloomy mode, these intellectuals emphasized the demonic and the barbaric character of the Nazi regime, as well as the danger it posed in replacing the modern age of Enlightenment and bringing about the end of human civilization.

These intellectuals were genuinely afraid that the Nazis would return humankind and modern culture to the primitive dark ages of the seminal, tribal, barbaric, pre-Enlightenment, and premonotheist. And yet, it was 'Aqqad who in particular did not ignore Nazi anti-Semitism and its murderous consequences. Already in the first chapters of his book, he offers a striking expression of this sentiment. He shows how *Mein Kampf* drew its anti-Semitism directly from classical anti-Semitic texts such as the writings of Frederick Neumann, Arthur Comte de Gobineau, and Houston Stewart Chamberlain in the late nineteenth century.[50] However, in 'Aqqad's estimation, Hitler empowered these early anti-Semitic formulas in *Mein Kampf* in a most demonic fashion: the cult of deification of the "sanctity of the Aryan master race" and its superiority over other racial and ethnic groups in the world, particularly "over the lowly Semites." This superiority assumes that "inferiority" means "repression, persecution, or elimination" of the "inferior" and "the despicable" by the "superior."[51] Even on the practical level, Hitler carefully studied the "hatred of the Jews [*'udwat al-yahud*]" and the "murders and massacres of the Jews [*mazabih al-yahud*]" from the terrible pogroms and the blood libel that occurred in "Central and Eastern Europe" at the end of the nineteenth and the beginning of the twentieth centuries.

The persecution of Jews in Germany in the 1930s and the fostering of a redemptive anti-Semitism that justified it was, in 'Aqqad's terms, both a continuation of this Jew hatred and a new, more "violent, aggressive, and murderous" phase of Nazi anti-Semitism: the mobilization of all resources and agencies of the Nazi state in discrimination, persecution, and murder. 'Aqqad defined it as "the religion of racist chauvinism [*din al-'asabiyya al-jinsiyya*]."[52] 'Aqqad viewed this "racist religion" as the key to understanding Hitler, Nazism, and its practices: the creation of a terrorist state, the extinction of "inferior races," particularly Semites, and the rampant imperialism seeking to destroy the Versailles international order and to replace it with "a new Nazi order [*al-nizam al-Nazi al-jadid*]" of universal Nazi control over the entire human race.[53]

In a more specific way, 'Aqqad understood very well the immediate threat of Nazism to "the Semites," including Jews, Arabs, Muslims, and "all the Eastern peoples." He repeated his claims that Nazism was a "crime against humanity" and Hitler "a colossal criminal," a "Satan," unbridled and limitless.[54] "Everything Hitler did was driven by one goal: satisfying constant and obsessive passions of hatred, violence, hubris, crime, and murder, stemming from his twisted, ugly, contemptible soul."[55] The murderous anti-Semitism, "complete subjugation of the Semites [Semites in general and Jews in particular] to Aryan power"[56] involving liquidation and complete extinction, was the main source of satisfaction/testament of these dark passions. As mentioned, 'Aqqad could not have known about the final solution. However, *Hitler fi al-Mizan* did include warnings that such horrible crimes were conceivable in the worldview and actions of Hitler and Nazism.

## Ahmad Hasan al-Zayyat

Ahmad Hasan al-Zayyat was also one of the most prominent intellectuals in Egypt and the Arab world in the 1930s and during World War II. He was the editor of one of the most popular cultural weeklies of the time, *al-Risala*. As such, his anti-Nazi and anti-Fascist views, expressed from 1933 to 1945, reflected a broader public sentiment. In those years, he and other contributors to *al-Risala* leveled profound and systematic criticisms against Mussolini and Fascist Italy, particularly regarding the brutal conquest of Ethiopia (Abyssinia), and its Italian occupation. Simultaneously, *al-Risala* attacked Nazi racism and Hitler's ambition to conquer a lebensraum in order to expand the "living space of the German race."[57] However, with the outbreak of World War II and Zayyat's clear awareness that Hitler was responsible for it, he escalated his personal attacks on the Führer. He now presented Hitler as a deadly combination of "infidel," "evil," and "demon" whose total aim was the annihilation of enlightened man and society.[58]

On 9 October 1939, about a month after the outbreak of the war, Zayyat published a major editorial, "The Crime of Nazism against Humanity."[59] The title of the article speaks for itself: here Zayyat consolidated his positions and sentiments from 1933 onward in one strong essay. This and other essays depict Nazism as an unprecedented and colossal threat to human civilization that originated from monotheism and was reshaped by the Enlightenment. Although Zayyat and *al-Risala* predicted the possibility of a world war during the years 1937 to 1939, there was hope that international intervention would manage to prevent such a catastrophe. Once the war erupted, Zayyat was devastated, as he clearly understood the monstrous nature of war and the unprecedented death and destruction it would bring to humankind. His opening words in this essay reflect his shock and profound distress with the outbreak of war. He begins his editorial by stating, "Oh, what a distortion of reason! Oh, what a perplexity of logic!" "Today," he laments, "human history is confronted with a horrific and overwhelming earthquake that man has never seen since God's creation of earth." In his neoclassical, archaic style, Zayyat employs the sharpest language, at times apocalyptic, to exclusively blame Hitlerian Nazism (*al-naziyya al-Hitlariyya*) for the outbreak of the war and its horrific results.

Zayyat admits that human reason remains powerless and inadequate in comprehending how humankind was led into such a horrendous war. The Nazis had conquered the great German nation, which had brought to humanity the finest intellectual works in science, philosophy, literature, and art. Zayyat wrote, "The Nazis silenced the thoughts of German people, eradicated the people's will, recreated it as a mob of elephants of hell [*afyal jahannam*], who aspire to conquer the whole world—the military forces as well as civil populations—either by totally destroying them or by planting terror and hunger!" One might be more empathetic to "Hitlerian Nazism," if one could find in its "authoritative dictatorship one good principle or one positive school of thought, and we can find an excuse for the total enslavement of the German people to Nazism, which brings chaos to humankind." However, Nazism is a "gross deviation of chauvinism and racism, of egoism/hubris and peril [*dalalat min dalalāt al-ʿasabiyya wa al-ʿunsuriyya wa al-athara wa al-ghurur*]." Zayyat is amazed by the follies of history. How could the enlightened German nation be reduced to a barbaric crowd of warriors, and even more troubling, how could Europe and the enlightened mankind let such a demonic phenomenon flourish and drag the world into such a devastating war?

Zayyat viewed Nazism as a demonic power that was waging total war against two major cultural traditions that an enlightened humanity had created. Nazism seriously challenged the monotheistic religious traditions of Judaism, Christianity, and Islam, and waged war on secular human civilization, as it was shaped in the Renaissance and the scientific revolution, particularly during the Enlightenment. Zayyat and *al-Risala* included the Arab Renaissance (*al-nahda*) in these modern secular trends. He vehemently rejects Hitler's theory of race as conceptually outlined in *Mein Kampf* and as implemented in Germany through race laws and regulations in the 1930s. Appealing to broad communities of readers, Muslims, Christians, and Jews, Zayyat employs macabre parody as a literary device to transmit his message. He attacks Hitler and *Mein Kampf* by presenting Hitler as a self-proclaimed prophet and *Mein Kampf* as his holy book. In Zayyat's sarcastic analogy, Hitler assumes that his book descended to him and humankind from the heavens, "thus, it is *Sharʿia* that invalidated all other holy books except for *Mein Kampf*; it erased all ruling authorities except Nazi rule, and obliterated all races other than the German [Aryan] race." Therefore, in this macabre construction, Hitler is an apostle (*rasul*) and *Mein Kampf* is a message (*risala*), a new shariʿa brought from heaven to the "new chosen people," the German Aryan race. In Hitler's racist doctrine, the Semites, the Semitic race, "is the scum of the human race [*huthalat al-nas*]." For Hitler, the religious messages of the Semites are inferior and indeed invalid compared to the sealed message of superiority that the Aryans brought to the world. "How can the Semites not be inferior to the Aryans? For they [the Aryans] are the epitome of the races and their revelation and apostle are superior to anything in the world?"

Thus, Hitler's murderous and barbaric racism shows Semites (Muslims, but mainly Jews) as "scum of the human race" in order to grant legitimacy to the "right" of the "supreme Aryan race" to control them and to kill them. The "filth" had to be purged and annihilated. Indeed, Zayyat, like 'Aqqad, was unable to predict the final solution. However, in realizing the "crimes of Nazism and Hitlerism against humanity," it was not impossible for him to conceive of such a possibility.

Zayyat used this literary strategy to reject all the racist theories and concepts in *Mein Kampf*, as well as the racist policies of the Nazi regime. Hitler is a false prophet, and his book is not shari'a but a demonic message of brutal, inhumane, barbaric racism. In contrast, Zayyat reasserts the distinctiveness of the universal messages, which the so-called Semites brought to the world through "Moses and Judaism, Jesus and Christianity, and Muhammad and Islam." The three Semitic monotheistic religions, he reminds the Führer, introduced the world to new laws and norms for human behavior. They brought messages of virtue, humanism, compassion, justice, love, and freedom, thereby easing human adversity and predicaments. In particular, they created universal equality and the right to live for all races: "no race is superior to another, no race may oppress another, and no nation shall commit injustice toward another." In other words, for Zayyat, the Semitic universal messages prove the complete falsity and hollow deception of *Mein Kampf*. Zayyat adds, "Who is a German deity who purifies the Aryans [four heroes], Hitler, Goering, Hess, and Ribbentrop, to exterminate the world nations, crushing human civilization, and annihilating all the brilliant achievements of mankind?" They undermine both God's law and the secular enlightened human conscience and seek to replace them with a totalitarian political order "that does not honor agreements, disregards treaties, and has neither laws nor principles," bringing about apocalyptic anarchy. Zayyat rhetorically asks, scorning this presumption, is this Hitler's superior pure Aryan race? In his poetics of evil, Zayyat defines Nazi racism, the brutal redemptive anti-Semitism, as the "Nazi doctrine," which "humiliates human races, denies the natural rights of peoples, disregards laws and norms," and aims only to rule by power, deception, manipulation, corruption, and trickery, while entirely rejecting all other worldviews.

Reasserting his prewar arguments, Zayyat presents Hitler as an international provocateur and manipulator, obsessed with undermining the contours of the international order that emerged after the Great War. Zayyat challenged Hitler by asking what Luther, Kant, Göthe, Beethoven, and "their enlightened German descendants" would say about the Führer's conduct. How would they respond to the tyrant, "the same frustrated artist, who lies in the name of the German state, signs agreements on behalf of his nation's honor and then disregards them, and turns his nation of hardworking people into a demonic enemy of peace that instills terror in every heart, and sews misery in every home?" How would the great ancestors of the German nation regard Hitler, who, after ardently opposing communism as the most loathsome doctrine and notorious regime, "lets the swastika slowly but surely be squashed between the hammer of communism and its sickle?" For example, Zayyat vehemently attacked the nonaggression pact between Soviet Russia and Nazi Germany in late August 1939, known as the Ribbentrop–Molotov Pact. *Al-Risala*'s contributors, similar to those in many other Egyptian papers and magazines, were convinced that Hitler's aim in provoking the war was to establish a "new world order [*al-nizam al-'alami al-jadid*]," the Nazi order.

Zayyat firmly rejects Nazi dictatorship (*al-tughyan al-nazi*). He reiterates that the Nazi regime repressed all civil rights and liberties, silenced all opposition, controlled the press, and turned Germany into a police state. Reminding the reader of his positive assessment of Hitler's domestic performance just a few months before, he conceded his grave mistake. Zayyat toiled to quote the paragraphs in which he had erred when he praised Hitler for his leadership abilities in an early May 1939 edition of *al-Risala*. He recounted that at that time, "I did not expect that God would strike Hitler with the lowest human defect—with a most devastating form of rapid extermination. His head is taken by hubris, his soul is full of obstinacy to the point that his passions are limitless and his whims are unstoppable." Similarly, Zayyat emphasizes that Hitler, who was initially admired by the youth of many nations of the world, was now viewed as a "warmonger" whose aim was to drag the world into the "blaze of war."

Zayyat returns to one of his central themes: the real victims of the war that Hitler imposed on the world are "the small peoples [*al-shu'ub al-saghira*]," including Egypt and the Arab peoples. The Nazi dictatorship "aims at controlling the world based on enslaving the weak [*'ala asas isti'bad al-da'if*] exploiting all natural and human resources for a single-race rule and the will of one dictator." Therefore, for Zayyat, the option of "the enemy of my enemy is my ally" is false and nonexistent.

He emphasizes that the only guarantee for the continued existence of these nations is a stable international order, a strong League of Nations, "honor, justice, and peace among nations." The only hope for a humanity rooted in monotheism and enlightenment is embodied solely in democracy.

Having ardently rejected Nazism, Zayyat attempted to reassert human freedom, liberal democracy, religious, racial, and ethnic tolerance, as well as a multiparty pluralistic parliamentary government. For him, the traditional-religious and modern-secular legacies that brought culture, morality, and social and political orders to humanity can "only be safeguarded and sustained by the free democratic powers." Therefore, in this global war, "a life of liberty for the small nations [*al-umam al-saghira*] is possible only through active participation in the unyielding and committed defense of democracy." Accepting reality, Zayyat adopted a pragmatic approach according to which the "only guarantee for the survival of the minority within the majority, of the weak under the wings of the strong, is anchored in the social virtues which first emerged in the monotheistic religions and were then developed and refined in the shelter of democracy." Nevertheless, Zayyat apocalyptically warned, "If heaven forbid," the totalitarian dictatorship should prevail, "human rights will be trampled and human brotherhood will be replaced by one-race ethnocentrism. Rather than equality among nations, a single nation will control the world, and a single dictator will suppress human liberty, we will witness a new world conquered by evil, and we do not want to live in such a world!"

Zayyat's conclusion is clear-cut: death is preferable to living in a world in which Nazism has triumphed. Hence, in a world confronting a fateful, zero-sum game of war, democracy must win and Nazism must be defeated. For democracy to triumph, Egypt and the Arab world must support the democratic camp and the Allies. More generally, it appears that for Zayyat, the historical anticolonial, anti-British struggle for independence must be postponed until the war against Nazism is won. Zayyat and *al-Risala* continued to express these attitudes and sentiments in the years to follow, from 1940 to 1943.[60]

## Conclusion

Hakim, 'Aqqad, and Zayyat's frequent usage of the negative stereotypes of "demon" and "infidel" to characterize Hitler, Nazism, and World

War II was not coincidental. It faithfully reflected a well-planned strategy on the part of the Egyptian intellectual community toward Hitler, the Axis, and the war.[61] These negative images functioned as stimuli in the general intellectual effort to demonize Hitler and to discredit him in the public sphere within the community of readers and print culture consumers in Egypt and the Arab world. On the one hand, the specific image of demon/Satan appears to have been created for a highly educated community. Its aim was to communicate the terrifying danger that Hitler and Nazism presented to humanity at large but also to Egypt and the Arab world. The war that Hitler imposed on humankind, many intellectuals warned, was a war of total annihilation, destined to end human civilization, as we know it. On the other hand, the image of the infidel seemed to be designed for transmitting the intellectual message to the less educated, broader sectors of society, both literate and illiterate. Here, the use of religious rhetoric and Islamic language—infidel, paganism, and the pre-Islamic era (*jahiliyya*), in contrast with the believer, Islam, Muhammad and shari'a (or Jesus and Christianity, Moses and Judaism)—intended to capture the imagination of the average people and to impress upon them the grave danger that Hitler posed to all three monotheistic religions, Islam, Judaism, and Christianity. Needless to say, these images were in no way disconnected from the realities of the war, and from Hitler and Nazi Germany's policies and aims. In fact, it was Nazi Germany's destructive actions in the war that provided these intellectuals with abundant evidence to both reassert and to promote this anti-Nazi, anti-Hitler negative imagery. The intellectuals demonstrated an in-depth knowledge of battlefield developments in Europe and around the world. They were also successful in identifying the mood of their community of readers, and thus, the messages they disseminated seemed to have been appealing. Though it is difficult to quantify to what extent these anti-Hitler and anti-Nazi images were accepted and assimilated, it seems that their impact was significant.

I have tried to show that Hakim, 'Aqqad, and Zayyat were not the exception but rather the rule. A historian who is interested in the modes in which the Egyptians imagined and perceived Hitler and Nazism can surely see that mainstream intellectuals, journalists, and other middle-class *effendi* voices in Egypt's public sphere developed profoundly negative attitudes and sentiments toward the German dictator. In contrast to the widely held perception shared by many historians and observers that the Egyptian public tended to develop pro-German positions and sentiments, this chapter attempts to show that prominent public intellectuals were vehemently anti-Fascist, anti-Nazi, and anti-Hitler. Their overall aim was, in fact, to demonize Hitler in the broader readership communities in Egypt and the Arab world. The Allied defeat of Rommel and Axis forces in the North African Campaign by May 1943, as well as Nazi Germany's eventual defeat in Europe in 1944–1945, tended to legitimize these negative images and representations. These major defeats actually, even if retrospectively, justified the intellectual struggle against the Nazis during the war, even when it seemed as though Hitler would emerge victorious. In this respect, these three liberal intellectuals, examining this phenomenon from a variety of angles and via different genres, demonstrated courage, integrity, and complete commitment to Britain and the Allied cause until the victory over the Nazi threat was complete.

**Israel Gershoni** is Professor in the Department of Middle Eastern and African History at Tel Aviv University. His primary field of interest is the modern intellectual history of Egypt and the Arab Middle East. His most recent books include *Confronting Fascism in Egypt: Dictatorship versus Democracy in the 1930s* (2010), coauthored with James Jankowski; *Dame and Devil: Egypt and Nazism, 1935–1940*, 2 volumes (in Hebrew, 2012); and editor of *Arab Responses to Fascism and Nazism: Attraction and Repulsion* (2014).

## Notes

1. See my previous work on the subject, "Egyptian Liberalism in an Age of 'Crisis of Orientation': *Al-Risala*'s Reaction to Fascism and Nazism, 1933–1939," *International Journal of Middle East Studies* 31, no. 4 (1999); "Beyond Anti-Semitism: Egyptian Responses to German Nazism and Italian Fascism in the 1930s," EUI RSC Working Paper no. 2001/32 (Florence, 2001), 1–26; "'Der verfolgte Jude': Al-Hilals Reaktionen auf den Antisemitismus in Europa und Hitlers Machtergreifung," in *Blind für die Geschichte? Arabische Begegnungen mit dem Nationalsozialismus,* ed. Gerhard Höpp, Peter Wien and René Wildangel (Berlin, 2004); "Liberal Democracy versus Fascist Totalitarianism in the Egyptian Intellectual Discourse: The Case of Salama Musa and al-Majalla al-Jadida," in *Nationalism and Liberal Thought in the Arab Middle East: Ideology and Practice,* ed. Christoph Schumann (London, 2010); "Eine Stimme der Vernunft: Muhammad Abdallah Inan und die Zeitschrift Al-Risala," in *Konstellationen: Über Geschichte, Erfahrung und Erkenntnis—Festschrift in Honor of Professor Dan Diner,* ed. Nicholas Berg, Omar Kamil, Markus Kirchhoff, and Susanne Zepp (Göttingen, 2011); "Why the Muslims Must Fight against Nazi Ger-

many: Muhammad Najati Sidqi's Plea," *Die Welt des Islams* 52, 3-4 (2012). For a more comprehensive discussion of the subject, see Israel Gershoni and James Jankowski, *Confronting Fascism in Egypt: Dictatorship versus Democracy in the 1930s* (Stanford, CA, 2010). These works recorded the view of many intellectuals as expressed in numerous articles, books, and writings that to my humble estimation represent mainstream educated publics in Egypt. They also recorded the anti-Nazi and anti-Fascist official mind of the Egyptian political elite, particularly governments, parties, and parliament. Simultaneously, they also try to demonstrate that pro-Fascist and pro-Nazi voices and activities that existed in Egypt stood at the periphery of the field of cultural production and the political arena at the time.

2. For further details, see Israel Gershoni, *Or Bazel: Egypt and Fascism, 1922–1937* [in Hebrew] (Tel Aviv, 1999); Israel Gershoni and Götz Nordbruch, *Sympathie und Schrecken: Begegnungen mit Faschismus und Nationalsozialismus in Ägypten, 1922–1937* (Berlin, 2011); Gershoni and Jankowski, *Confronting Fascism in Egypt*; Israel Gershoni, *Dame and Devil: Egypt and Nazism, 1935–1940* [in Hebrew], 2 vols. (Tel Aviv, 2012); Israel Gerhsoni, ed., *Arab Responses to Fascism and Nazism: Attraction and Repulsion* (Austin, TX, 2014).

3. See the works in notes 1 and 2.

4. Nadav Safran, *Egypt in Search of Political Community: An Analysis of the Intellectual and Political Evolutions of Egypt* (Cambridge, MA, 1961), 187–208; Panayiotis J. Vatikiotis, *The Modern History of Egypt* (London, 1969), 315–361; Panayiotis J. Vatikiotis, *Nasser and His Generation* (London, 1978), 23–112; Afaf Lutfi al-Sayyid Marsot, *A Short History of Modern Egypt* (Cambridge, 1985), 99–101; Elie Kedourie, *The Chatham House Version and Other Middle Eastern Studies* (London, 1970), 215–224; Sylvia G. Haim, *Arab Nationalism: An Anthology* (Berkeley, CA, 1962), 41–43, 49–51; Bernard Lewis, "The Nazis and the Palestine Question," in *Semites and Anti-Semites: An Inquiry into Conflict and Prejudice* (London, 1986), 143–162; Bernard Lewis, *The Middle East: A Brief History of the Last 2,000 Years* (New York, 1995), 348–351; Lukasz Hirszowicz, *The Third Reich and the Arab East* (London, 1966), 13–268, 307–319; Eliezer Be'eri, *The Officer Class in Politics and Society of the Arab East* (Tel Aviv, 1966), in Hebrew, 39–44, 63–77, 250–271, published in English as *Army Officers in Arab Politics and Society*, trans. Dov Ben-Abba (Jerusalem, 1969), 15–129, 373–400; 'Abd al-Rahman al-Rafi'i, *Fi A'qab al-Thawra al-Misriyya*, vol. 3 (Cairo, 1951); Muhammad Husayn Haykal, *Mudhakkirat fi al-Siyasa al Misriyya*, vol. 2 (Cairo, 1953).

5. See, e.g., Jeffrey Herf, *Nazi Propaganda for the Arab World* (New Haven, CT, 2009); Matthias Küntzel, *Jihad and Jew-Hatred: Islamism, Nazism and the Roots of 9/11* (New York, 2007), vii–xxv, 1–60, 146–150; Barry Rubin and Wolfgang G. Schwanitz, *Nazis, Islamists, and the Making of the Modern Middle East* (New Haven, CT, 2014); Wajih 'Abd al-Sadiq Atiq, *Al-Malik Faruq wa-Almaniya al-Naziyya: Khams Sanawat min al-'Alaqa al-Sirriyya* (Cairo, 1992); Wajih 'Abd al Sadiq Atiq, *Al-Jaysh al-Misri wa-al-Alman fi Athna al-Harb al-'Alamiyya al-Thaniyya* (Cairo, 1993). For a substantial response to Jeffery Herf's arguments and similar claims, see Francis R. Nicosia, *Nazi Germany and the Arab World* (New York, 2015).

6. See, e.g., Anouar Abdel-Malek, *Egypt: Military Society—The Army Regime, the Left, and Social Change under Nasser* (New York, 1968), 18–22, 44–46.
7. Musa goes on to fundamentally change his position on the eve of and during the war. See, in detail, Gerhsoni, "Liberal Democracy versus Fascist Totalitarianism."
8. Vernon Egger, *A Fabian in Egypt: Salamah Musa and the Rise of the Professional Classes in Egypt, 1909–1939* (New York, 1986), 198 and, more broadly, 194–207.
9. Joel Beinin and Zachary Lockman, *Workers on the Nile: Nationalism, Communism, Islam, and the Egyptian Working Class, 1882–1954* (Princeton, NJ, 1987), 286 (emphasis added) and, more broadly, 285–340.
10. For a comprehensive and critical discussion of this historical lacuna, see Gershoni and Jankowski, *Confronting Fascism and Nazism in Egypt*, 3–13, 267–288; Gershoni, *Arab Responses to Fascism and Nazism*, 1–31.
11. See, in detail, Gershoni, *Dame and Devil*, 2 vols.
12. See, e.g., Hakim's following artistic and journalistic works: *Tahta Shams al-Fikr* (Cairo, 1938); *Praksa aw Mushkilat al-Hukm* (Cairo, 1939); *'Ahd al-Shaytan* (Cairo 1938, 1942); *Min al-Burj al-'Aji* (Cairo, 1941); *Tahta al-Misbah al-Akhdar* (Cairo, 1941, 1942); *Shajarat al-Hukm* (Cairo, 1945). For a more systematic examination of Hakim's attitudes toward Hitler, Mussolini, Nazism, and Fascism, see, Israel Gershoni, "Confronting Nazism in Egypt: Tawfiq al-Hakim's Anti-totalitarianism, 1938–1945," *Tel Aviver Jarbuch für Duetsch Geschichte* 26 (1997).
13. Tawfiq al-Hakim, *Sultan al-Zalam* (Cairo, 1941), 9–10, 27–28. All translations in this chapter are my own unless otherwise indicated.
14. Ibid., 39.
15. Ibid., 41.
16. Ibid., 41.
17. Ibid., 28, 32, and, more broadly, 9–47.
18. Anwar El Sadat, *Revolt on the Nile* (London, 1957), 34 and, more broadly, 26–57.
19. See, in detail, Israel Gershoni, "An Intellectual Source for the Revolution: Tawfiq al-Hakim's Influence on Nasser and His Generation," in *Egypt from Monarchy to Republic: A Reassessment of Revolution and Change*, ed. Shimon Shamir (Boulder, CO, 1995), 213–249.
20. Hakim, *Sultan al-Zalam*, 35, 38.
21. Ibid., 36, and for more on these themes, 34–39.
22. Ibid., 50, 57, and, more generally, 38–57.
23. Tawfiq al-Hakim, *Himari Qala Li* (Cairo, 1945), 6–15; Tawfiq al-Hakim, "Himari wa Hitlar," in *Himari Qala Li* (Cairo, 1945), 38–39.
24. Ibid., 39 and, more broadly, 26–39; see also 40–58.
25. Ibid., 38.
26. Ibid.
27. Ibid., 37–39 and, more broadly, 26–39.
28. Ibid., 37–39, and more broadly, 26–39.
29. Ibid.
30. Ibid., 58–69.
31. 'Abbas Mahmud al 'Aqqad, *Hitlar fi al-Mizan* (Cairo, 1940), 76–125.

32. Ibid., 85.
33. Ibid., 82–88.
34. Ibid., 85.
35. Ibid., 87.
36. Ibid., 88.
37. Ibid., 88–90.
38. Ibid., 90.
39. Ibid., 50; see also 95–106.
40. Ibid., 75–147.
41. Ibid., 152–153.
42. Ibid., 151.
43. Ibid., 152–153.
44. Ibid., 152; see also 3–74, 149–223.
45. Ibid., 159.
46. Ibid., 159–160.
47. Ibid., 154–161, 163.
48. Ibid., 162–163, 172.
49. Ibid., 150–193. For 'Aqqad's consistent anti-Fascist and anti-Nazi positions during the 1930s and early 1940s, see Gershoni, *Or Bazel*, 75–83, 297–329; Gershoni, *Dame and Devil*, 2:93–227, 264–285.
50. Gershoni, *Dame and Devil*, 2:23–24.
51. Ibid., 23–27.
52. Ibid., 23–25.
53. Ibid., 46–62.
54. Ibid., 140–148, 150–161, 210–223.
55. Ibid., 143.
56. Ibid., 156.
57. Gershoni, *Or Bazel*, 299–329; Gershoni, "Egyptian Liberalism in an Age of 'Crisis of Orientation.'"
58. Gershoni, *Dame and Devil*, 2:157–227.
59. Ahmad Hasan al-Zayyat, "Jarirat al-Naziyya 'ala al-Insaniyya," *al-Risala*, 9 October 1939, 1927–1928. The quotations and references that follow are taken from this article.
60. See all the issues of *al-Risala* and Zayyat editorials from November 1939 to June 1943. See, in particular, the following articles by Zayyat from late 1939 and 1940: "Siyasat al-Samak!," *al-Risala*, 11 December 1939, 2251–2252; "Muhammad al-Za'im," *al-Risala*, 4 March 1940, 361–362; "Ba'd Isdal al-Sitar 'ala Ma'sat Finlanda: Fashl al-'Aql," *al-Risala*, 18 March 1940, 481–482; "al-Fikr wa al-Harb . . . ," *al-Risala*, 27 May 1940, 881–882; "Al-Harb bayna al-Ams wa al-Yawm," *al-Risala*, 10 June 1940, 961–962; "Fransa Tanharu?!," *al-Risala*, 24 June 1940, 1037–1038; "Ummat al-Tawhid Tattahidu . . . ," *al-Risala*, 11 November 1940, 1673–1674; "Injiltra hiya al-Mathal," *al-Risala*, 25 November 1940, 1729–1730. See also Zayyat's "final" essay about the war celebrating the "End of the Two Dictators," Hitler and Mussolini, "Nihayat Diktaturayn," *al-Risala*, 7 May 1945, 473–474.
61. For an extensive discussion of a broader anti-Nazi and anti-Fascist intellectual discourse, see Gershoni and Jankowski, *Confronting Fascism in Egypt*.

# Bibliography

Abdel-Malek, Anouar. *Egypt: Military Society—The Army Regime, the Left, and Social Change under Nasser.* New York, 1968.

'Aqqad, 'Abbas Mahmud al. *Hitlar fi al-Mizan* [Hitler in the balance]. Cairo, 1940.

Atiq, Wajih 'Abd al-Sadiq. *Al-Jaysh al-Misri wa-al-Alman fi Athna al-Harb al-'Alamiyya al-Thaniyya.* Cairo, 1993.

———. *Al-Malik Faruq wa-Almaniya al-Naziyya: Khams Sanawat min al-'Alaqa al-Sirriyya.* Cairo, 1992.

Be'eri, Eliezer. *The Officer Class in Politics and Society of the Arab East.* [In Hebrew.] Tel Aviv, 1966. Published in English as *Army Officers in Arab Politics and Society,* translated by Dov Ben-Abba (Jerusalem, 1969).

Beinin, Joel, and Zachary Lockman. *Workers on the Nile: Nationalism, Communism, Islam, and the Egyptian Working Class, 1882–1954.* Princeton, NJ, 1987.

Egger, Vernon. *A Fabian in Egypt: Salamah Musa and the Rise of the Professional Classes in Egypt, 1909–1939.* New York, 1986.

Gershoni, Israel, ed., *Arab Responses to Fascism and Nazism: Attraction and Repulsion.* Austin, TX, 2014.

———. "Beyond Anti-Semitism: Egyptian Responses to German Nazism and Italian Fascism in the 1930s." EUI RSC Working Paper no. 2001/32. Florence, 2001.

———. "Confronting Nazism in Egypt: Tawfiq al-Hakim's Anti-totalitarianism, 1938–1945." *Tel Aviver Jarbuch fur Duetsche Geschichte* 26 (1997): 121–150.

———. *Dame and Devil: Egypt and Nazism, 1935–1940.* [In Hebrew.] 2 vols. Tel Aviv, 2012.

———. "Egyptian Liberalism in an Age of 'Crisis of Orientation': *Al-Risala*'s Reaction to Fascism and Nazism, 1933–1939." *International Journal of Middle East Studies* 31, no. 4 (1999): 551–576.

———. "An Intellectual Source for the Revolution: Tawfiq al-Hakim's Influence on Nasser and His Generation." In *Egypt from Monarchy to Republic: A Reassessment of Revolution and Change,* edited by Shimon Shamir, 213–249. Boulder, CO, 1995.

———. "Liberal Democracy versus Fascist Totalitarianism in the Egyptian Intellectual Discourse: The Case of Salama Musa and al-Majalla al-Jadida." In *Nationalism and Liberal Thought in the Arab Middle East: Ideology and Practice,* edited by Christoph Schumann, 145–172. London, 2010.

———. *Or Bazel: Egypt and Fascism, 1922–1937.* [In Hebrew.] Tel Aviv, 1999.

———. "Eine Stimme der Vernunft: Muhammad Abdallah Inan und die Zeitschrift Al-Risala." In *Konstellationen: Über Geschichte, Erfahrung und Erkenntnis—Festschrift in Honor of Professor Dan Diner,* edited by Nicholas Berg, Omar Kamil, Markus Kirchhoff, and Susanne Zepp, 105–124. Göttingen, 2011.

———. "'Der verfolgte Jude': Al-Hilals Reaktionen auf den Antisemitismus in Europa und Hitlers Machtergreifung." In *Blind für die Geschichte? Arabische Begegnungen mit dem Nationalsozialismus,* edited by Gerhard Höpp, Peter Wien, and René Wildangel, 39–72. Berlin, 2004.

———. "Why the Muslims Must Fight against Nazi Germany: Muhammad Najati Sidqi's Plea." *Die Welt des Islams* 52 Number 3-4 (2012): 471–498.

Gershoni, Israel, and James Jankowski. *Confronting Fascism in Egypt: Dictatorship versus Democracy in the 1930s*. Stanford, CA, 2010.

Gershoni, Israel, and Götz Nordbruch. *Sympathie und Schrecken: Begegnungen mit Faschismus und Nationalsozialismus in Ägypten, 1922–1937*. Berlin, 2011.

Haim, Sylvia G. *Arab Nationalism: An Anthology*. Berkeley, CA, 1962.

Hakim, Tawfiq al-. *'Ahd al-Shaytan*. Cairo, 1938, 1942.

———. *Himari Qala Li*. Cairo, 1945.

———. "Himari wa Hitlar." In *Himari Qala Li*, 38–39. Cairo, 1945.

———. *Min al-Burj al-'Aji*. Cairo, 1941.

———. *Praksa aw Mushkilat al-Hukm*. Cairo, 1939.

———. *Shajarat al-Hukm*. Cairo, 1945.

———. *Sultan al-Zalam*. Cairo, 1941.

———. *Tahta al-Misbah al-Akhdar*. Cairo, 1941, 1942.

———. *Tahta Shams al-Fikr*. Cairo, 1938.

Haykal, Muhammad Husayn. *Mudhakkirat fi al-Siyasa al-Misriyya*. 2 vols. Cairo, 1953.

Herf, Jeffrey. *Nazi Propaganda for the Arab World*. New Haven, CT, 2009.

Hirszowicz, Lukasz. *The Third Reich and the Arab East*. London, 1966.

Kedourie, Elie. *The Chatham House Version and Other Middle Eastern Studies*. London, 1970.

Küntzel, Matthias. *Jihad and Jew-Hatred: Islamism, Nazism and the Roots of 9/11*. Translated by Colin Meade. New York, 2007.

Lewis, Bernard. *The Middle East: A Brief History of the Last 2,000 Years*. New York, 1995.

———. "The Nazis and the Palestine Question." In *Semites and Anti-Semites: An Inquiry into Conflict and Prejudice*, 140–163. London, 1986.

Marsot, Afaf Lutfi al-Sayyid. *A Short History of Modern Egypt*. Cambridge, 1985.

Rafi'i, 'Abd al-Rahman Al-. *Fi A'qab al-Thawra al-Misriyya*. 3 vols. Cairo, 1951.

Rubin, Barry, and Wolfgang G. Schwanitz. *Nazis, Islamists, and the Making of the Modern Middle East*. New Haven, CT, 2014.

Sadat, Anwar El. *Revolt on the Nile*. London, 1957.

Safran, Nadav. *Egypt in Search of Political Community: An Analysis of the Intellectual and Political Evolution of Egypt*. Cambridge, MA, 1961.

Vatikiotis, Panayiotis J. *The Modern History of Egypt*. London, 1969.

———. *Nasser and His Generation*. London, 1978.

*Chapter 4*

# THE PERSECUTION OF THE JEWS IN GERMANY IN EGYPTIAN AND PALESTINIAN PUBLIC DISCOURSES, 1933–1939

*Esther Webman*

BETWEEN THE END OF THE Great War in 1918 and World War II, Middle Eastern Arab societies were making their first strides in shaping and consolidating their newly established states under French and British colonial rule, enjoying different degrees of autonomy. They struggled against colonialism while striving to construct their nascent nationalism, searching for their respective political and cultural identities in response to the challenges of modernism, secularism, and Western culture. Two trends were emerging, representing two contradicting and competing worldviews: Arabism, a substantially modern, secular nationalism with a Western orientation; and Islamism, a modern anti-Western political Islamic movement. At the same time, Zionism, the Jewish national movement, was striving to build a national home for the Jewish people in Palestine against a growing resistance by the local Arab population. Arab leaders and intellectuals perceived Zionism from its very early stages as a foreign intrusion and another form of Western colonialism. Yet, it should be noted that their involvement in the conflict between Arabs and Jews in Palestine was very limited until the mid-1930s. It increased in the wake of the Arab revolt of 1936–1939,[1] which erupted in April 1936 with an attack on a Jewish bus, and intensified following the publication in July 1937 of the recommendations of the Peel Commission.[2] The recommendations called for the partition of Palestine between Arabs and Jews. Arab Palestinian rebels demanded an end to Jewish immigration to Palestine and to Jewish land acquisition, and the establishment of an Arab national government. In an effort to appease Arab public opinion and quiet the revolt in view of the looming war in Europe, Britain issued a White Paper in May 1939, restricting Jewish immigration.[3] The mainstream attitudes toward the Nazi persecution of the Jews are examined against this background.

The Egyptian and Palestinian perceptions of Nazism before World War II have been preoccupying historians, especially since the 1990s, but they have referred to the reactions to the persecution of the Jews during that period only in passing.[4] This chapter seeks to fill some of this void. It explores and compares the Egyptian and Palestinian mainstream public discourses on the persecution of the Jews in Germany between the ascension of Nazism to power in 1933 and the outbreak of the war in Europe in September 1939. By focusing on several landmarks in the history of the Nazi regime and its policy toward the Jews,[5] it attempts to provide answers to several questions: Did the Arab press deal with the Nazi persecution of the Jews and how? How were the persecutions perceived and represented? Were there any changes in the attitudes over time? Were there any differences between the Egyptian and the Palestinian attitudes? Why? And did these attitudes affect in any way later Arab discourses on the Holocaust?[6]

This chapter is based on two basic assumptions: first, Egyptian and Palestinian, as well general Arab, responses to the Nazi persecution of the Jews had been influenced and shaped by developments in the region, by the national struggle for independence from the British and French colonial yoke, and particularly by the Arab-Israeli conflict; second, the mainstream discourses in Egypt and in Palestine would differ, as Palestine was naturally more affected by the Jewish immigration and reacted accordingly. It shows that the attitudes toward the persecution of the Jews in the prewar era were ambivalent and complex, as they were later in the postwar Holocaust discourse. They were entangled with the discourse of conflict in Palestine, and evinced some prevalent anti-Semitic perceptions, particularly in the Palestinian discourse.

The press of that period serves as the major source for the reconstruction of the public discourse of the times, "from within the times." Because of the vast number of publications, this study focuses on two major daily newspapers, the Egyptian *al-Ahram* and the Palestinian *Filastin*, representing their respective mainstream public discourses. *Al-Ahram* was established in December 1875 in Cairo by two Christian

Lebanese brothers, Salim and Bishara Taqla. It became a leading Arab newspaper and, up to the Egyptian revolution led by the Free Officers Movement in July 1952, retained an independent, impartial editorial policy, including during the years of World War II. In the 1930s, it had an estimated circulation of up to one hundred thousand copies. *Filastin* was established in Jaffa in 1911 (then under Ottoman rule) by Greek Orthodox 'Isa Daud 'Isa. The paper was closed on the eve of the Great War in 1914 and resumed publication in 1920 under the British Mandate. With the establishment of the State of Israel in 1948, its headquarters moved from Jaffa to Jerusalem, where it continued publication until 1967. It maintained a clear national Palestinian editorial line, and reached a circulation of up to seven thousand copies in the 1930s. It had a limited impact outside of Palestine.[7]

*Al-Ahram* and *Filastin* during the period under review clearly showed a keen interest in the developments in Europe. They relied on international news agencies for reports on international affairs, but *al-Ahram,* being larger and better off financially, was also able to send special envoys to European capitals, thus exposing firsthand information and assessments. *Filastin,* on the other hand, was limited to envoys mostly in the neighboring Arab countries. It compensated for its limitations by quoting *al-Ahram* and translating a variety of articles from Western sources. Both newspapers followed Hitler's ascension to power and the consolidation of his regime, were well aware of the deep animosity toward the Jews embedded in Nazi ideology and Hitler's worldview, and closely followed the anti-Jewish measures in Germany and their consequences. The number of editorials that reflected a clear political or ideological stance was relatively small, yet the mere transmission of information was of great importance. The coverage of events was mostly factual and neutral; however, the titles, how the information was presented, and sometimes short interventions by usually unidentified writers revealed the inclination of each paper and its writers.

## The Formation of Hitler's First Government, 30 January 1933

Both *al-Ahram* and *Filastin* reported on Hitler's new government, including the unrest it caused and the anxiety it aroused among socialists, communists, and Jews in Germany. The German political crisis between 1930 and 1933 was clearly presented, as well as the competing camps,

Hitler's maneuvering, and his potential danger.[8] Both papers saw the government as right wing, and *al-Ahram* even defined it as "extreme nationalist,"[9] which intends to fight the capitalists, communists, and socialists, as well as the Jews. They published the content of the pamphlet disseminated by the new government on 1 February, details on Hitler's speech, and the possibility of the dissolution of the Reichstag and a proposed four-year plan.[10] However, because members of the Nazi Party constituted only one-third of the government, the papers wondered if Hitler would "be able to fulfill anything from his extremist plans."[11] They determined, as apparently did the European news agencies, the source of most of these reports, that he "will not embark on dangerous adventures internally or externally."[12]

Both papers referred to the anxiety in the German Jewish community. *Al-Ahram*'s envoy in Berlin quoted German Minister of the Interior Wilhelm Frick as saying, in response to a question about the Jews' concerns and attempts to achieve travel permits, that there was no intention to take any measures against them, but if they wanted to leave, "we will not be angry."[13] *Filastin* seemed particularly interested in the Jewish issue and its impact on immigration to Palestine. In a short item on the Jews of Germany on 3 February, it quoted President of the Jewish Agency for Palestine Nahum Sokolow as referring to the ascension of Hitler to power at an event in Tel Aviv and urging his audience that "we have to exert all our efforts to pave the ground for receiving Germany's Jews in Palestine."[14] Already in its reports on 31 January, the paper emphasized that the struggle against the Jews through laws and eviction was part and parcel of Hitler's program. This was well known worldwide, "and we will see what Hitler would be able to do in this regard," it added. The article concluded by promising to publish in another issue "a translation of Hitler's [book] and present his party's goals."[15] Two days later, the paper summarized from Hebrew newspapers the reactions of the Jewish Yishuv in Palestine to the new German government, and pointed to its fears and alarm regarding a wave of anti-Semitism against German Jews. It also quoted the liberal daily *Haaretz* dismissing those fears but mentioned rumors about the appointment of Goebbels as the head of security, defining him as "known for his deep hatred toward [Jews]."[16] Although there were no immediate measures against the Jews before April 1933, both papers were clearly aware of Hitler's enmity toward the Jews, despite the initial doubts that he would take any action, and they conveyed the justified anxiety among the Jews in Germany.

## The 1 April 1933 Boycott

By the end of March 1933, both papers had dealt extensively with the looming German plans to boycott Jewish stores, doctors, and lawyers in reaction to the Jewish campaigns in the United States, Poland, Egypt, and Palestine to boycott German goods, and stressed the German refutation of persecution of the Jews.[17] In an article titled "Hitler and the Jews," *Filastin* quoted the Central Council of German Jews as denying the allegations on the situation of the Jews and declaring that "at the beginning of Hitler's coup [*inqilab*] few extremists [*mutatarrifin*] attacked individual Jews, but the government made an effort to stop such attacks." In another item on the same day, it also quoted Hermann Goering as asserting that "the government has no intention to discriminate against the Jews and meddle with their freedoms."[18] But the paper also gave full details of the various worldwide Jewish protests. In its report of 29 March, it even quoted an American Jewish association's statement defining Hitler's regime as "based on a barbaric power."[19] Both papers continued to survey Jewish reactions, putting a special emphasis

**Figure 4.1.** Photograph of the visit of the Palestine Symphony Orchestra in Egypt, January 1937. Egyptian Prime Minister Mustafa Nahhas shakes hands with the orchestra's General Manager, Shlomo Lewertov. *Courtesy:* Association of Jews from Egypt, Tel Aviv.

on the Jewish communities in Egypt, Lebanon, Iraq, and particularly Palestine.[20]

*Al-Ahram* also focused its attention on the activities of the Jewish community in Egypt in response to Hitler's rise to power and the imminent danger to the Jews in Germany.[21] It reported on the formation of the Jewish Defense League in Egypt, its call for boycotting German goods in solidarity with German Jews, its demonstrations, and the Jewish leaders' statements in court to defend a Jewish newspaper sued by the German legation in Egypt for its criticism of the German government.

Its report on the League on 29 March also quoted the official German declaration refuting all information on atrocities against the Jews in Germany, and concluded that "all the rumors about the atrocities allegedly committed against the Jews in Germany, and which caused here in Egypt concern and sorrow for the fate of German Jews, are a pure fabrication [*iftira' mahdh*] that has no basis in reality."[22] On 31 March, the paper referred to "the situation of the Jews in Germany" in an article dealing with the disarmament conference between Russia and England, which took place at that time. It also stated that the number of German Jews did not exceed half a million people, "but their influence is very significant, particularly in the economy and finance." In conclusion, the article asserted that Jewish solidarity initiatives in Egypt might create problems for Jews in Germany, and predicted that Palestine's doors would not be opened for German Jews.[23]

On the day of the boycott of Jewish businesses in Germany, 1 April, both papers gave full details on the boycott measures and on Jewish reactions, and pointed to the behind-the-scenes efforts to end the "dispute" (*niza'*) between the Jews and Germany.[24] A long account delivered by *al-Ahram*'s special envoy in Berlin introduced the leaflets disseminated across Germany, which explained the reasons for the boycott decision and justified the new measures by the German state. *Filastin* published similar information as well. Probably drawing their inspiration from *The Protocols of the Elders of Zion,* the leaflets revealed the German fear of Bolshevism and the belief in the alleged Jewish power to mobilize public opinion against Germany through the international media, allegedly under Jewish control.[25] *Al-Ahram* also quoted an article by Julius Streicher, the organizer of the boycott, warning the Jews that if the campaigns against Germany did not stop completely, the boycott against them would be forcefully resumed. If they wanted war, "the war will continue until they realize that Germany under Nazi rule does not know fear."[26] An editorial published the next day described the increasing use of boycotts, defining them as a detrimental weapon like the sword and the cannon. It quoted Goebbels's warning that if Germany resumed the boycott, it "will seek to annihilate the Jews in Germany," and concluded that the Jews might be more susceptible to the potential damage of boycotts than Germany, wondering if "yesterday's experience will be enough to calm the atmosphere" and return things to normal.[27]

*Filastin* dedicated its editorials to the persecution of the Jews and its ramifications for Palestine. "We do not support any movement engaged in the persecution of nations no matter what its reasons are, but similarly we do not tend to deceive people and encourage those who mislead with their deeds and their disinformation," it claimed in a column on 1 April, entitled "Allegations on the Persecution of the Jews" (*maza'im idtihad al-yahud*). While accusing the Jews of carrying out harsh campaigns against Germany, it asserted that "the Jew does not recognize any homeland except his Jewishness, and beware of this deficiency in his character that prompts people to fear him and distrust him." This was a common anti-Semitic sentiment. Arguing that the Nazis did not harm or persecute one Jew, the editorial concluded, "Those persecuted were communists and propagators of destructive communism." Since most of those propagators were allegedly Jews, it exonerated the Nazis of any fault.[28]

Another editorial a few days later on "Germany and the Jews" claimed that Great Britain knew how to exploit the Jewish wealth and issued the Balfour Declaration, which aroused the powers of "international Judaism" against Germany and its allies. It accused the Jews in the Ottoman Empire of spying on the empire, leading to the arrest of no fewer than 1,400 Jews in Palestine. Under the subtitle "Hitler and the Founders of the National Home," it reported that the World Zionist Organization added Hitler's picture to the gallery of founders of the Jewish national home, despite his severe persecution of the Jews. "No one of the founders of the national home has succeeded in opening the doors of Palestine for immigration more than Hitler," it quoted its so-called official reliable Zionist source. Before the persecution of the Jews in Germany began, Britain was cautious to avoid the occupation of all of Palestine, but today, in the name of "the victory of humanism" and "the call of conscience," the situation has changed. And we ask: "Why are the British keen to support a group allegedly exposed to persecution in Germany when it is this group's intention to arrive in Palestine to persecute the Arabs in their own homes?"[29] This kind of argumentation has intensified over the years since 1945, leading some to believe that the

Holocaust was the major cause for the Palestinian catastrophe (Nakba) and the establishment of the Jewish state.

## The Book Burning of 10 May 1933

While the Nazi regime's consolidation of power and its attitude toward German Jews continued to preoccupy the two papers, the book burning on 10 May 1933 received brief coverage. *Al-Ahram* reported on 8 May that a group of students in Germany had collected hundreds of non-German publications from public libraries and intended to burn them.[30] On the same day, it also published a denial of attorney Léon Castro, head of the Egyptian Jewish Association, that Egyptian Jews were trying to get permits for two hundred Jewish doctors to immigrate to Egypt from Germany. He was quoted as saying they were involved in collecting aid for their coreligionist immigrants, but they were fully committed to Egypt. *Filastin* also referred to this issue, but it also presented the declaration of the Egyptian Medical Association, which rejected the immigration of doctors to Egypt, claiming they might have a negative effect on the Egyptian doctors.[31]

*Filastin* was much more comprehensive in its reports on the book burning. It published several items on the same day, identifying the participants as Hitlerite students who collected books that "did not conform to the German spirit," and added that the German Ministry of Education issued new instructions forcing writers and poets identifying with leftist views that represent a "Jewish mentality" to resign from their positions.[32] Other items dealt with Jewish immigration, the subject that mostly preoccupied the Palestinian paper, reporting on the efforts of the British and American Jews, as well as the Jews of Palestine, to search for ways to help German Jews to emigrate and to renew the struggle against Germany.[33] In contrast to the Egyptian paper, *Filastin* was less inhibited in expressing its interpretation of the events and presenting Hitler's views. On 10 May, it published an item titled "Exaggerating the Incidents of the Nazis against the Jews," and on the next day it brought a translation of an English article (without mentioning the writer's name or the source), introducing Hitler's book *Mein Kampf* and explaining his aversion toward the Jews. One of the subtitles of the article was "The Social Flaws of the Jews." Quotations such as "when I studied the activities of the Jews in the press, the arts, the humanities, and literature, I was able to perceive where the world's complaints against the Jews come from," or "I found out that all that the Jews produced in those arts is a catastrophic danger, worse than the danger of the black plague in the past,"[34] were conducive to the later adoption of such claims in the Arab discourse on the Jews and the Arab-Israeli conflict. Articles such as these did not appear in *al-Ahram*.

## The Nuremberg Race Laws of 15 September 1935

The Nuremberg Race Laws were presented in detail in both papers as decrees redefining the relationship between Germans and Jews. The reports extensively quoted Hitler's speech and other German officials at the Nazi Party convention in Nuremberg, and explained the reasons for the enactment of the new laws.[35] *Filastin*, however, seemed to have basically adopted the German narrative blaming the Jews for what befell them and accusing them of provocative behavior. In one article, it commented that "the Germans do not oppose the Jews as long as they want to be Jews and behave accordingly," and that the new law even "serves the Jews in Germany and helps them to become an independent people."[36] An editorial on 27 September, titled "The Ethnic Cleansing of Jews from Germany," contended that "the Jews launched an anti-German campaign, which led the Germans to revenge and to get rid of all German Jews." The Nazi decision, it said, bodes well for the extremist Zionist policy, which aims at Judaizing Palestine and East Jordan. "We do not claim that the Nazis cooperate with the Zionists in realizing their destructive political aspirations against the Arabs," it concluded, "but we see that this is a Jewish ploy [*hila*] that succeeds in exploiting the feelings of anger against the Jews in Germany for their own plans."[37]

In contrast to *Filastin*'s commentaries, *al-Ahram*'s special envoy to Nuremberg dispatched an extraordinary opinion article on 21 September on the Nazi Party rally, which did not touch on the issue of the Jews. In a sharp assessment, conveying fear and admiration, he described the event in terms of a religious pilgrimage and the Nazi movement as a cult-worshiping power. This display of force could be interpreted as a sign of war, he admitted, but because of his familiarity with the German people, his fears had been allayed, and he was left fascinated by the exhibition of power, which "is one of the causes of respect and glory" from time immemorial.[38]

## The Évian Conference, 6–15 July 1938

The Évian Conference was a significant wake-up call for the Arabs, particularly for the Palestinians. Its convening came a year after the publication of the Peel Commission's recommendations for the partition of Palestine, exacerbating Arab fears of growing Jewish immigration to Palestine. These fears were heightened by the reluctance of the participant states at Évian to absorb Jewish refugees, as well as by increasing Jewish demands to open Palestine for Jewish immigration. The conference, which was convened 6–15 July 1938 at the initiative of US President Franklin D. Roosevelt to discuss the issue of increasing numbers of Jewish refugees fleeing Nazi persecution, drew the attention of both papers. They closely followed its deliberations, describing the moral dilemma of the participants who recognized the need to assist the refugees but still rejected their plea for financial and racial reasons. They naturally focused on Jewish and Zionist efforts to obtain agreement on pressuring Germany to allow the refugees to emigrate with some of their property, and on Palestine as the best destination for Jewish immigrants from Germany.[39]

Before the opening of the conference, *Filastin* dedicated its front pages to both the upcoming conference and the annual convention of American Jewish organizations held in the United States, emphasizing in the main headline that "Roosevelt is sympathetic to the establishment of a national home"[40] to save the Jews from "the Hitlerite hell" (*al-jahim al-hitleri*).[41] The report on the American Jewish convention included details on a Jewish Agency memorandum submitted to the convention under the subtitle "Only Palestine Would Solve the Problem of Jewish Immigration."[42] *Al-Ahram* as well referred to the memorandum, wondering if anyone at the conference would side with the Zionists' desire, and concluded, "The conference is supposed to find a social and economic solution for the Jewish problem and not to enable the Jews to establish a national home on the ruins of another people."[43]

Both papers were particularly interested in the British delegation's position on the issue of Jewish immigration to Palestine, and frequently referred to its statements and to reports on the conference in the British papers. On 6 July, *Filastin* quoted British "reliable circles" as saying that the British delegation was trying to prevent long discussions about Jewish immigration to Palestine, focusing instead on finding ways to negotiate with Germany the export of Jewish assets. *Filastin* emphasized that Lord Winterton, head of the British delegation, asserted in his speech at the opening session that "the countries that persecute the Jews should not get the wrong idea that the result of the persecution of minorities will be their evacuation from their country." *Al-Ahram*, on the other hand, highlighted the British government's determination to examine the possibility of sending Jews to its colonies.[44]

Winterton's speech at the closing session of the conference was extensively covered. He asserted that Palestine should not be tied to the general problem of the refugees. Doubting the capacity of Palestine to absorb a large and growing number of refugees, he considered it "improper to decide the fate of the refugees based on what can be expected from the solution of the Palestine problem." On 17 July, *Filastin* also remarked that Winterton spoke of Palestine because of the pressure exerted on him by the American delegation, and that the British government designed a plan for Palestine that it intended to implement.[45]

Both papers' extended coverage of the conference also presented the German perception of the conference, as well as the Arab reaction. *Al-Ahram* quoted at length Alfred Rosenberg's article in the Nazi Party daily, *Völkischer Beobachter*, titled "The Jews and Where Will They Be Sent?" He explored options for the migration of the Jews, rejecting Palestine as a viable possibility because the Jews who were already there caused constant riots and disorder. He suggested finding a territory outside Europe to absorb them and allow them to establish their independence.[46] Both papers reported on new German measures against the Jews[47] but considered any increase in the number of Jewish refugees in Palestine as a source of unrest and conflict throughout the Arab and Islamic East.[48]

There were very few references to the Arab position on the conference. In one of its early reports, *Filastin* revealed that Arab circles in Paris watched the conference with interest, and dismissed the possibility that it would deal with the migration of German Jews to Palestine.[49] They published a telegram by the defense committees on Palestine in Syria to the conference, warning that support for the Zionist policy would entail "the dissemination of hatred and enmity against the Jews in all Arab countries. The Arabs did not assault anybody and did not persecute the Jews, and it is unjust that they bear the guilt of Europe's crimes of persecution against the Jews and be asked to give up their country and their existence in their country."[50] The telegram unwittingly exposed an anti-Semitic belief in the power of "Jewish propaganda and machinations" (*bil-di'aya wal-dasa'is*). Lebanese parliament representatives sent a similar protest against Jewish immigration to Palestine.[51] The letter and the spirit of the claims raised in the Syrian telegram became seamlessly part of Arab responses to the Holocaust. The link between the situation in Palestine and the fate of the Jews in Arab lands, as well as the argument that the Arabs were forced to bear the brunt of Europe's misdeeds toward the Jews, constitute two basic motifs in the Arab Holocaust discourse.[52]

Although both papers attached great importance to the conference, most of the *al-Ahram* reports appeared in inside pages, and their titles remained as neutral as possible, such as "The Évian Conference for the Inquiry of the Jewish Immigration Problem"[53] or "The Évian Conference and the Jewish Emigration."[54] It also provided information on the intensification of attacks against the Jews in Germany and elsewhere.[55] *Filastin*, on the other hand, carried bolder headlines, which not only seemed to argue with Jewish leaders' aspirations but also exposed the bare truth about the conference itself. Some examples include "At the Évian Conference for Refugees, Australia Rejects Jewish Immigration from Germany,"[56] "The Disappointment at Évian: The Delegations of Some Countries Reject the Refugees! Failure Was Not Taken into Account by the Jewish Leaders!!,"[57] and "Did the Conference Fail? The Countries are Ready to Propose but not to Implement."[58]

Both papers referred to the situation of the Jews in Italy. They quoted *Stampa*, the Italian daily that explained the reasons for the persecution of the Jews. *Stampa* asserted that the Jewish assault on trade, the economy, and the medical profession had caused economic and social damage to European society, and therefore no one was ready to provide the Jews with shelter.[59] *Al-Ahram* also reported on the Italian Manifesto of Race of 14 July and the anxiety it caused among the Italian Jews. The Manifesto stipulated that the Italians were Aryans, whereas the Jews as non-Italians were the only people who could not be integrated in the Italian society. This was a prelude to the racial laws promulgated in November 1938. *Filastin* mentioned the Manifesto when it reported on the reaction of international Judaism in a short item entitled "The Reason for the Fascists' Anger toward the Jews."[60]

In its editorial of 15 July, entitled "Évian—Filastin," *Filastin* reassured its readers that no one had invoked "the name of Palestine or the sending of some of the refugees there" at the conference except of the Zionists. However, it warned that the danger still existed, because the conference was scheduled to reconvene, and, undoubtedly, the Zionists would try again to push their agenda.[61] *Al-Ahram*, on the other hand, published an editorial a day after the conclusion of the conference, which discussed very clearly, perhaps for the first time, "the Palestine Problem and the Arab and Jewish Positions and Its Impact on the Arab and Islamic Worlds." It introduced the Arab and Jewish positions, wondering, "Why is this enmity between two Semitic peoples that lived for centuries in harmony and peace?" It accused Zionism of wanting Palestine to be theirs, as well as "International Judaism" and England, "but the Arabs ultimately say 'No' and the Islamic world repeats it." It wondered why England refused to keep the Jews and allocate them a piece of its vast lands, and why it was "mute in front of the strong that persecute them [the Jews] and inflict harm on their behalf on a weak people [the Arabs] that trusted it and considered it to be its friend."[62] The spirit of this editorial was also conveyed in a *Filastin* editorial that reported on an Arab League memorandum to the American delegation at Évian, which concluded, "Do we need to ask in the spirit of American justice and democracy that you refrain from adopting the Jewish arguments and aspirations in Palestine, and that your sublime humanistic feelings serve the realization of their goals in this country?"[63]

The reactions of both papers to the Évian Conference clearly show an increase in the Arab concern over Palestine, specifically over the possibility that the persecuted Jews in Germany would have nowhere else to go. As a result, they raised the call to separate the solutions to the Jewish refugee problem and the Palestine problem. This demand became part of the Arab official and public discourses after the war, when the United States sought to resolve the issue of Jewish displaced persons in Europe.[64]

## Kristallnacht, 9–10 November 1938

Interest in the events in Germany and the fate of the Jews continued unabated in Egypt and Palestine, and was clearly demonstrated in the detailed accounts of the Kristallnacht pogrom in both papers. They described the violent reactions against the Jews in the wake of the assassination of the German embassy's third secretary in Paris, Ernst vom Rath, on 7 November 1938 by the young Polish Jew, Herschel Grynszpan. These included demonstrations, violent attacks, the burning of synagogues, the demolition of Jewish-owned stores, the arrest of thousands of Jews, and the government's extreme new measures against them.[65] They also cited official German sources to explain the reasons behind the outburst of rage. "The Jews challenged us and we will fight them mercilessly," *al-Ahram* quoted the German newspapers on 10 November. They should blame themselves "if the thousands of Jews living in Germany in peace among their hosts will be held responsible for what the Jew Grynszpan had done."[66] The paper's special envoy to Berlin wrote the next day that there was an expectation of an official declaration on "harsh measures" against the Jews, and that the Germans perceived the assassination not as "an individual's act but a proof of the Jewish world's conspiracy against Nazism and Germany."[67]

*Filastin* also covered the German media's reactions and reported in detail Hitler's speeches and Goebbels' statements.[68] On 10 November, it quoted Hitler's speech in Munich on the retrieval of German rights, in which he criticized the hypocrisy of British policies: "The British representatives speak frequently about democracy, but I tell you that this spirit should be applied in Palestine, which is dominated by a regime that has nothing to do with democracy, but is 'based on sheer force.'"[69] Two days later, it published an article from a German official paper responding to the publication of the White Paper. Under the title "Like the German People, the Arabs Should Get Their Rights," the paper stressed that Germany has no interests in Palestine and would like to see all peoples achieving their rights and independence, adding that

**Figure 4.2.** Photograph of a gathering of Muslim, Christian, and Jewish employees of the newspaper *La Bourse Egyptiene*, from the late 1930s. *Courtesy*: the Tam family, Tel Aviv.

"the Jewish problem should be solved but not at the expense of Palestine and its small space."[70] German papers were also quoted as threatening the British parliament that if it intended to discuss the recent events in Germany against the Jews, considered an internal German issue, the Reichstag would conduct a debate on the British policy in Palestine.[71] In contrast to this report, *al-Ahram* preferred to quote at length a 14 November interview of the BBC with Goebbels in which he discussed "The Problem of the Jews" and the new measures against them, and suggested "that English papers treat Germany's internal problems in the same way in which German papers deal with England's internal events," wishing in conclusion for an improvement in British-German relations.[72]

Both papers also gave details of the persecution of the Jews, the arrests of thousands of Jews, the raids on their homes and stores, and the difficulties they faced in paying the fine imposed on them for the damages incurred during the night of violence. *Al-Ahram* even quoted an announcement published in a German paper, calling for active participation in the demonstrations held that day to express "contempt to those Jews, the malicious murderers, who killed vom Rath for no reason except for being a German." Whereas the headline of *al-Ahram*'s article was "The Persecution of the Jews in Germany," *Filastin* chose a more neutral headline—"Germany and the Jews," providing information on how the money would be collected.[73] Days after the Kristallnacht, the papers continued to cover the imposition of the new measures against the Jews in Germany, but *Filastin* seemed more focused on Jewish emigration from Germany. In its report on 13 November, it quoted Chaim Weizmann, president of the World Zionist Organization (WZO), as saying at the meetings of the WZO in London that "Palestine is the only hope" for Jewish immigration.[74]

A stark example of the differences between the two papers is *Filastin*'s preoccupation with Nazism and Hitler. Whereas it cited French and British experts on European history—introducing details on Hitler's personality, biography, and worldviews, without expressing its opinion[75]— *al-Ahram* could allow itself, despite its awareness of the Palestine problem, to uphold a moral stance against the persecution of the Jews. In an editorial in response to Kristallnacht, titled "The Policy of Force and Violence in the World: New Principles Undermine the Bases of Social Order," *al-Ahram* criticized and condemned the persecution of the Jews in Germany. It considered Germany's conduct disturbing, threatening "to return humanity to the remotest barbaric eras," and breaching all human moral and religious values. It regarded England as the most suited power to stand against this policy of force and violence in service of humanity but concluded that its moral failure in Palestine impairs its ability to preach for "justice, fairness, and compassion."[76]

## Conclusion

The coverage of the events in the period under review from the leading Egyptian and Palestinian mainstream newspapers "makes clear that a usually very informed debate about Europe provided a multifaceted perspective to readers."[77] It leaves no doubt as to the flow of information and the level of knowledge about the Nazi atrocities against the Jews in Germany during the 1930s. The presentation and the discussion of these issues also confirmed several initial assumptions.

Arab responses to the events in Europe were influenced and shaped by developments in the region, specifically by the national struggle for independence and the Arab-Zionist conflict in Palestine. Egyptian and Palestinian interest in Nazi Germany, Nazi ideology, and its animosity toward the Jews stemmed not only from the narrow prism of the evolving Arab-Israeli conflict but also from a broader vision of their future political, cultural, and social postcolonial worlds. However, the Nazi persecution of the Jews was seen, particularly by the Palestinian newspaper, through the prism of its possible adverse implications for Palestine. Jewish immigration preoccupied the Palestinian paper relatively more from the very beginning of the Nazi regime's measures against the Jews; this affected its reports, leading to attempts to minimize the scope of the persecutions or doubt their accuracy altogether. The Egyptian paper's interest in the issue of Palestine and Jewish immigration intensified during this period as Egyptian involvement in Arab affairs grew.

It has been assumed that there were differences between the Palestinian and the Egyptian discourses. Indeed, there were nuances in the reporting, in the choice of issues and emphasis, and in the phrasing of titles and subtitles. The Egyptian paper seems to have been less emotionally involved, and hence its coverage of the Jewish situation in Europe more comprehensive. The titles were more neutral than those in the Palestinian paper, which did not hesitate to assert its views in its titles. *Filastin* was more attentive to the pronouncements of Jewish Zionist leaders, closely surveyed them, and interpreted their implications for Palestine. It often published the reports on the events in the front page, which *al-Ahram* rarely did. The Egyptian paper could allow itself, despite its awareness of the Palestine problem, to uphold a moral stance toward the persecutions of the Jews, whereas the Palestinian paper reacted perhaps out of a "defense mechanism," realizing their adverse implications for Palestine and its Arab inhabitants. As a result, they also seemed keen on emphasizing the alleged reasons behind Germany's policy against the Jews in order to undermine Jewish moral claims.

My previous research has dealt with the period of almost seventy years since the end of World War II in 1945. It had been established that the years between the end of the war and the founding of the state of Israel in 1948 constituted a formative period that laid the foundations of the post-1945 discourse on the Holocaust. This chapter does not challenge this assumption. However, it demonstrates that the representation of the Holocaust after the war is rooted in the prewar discourse on the persecution of the Jews, which had been entangled with the conflict in Palestine. Several arguments that appeared during this earlier period seemed to persist, and later became part of the Arab post-Holocaust discourse. One has been the Arab call to separate the Palestine problem from the Jewish refugee problem. Arab representatives, as well as the British, held this position before and after the war, first at the Évian Conference and then in reaction to the deliberations on the fate of the more than two hundred and fifty thousand displaced persons in Europe after the war. Another theme that also emerged in the wake of the Évian Conference was the argument that the Arabs did not persecute the Jews and that it was unjust that they suffer the consequences of Europe's crimes. This was clearly drafted in the Syrian memorandum to the conference, and after the war, it became a prominent motif in Arab Holocaust discourse. Another theme is the accusation of Zionist exploitation of the Nazi atrocities for achieving the movement's political goals, which became ever more pronounced after the war. As the solution of the Jewish refugee problem seemed to lead to Palestine, and after the war to the establishment of a Jewish state, Arab preoccupation with the persecution of the Jews and later with the Holocaust focused on their political ramifications, on their perceived political exploitation by the Zionists, leading to attempts to minimize the scope of Nazi persecution and the Holocaust or to deny them altogether.

Anti-Semitic beliefs, which mostly emanated from Western sources translated into Arabic, penetrated the discussions in both papers but were particularly evident in the Palestinian daily *Filastin*. Beliefs in alleged Jewish power and control of the media, in the Jewish conspiratorial and treacherous character, and in inherent Jewish corruption became part and parcel of the postwar public discourse on the Arab-Israeli conflict, Zionism, and the Holocaust. Few editorials took a clear stance, denouncing or praising Nazi Germany. Some of the reports in both papers, however, quoted German sources either to present a full picture of the events or, particularly in *Filastin,* to balance the accounts of the measures against the Jews by explaining or even justifying them while blaming the Jews for what befell them. But the comments were made in context. After the war, the animosity toward the Zionists and the Jews prompted various writers, mostly Islamists, to adopt the German arguments as facts detached from their original context and to present the Jews as the instigators of war against Germany, deserving punishment, and Nazi Germany as an innocent victim of a broad Jewish-Zionist conspiracy.

The discourse on the persecution of the Jews and later the Holocaust developed in response to the emerging reality in Palestine and the Middle East. The arguments raised were rooted in this reality and maneuvered between the acknowledgment of the Nazi atrocities and the growing body of information about them, and the need to check, dismiss, or even supress this information. The linkage between the solution of the Jewish crisis in Europe and the solution of the Palestine problem created by the resolutions of the various conferences and commissions before and after the war encouraged the trend to obfuscate the meaning of the persecutions and the Holocaust, to ignore them, and to deny their human aspects. The diverse prewar discourse, which continued at least in the Egyptian press in the immediate postwar years, was substituted by suppressed knowledge, ignorance, and a more monolithic discourse that uses the Holocaust as another tool in the Arab-Israeli rhetoric of conflict.

**Esther Webman** is head of the Zeev Vered Desk for the Study of Tolerance and Intolerance in the Middle East, and a senior research fellow at the Dayan Center and the Stephen Roth Institute at Tel Aviv University. Her research focuses on Arab discourse analysis, mainly Arab anti-Semitism and Arab perceptions of the Holocaust. She has published extensively on these topics. She was a visiting scholar at the Oxford Centre for Hebrew and Jewish Studies as a Skirball fellowship recipient, at Boston University as a Fulbright recipient, and at Yad Vashem. Her book, coauthored with Meir Litvak, *From Empathy to Denial: Arab Responses to the Holocaust* (2009) won the 2010 Washington Institute Book Prize and was published in Hebrew in 2015. She is the editor of *The Global Impact* *of* The Protocols of the Elders of Zion: *A Century-Old Myth* (2011) and *Antisemitism: The Generic Hatred* in Arabic (2017).

## Notes

1. On the Arab Revolt, see, e.g., Tom Bowden, "The Politics of the Arab Rebellion in Palestine 1936–39," *Middle Eastern Studies* 11, no. 2 (1975); Charles Townshend, "The First Intifada: Rebellion in Palestine 1936–1939," *History Today* 39, no. 7 (1989).
2. On the Peel Commission's recommendations, see Jewish Virtual Library, *British Palestine Mandate: Text of the Peel Commission Report (July 1937)*, http://www.jewishvirtuallibrary.org/jsource/History/peel1.html.
3. On Arab attitudes toward Zionism, see, e.g., Neville J. Mandel, *The Arabs and Zionism before World War I* (Berkeley, CA, 1976); Thomas Mayer, *Egypt and the Palestine Question, 1936–1945* (Berlin, 1983); Yehoshua Porath, "Anti-Zionist and Anti-Jewish Ideology in the Arab Nationalist Movement in Palestine," in *Antisemitism through the Ages*, ed. Shmuel Almog (Oxford, 1989); Itamar Rabinovich, "Egypt and the Palestine Question Before and After the Revolution," in *Egypt from Monarchy to Republic: A Reassessment of Revolution and Change*, ed. Shimon Shamir (Boulder CO, 1995); Benny Morris, *Righteous Victims: A History of the Zionist-Arab Conflict, 1881–2001* (New York, 2001).
4. See, e.g., Israel Gershoni and James Jankowski, *Confronting Fascism in Egypt: Dictatorship versus Democracy in the 1930s* (Stanford, CA, 2010); Israel Gershoni, *Dame and Devil: Egypt and Nazism, 1935–1940* [in Hebrew], 2 vols. (Tel Aviv, 2012); Moshe Shemesh, "*Filastin*'s Position toward the Axis and the Democratic States" [in Hebrew], *Iyunim Bitkumat Israel* 2 (1992); René Wildangel, "The Invention of 'Islamofascism': Nazi Propaganda to the Arab World and Perceptions from Palestine," *Die Welt des Islams* 52, no. 3-4 (2012); René Wildangel, "More Than the Mufti: Other Arab-Palestinian Voices on Nazi Germany, 1933–1945, and Their Postwar Narrations," in *Arab Responses to Fascism and Nazism: Attraction and Repulsion*, ed. Israel Gershoni (Austin, 2014); Mustafa Kabha, "The Palestinian National Movement and Its Attitude toward the Fascist and Nazi Movements 1925–1945," *Geschichte und Gesellschaft* 37, no. 3 (2011).
5. These include the formation of Hitler's first government, the April 1933 boycott, the book burnings in May 1933, the Nuremberg Race Laws of September 1935, the Évian conference in July 1938, and Kristallnact in November 1938. For a comprehensive account of this period, see Saul Friedländer, *Nazi Germany and the Jews: The Years of Persecution, 1933–1939*, vol. 1 (New York, 1997).
6. On the representation of the Holocaust in Arab public discourse, see Azmi Bishara, "The Arabs and the Holocaust: The Analysis of a Problematic Conjunctive Letter" [in Hebrew], *Zmanim* 53 (1995); Meir Litvak and Esther Webman, *From Empathy to Denial: Arab Response to the Holocaust* (London, 2009); Gil-

bert Achcar, *The Arabs and the Holocaust: The Arab-Israeli War of Narratives* (London, 2010).
7. On the newspapers, see Ami Ayalon, *The Press in the Arab Middle East: A History* (New York, 1995); Ami Ayalon, *Reading Palestine: Printing and Literacy, 1900–1948* (Austin, TX, 2004); Mustafa Kabha, *Journalism in the Eye of the Storm: The Palestinian Press Shapes Public Opinion 1929–1939* [in Hebrew] (Jerusalem, 2004).
8. *Al-Ahram*, 29–31 March 1933, 1–2 February 1933; *Filastin*, 29 January 1933, 31 January 1933, 1–2 February 1933.
9. *Al-Ahram*, 31 January 1933; *Filastin*, 31 January 1933. All tranlations in this chapter are my own unless otherwise indicated.
10. *Al-Ahram*, 2–3 February 1933; *Filastin*, 3 February 1933.
11. *Filastin*, 1 February 1933.
12. *Al-Ahram*, 31 March 1933, 2 February 1933; *Filastin*, 3 February 1933.
13. *Al-Ahram*, 2 February 1933. A similar report was also published a day earlier, alluding to the concern among the Jews and their determination to emigrate: *al-Ahram*, 1 February 1933. See also, *Filastin*, 3 February 1933.
14. *Filastin*, 1 February 1933, 3 February 1933.
15. *Filastin*, 31 January 1933.
16. *Filastin*, 2 February 1933.
17. *Al-Ahram*, 28–31 March 1933; *Filastin*, 28 March 1933, 30 March 1933.
18. *Filastin*, 28 March 1933.
19. *Filastin*, 29–31 March 1933.
20. *Filastin*, 1 April 1933, 4–5 April 5, 1933; *al-Ahram*, 5 April 1933.
21. For a short account on the reaction of the Egyptian Jewish community to Hitler's rise to power, see Hagar Hillel, *Israel in Cairo: A Zionist Newspaper in Nationalist Egypt, 1920–1939* [in Hebrew] (Tel Aviv, 2004), 154–170.
22. *Al-Ahram*, 28–30 March 1933.
23. *Al-Ahram*, 31 March 1933.
24. *Al-Ahram*, 1 April 1933. See also *al-Ahram*, 2–3 April 1933; *Filastin*, 31 March 1933, 1–2 April 1933, 4–5 April 1933.
25. *Al-Ahram*, 1 April 1933; *Filastin*, 31 March 1933.
26. *Al-Ahram*, 1 April 1933. See also *al-Ahram*, 4 April 1933.
27. *Al-Ahram*, 2 April 1933.
28. *Filastin*, 1 April 1933.
29. *Filastin*, 4 April 1933.
30. *Al-Ahram*, 8 May 1933.
31. Ibid.; *Filastin*, 9 May, 1933.
32. *Filastin*, 9 May 1933. More information on the events was published in *Filastin*, 12 May 1933.
33. *Filastin*, 9 May 1933. See also *Filastin*, 10–11 May 1933; *al-Ahram*, 10 May 1933, 15–16 May 1933.
34. *Filastin*, 10–11 May 1933.
35. *Al-Ahram*, 13–14 September 1935, 17–18 September 1935; *Filastin*, 13 September 1935, 17 September 1935, 26 September 1935.
36. *Filastin*, 17 September 1935.

37. *Filastin*, 13 September 1935.
38. *Al-Ahram*, 21 September 1935. See also Gershoni and Jankowski, *Confronting Fascism in Egypt*, 66–68.
39. *Al-Ahram*, 5–6 July 1938, 8–11 July 1938; *Filastin*, 7 July 1938, 10 July 1938, 12–13 July 1938, 15–16 July 1938.
40. *Filastin*, 5–6 July 1938.
41. *Filastin*, 6 July 1938.
42. Ibid.
43. *Al-Ahram*, 6 July 1938.
44. *Filastin*, 7 July 1938; *Al-Ahram*, 7 July 1938. See also *al-Ahram*, 15 July 1938; *Filastin*, 14–17 July 1938.
45. *Al-Ahram*, 16 July 1938; *Filastin*, 16–17 July 1938, 20 July 1938.
46. *Al-Ahram*, 9 July 1938.
47. *Al-Ahram*, 10 July 1938; *Filastin*, 15 July 1938.
48. *Al-Ahram*, 9 July 1938; *Filastin*, 10 July 1938.
49. *Filastin*, 7 July 1938.
50. *Al-Ahram*, 12 July 1938; *Filastin*, 14 July 1938.
51. *Al-Ahram*, 14 July 1938; *Filastin*, 14 July 1938.
52. See Litvak and Webman, *From Empathy to Denial*, 35–57.
53. *Al-Ahram*, 9 July 1938.
54. *Al-Ahram*, 14 July 1938.
55. *Al-Ahram*, 6 July 1938, 10–12 July 1938, 18–19 July 1938.
56. *Filastin*, 8 July 1938.
57. *Filastin*, 9 July 1938.
58. *Filastin*, 10 July 1938.
59. *Al-Ahram*, 13 July 1938; *Filastin*, 14 July 1938.
60. *Al-Ahram*, 15–17 July 1938; *Filastin*, 23 July 1938. In its issue of 12 November 1938, *Filastin* quoted *The Jewish Chronicle* on the new racial laws against the Jews in Italy. For a discussion of the Italian racial laws, see Gene Bernardini, "The Origins and Development of Racial Anti-Semitism in Fascist Italy," *Journal of Modern History* 49, no. 3 (1977).
61. *Filastin*, 15 July 1938.
62. *Al-Ahram*, 17 July 1938. See also Gershoni, *Dame and Devil*, 1:199–200.
63. *Filastin*, 21 July 1938.
64. See Litvak and Webman, *From Empathy to Denial*, 35–46.
65. *Al-Ahram*, 9–11 November 1938, 13 November 1938; *Filastin*, 10–12 November 1938, 15 November 1938, 17 November 1938.
66. *Al-Ahram*, 10 November 1938.
67. *Al-Ahram*, 11 November 1938.
68. *Filastin*, 11–14 November 1938.
69. *Filastin*, 10 November 1938.
70. *Filastin*, 12 November 1938.
71. *Filastin*, 13 November 1938.
72. *Al-Ahram*, 14 November 1938.
73. *Al-Ahram*, 13 November 1938; *Filastin*, 13 November 1938.
74. *Al-Ahram*, 15 November 1938; *Filastin*, 12–18 November 1938.

75. *Filastin,* 13 November 1938, 15 November 1938, 18 November 1938.
76. *Al-Ahram,* 15 November 1938. See also Gershoni, *Dame and Devil,* 1:183–84, 198.
77. Wildangel, "The Invention of 'Islamofascism,'" 539.

# Bibliography

Achcar, Gilbert. *The Arabs and the Holocaust: The Arab-Israeli War of Narratives.* London, 2010.
Ayalon, Ami. *The Press in the Arab Middle East: A History.* New York, 1995.
———. *Reading Palestine: Printing and Literacy, 1900–1948.* Austin, TX, 2004.
Bernardini, Gene. "The Origins and Development of Racial Anti-Semitism in Fascist Italy." *Journal of Modern History* 49, no. 3 (1977): 431–453.
Bishara, Azmi. "The Arabs and the Holocaust: The Analysis of a Problematic Conjunctive Letter." [In Hebrew.] *Zmanim* 53 (1995): 54–71.
Bowden, Tom. "The Politics of the Arab Rebellion in Palestine 1936–39." *Middle Eastern Studies* 11, no. 2 (1975): 147–174.
Friedländer, Saul. *Nazi Germany and the Jews: The Years of Persecution, 1933–1939.* Vol. 1. New York, 1997.
Gershoni, Israel. *Dame and Devil: Egypt and Nazism, 1935–1940.* [In Hebrew.] 2 vols. Tel Aviv, 2012.
Gershoni, Israel, and James Jankowski. *Confronting Fascism in Egypt: Dictatorship versus Democracy in the 1930s.* Stanford, CA, 2010.
Hillel, Hagar. *Israel in Cairo: A Zionist Newspaper in Nationalist Egypt, 1920–1939.* [In Hebrew.] Tel Aviv, 2004.
Kabha, Mustafa. *Journalism in the Eye of the Storm: The Palestinian Press Shapes Public Opinion 1929–1939.* [In Hebrew.] Jerusalem, 2004.
———. "The Palestinian National Movement and Its Attitude toward the Fascist and Nazi Movements 1925–1945." *Geschichte und Gesellschaft* 37, no. 3 (2011): 437–450.
Litvak, Meir, and Esther Webman. *From Empathy to Denial: Arab Responses to the Holocaust.* London, 2009.
Mandel, Neville J. *The Arabs and Zionism before World War I.* Berkeley, 1976.
Mayer, Thomas. *Egypt and the Palestine Question, 1936–1945.* Berlin, 1983.
Morris, Benny. *Righteous Victims: A History of the Zionist-Arab Conflict, 1881–2001.* New York, 2001.
Porath, Yehoshua. "Anti-Zionist and Anti-Jewish Ideology in the Arab Nationalist Movement in Palestine." In *Antisemitism through the Ages,* edited by Shmuel Almog, 217–226. Oxford, 1989.
Rabinovich, Itamar. "Egypt and the Palestine Question Before and After the Revolution." In *Egypt from Monarchy to Republic: A Reassessment of Revolution and Change,* edited by Shimon Shamir, 325–343. Boulder, CO, 1995.
Shemesh, Moshe. "*Filastin*'s Position toward the Axis and the Democratic States." [In Hebrew.] *Iyunim Bitkumat Israel* 2 (1992): 245–278.

Townshend, Charles. "The First Intifada: Rebellion in Palestine 1936–1939." *History Today* 39, no. 7 (1989): 13–19. http://www.historytoday.com/charles-townshed/first-intifada-rebellion-palestine-1936-39.

Wildangel, René. "The Invention of 'Islamofascism': Nazi Propaganda to the Arab World and Perceptions from Palestine." *Die Welt des Islams* 52 , no. 3–4 (2012): 526–543.

Wildangel, René. "More than the Mufti: Other Arab-Palestinian Voices on Nazi Germany, 1933–1945, and Their Postwar Narrations." In *Arab Responses to Fascism and Nazism: Attraction and Repulsion,* edited by Israel Gershoni, 101–126. Austin, TX, 2014.

*Chapter 5*

# DEFINING THE NATION

Discussing Nazi Ideology in Syria and Lebanon during the 1930s

*Götz Nordbruch*

THIS CHAPTER FOCUSES ON INTELLECTUAL encounters with Nazism in Lebanon and Syria under French mandate rule. It situates these encounters in the context of an evolving local political culture that was shaped by profound transformations of the social and political order.[1] Previous studies have often concentrated on formal relations and informal contacts between local political actors and representatives of the new German regime.[2] While an inquiry into these networks and exchanges provides important insight into the strategic interests of both sides, most studies do not relate these contacts to the specific ideological context of the time. As Basheer Nafi put it in his study about these relations: "Almost all the Arab leaders who became involved in the Arab-Axis imbroglio were men of practical politics, with little affinity for ideological complexities."[3]

Nafi's conclusion that pro-German declarations were in fact expressions of *Realpolitik* rather than of ideology resonates with the saying "the enemy of my enemy is my friend," which continues to be alluded to in popular interpretations of Arab-German relations. Yet, in countries such as Egypt, Palestine, or Iraq, the choice of international allies was closely tied to ongoing local political battles. Alliances with regional actors and the affiliation to one of the evolving international camps were among the most controversial questions debated in the local public. These debates were not limited to pragmatic assessments of balances of power;

they echoed an awareness that any such affiliation would have cultural and ideological implications for the local political scene.

This was true for Lebanon and Syria as well. Political moves toward Germany were scrutinized in an increasingly politicized press, forcing the respective actors to legitimize their reasoning and to tie their preferences to their political vision. Assessments of the new German regime that were articulated in the press and in various political and cultural circles can be interpreted as part of an intellectual quest for orientation, a quest that was shaping these years between the breakup of the Ottoman Empire and the achievement of national independence following World War II.

The evolving political culture and the challenge of state building in the 1930s and early 1940s is key to understanding the contradictory approaches followed by Arab intellectuals and politicians to both the ideology and the politics of the National Socialist regime. For many observers in the Middle East, Germany's situation after World War I very much resembled their own, as victims of peace settlements imposed by the victors following the war. Arab societies felt betrayed by the European colonial powers and saw themselves in a sense as fellow victims of a *Diktat* (dictated peace).

Arab observers closely followed events in German society with Adolf Hitler's rise to power. For many, Nazism was a potential role model that promised a constructive orientation for a humiliated Arab nation and for the state building that nationalists of different political orientations in the Arab lands were eager to achieve.[4] The rise to power and the success of Hitler gave reason to reflect on possible lessons that could be drawn from the German experience. An important finding of recent studies on Arab encounters with Nazism is that the rise and fall of National Socialism was an important catalyst for discussions about their future political order. Refering to debates among Egyptian intellectuals, Israel Gershoni concludes, "In the specific context of the era, a crucial key to our understanding of the intellectual elite's position in relation to liberalism as a distinct system of values, and as a basis for a political culture and government, can be found in the attitudes it developed towards fascism and Nazism."[5]

However, it should be kept in mind that Nazism was only one point of reference. Italian Fascism, Kemalism in Turkey, communism, the French Republic, and the American New Deal were other social, economic, and political models that were widely discussed among Arab observers. This chapter focuses on notions of community and nation, as well as the specific context of the time in which National Socialist ideology was one starting point to discuss the relation between the individual and the community, and the definition of communal identity.

## Rethinking Society in a Global Context

Facing profound transformations during these years of the interwar period, the local public in Syria and Lebanon was engaged in a controversial search for milestones for the future.[6] The end of the Ottoman Empire coincided with modernization processes that were shaking the traditional order. Already at the end of the nineteenth century, the "searching for one's self" (*quête de soi-même*)[7] had been at the core of the early Arab renaissance movement (*al-nahda*). Urbanization, the extension of school education, and the beginning industrialization were paralleled by the emergence of new political and social actors. Students, workers, and women were harbingers of a mass politics that was to take root in the Levante.[8]

On an intellectual level, these transformations resounded in calls for restoration, reform, or revolution. Individual and collective identities had to be redefined; the same was true for the relations between the individual and the community, between the state and religion. In short, at the center of the debate was the vision for the future social and economic order. Defining the nation was a key challenge to contemporary attempts of state building.

Inspiration for these reflections came from a variety of sources. This should not come as a surprise, since regional transformations much resembled those experienced in other regions of the world as well.[9] The importance of local religious and cultural traditions as milestones and intellectual guidelines was best visible in the extensive coverage of early Arab and Islamic thinkers in the numerous cultural magazines. Classical Arab writers such as al-Mutanabbi were as much dealt with as were contemporary intellectuals as Jamal al-Din al-Afghani and Rashid Rida. No less important were other sources that were not immediately linked to the local intellectual and cultural context. In fact, one of the most striking traits of the intellectual debates of these years was their openness to local *and* nonlocal sources of thought and ideological currents. In journals such as *al-Hadith, al-Taliʿa,* and *al-Maʿrid,* articles about Amin al-Rihani and Khalil Jibran could be found framed with reviews of the works of André Gide, Gustave Le Bon, Friedrich Nietzsche, and Karl

Marx. Equally multifaceted were the discussed topics. Contributions on Arabic poetry and early Islamic history were published side by side with debates about the theories of Charles Darwin, the role of women in Soviet society, and Kemalist reforms in Turkey.

Nazism and its ideological claims figured among these references. As stated above, Germany supposedly shared the experiences of the Arab mandate states as oppressed and deprived of legitimate rights over their respective territories and their sovereignty. Writing in this spirit, one commentator of the Damascus newspaper *al-Qabas* described Hitler as "the leader [*zaʿīm*] who has promised himself to lead the German people by his hands through the darkness of these tyrannical international politics into the safe harbour where Germany will feel free, powerful, and sovereign."[10] According to this view, Nazism and Hitler had been able to reestablish Germany's glory and had prepared the German nation for the challenges of the time. In short, for many, Nazism appeared as a legitimate project of national revival.

Early reports about the rise of the National Socialist movement can be traced to the mid-1920s. With Hitler's appointment as Reich Chancellor in January 1933, Nazism had turned into an almost daily topic in the local press. In most cases, early information and comments were directly related to specific policies pursued by the Nazi regime. Fascination with Hitler's personality and his mobilization against his enemies were additional features of this coverage. Noticeable in this regard is the detailed information available to the broader public. Drawing primarily on European newspapers, press agencies, and radio broadcasts, most papers closely followed developments in Germany and some of the reactions of its European neighbors. With ever more details available, the commentators of local daily newspapers such as *al-Nahar* and *al-Qabas* interpreted German moves and questioned their political and ideological motives.

By the mid-1930s, references to Nazism exceeded the limits of daily politics and immediate assessments of international events. By then, major journals that provided a forum for increasingly diverse intellectual discourse frequently discussed and elaborated on facets of National Socialist thought. Throughout the years that followed, specific aspects of Nazism were addressed as potential starting points for broader questions that preoccupied local societies. In this context, National Socialist organization and youth formations, the German concept of the *Volk*, and the role of the *Führer* as an undisputed representation of the people's will furnished important stimuli that were to resonate in evolving local ideological currents.

What is important is that Nazism was not necessarily perceived as distinct from other ideological currents that had emerged during these years. More specifically, an apologetic view of Nazism did not oblige rejection of ideas articulated among French, Turkish, or Russian intellectuals, or vice versa. Intellectuals like Edmond Rabbat, Mishal 'Aflaq, Antun Sa'ada and others drew on a variety of sources that were not exclusively linked to one particular current or national context. For them, the intellectual choice was not between Nazi Germany and, say, France; in their perspective, the choice was between essentialist constructions of the community on the one hand and republican understandings on the other, or between authoritarian concepts of rule and their liberal democratic antagonists. In this regard, the near unanimous rejection of the National Socialist concept of "race" did not imply rejection of essentialist conceptualizations of the Arab nation. While racial theories were generally rejected, theories of geographically, linguistically, or culturally determined "historical races"—which were often formulated with recourse to French, British, and Italian thinkers—had become ever more popular within local nationalist circles.

What is striking, then, is the reluctance of many contemporary thinkers to acknowledge their references to nonlocal intellectual sources. While authors such as Michel 'Aflaq and Antun Sa'ada clearly drew on European sources, they vehemently defended their thoughts as authentic and distinct, and rejected all accusations of "non-Arab" or "non-Syrian" inspiration. As for Nazism itself, which pretended to reflect an authentic message of the German *Volk,* assertions of authenticity were central to most local nationalist currents.

The quest for collective identity became particularly urgent throughout the upheavals of the 1920s and 1930s. In this context, the German concept of the nation offered a potential starting point. The Damascene teachers' journal *Majallat al-Mu'allimun w-al-Mu'allimat* provides examples for such a search for outside inspiration. The publication aimed at developing national education and offered comparative approaches on questions of teaching, socialization, and methods of instruction. In late 1935, the journal published an article that explicitly drew on the experience of other nations' revivals. Germany provided one example:

> Talk about the youth can be heard every day and at every place. Never had the youth been encumbered with responsibilities and duties as it has during this age—the age of crisis, radical changes, and oddities. It is a law of nature that in a time of difficulties and crisis, one looks

for help from an active element that is full of vitality, warding off the unexpected danger or preserving the threatened entity. The revolution of the German people did not come without the help of the iron youth; it is the result of the alarm of the German youth and its distress following the world war, its suffering of the pains of unemployment and the bitterness of poverty. This revolution is not restricted to a liberation from foreign treaties and bondage, but compounds of an inner revolution aimed at ending the past age and to following new ways of life.[11]

The image of an "inner revolution" that was to be inspired in the hearts of the next generations reflected a prevailing mood of a *fin-de-siècle*; change was not about reform but about a revolution of values and traditions, about the creation of "new ways of life." Articles increasingly focused on the Hitler Youth and its role and links within German society. Interest, however, had become much broader, questioning the very educational reason for paramilitary organization and the role of the youth—these "soldiers of war and guardians of peace"[12]—within a nation's struggle for revival. Introducing one of the various contemporary publications dealing with educational questions, Munir al-Nusuli—son of the eminent leader of the Lebanese boy scouts movement, Muhyi al-Din al-Nusuli—declared, "The best service for man to serve his nation [*umma*] is his sympathy for its children and to strive for sincere national [*qawmiyya*] education."[13] In a chapter dedicated to the links between education and politics, Nusuli further wrote:

> It is necessary that the government has goals that it is striving for with wise determination. The president has the first responsibility to ensure the implementation of the curriculum on all levels. He must be an honest supervisor [*mufattish*] of this nation from whose midst he has been chosen. . . . In this book, we cannot go deeper into this issue; we can only focus on its educational side—a side which we consider of highest importance for society. Did not the modern nations that had recently experienced a renaissance—Italy, Germany, and Turkey—prove right what we just said?[14]

National revival required new organizations and new educational patterns; in the first place, however, it meant the formulation of a philosophy of the nation that would reintroduce glorious national traditions, values, and myths into the minds and souls of its children. Such a quest to revive an original national culture included a quest for the very definition of origin, of the foundations of community that was to be pursued. The notion of an "authentic culture" provided a possible answer. Articles frequently appeared that attempted to determine shared cultural foundations and to identify their traces in contemporary Levantine societies.

## Nationalism and the Question of Minorities

Questions regarding the constituency of the nation, the definition of borders, and the relations with religious and ethnic minorities were at the core of ongoing struggles over an appropriate nationalist orientation. Differing with regard to their territorial claims and their sectarian or anti-sectarian definitions of the nation, the diverse ideological elaborations of the nation echoed similar debates in Europe. Various territorial, historical, cultural, but also biologistic considerations offered quasi-scientific proof for the suggested delimitations of community. In light of the fragmentation of the populations in the mandates, historical experiences of nation building in Europe were of significant interest. Here, the difference between a French voluntarist definition of the nation and a German nationalist imagination of an ethnocultural *Volk* was noticed as an ideally typical distinction within European debates.[15] Of particular importance in the local context, then, was the question of the religious foundations of national identity. The impact of the respective status as a religious or ethnic community for the definition of communal bonds was markedly visible in the disputes among Lebanese and Syrian nationalists. Emphasizing the Christian particularities of Lebanon, proponents of a distinct Lebanese nation referred to religion as a major argument to justify their opposition to pan-Arab nationalist territorial ambitions. In contrast, Arab nationalist voices in various cases tended to advance explicit nonsectarian arguments to justify their vision: "Religion is for God, the nation is for all!"[16] was the motto forwarded by the National Bloc–affiliated daily *al-Qabas,* not least as a challenge to claims raised by religious and ethnic minorities.

The question of minorities within the state and the nation, which had long preoccupied the local public itself, characterized local perceptions of Europe and European politics as well. The discrimination against Muslims in Europe, for instance, was a major concern at the European Islamic conference in Geneva in 1935.[17] In contrast, European protection and support for minorities in the Middle East had long since been criticized as an instrument and pretext for colonial interventions; the "creation" of minorities by European powers was designed to generate a division of local populations according to the Europeans' immediate political or economic interests. Political and religious demands of the Armenian and Assyrian populations were thus reason for suspicion, as their demands were nothing but "a cause cooked in the kitchen of imperialism, for the sake of imperialism."[18] Related, then, was the suspicion against humanitarian arguments that were put forward to legitimize the European position. Calls for the granting of Lebanese and Syrian citizenship to Armenian and German Jewish refugees, for instance, appeared as being in outright contradiction to the strict regulations that were governing citizenship laws imposed on the Arab population itself. In light of the politics pursued by the mandate powers toward their local subjects, humanism seemed a cynical argument at best.[19]

In this context, international reactions to Germany's policies against Jews differed from previous experiences with European policies in the Middle East. While the debates in the League of Nations and the criticism leveled against Germany for its anti-Jewish policies were seen by some as a result of Jewish pressure, others openly wondered about the lack of concern and the missing calls for military action.[20] Since the countries in the Middle East had on various occasions faced foreign interventions in the name of a protection of ethnic and religious minorities, the international reactions to Nazism seemed strikingly halfhearted.

National Socialist policies toward the Jews did not originate in actual conflicts between non-Jews and Jews. Jews—or, more specifically, those who had been labeled as Jews according to the National Socialist doctrine—were persecuted not as an identifiable group with distinct traits but as an imagined community perceived not only as a hostile opposite but also as the negation of the German people as such. In National Socialist thought, the perception of an assumed "Jewish threat" for the German people thus differed fundamentally from the perception of other "races." While these races were seen as biologically and culturally less developed, the former, together with the "Gypsies," were systematically persecuted as the ultimate enemies of the "Aryan race."[21]

The centrality of this imagination of a German-Jewish antagonism within National Socialist ideology had been noticed even before the National Socialist rise to power. Already at the beginning of the 1930s, newspapers had covered expressions of anti-Jewish hostility as a basic tenet of Nazism. The deprivation of Jews of their civil rights was described here as a key aspect of Hitler's political program. Accordingly, the coverage of Hitler's takeover of power placed a particular emphasis on the immediate measures taken by the NSDAP to implement its anti-Semitic visions. Reports about the introduction of discriminatory laws and the boycott movement against Jewish businesses offered frequent information about the worsening situation for Jews in Germany.[22]

Repression against Albert Einstein, the internationally known German-Jewish scientist, was one focus of this coverage.[23] Being a nonreligious Jew who was widely perceived as a symbol of German science, Einstein nevertheless fell victim to National Socialist imagination of destructive Jewish influences. The persecution of his person illustrated the character of such anti-Semitic measures that were not limited to specific groups of non-German, religious, or poor Jews but directed against a racially defined Jewish collective. For one, the Beirut newspaper *al-Ahrar* hinted at this fact, which was crucial in determining the overarching concept of these persecutions. The sanctions were not restricted to impoverished Eastern European Jews who had only recently immigrated to Germany, the paper noted. Instead, anti-Semitic regulations were explicitly "forced on every Jew, even those who are baptized [but] who have a grandparent of Jewish origin."[24]

Despite the particular importance of this hatred toward Jews in National Socialist ideology, Nazism was not perceived as having invented anti-Semitic hostilities. Attacks and discrimination against Jews were interpreted as originating in a widespread animosity within European societies. Reports about the "German people's hatred of the Jews"[25] to a certain extent were thus paralleled by articles about anti-Jewish incidents in Austria, France, Turkey, Poland, or Romania.[26] In these perceptions, the National Socialist movement was neither the first nor the cruelest in its articulation of anti-Jewish sentiments.

In fact, anti-Jewish incidents were not unknown to Levantine societies. The Jewish communities of Lebanon and Syria counted among the smaller religious minorities concentrated in the urban centres of Beirut, Damascus, and Aleppo.[27] In Lebanon, confessional regulations established by the Lebanese constitution of 1926 defined their legal status, granting legal guarantees not only for Jews but for other religious groups as well. The acknowledgment of the Jewish community "as one minority among many, rather than [as] second-class citizens or even [as] the enemy within,"[28] considerably strengthened its position vis-à-vis the state and other communities. Throughout the mandate period, Jews were thus part of the political struggles over the balancing of communal interests and the formulation of a policy toward the French authorities. While the majority of Lebanese Jews remained critical of the Zionist project, leading Maronite personalities occasionally defended the formation of a Jewish state in Palestine as an important factor to counter a Muslim dominance in the region.[29] In Syria, however, the situation differed in several aspects. The dominant currents of pan-Arab nationalism focused on ethnocultural definitions of the collective in which references to distinct religious communities were substituted by shared Arab cultural and historical characteristics. Despite its formal secularism, however, Arab nationalism in the Syrian context, with its overwhelmingly Sunni majority, continued to imply for many a "defence of Islam against foreign aggression."[30] While the developing confessional system in Lebanon formally placed Jews on an equal basis with others, the dominant nationalist discourse in Syria avoided references to particular religious or ethnic divisions of the supposed Arab or Syrian collective. In both countries, however, the perception of Jews—as of any other minority—was closely linked to the ongoing construction processes of national identities.

Adding to the resulting ambivalences of the image of minorities were religious resentments.[31] Classical Christian anti-Judaism and the ambiguous depictions of the Jews in Islamic traditions noticeably echoed in reactions to the anti-Semitic measures implemented in Germany. In the light of growing tensions with Zionism and, by the 1930s, the frequent campaigns against Jewish immigration to the region, perceptions of National Socialist anti-Semitism were tied to prevalent images of the Jews. In fact, critical coverage of the persecutions in Germany did not necessarily obstruct the deliberate publication of anti-Jewish prejudices. Anti-Jewish jokes featured in various newspapers, most prominently in the two leading satirical magazines *al-Dabbur* and *al-Mudhik al-Mubki*. They reflected the existence of commonly known stereotypes and, more often than not, open resentments.[32] Such perceptions of Jews necessarily reflected the public assessments of the anti-Semitic persecutions in Germany, and its notion of the nation. National Socialist discrimination was thus not only an issue of individual rights against the state; it was also interpreted within the existing patterns of the interreligious and interethnic conflicts of the region.

## Antun Sa'ada: The Quest for Authenticity

The second half of the 1930s witnessed a further development of the theoretical elaborations of Arab nationalist thought. The writings of

Antun Sa'ada, Edmond Rabbath, Constantin Zurayq, and Raif Khuri illustrate the broad range of intellectual approaches to the nation in the Syrian and Lebanese contexts. Despite their differences, all of these writers, explicitly or implicitly, offer insights into contemporary perceptions of romantic German and National Socialist thought. While they were of Christian background, their intended audiences were not limited to members of the Christian denominations in Lebanon and Syria. As leading activists and intellectuals in different political parties, their ideas were shared by larger segments of the various nationalist currents.

Antun Sa'ada, the founder of the Syrian Nationalist Party (Al-Hizb Al-Suri Al-Qawmi), was a protagonist of nationalist thought.[33] His historical work *The Evolution of Nations* [*Nushu al-umam*], which was largely written during a prison term in 1936 and published in 1938, provided a detailed explanation of his reflections and his vision of a Syrian nation. In his introduction, Sa'ada highlights the relevance of the nation for the individual, as well as its importance for the well-being of humankind. Sa'ada's claim of a distinct Syrian nation, which lies at the core of his work, clearly differed from other nationalist conceptions of the time. His reference to Syria as a unique nation in the lands between the Tartus Mountain in the north, the Suez Canal in the south, and the Syrian Desert in the east obviously contradicted most communal identities that were based either on Arab or Lebanese particularities or, religiously, on Maronite Christian or pan-Islamic loyalties.

For Sa'ada, modern science had proved wrong the belief in racial purity of nations: "every nation is composed of a variety of different racial groups; the nation is a mixture of different human races [*sulalat*]."[34] Hence, and in contrast to European racial theories, Sa'ada focused not on racial particularities but on the distinctiveness of each nation. While nations were originally formed out of different races, over time, their geographical and spiritual conditions—nature and spirit—had determined their essence: "Races are a natural fact which preceded history; the nation, instead, is something that had developed over time, and is a product of thoughts, emotions, and wills of human minds. It is an artificial composition."[35]

Central to Sa'ada's concept of the Syrian nation was his claim of purity, as well as his vehement objection to Zionism and the Jews. Given his attempt to nationalize Islam and Christianity as expressions of the Syrian spirit, the existing conflict with the Jews was a relevant function of his imagination of an authentic Syrian nation. In *Nushu al-umam,* Sa'ada argues that Jewish claims of nationhood are as baseless, as would be any similar claim based on Muslim or Christian identity. It was Jewish nationalism, however, that he perceived as the most dangerous threat to the existence of the Syrian nation.[36] In the first edition of *Suriyya al-Jadida*, a newspaper linked to the Syrian Nationalist Party that had been published since March 1939 in Brazil, Sa'ada dedicated an editorial to the renaissance of the Syrian *umma* (people), in which explicit reference to an assumed Syrian-Jewish antagonism was made. According to Sa'ada, the Syrian nation had recently witnessed a revival, discarded outdated loyalties, and regained its national spirit. Yet, this revival was not complete, and the "mental diseases" of the past continued to plague parts of its people. Despite the dawn of a "new age," Sa'ada saw it necessary to draw attention to these remaining threats obstructing the path of revival:

> How many people out there see the transition to a new state [of community/history] as something unimportant, for they perceive this transition through their ailing frames of mind, through their hidden haughtiness, their overdue traditions, their tight psyches, their oppressive illusions [they perceive this transition] through [the lens of] all these forms of mental-spiritual illnesses that had given them so much pleasure, [so much so] that for these persons a life without them has become inconceivable? All of these persons feel that the national renaissance has frustrated their hopes just as the coming of the messiah frustrated the hopes of the Jews. The Jews had hoped for a salvation from their [bad] situation by the hands of the messiah who would come to satisfy their particular desires. The Syrian land, however, was not serviceable for these sick Jewish particularities, and the messiah came to salvage Syria and the world from these very Jewish particularities.[37]

While in this view Jews lacked all necessary elements to form a nation, their very existence posed a threat to others. More specifically, as a non-nation, they personified the existing threats faced not only by the Syrian nation but by others as well. Here, sectarianism and Jewishness were identified as the negation of the nation as such; for Sa'ada, the Jew was a metaphor for the destructive influences of non- and antinationalist thought.

In the light of these views, local critics frequently accused Sa'ada and his Syrian Nationalist Party of being inspired by Nazi Germany and its ideological claims. Yet, Sa'ada himself, and many of his followers, publicly disputed such accusations and insisted on the original character of Syrian nationalist ideology. Sa'ada personally responded to his critics; already in June 1935, during one of his first public speeches as the leader of the Syrian Nationalist Party, Sa'ada declared: "I want to use this opportunity to say that the system of the Syrian Nationalist Party is neither a Hitlerite nor a Fascist one, but a pure nationalist one. It is not based on useless imitation, but is [instead] the result of an authentic invention—[an invention] that is a privilege of our people."[38] Central to this statement was the claim of an authentic character of the Syrian Nationalist Party; it was not meant to clarify how its own nationalist idea differed from Nazi German ideology.

## Edmond Rabbath and Constantin Zurayq: Unifiying the Arab Nation

Edmond Rabbath's work *Unité Syrienne et Devenir Arabe* differed in various aspects from Syrian nationalist thought as formulated by Antun Sa'ada. As a member of the National Bloc and the Syrian parliament, the Greek-Orthodox Christian from Aleppo stood for a secular current of pan-Arab nationalism.[39] Although far less influential than Constantin Zurayq and his work *Al-wa'i al-qawmi* (National consciousness, 1939), Rabbath's defense of the existence of an Arab character of the Syrian nation marked an important contribution to intellectual efforts against mainstream French perceptions of Levantine conditions. Henri Lammens's *La Syrie: Précis Historique,* which was published in 1921, had furnished French official rhetoric with important arguments for their rejection of the idea of Arab unity and of pan-Arab nationalist politics. Rabbath provided detailed responses that were meant to refute these claims of an existing distinct Syrian history and to substantiate the Arab character of Syria and its shared history and descent within the broader Arab world. Rabbath explicitly stated:

> There is no Syrian nation. There is an Arab nation, the product of this cluster of peoples who once formed the Arab Empire. The combination of so many different elements, merged, lumped together in the melting pot of a specific and absorbent civilization, was born a new national entity. It is a lively unit, united in its most divergent parts, similar in its remotest fractions. One blood tempering its flesh. A homogeneous spirit animates its functional life. It is held together by collective sentiments. Jointly experienced glories and sufferings,

shared interests bring together its membra disjecta. A traditional ideal, identical destinies complete their merger.[40]

Nevertheless, although Rabbath supported the idea of an ethnic "amalgam" that was based on the origin of the Arab nation, an idea that went counter to basic National Socialist thought, he introduced this core paragraph of his work with a quotation from Hitler's *Mein Kampf*: "Men who share the same blood have the same fatherland."[41] Focusing on unity instead of purity, Hitler's idea of an essential territorial link between the nation and its land was shared by Rabbath: "The nation is based on a unity of origin and civilization, a combination of complex and interrelated factors that act simultaneously and penetrate each other, within a coherent physical and delimited environment."[42] Noteworthy, however, is the fact that Rabbath's thoughts hardly fit into potential antagonism between Germany and France. Writing in 1937 in the wake of the signing of the Franco-Syrian Treaty of Independence,[43] the French-educated Rabbath explicitly drew on French historical experiences; for him, quoting Hitler did not imply a rupture with France. Instead, Rabbath's assumption of historically formed nations led him to highlight France's very own national history: "Hybrid races can compose a united nation. And this is the glory of France to provide this beautiful example of a highly homogeneous people, despite the diversity of the old races that make up its constituency."[44] As an example of an "ethnic synthesis," France continued to serve as a reference for him. In this context, Rabbath's reference to Hitler did not imply an adoption of Nazi ideas of racial superiority; rather, it was about the nation's right to its natural land and national unity that he believed Hitler and Nazism stood for.

Constantin Zurayq's widely noted work *Al-waʿi al-qawmi* resembled Rabbath's assumptions in various ways. While Rabbath's writing can be read as a defense of Arab nationalism against French objections, Zurayq explicitly addressed an Arab audience. His various functions at the American University in Beirut and in the Arab Nationalist Party (al-Hizb al-Qawmi al-ʿArabi), but no less so his role as an intellectual mentor of the cultural club al-ʿUrwa al-Wuthqa (The strongest bond) and its magazine, gave him an important position from which to promote his thoughts.[45] The consolidation of the strength of the Arab nation was his main intention as he pursued his work. Zurayq had called for the formulation of a "national philosophy" that would allow overcoming a prevailing "intellectual anarchy"[46] within Arab society and promote the

*Defining the Nation*

**Figure 5.1.** Photograph of Constantin Zurayq (no date) (US-PD). *Source:* https://en.wikipedia.org/wiki/Constantin_Zureiq.

unification of the Arab nation and the creation of a shared pan-Arab ethnocultural communal identity.[47]

Reflecting idealistic notions of the Arab nation, his historical deduction of an identifiable core of this nation reflected widespread assumptions of an existing and distinct Arab civilization. Similar to Rabbath, the Christian-Orthodox historian did not question the importance of Islamic history for the Arab nation. The importance of Islam, however, was not seen in its religious practices or in its concrete religious interpretations and commandments; rather, it stood for a communal spirit, a spiritual culture that was to provide guidelines not only for Muslims but also for Arab society as a whole.[48] The "noble message"[49] that is distinct to the Arab nation and that it must fulfill, among the nations, is the result of its shared history and civilization. In this, the Arab nation is no different from others:

> This is the awareness, which a German possesses when he speaks to you about his nation and about its future: all the elements of his life—sciences, art, literature, military might, the economic order—they all gained new strength and are tinted in splendid colours. They are united in one image, which is the message that entails the destiny [*qadar*] of the German nation, and of the German nation alone. . . . Such principles fill the minds of the British, the French, the Japanese, and of all those who strive for a place for their nations on this earth, for a mentioning [of their nation] in history. This is nothing to be afraid of; such awareness of the message of the nation may in many cases have adopted extremist forms. It may be taken as a cover for material-earthly ambitions—as it was done by Western states throughout their colonial history and during the World War, and as it is done by Japan during these days—but the danger in our case is not one of excess and exaggeration, but of neglect and imperfection. We are not befallen by a love to control and to impose rule, but by a lack of determination, and a weakness of faith. We, if we would adopt this thinking [about the message of the Arab nation], and would feel this awareness, our jihad for freedom and independence would acquire a new meaning.[50]

Zurayq's explicit reference to Germany and its supposed message, whose positive depiction strikingly contrasted to the singled-out critique of extremist Japanese nationalism, echoed fascination for Germany's forceful reemergence among the peoples. While such fascination evidently drew on German romantic nationalist thought of the nineteenth century, it did not necessarily imply a rebuttal of National Socialist concepts and thoughts.

Rabbath and Zurayq's quest for a unified Arab nation was characteristic for Arab nationalist views of the time. While significant differences existed, other protagonists of Arab nationalist thought such as Satiʽ al-

Husri or, later, Michel 'Aflaq, one of the intellectual founders of the Arab Socialist Ba'ath Party, shared this quest for a collective identity based on Arab culture that went beyond the divisions of religion, clans, and social structure.[51]

## Raif Khuri: The Nation as an Outcome of History

Nationalist writers spent considerable effort trying to define the particularities of their communities whose cultural, ethnic, territorial, and linguistic borders they sought to determine. From a materialistic perspective, such attempts necessarily appeared to be problematic. Since the 1930s, Marxist-inspired circles in Lebanon and Syria were engaged in controversial debates with mainstream nationalists about the appropriate definition of the nation, as well as its relation to other relevant cleavages along the lines of "class" and colonial domination. Raif Khuri, a Lebanese intellectual with a Marxist orientation, contributed various works in which different facets of these questions were addressed; his major contribution, however, was a systematic critique of Zurayq's *Al-wa'i al-qawmi*.[52]

Despite considerable respect for Zurayq and his work, Khuri's rejection of Zurayq's nationalist thought was uncompromising. Referring to the assumption of a distinct Arab civilization, Khuri responded with sharp irony and humor. Writing in his book *Signposts of National Consciousness* [*Ma'alim al-wa'i al-qawmi*], a direct response to Zurayq's attempt to outline an Arab nationalist philosophy, Khuri declared: "The Arabs don't want to have railways, for instance, because there are so many railways in America. [Arab nationalists are afraid that] if they would [also] use railways, their civilisation would not be 'distinctly Arab nationalist' anymore."[53] Khuri explicitly objected to nationalist assumptions of an existing "Arab message" or a "distinct Arab secret," which, according to mainstream nationalist discourse, distinguished the Arab national spirit from others. In a speech held in the framework of an anti-Fascist conference in 1935 in Beirut, Khuri discussed the notion of Arab national identity and challenged Arab nationalist visions by highlighting the universal challenges of the time. For him, the challenges of the time imposed not a quest for national authenticity but a defense of universal values and a shared human history and future:

> Our particular secret, the particular secret of the Arabs, is the love of freedom and the fight against ignorance, humiliation, and the oppo-

sition against the oppressors. This secret, however, is neither a secret, nor is it in any way particular. If this is a source of pride and hope, the Arabs share these principles with all the peoples of the world, principles that mark the glory and the pride of the peoples. The Arabs share that general goal, the goal that human kind is longing and striving for—and they will be victorious."[54]

Speaking at a conference that was meant to address the mounting threats of Nazism and Fascism in Europe, as well as in the Middle East, Khuri insisted on the universal character of this challenge. For him, nationalism and the assumption of an authentic and quasi-natural nation risked blurring past and present crossings and encounters among different societies. He thus rejected any notion of nationally specific philosophy and thought. To speak of a German, French, or Arab philosophy only indicated that a particular philosophical current was most evident among German, French or Arab thinkers but that its claims were in essence universal. The assumption of an authentic core of any nation contradicted basic developments of human society: "The question of the nation is not a question of racial origin; it is, in general, a question of historical development and circumstances, and the outcome of history."[55]

This question of how to define the nation was not only a philosophical one. For Khuri, the assumption of a unified national interest was not only a distortion of social reality; it also included an implicit statement about the future political order. In light of the various cleavages within all societies, an a priori claim of a national consensus would divert attention from a political system that would allow the balancing of conflicting social and political interests. If such cleavages were ignored, calls for a democratic order would necessarily appear secondary. Therefore, it should not come as a surprise that Khuri's critique of Arab nationalist thought was formulated in the context of a conference that was meant to address the mounting challenges of Nazism and Fascism in Europe and beyond. For him, nationalism, understood as a claim of authentic and distinct communities that would submit the individual to the consensus of the nation, was a threat to individual and collective liberation.

## Conclusion

This overview does not give a complete picture of the local intellectual scene and the variety of options forwarded by its protagonists in an effort to define the nation. Yet it highlights that these debates clearly echoed many of the concerns that other intellectuals in other parts of the world were facing. In various ways, the challenge to build a state, to define its origins, to define the relation between the individual and the community, and to distinguish this state from others was also a key challenge to intellectuals in Europe. Nazi Germany was no exception. What is striking is that most of the intellectuals in Syria and Lebanon were aware of these debates in Europe but also in Turkey, Iran, and Russia. They were eager to learn from these debates and to scrutinize them for potential signposts that could be adapted to the Levantine context. This does not imply that Syrian and Lebanese intellectuals simply imported solutions formulated by others; on the contrary, these intellectuals exemplify the tendency to merge intellectual debates that were becoming less confined to geographic borders.

National Socialism was an ideology deeply linked to German society and its particular history; yet, the answers it provided were not confined to German borders. The simple fact that intellectuals—though not only intellectuals—in Beirut, Damascus, or Aleppo felt obliged to discuss Nazi German works and thoughts illustrates the simultaneity of social transformations of this period that were not limited to central Europe. Raif Khuri most clearly represents such increasing globalization of political thinking. In 1943, at the height of World War II, he published an outstanding work titled *Modern Arab Thought. Political and Social Vestiges of the French Revolution* (*Al-fikr al-'arabi al-hadith. Athar al-thawra al-firansiyya fi tawjihihi al-siyasi wa al-ijtima'i*), in which he traces the impact of the French Revolution on the Arab world.[56] National Socialist ideology was one piece in this increasingly global puzzle of political thinking to which Syrian and Lebanese intellectuals contributed and responded, though it was by far not the only one.

**Götz Nordbruch** is an independent scholar and co-director of a German-based organization that develops civic education and prevention programs on issues related to Islam, racism, and religious extremism in Germany and Europe. He was Assistant Professor at the University of Southern Denmark, Odense, and a postdoctoral fellow at the Institut de recherches et d'études sur le monde arabe et musulman, Aix-en-Provence. His research interests focus on Islam in interwar Europe and Arab encounters with National Socialism. His recent books include *Transnational Islam in Interwar Europe: Muslim Activists and Thinkers* (2014, edited with Umar Ryad), *Sympathie und Schrecken: Begegnungen* *mit Faschismus und Nationalsozialismus in Ägypten, 1922–1937* (2011, coauthored with Israel Gershoni), and *Nazism in Syria and Lebanon: The Ambivalence of the German Option, 1933–1945* (2009).

## Notes

1. Segments of this article have been published in Götz Nordbruch, *Nazism in Syria and Lebanon: The Ambivalence of the German Option, 1933–1945* (London, 2009), 21–23, 71–77, 135–136, used here with permission from Taylor & Francis.
2. See, e.g., Wolfgang G. Schwanitz, "The German Middle Eastern Policy, 1871–1945," in *Germany and the Middle East 1871–1945*, ed. Wolfgang G. Schwanitz (Princeton, NJ, 2004), 1–23; Chantal Metzger, *L'Empire Colonial Français dans la Stratégie du Troisième Reich (1936–1945)*, 2 vols. (Bruxelles, 2002); Renate Dieterich, "Rashid ʿAli al-Kailani in Berlin: Ein irakischer Nationalist in NS-Deutschland," in *Al-Rafidayn: Jahrbuch zur Geschichte und Kultur des modernen Iraq—Band III*, ed. Peter Heine (Würzburg, 1993), 47–79.
3. Basheer M. Nafi, "The Arabs and the Axis: 1933–1940," *Arab Studies Quarterly* 19, no. 2 (1997): 18.
4. See Kazim al-Sulh, "Li-madha ʿarrabna wa nasharna kitab hitlir kifahi," *Al-Nida*, 22 May 1934; "Al-shabab fi almaniya," *Al-Qabas*, 3 September 1935; "Khitab al-ustadh jamil bayhum fi bayrut," *Al-Ayyam*, 10 January 1936; "Hitlir baʿd al-istifta al-shaʿbi fi almaniya," *Al-Qabas*, 23 August 1934.
5. Israel Gershoni, "Egyptian Liberalism in an Age of 'Crisis of Orientation': *Al-Risāla*'s Reaction to Fascism and Nazism, 1933–1939," *International Journal for Middle East Studies* 31, no. 4 (1999): 554.
6. The scenery of this generation of intellectuals of the decades between 1908 and the late 1930s is reconstructed in Leyla Dakhli, *Une génération d'intellectuels arabes: Syrie et Liban (1908–1940)* (Paris, 2009).
7. Anne-Laure Dupont and Catherine Mayeur-Jaouen, "Monde Nouveau, Voix Nouvelles: Etats, Sociétés, Islam dans l'Entre-Deux-Guerres," *Revue des Mondes Musulmans et de la Méditerranée* 95–98 (2002): 24. All translations in this chapter are my own unless otherwise indicated.
8. See Keith David Watenpaugh, *Being Modern in the Middle East: Revolution, Nationalism, Colonialism, and the Arab Middle Class* (Princeton, NJ, 2006), 211–221; Philip S. Khoury, *Syria and the French Mandate: The Politics of Arab Nationalism 1920–1945* (Princeton, NJ, 1987), 311, 409–414; Ulrike Freitag, *Geschichtsschreibung in Syrien 1920–1990: Zwischen Wissenschaft und Ideologie* (Hamburg, 1991), 46–57. For the changing educational system and its effects on the formation of a new middle class, see Christoph Schumann, *Radikalnationalismus in Syrien und Libanon: Politische Sozialisation und Elitenbildung 1930–1958* (Hamburg, 2001), 192–196.
9. Benjamin Thomas White convincingly illustrates these parallels in reference to the development of notions of "minorities" and the nation-state in *The Emer-*

gence of Minorities in the Middle East: The Politics of Community in French Mandate Syria (Edinburgh, 2012).

10. "Hitlir ba'd al-istifta' al-sha'bi fi almaniya," *Al-Qabas*, 23 August 1934. The article is signed with "a political writer for al-Qabas," most probably a reference to the nationalist activist and member of the National Bloc Munir al-'Ajlani.
11. Ibrahim Kaylani, "Nahdatuna al-Haditha: Al-shabab al-suri," *Majallat al-Mu'allimun wa-l-Mu'allimat* 1 (1935): 29.
12. Sharfi al-Kaylani, "Risalat al-shabab," *Al-Tamaddun al-Islami* 5 (Rajab 1357h [September 1938]), 137.
13. Munir al-Nusuli, *Fi sabil al-istiqlal: Natharat fi-l-tarbiyya al-haditha* (Beirut, 1937), vi.
14. Nusuli, *Fi sabil al-istiqlal*, 66–67.
15. "Al-wataniyya al-almaniyya," *Al-Nida*, 10 August 1933.
16. Wajih al-Haffar, "Al-din li-llah wa-l-watan li-l-jami'," *Al-Qabas*, 7 July 1935.
17. See Politisches Archiv des Auswärtigen Amts (hereafter PAAA), CGB 50, German Consulate Geneve to AA, "Kongreß der mohamedanischen Minderheiten in Europa in Genf," 25 September 1935.
18. With regard to the Assyrians, the newspaper *Al-Ahrar* claimed that this community was created by the colonial powers as "the latest tool to block the jihad of the Arabs for freedom." See "Al-umma al-ashuriyya," *Al-Ahrar*, 11 August 1933.
19. Jibran Tuwayni, the editor of *Al-Nahar*, for instance, declared: "We [the Arabs, in contrast to the refugees] do not ask Europe's 'humanism' to grant us mercy or sympathy. We claim a legitimate right." See Jibran Tuwayni, "Ya'tifuna 'alayhim wa ya'tunahum al-jinsiyya," *Al-Nahar*, 11 August 1933.
20. See, e.g., "Jam'iyyat al-umam tantasir li-yahud almaniya," *Al-Sha'b*, 8 October 1933. This report about the proceedings of a session of the League of Nations related to the situation of the Jews in Germany is subtitled, "Is it because they are rich?!"
21. See Klaus Holz, *Nationaler Antisemitismus: Wissenssoziologie einer Weltanschauung* (Hamburg, 2001), 386.
22. See the long article by the Swiss-German author Emil Ludwig about anti-Semitic policies in Germany, "Idtihadat al-alman li-l-yahud," *Al-Nida*, 11 April 1933. Ludwig's articles about various subjects were often translated by Syrian and Lebanese newspapers.
23. See "Falsafat al-'alim Aynshtayn," *Al-Nida*, 29 March 1933. The persecutions that Einstein had faced were also mentioned in "Kitab jadid li-l-'alim albir Aynshtayn," *Al-Ma'rid*, 31 May 1934.
24. "Al-mutamar al-yahudi al-iqtisadi al-'alami," *Al-Ahrar*, 24 July 1933; "Hitlir yara yahudan fi kull makan," *Al-Sahafi al-Taih*, 25 August 1933.
25. "Karahat al-sha'b al-almani li-l-yahud," *Al-Sahafi al-Taih*, 22 January 1933.
26. "Idtihad al-yahud fi nimsa wa rumaniya," *Al-Sha'b*, 11 December 1933; "Al-gharam li-l-yahud," *Al-Sahafi al-Taih*, 26 January 1933. *Al-Ma'rid* published a historical account of the Dreyfus-affair in France, "Qadiyyat drayfus," *Al-Ma'rid*, 21 and 28 February 1932.
27. By 1945, an estimated thirty thousand Jews were living in Syria. See Khoury, *Syria and the French Mandate*, 15. According to the census of 1932, the num-

ber of Jews living in Lebanon amounted to 3,600. See Kirsten Schulze, *Jews of Lebanon: Between Coexistence and Conflict* (Brighton, 2001), 35.
28. Schulze, *Jews of Lebanon*, 34.
29. Laura Zittrain Eisenberg, *My Enemy's Enemy: Lebanon in Early Zionist Imagination, 1900–1948* (Detroit, 1994), 61–67; Schulze, *Jews of Lebanon*, 41, 52; Hasan Hallaq, *Mawqif lubnan min al-qadiyya al-filastiniyya 1918–1952* (Amman, 2002), 34–49.
30. Khoury, *Syria and the French Mandate*, 301.
31. Important in this context were traditional Christian anti-Jewish accusations such as the blood libel. Most of the early anti-Jewish literature in Lebanon, as in other parts of the Arab world, in fact originated from within the Christian community. See Schulze, *Jews of Lebanon*, 18–20, 37.
32. See, among others, "Nuwadir al-'uzama," *Al-Mudhik al-Mubki*, 15 July 1933; "Musawama yahudiyya," *Al-Mudhik al-Mubki*, 11 November 1933; "Fatawa al-dabbur," *Al-Dabbur*, 7 August 1933. With regard to the emerging conflict in Palestine, Jibran Tuwayni wrote in *Al-Nahar*: "The nations that are [now] celebrating the birth of the Christ are surrendering the land of Christ—the grave of Christ—to the descendants of those who persecuted Christ and crucified him." See Tuwayni, "Mutanaqidat," *Al-Nahar*, 28 December 1933.
33. For Sa'ada's biography, see Christoph Schumann, "Symbolische Aneignungen: Antun Sa'adas Radikalnationalismus in der Epoche des Faschismus," in *Blind für die Geschichte? Arabische Begegnungen mit dem Nationalsozialismus*, ed. Gerhard Höpp, Peter Wien, and René Wildangel (Berlin, 2004), 158–161; and, in less detail, Bassam Tibi, *Vom Gottesreich zum Nationalstaat: Islam und panarabischer Nationalismus* (Frankfurt, 1987), 180–182. While Tibi explicitly identifies Sa'ada as "Germanophil," it is interesting to note that Sa'ada's fascination for Germany, which is visible already in his earlier writings, is often neglected. Ibid., 183. The French authorities called the party "Parti Populaire Syrien" (PPS). In 1947, the party changed its name to "Syrian Social Nationalist Party" (SSNP). See Labib Zuwiyya Yamak, *The Syrian Social Nationalist Party. An ideological analysis* (Cambridge, MA, 1966), 167.
34. Antun Sa'ada, "Ma'na al-umma wa sifatuha," *Al-Majalla*, May/June 1933, reproduced in Sa'ada, *Al-a'mal al-kamila: Al-juz al-thani 1932–1936* (Beirut, 2000), 58. To define the term "sulala," Sa'ada explicitly used the English term "race." Sa'ada's views continue to be controversially discussed in today's historiography of nationalist thought in the Arab world. Bassam Tibi for instance claims that Sa'ada had in fact adopted a "pseudoscientific, biological definition of the nation, that was prevalent during the Third Reich." See Tibi, *Vom Gottesreich zum Nationalstaat*, 183. Hazim Saghiyya shares this view. While other Arab nationalist thinkers had been inspired by German nationalist thinkers of the nineteenth century, Saghiyya sees Sa'ada as directly influenced by biologistic and pseudoscientific racial theories. See Saghiyya, *Qawmiyyu al-mashriq al-'arabi: Min Drayfus ila Gharudi* (Beirut, 2000), 220. Christoph Schumann, in contrast, insists that Sa'ada's objection to the concept of racial purity marks a significant difference with National Socialist racial thought. See Schumann, "Symbolische Aneignungen," 161–165. Labib Zuwiyya Yamak, in an early and still valuable analysis of Sa'ada's thought, argues: "Thus in denying the single

racial origin of the Syrian nation, Saʿada has not really wandered very far from the theory of racial superiority of certain ethnic stocks which he himself discredited as a social scientist in his major work on the origins of nation [*nushu al-umam*]. . . . What Saʿada really did therefore was to deny racialism in theory while accepting it in practice." See Yamak, *The Syrian Social Nationalist Party*, 83.

35. Saʿada, "Maʿna al-umma wa sifatuha."
36. With regard to Saʿadaʾs concept of "race" and "nation," historiographical interpretations of Saʿadaʾs image of the Jews are far apart. While Schumann relates to Saʿadaʾs vehement attacks on Zionism and Jews as an expression of Saʿadaʾs antisectarian approach to the nation, Saghiyya explicitly highlights the perceived existential and overly historical confrontation between the Syrian nation and the Jews. See Schumann, "Symbolische Aneignungen," 170–173; Saghiyya, *Qawmiyyun*, 233–250. In his analysis of Saʿadaʾs image of the Jews, Saghiyya focuses on sources published in the years following World War II.
37. Antun Saʿada, "Suriyya al-jadida," *Suriyya al-Jadida*, 11 March 1939.
38. Antun Saʿada, "Al-khitab al-manhaji al-awwal," in *Al-aʿmal al-kamila: Al-juz al-thani 1932–1936* (Beirut, 2000), 104. In his speech, Saʿada also addressed the increasing Italian and German propaganda in the region. While warning the party members not to fall victim to such propaganda, he nevertheless argues that relations with any country that are based on mutual equality might be useful and in the interest of the nation.
39. For Rabbath, see also Freitag, *Geschichtsschreibung*, 108–112.
40. Edmond Rabbath, *Unité syrienne et devenir arabe* (Paris, 1937), 33.
41. Ibid.
42. Ibid., 43.
43. The signing of the treaty in September 1936 following the election of the Popular Front–led government in France had raised some hopes that France would ultimately relinquish power in Syria. Yet, in the light of mounting tensions in Europe and persisting opposition against granting Syria independence, the French government quickly backed off its promises.
44. Rabbath, *Unité syrienne*, 51.
45. For Zurayqʾs position and his involvement in the ANP and al-ʿUrwa al-Wuthqa, see Shafiq Juha, *Al-haraka al-ʿarabiyya al-sirriyya: Jamaʿat al-kitab al-ahmar, 1935–1945* (Beirut, 2004), 85–95.
46. Constantin Zurayq, "Al-waʿi al-qawmi," *Al-Hadith* 8 (August 1939), 669.
47. Although Zurayq shared the idea of many pan-Arab nationalists that the Arab nation needed to be recreated, he insisted on the necessity to modernize society and to evaluate Western technology and political institutions in an attempt to profit from its experience. In addition, Zurayqʾs concept of Arab nationalism was not entirely reduced to the interests of the collective; rather, he perceived nationalism as a means rather than a goal. For him, the individual and the interest of the individual remained a major determinant of politics and thought, highlighting the ambiguity of his thought about the individual and the nation. See, e.g., Hani Faris, "Constantine K. Zurayk: Advocate of Rationalism in Modern Arab Thought," in *Arab Civilisation: Challenges and Responses*, ed. George N. Atiyeh and Ibrahim M. Oweiss (New York, 1988), 20–21. Saghiyya points to Zurayqʾs particular focus on Palestine as a core Arab problem. With

regard to Zurayq's later writings, he draws attention to its preoccupation with a putative "might of the Jews." See Saghiyya, *Qawmiyyun*, 158.
48. Freitag, *Geschichtsschreibung*, 113.
49. Zurayq, "Al-wa'i al-qawmi," 651.
50. Ibid.
51. See Tibi, *Vom Gottesreich zum Nationalstaat*, 130–148.
52. For Khuri's work, see also Götz Nordbruch, "Defending the French Revolution during World War II: Raif Khoury and the Intellectual Challenge of Nazism in the Levant," *Mediterranean Historical Review* 21, no. 2 (2006).
53. Raif Khuri, *Ma'alim al-wa'i al-qawmi* (Beirut, 1941), 12. See also 'Abd al-Razzaq 'Id, "Raif Khuri wa 'ma'alim al-wa'i al-qawmi': Juzur al-tabi'iyya fi al-fikr al-qawmi," *Al-Nahj* 20 (1988), 216–225.
54. Raif Khuri, *Turath al-qawmi al-'arabi* (Beirut, 1942), 163.
55. Raif Khuri, *Ma'alim al-wa'i al-qawmi*, 61.
56. Raif Khoury, *Modern Arab Thought: Channels of the French Revolution to the Arab East* (Princeton, NJ, 1983).

# Bibliography

Auswärtiges Amt. Politisches Archiv (Berlin). Generalkonsulat Beirut.

Dakhli, Leyla. *Une génération d'intellectuels arabes: Syrie et Liban (1908–1940)*. Paris, 2009.

Dieterich, Renate. "Rashid 'Ali al-Kailani in Berlin: Ein irakischer Nationalist in NS-Deutschland." In *Al-Rafidayn: Jahrbuch zur Geschichte und Kultur des modernen Iraq—Band III*, edited by Peter Heine, 47–79. Würzburg, 1993.

Dupont, Anne-Laure, and Catherine Mayeur-Jaouen. "Monde Nouveau, Voix Nouvelles: Etats, Sociétés, Islam dans l'Entre-Deux-Guerres." *Revue des Mondes Musulmans et de la Méditerranée* 95–98 (2002): 9–39.

Eisenberg, Laura Zittrain. *My Enemy's Enemy: Lebanon in Early Zionist Imagination, 1900–1948*. Detroit, 1994.

Faris, Hani. "Constantine K. Zurayk: Advocate of Rationalism in Modern Arab Thought." In *Arab Civilisation: Challenges and Responses*, edited by George N. Atiyeh and Ibrahim M. Oweiss, 1–41. New York, 1988.

Freitag, Ulrike. *Geschichtsschreibung in Syrien 1920–1990: Zwischen Wissenschaft und Ideologie*. Hamburg, 1991.

Gershoni, Israel. "Egyptian Liberalism in an Age of 'Crisis of Orientation': *Al-Risāla*'s Reaction to Fascism and Nazism, 1933–1939." *International Journal for Middle East Studies* 31, no. 4 (1999): 551–576.

Hallaq, Hasan. *Mawqif lubnan min al-qadiyya al-filastiniyya 1918–1952*. Amman, 2002.

Holz, Klaus. *Nationaler Antisemitismus: Wissenssoziologie einer Weltanschauung*. Hamburg, 2001.

Juha, Shafiq. *Al-haraka al-'arabiyya al-sirriyya: Jama'at al-kitab al-ahmar, 1935–1945*. Beirut, 2004.

Kaylani, Ibrahim. "Nahdatuna al-haditha: Al-shabab al-suri." *Majallat al-muʿallimun wa-l-muʿallimat* 1, no. 10 (1935): 29–30.

al-Kaylani, Sharif. "Risalat al-shabab." *Al-Tamaddun al-islami* 5, (Rajab 1357h [September 1938]): 136–137.

Khoury, Philip S. *Syria and the French Mandate: The Politics of Arab Nationalism, 1920–1945.* Princeton, NJ, 1987.

Khoury, Raif. *Modern Arab Thought: Channels of the French Revolution to the Arab East.* Princeton, NJ, 1983.

Khuri, Raif. *Maʿalim al-waʿi al-qawmi.* Beirut, 1941.

———. *al-Fikr al-ʿarabi al-hadith: Athar al-thawra al-firansiyya fi tawjihihi al-siyasi wa al-ijtimaʿi.* Beirut, 1943.

———. *Turath al-qawmi al-ʿarabi.* Beirut, 1942.

Metzger, Chantal. *L'Empire Colonial Français dans la Stratégie du Troisième Reich (1936–1945).* 2 vols. Bruxelles, 2002.

Nafi, Basheer M. "The Arabs and the Axis: 1933–1940," *Arab Studies Quarterly* 19, no. 2 (1997): 1–24.

Nordbruch, Götz. "Defending the French Revolution during World War II: Raif Khoury and the Intellectual Challenge of Nazism in the Levant." *Mediterranean Historical Review* 21, no. 2 (2006): 219–238.

———. *Nazism in Syria and Lebanon: The Ambivalence of the German Option, 1933–1945.* London, 2009.

Nusuli, Munir al-. *Fi sabil al-istiqlal: Natharat fi-l-tarbiyya al-haditha.* Beirut, 1937.

Saʿada, Antun. *Nushu al-umam.* Beirut, 1938.

———. "Al-khitab al-manhaji al-awwal." In *Al-aʿmal al-kamila: Al-juz al-thani 1932–1936.* Beirut, 2000: 104–105.

Saghiyya, Hazim. *Qawmiyyu al-mashriq al-ʿarabi: Min Drayfus ila Gharudi.* Beirut, 2000.

Schulze, Kirsten. *Jews of Lebanon: Between Coexistence and Conflict.* Brighton, 2001.

Schumann, Christoph. *Radikalnationalismus in Syrien und Libanon: Politische Sozialisation und Elitenbildung 1930–1958.* Hamburg, 2001.

———. "Symbolische Aneignungen: Antun Saʿadas Radikalnationalismus in der Epoche des Faschismus." In *Blind für die Geschichte? Arabische Begegnungen mit dem Nationalsozialismus,* edited by Gerhard Höpp, Peter Wien, and René Wildangel, 155–189. Berlin, 2004.

Schwanitz, Wolfgang G. "The German Middle Eastern Policy, 1871–1945." In *Germany and the Middle East 1871–1945,* Wolfgang G. Schwanitz, 1–23. Princeton, NJ, 2004.

Tibi, Bassam. *Vom Gottesreich zum Nationalstaat: Islam und panarabischer Nationalismus.* Frankfurt, 1987.

Watenpaugh, Keith David. *Being Modern in the Middle East: Revolution, Nationalism, Colonialism, and the Arab Middle Class.* Princeton, NJ, 2006.

White, Benjamin Thomas. *The Emergence of Minorities in the Middle East: The Politics of Community in French Mandate Syria.* Edinburgh, 2012.

Yamak, Labib Zuwiyya. *The Syrian Social Nationalist Party: An Ideological Analysis.* Cambridge, MA, 1966.

Zurayq, Constantin. *Al-waʿi al-qawmi.* Beirut, 1939.

*Chapter 6*

# MOSUL AS PARADISE

Nazis, Angels, Jewish Soldiers, and the Jewish Community in Northern Iraq, 1941–1943

*Orit Bashkin*

IN 1943, A POLISH JEWISH soldier stationed with the British Army in Iraq visited a brothel in Baghdad. The solider wore a small mezuzah on his neck, a gift from a friend, and a reminder of the European Jewish world he would never see again. At the brothel, upon seeing the mezuzah, a prostitute started crying. Although she could not speak to the soldier, she intimated that she, too, was Jewish. She asked him to visit her daily, promising that he would never have to pay for her services. The soldier was saddened, though, because he had never seen a Jewish prostitute before.[1]

Around the same time, in Mosul, to the north of Baghdad, Jews began to build a neighborhood of posh villas. The money they had earned from providing services to British Army units stationed in Northern Iraq made this possible. The Jews, jokingly, called the new district the "Hitler neighborhood." Although Mosuli Jews also added the Biblical curse *yimah shemo* ("May his name be cursed [from this world and the next]") after uttering the name of Hitler, they were very much aware that the war against the murderous tyrant had brought much wealth to their city.[2]

Building on these anecdotes, this chapter examines the realities of World War II in Northern Iraq. I argue that in Iraq, as elsewhere in the Middle East, the reception of Nazi, Fascist, and antidemocratic views depended on the ideological, ethnic, and religious fabric of each "region" (rather than each "state") and the region's relationships with

*Mosul as Paradise*

Majority Groups in Iraq

**Map 6.1.** Map of Iraq during World War II, with areas of religious and ethnic concentration. Courtesy of Gregory T. Woolston, Cartographer.

the state. The Jewish community of Northern Iraq lived among Kurds, Arabs, and Turkmans. At times, the tense relationships between these communities and the political powers in Baghdad that tried to exercise power over them led to friction and riots. At other times, however, Jews worked and lived together with different ethnic and religious communities. During World War II, many of the crimes committed against Jews in Northern Iraq could indeed be traced to Nazi and Fascist influences, but they were also connected to regional politics, as policemen, regional governors, and other officials tried to profit from these difficult times at the expense of the Jewish community. Most of the incitement, in other words, had more to do with attempts at blackmail rather than targeting Jews in the name of an anti-Semitic and pro-Nazi ideology. Moreover, as was the case in Baghdad and Basra, Muslims—both Kurds and Arabs—often helped Jews; they refuted unjust accusations against the latter and challenged xenophobia and racism. These friendships allowed the Jews later on to joke about the events, much as they did in the case of the neighborhood named after the greatest enemy of the Jewish people.

I also argue that the war generated new ideas about Jewish solidarity. Accounts of young Iraqi Zionists from the 1940s and 1950s convey the notion that Iraqi Jews had accepted the ideas that all Jewish communities were bound to face anti-Semitism.[3] However, as Jews in Iraq from 1941 to 1945 learned more about the horrors that had occurred and were occurring in Europe, they did not always reach the same conclusion as the Zionists. Jews in Northern Iraq encountered many Ashkenazi Jews, especially soldiers stationed in British units, who provided them with firsthand information about the Holocaust. These interactions, however, did not lead to a desire to immigrate to Palestine, and may have actually convinced the Jews in northern Iraq that their lot was far better than that of their European brethren. These interactions nevertheless resulted in a greater sense of solidarity between different communities of Jews and to the realization that the war was a global one against the Jewish people in which Iraqi Jews should play a role.

## Agas as Angels: The North during the Rashid 'Ali al-Kaylani Revolt

Northern Iraq was a unique demographic unit comprised of a sizable Kurdish population (the majority) and Turkish-speaking and Arabic-speaking populations, as well as Christians and Jews. It was characterized by a mixture of languages, notably Kurdish, Turkish, and Arabic, as well as various dialects of Aramaic spoken by Christians and Jews. The Jewish population of the North included the Arabized Jewish community of Mosul, the Turkified communities in Kirkuk and Sulimaniya, and the bilingual Kurdish-Aramaic communities in provincial towns such as Khanaqin, Zacho, Dohuk, and Irbil. Many Jews in these towns spoke Arabic as well. There were also rural Jews in the hinterlands of each city and town who mostly spoke Kurdish and Aramaic. Many Jewish villagers in the North migrated to the northern cities during the interwar period. In those cities, Jews worked as clerks, merchants, shopkeepers, and goldsmiths, while in the villages Jews were peasants, peddlers, and traders. The stability of these Jewish communities often relied on collaboration with local Kurdish tribal elites; northern Iraqi Jews did form relationships with the Arab-Sunni state, but they still relied on social links with certain members of local elites, such as Kurdish tribal leaders known as agas, landowners, and notables. Because their cultural practices, such as their modes of dress and food, resembled those of their Kurdish neighbors with whom they lived and traded, many Jews who lived in Northern Iraq were identified as "Kurdish Jews" by European travelers, south-central Iraqi Jews, and often themselves. These Jews differed considerably from Iraqi Jews who spoke Arabic and lived in south and central Iraq; the latter were more urbanized and educated, and their Westernized elites, especially those of Baghdad, came to adopt the Arab national narratives current in modern Iraq.[4]

Adherence to the ideas of Pan-Arab nationalism, typically associated with the Baghdadi political center, was strongest in the Muslim and Christian Arab communities in Mosul. But because the Pan Arab leadership of the new state viewed Kurds, Turkmen, and the Assyrian survivors of the 1933 genocide with much suspicion, many of the non-Arab communities in the north were hostile to the Arab state's attempt to hegemonize the multilingual and multiethnic nature of the north, an outlook that affected their reactions to Fascist and Nazi ideologies. In Baghdad, admiration of Nazi Germany and Fascist Italy was common among a group of Pan-Arab intellectuals, and policy makers, whose voices became hegemonic in the 1930s. This camp hoped that the implementation of Fascist models in Iraq would allow the state to mold the souls and bodies of the nation's subjects, achieve military successes, and improve Iraq's global position by siding with England's geopolitical rivals, namely, Germany and Italy.[5] Reeva Simon has pointed out that Pan-Arab politicians

> borrowed from the German *Volk* historians . . . the theory of a primeval ancestor nation transmitting civilization to the rest of the world during its meanderings from an original homeland to its present abode which had been "Turkified" by the Ottomans . . . Similarly, the pan-Arabs extolled both the historic role of the pre-Islamic Arabs and the geographic unity of the territory which was to be the modern Arab nation.[6]

These ideas were for the most part rejected by non-Arab communities outside the Baghdadi center.

The danger of Nazi influence on the Iraqi state and society seemed alarming to British officials because of the country's political instability.

Iraq had experienced a period of continual political instability following the military coup orchestrated by Bakir Sidqi (October 1936–August 1937). After the coup's failure, a group of four nationalist colonels wielded tremendous political power so they could ensure the installation of prime ministers sympathetic to their concerns. In September 1939, the pro-British Nuri al-Sa'id was appointed prime minister and declared that Iraq would not enter World War II unless attacked. He confirmed that Iraq would help Britain in the war, though only to the degree specified in the Anglo-Iraqi Treaty of 1930. Disagreements between Iraq's pro-British elites and more radical powers regarding Iraq's relationship with Germany led to the appointment of Rashid 'Ali al-Kaylani as Prime Minister in March 1940. He resigned, rather than cut off relations with Italy, at the end of January 1941 but was returned to his post as the result of pressure from the military. Upon his return to power, Kaylani announced the establishment of a military regime, at which point Sa'id and the pro-British Iraqi political elite fled Iraq. This turn of events did not please the British, who were aware of the nationalist inclinations of the new government. Kaylani was unable to navigate between British pressure on the one hand and the nationalist and pro-German demands of some of his supporters on the other. He promised British officials he would honor previous agreements with them, but they did not consider him trustworthy. British forces entered Iraq in April and after a short military campaign, lasting through April and May, reoccupied the country.[7]

The revolt significantly impacted the lives of Jews in Baghdad and in southern and central Iraq. They were suspected of being pro-British and consequently subject to sporadic mob violence, arrests, and searches of their homes by the authorities. From 7 to 8 May, Jewish stores were looted in Basra following the departure of the pro-Kaylani forces. From 1 to 2 June, as Kaylani and forces loyal to him left Baghdad but before the British entered the city, Jews were attacked by groups comprised of policemen, soldiers, and civilians. The rioters, in a series of assaults that came to be known as the *Farhud*, attacked the poor sections of the Jewish quarter and some of the city's mixed neighborhoods. When the *Farhud* ended, somewhere between 135 and 189 Jews had been killed and between 700 and 1,000 wounded, there were at least 10 cases of rapes, and around 550 stores and 900 apartments had been looted.[8]

Northern Iraqi Jews also suffered during the days of Rashid 'Ali's coup because of their assumed connections to the British. The situation in Mosul was especially tense. British reports on the north mention extreme anti-British propaganda and rumors that the British intended to kidnap the young Iraqi king, Faysal II. During the time of the revolt, coffee shops in the city were packed with customers who came to listen to the news. Every day the radio would announce the victories of the great Iraqi Army, whether actual or not, boosting the morale the public. The killings of many Mosuli civilians by British bombs complicated the situation even further. As in Baghdad, Jews were accused of supporting the British; those sweeping their rooftops were accused of sending coded messages to the British, as was a man who shined shoes. Four men who talked about politics were arrested because they were suspected of praising the British. Shop owners were asked to contribute large sums of money to the army to show their loyalty to the nation and its army. Getting those arrested during the searches out of jail required bribes. Jewish French education in the Alliance Israélite Universelle (AIU) schooling network in Mosul came to a halt, and Eli Zliberstein, a French citizen and the director of the AIU, was arrested on charges of collaborating with the enemy.[9]

In other regions, Jews faced similar challenges. Reports tell of Jews locking themselves indoors on many occasions, being afraid to leave their houses. In the Kurdish Jewish village of Sandur, eight to ten Jews were killed in the winter of 1941. The reason for the murders had to do with a cow stolen from a Jewish household by three members of a neighboring village. The conflict over the ownership of the animal deteriorated, and the thieves then attacked the Jews from whom the cow was stolen. The general lack of security in the north allowed the killers to attack the Jews, knowing no state authority could come to their victims' rescue. In Kirkuk, the Jewish daughter of the local Ford Motor Company Agency dealer was hanging her laundry to dry when a mob suspected her of signaling to the British airplanes and attempted to attack her. In Sulimaniya, a mob tried to break into the home of a Jewish family but was stopped by the police. In Dohuk and Sandor, fears circulated that neighboring Kurdish tribes would loot Jewish property. In Koi Sanjaq, Muslims attacked the Jewish neighborhood. Mostly, these anti-Jewish efforts failed, and no causalities were listed, but they testify to the nature of the anti-Jewish activity in the north, as popular anti-British sentiment and local feuds were translated into mob violence.[10]

The worst consequences of the Kaylani coup were the blackmailing attempts by some local authorities. In late May 1941, the governor of the Mosul province, Qasim Maqsud, called together fourteen leaders of the Jewish community, among them Rabbi Suleiman Barazani, to tell them that it had been decided in a meeting of the military council established by the city that the Jews were pro-British and therefore needed to pay a large sum of money as a sign of loyalty to the state. Maqsud had once been on good terms with the Jewish community. Stories about how his wife had given birth to a boy thanks to a rabbi's blessing circulated in the city. A rabbi, in fact, circumcised his son.[11] Sasson Tzemah, the Jewish parliamentary representative for the province (*wilayat*) of Mosul, described how Maqsud had changed: "The Jews limited their interaction with the population and the government and sealed themselves in their homes. The meetings with [Maqsud] were short and few, and were made on his initiative." When he called the fourteen leaders to his office, he asked for money in a specific form, saying, "Not Dinars, but Liras, not Iraqi, but Ottoman, not in bills, but in gold coins."[12] It is clear what Maqsud had in mind. By late May, he had realized that the coup was about to fail, and was seeking to extort from the Jews' liquid assets in case he needed to flee. The Jewish community, however, kept asking for more time to collect such a large sum of money. By June, Maqsud was out of the picture.

Officials elsewhere in the north made similar attempts. In Dohuk, the *qaim maqam* (District Governor) demanded one hundred golden liras from the Jewish community, but the regime collapsed before he saw the money. In Zacho, Jews were told by the *qaim maqam* to provide gold within fifteen days, but some Jews believed that he himself wanted to give them time.[13] These events indicate that the worst part for the community was not when the coup was at its zenith but rather when it had become apparent that the coup's days were numbered. However, in most cases, Jews were quick to take advantage of the weak positions of the officials in question and avoid paying the money to them.

Jews were able to weather this difficult time because they had some key allies in the north. First, in Mosul, Kirkuk, Sulimaniya, and the provincial towns, Jews labored to maintained good relations with the local administrators, mostly Arabs, who consequently came to their assistance. The representatives of the state wanted to prevent riots, which could deteriorate into major ethnosectarian conflicts, and therefore acted swiftly to deter mobs from violence. Hence, since the state authorities feared that any attack on Jews would escalate into major mayhem, which they could not control, the state's representatives defended local Jews. In Kirkuk, the police saved a Jewish woman from a local mob; she was taken to police headquarters, and the governor had her released within two hours. In Mosul, the police took up positions in the Jewish quarter on 1 June 1941 to safeguard its residents; policemen remained at these posts through the following day. The decision by a Jew, Habib Saleh Sha'ul, who worked in the local post office, to hide the telegram the post office received about the pogrom in Baghdad helped calm things down and prevent hysteria in the city.[14]

Second, friendships and partnerships with Muslims were crucial. In Mosul, Mustafa al-Sabunji, a local notable, advised the Jews not to give the *qaim maqam* the golden Ottoman liras. North of Mosul, Jews traditionally had a network of patronage with local agas and elites. As noted above, despite the support for the coup in Mosul, Pan-Arab nationalism never enjoyed a great deal of support in this region because of the large Turkish and Kurdish populations, and Jews were often the beneficiaries of this divide. In Koi Sanjaq, two Kurdish leaders sent eighteen armed men to rescue Jews from a mob that had surrounded their neighborhood.[15]

Third, Islamic religious sentiment, which saw Jews as protected minorities, prevented attacks on the Jews. When Haj Amin al-Husayni visited Mosul, he was told by Ra'uf al-Mufti, the chief judge, that the people of Mosul had no intention of harming Jews, because the latter were their neighbors and Islam commanded Muslims to guard the neighbor and the friend. The Mufti, Sheikh Ibrahim al-Rumi, promised the chief rabbi of Mosul that the Jews would be safe, and the police commander likewise guaranteed their safety. In Sulimaniya, the imam of the city, upon hearing that young men were planning to attack the Jewish population, attempted to dissuade them by saying that those who had looted houses in Baghdad were criminals who did not believe in Allah and His Messenger and that the Jews were under the protection of Islam.[16]

Sometimes, religious men and officials were able to redirect the mob's attention to the British and convince mobs that Jews were not British supporters. The first instance of this occurred in 1939, after the death of young King Gazi in a mysterious car accident. The belief that the "pro-British" Jews had had a hand in the accident, or simply anger at the "pro-British" Jewish community, led to hostility against Jews in Mosul. Shoshanna Irbili (later, Arbeli Almozlino) recalls that she feared for her safety in the school she attended and that her Christian teacher rescued her.[17] Rumors circulated in the city that the Muslim mob was nearing the Jewish neighborhoods. Jews locked themselves in their houses. A local notable, Ra'uf al-Naqib, addressed the mob, telling them they would take vengeance on the innocent. He suggested they take their grievances to the guilty party, the British Consul, the representative of the power that planned the killing. The Jews were saved. The British consul was less lucky. He was lynched by the mob.[18]

Two pieces of evidence about this period, from two different sources, shed light on the difficult conditions faced by the Jews. The first is a letter written by a Palestinian Jew, Shalom Rashba, who served in Iraq from 1942 to 1943 as part of a group belonging to the Zionist company Solel Boneh and the Special Construction Unit–Palestine, which carried out construction work in northern Iraq for the British. The letter he sent in 1942 to Aliya officials in Mandatory Palestine summed up his experiences in Kirkuk:

> I received the most peculiar impression from the fact that while passing the night in the streets of Kirkuk, which is a city in an Arab state, I heard, from many houses, and many coffeehouses, news broadcasts from radio stations in Ankara in Turkish. The attitude most people have with respect to the matter of the Allies and the Axis is influenced by these Turkish broadcasts, which [the people of Kirkuk] consider neutral. The local Jews think that the local Turk[men] in Kirkuk are pro-Nazi and they speak favorably of the Kurds. The pro-British sympathies among the Kurds, even if not terribly strong, are there nonetheless. After the Assyrians (who are 100 percent pro-British) the Kurds are the most loyal element to the British. . . . The Kurds have an account to settle with the local Arab people who control this country. . . . It should be noted that many of the Jews of Kirkuk intimated to us that after the lessons of the Rashid 'Ali days, they bought pistols and are unwilling, in the days of trouble, to be taken as lambs to the slaughter. It is hard to tell how serious and definite this is. During the revolt of Rashid 'Ali, Jews were locked in their quarters for a month and were afraid to leave the region. I know only of a young Jewish man (I befriended his elder brother—they both work for the Rafidain company) who in those days was the only one who would walk outside the Jewish quarter and follow what was happening. His brother served as an officer in Baghdad. The two brothers told me in secret that during the revolt, all the staff of the Iraqi Petroleum Company and the Rafidain Oil Company were put in jail. When German pilots stayed in the city for three weeks and grave times were upon the heads of the Jews, the local rabbi got in touch with the city Mutassarif and district manager, a Kurd and a friend of the British, and offered a personal bribe of 3000 dinars, given to the local police, to prevent

any outbreak [of violence] against the Jews. ... I should note that the local police [employs] a Jewish policeman at the rank of sergeant, whom I saw from time to time at the home of the rabbi. ... Finally, some words on the Jews living around Kirkuk: they are small communities in Sulimaniya, Irbil, and Dohuk. Some Jews used to live in Kurdish villages, but they have left them in recent years. The few who remained were forced out completely during the time of Rashid 'Ali.[19]

He notes the following about the Kurdish leaders:

During these days, Rashid 'Ali and Yunis Sabwa'i ... demanded that Sheikh Muhammad [Barazani] print a pamphlet calling on the Kurds to participate in the revolt. Sheikh Mahammaud, being pro-British, suggested something more useful than a pamphlet—that he himself would go to Sulimaniya and quickly organize armed Kurdish brigades who would support the revolt actively. Rashid 'Ali agreed and Sheikh Muhammad went on his way. But as he moved from Baghdad, he immediately called Major Lions [the political adviser in Kirkuk] and went around with him to places around Sulimaniya demanding that the Kurds, who are mostly under his influence, not support the revolt in any way. It is noted that this was an important service to the British. ...

As for the attitude of the Jews of Iraq to the British, we note suspicion and lack of trust. The Jews think that instead of the Assyrian pawn, the British selected the Jews as a pawn in recent years. The distrust is such that in Jewish circles, the stress on our need to fight in the war with the British may cast doubt on you, as possibly being an agent in the service of the British. This mood is mostly in Baghdad (based on impressions) but I witnessed some cases like that [here].[20]

A few comments are in order: first, according to the report, the danger to the Jews during the coup was both in urban spaces and in the countryside. The collapse of order and security exposed the Jews to tribal attacks, led to depopulation of the villages, and pushed Jews to bribe state officials in the cities. Second, the attitude toward the British was ambivalent. It was accepted that the Jews could rely on pro-British power during the revolt, but British neglect of the Assyrians (who had been massacred in 1933), and the long time it took the British to help Baghdadi Jews during the *Farhud* actually led to resentment toward the British after the fall of Rashid 'Ali's regime.

Third, the pro-Nazi and anti-Nazi stances were seen in sectarian and ethnic terms. Because the North was an in-between zone, pro-Fascist sentiments coming from Turkey[21] shaped the Jewish community's perception of the Turkmen of Kirkuk. The Kurds, not the villagers but the agas, and especially Sheikh Muhammad, were seen as more pro-Jewish because they were pro-British and hostile to Pan-Arabism. Supporting or rejecting Rashid 'Ali's coup was thus less about the position toward Germany and more about the north's ethnic makeup and the attitude of different groups toward the British and the Iraqi state. In other words, we need to locate the approach to the Jews in a web of Arab-Kurdish-Turkish-British relations, as much as we need to understand German influence in Iraq more broadly.

The second source that sheds light on the situation in the North are tales about the days of Rashid 'Ali al-Kaylani recounted by members of the Jewish community in Irbil, who eventually migrated to Israel. There are various versions of a legend recounting how Irbili Jews were rescued during the revolt, collected by folklorist Haya Gavish. One version tells the following story:

> In June 1941 Iraq had the fascist regime of Rashid 'Ali and in the holiday of Shavu'ot a thousand Jews were murdered in Baghdad. Gangs of gentiles in Irbil planned a massacre of Jews and came with weapons to kill the Jews and take their property. Hundreds came to the Jewish neighborhood. . . . When the rioting goyim approached, the Jews sat in their homes, reading the Psalms, for what else could be done? When the rioters came to the Jewish neighborhood, they saw two old men. The men stopped the leader of the mob and asked him: "Where are you going?" He said: "To kill the Jews, like in Baghdad, to take their property." The two men told him: "We will give you better advice: there is a *wali* [governor] in the city who sits in the *saray* [the governor's palace]. He will not allow you to take over the Jewish neighborhood. Go to the *saray* and harm the *wali,* and then the city is yours, and you can do with it whatever you want." They agreed. They went to the *saray* and killed . . . a few people.[22]

The story ends with the *wali* calling on the British, who stop the rioters and save the Jews. This version of the legend notes that both the Jews and non-Jews in the city believed that the two men were angels or God's messengers. Another version shifts the credit for saving the Jews from the angels to a local leader:

> In the period of Rashid 'Ali in 1941, there was a rich sheikh; Mula Effendi was his name. He lived three to four kilometers outside the city border and was very rich and very wise. He loved humanity—not just Jews but all humans. He loved mankind.... So one night, two hundred pro-Nazi youths planned to attack the Jewish quarter, and he, Mula Effendi, dreamt a dream that night. He woke up, and with no bodyguards, he stopped the riot. He told the rioters: "You will not harm the Jews! The Jews are saints! I will slaughter with my own hands whoever harms the Jews." And he, Mula Effendi, stopped the riot.[23]

Other versions mention some divine or supernatural power that convinced the rioters not to attack to the Jews but rather to go to the house of the governor and burn it; some mention a saint associated with a local shrine, while others suggest that Rabbi Shimon Bar Yochai, a 2nd century Jewish miracle worker, was involved in saving the Jews. Daniel Qassab, who was a high school teacher in the city, gave some context to the legend. A local mob did demonstrate in front of the *saray*, demanding the governor to give them the British spies (namely, the Jews) who were supposedly hiding in his office. The demonstration, however, was broken up and the inciters arrested. The chief Rabbi of the community also reported on a man who convinced an incited mob eager to attack the Jews to take the guns found in the *saray* instead of harming the Jews. The local police and powers from Kirkuk who arrived on the scene battled the mob; some escaped, but the majority were arrested. British bombing on the next day was seen as a sign that the Jews were receiving further aid. The rabbi believed, however, that the man who directed the mob's attention to the guns and away from the people was the prophet Eliyahu.[24]

The stories are from the realm of the mythical. But these versions have some recurrent elements: a local man (or a saint/angel/prophet dressed as a local man) stops the riots, the Jews can trust the powers in the governor's *saray* and in his power to crush the riots, and the sense that local anger toward the government could be manipulated for their own interests. In all versions, then, local power and knowledge of the local political landscape help the Jewish community. The grave fear that what happened in Baghdad would come to the north is evident in such stories, which provide inflated numbers of all Jews killed during the *Farhud*. Notably, because these stories are collected from informants living in Israel, many attribute Nazi beliefs to the rioters. The rescue from the calamity, however, is often narrated in religious terms.

In conclusion, the effects of the *Farhud* and Rashid 'Ali's coup in northern Iraq should be seen in a local context. It was a very difficult time for the Jews there, but local systems of patronage (tribal, regional, and city based) and religious values, especially the belief that Muslim protection of the Jews was a duty, helped the local Jewish communities. Moreover, the fact that the state had been both present and not present in the north, even before the coup, and therefore, officials who feared sectarian and ethnic riots could be bribed, created a situation in which Jews could rely on both willing and unwilling allies.

## Tropical Fruits and Broken Hebrew: Jewish Solidarity in Northern Iraq

Iraqi Jews had had contact with Ashkenazi Jews long before the arrival of the former in Israel. AIU teachers, merchants, agents of European newspapers published in Hebrew, and emissaries from Palestine all lived in Iraq and had different dealings with its Jewish community. In addition, Jewish refugees fleeing Nazi Germany had come to Iraq in the late 1930s.

Jewish soldiers were stationed in the north of Iraq as part of British units affiliated with the Anders' Army (the informal name for the Polish Armed Forces in the East). This force was organized in the USSR in 1941 and 1942 under the command of Lieutenant General Władysław Anders. Many of the Jews who had escaped from Nazi-occupied Poland by entering territories in the USSR sphere of influence had been jailed in Soviet prisoner and labor camps and were eager to join the army; they initially formed 40 to 60 percent of the Anders' Army's recruits. Polish officers, however, minimized the number of Jewish recruits and expelled others who had already been drafted. The Anders' Army's units were evacuated to Iran in the spring and summer of 1942 to serve under the British. In March and April, 31,500 soldiers and 12,500 civilians arrived in Iraq and were joined by an additional 45,000 soldiers and 25,000 civilians in August and September. About 3,500 Jewish soldiers and 2,500 Jewish civilians were included in these units, who were then incorporated into the British Eighth Army as the Polish II Corps. They trained at military bases in Iran and Iraq for nearly a year.[25]

In Iraq, the soldiers were stationed in Khanaqin, Kirkuk, and Mosul, guarding oil fields and refineries, as well as in Baghdad and Habaniya. Some Jewish soldiers left their wives and children in Teheran, while oth-

**Figure 6.1.** Photograph of members of the Polish II Corps (Anders' Army) attending an outdoor class at their military base in Iraq, 1942–1943. *Courtesy:* United States Holocaust Memorial Museum.

ers brought their wives to northern Iraq. Jewish soldiers also left their children in Teheran, where a thousand Jewish orphans were taken care of by the local community (and eventually sent to Mandatory Palestine). The Polish Jewish soldiers who came to Iraq had survived hellish conditions. They had lived in Nazi-occupied Poland, often leaving family members behind in ghettos and labor camps as they escaped to the USSR-controlled territories. They had managed to survive Russian jails and labor camps, and near starvation in Siberia, a location to which many were sent upon their arrival in the USSR. Finally, they, and their families who followed them, had made a torturous journey from Russia through central Asia to Iran and finally to Iraq. In that country, they were safe from both the Germans and the Soviets; some family members (mostly women and children) remained in Teheran, and they could reasonably hope they might be able to reconstruct their lives at some point.[26]

Upon the arrival of the Jewish soldiers at the British bases in Iraq, the Jewish community in northern Iraq did much to greet them. Rabbis turned to their congregations in their synagogues, asking them to help the Jewish soldiers, feed them, and host them and their families during holidays. Schools, like the AIU, were emptied during the holidays to host the soldiers. However, northern Iraqi Jews often did not know how to identify the Jewish soldiers from among the Indian, Polish, and British soldiers. Jewish children and young adults would walk in the streets saying "shalom" or "Shema' Israel"; once they were answered, they would invite the Jews to come to the synagogues or offer to host them. The soldiers, for their part, found it hard to understand the Hebrew spoken by northern Iraqi Jews. The Polish Jews searched for mezuzahs and siddurs in order to identify local Jews. On the holidays, they visited the synagogues. In 1942, many attended the synagogue in Khanaqin for Rosh Hashanah and were hosted by local Jews. Afterward, Jews built cantinas in the military base in Khanaqin and even learned some words in Polish.[27]

For many Polish Jewish soldiers, this was the first time they had seen non-European, Arabic-speaking, or Aramaic-speaking Jews. They could not understand the prayers, and conversed using a mishmash of Hebrew accents and a few words from Western languages. The local Jews, especially the "Kurdish Jews," dressed differently than the Jews of Poland. They were multilingual, as many spoke Turkish or Kurdish in addition to Arabic, but such languages were useless in their interaction with the Polish Jews. The European Jews did not like some things they saw. At the synagogues, European Jews preferred sitting on benches, while the local Jews sat on carpets. The Polish Jewish soldiers resented the separation of men and women in the Jewish households. Some Polish Jews also smoked on Yom Kippur and were scolded by the Arab Muslims in Mosul for breaking the holiday's laws.[28]

However, Jews in northern Iraq also offered hospitality, warmth, and a feeling of solidarity. The Polish Jewish soldiers toured the north and visited Jewish shrines, such as the Shrine of the Prophet Daniel. They also met other Ashkenazi Jews who worked for British companies in the North. Most importantly, they gained a renewed sense of Jewish communal life in Northern Iraq. The Iraqi Jews whom the Polish Jews met did not suffer persecution as they had; many Jewish Polish soldiers came from families torn apart by the realities of war, but in Iraq, family members lived together, and some enjoyed relative prosperity. Moreover, the Jews of northern Iraq actively sought out the Jewish soldiers and offered help. Local Jews hosted wives of soldiers at their homes; they baked matzah for soldiers for Passover, and there was a fierce competition to host the Polish Jews during the holidays. The soldiers marching in their uniforms to attend the prayers in the synagogues impressed Jews in Khanaqin. Moreover, now Jews were allied with the strongest power in the north, the British, as members of their religious community were serving in its army. The Jews in Kirkuk built cantinas around the camps and befriended Jewish soldiers. They invited them to at least one wedding. Jewish children would hold on to the soldiers in order to brag to their Muslim friends that they had friends among the British Army. Mosul witnessed the arrival of Jews in large numbers during the holidays. The military rabbi, Pinhas Rosengarten; the local rabbi, Suleiman Barazani; and the AIU teacher all knew each other well.[29]

In April 1943, news came about the Warsaw Ghetto Uprising. The local synagogue organized a communal prayer at the end of the holiday of Passover. According to Rabbi Rosengarten:

> On the day of the memorial, many soldiers gathered by the synagogue close to Mosul. A local crowd of women, children, and men flocked to the gathering site. . . . The Hakham spoke later. His sermon was in Arabic, peppered with the sayings of the Jewish sages on the begging of redemption, the Amalekites, Hamman, and other haters of the Jews across the centuries. Every once in a while, when the name of the Nazi murderer was mentioned, the public reacted by shouting: "*Arur!* [Damned!]" The women cried and wailed . . . standing for our mother Rachel, crying for the murder of her sons and daughters.[30]

For the Polish Jews, this must have been a strange way of commemorating what had happened; the Arabic speech and the cries of women were different from their own traditions. But for the local Jews, it was a sign of solidarity; they wanted to express the pain they shared with their Ashkenazi brethren. And for the Ashkenazi rabbi, the northern Iraqi Jewish women crying symbolized the Jewish Biblical matriarch, Rachel. All Jews were her children.

An interesting account of the personal connections formed with the Jews in northern Iraqi comes from the autobiography of David Azrieli, then a Polish soldier stationed in Khanaqin:

> It seemed like the small city of Khanaqin was occupied by a large military force, as the units of Anders' Army constructed a camp next to Khanaqin that resembled a small village in size. The first time we got a night off was the night of Rosh Hashanah. Adam and I went out of the camp searching for the synagogue. Finally, we found a small one, and sat carefully at the last rows. We listened silently for the prayers we knew, and the Hebrew words we recognized were chanted

to a strange tone. A man went up to us and said something in Arabic. After some failed attempts to understand each other, he pointed to the right page on the siddur and went back to his place. After the prayer, he came back to talk to us. Finally, with the help of some broken Hebrew, a few English words, and hand gestures, we realized he wanted to invite us to [his] home, to a holiday dinner. I shall never forget the sight of the holiday table—over a white map laid all kinds of tropical fruits and vegetables, the kinds of which I have never seen. . . . When I got used to the sight of the table, I noticed that [only] the men were sitting in the living room, and from the kitchen rose the voices of women who were busy preparing the meat. Every once in a while, one of the women or the girls peeped beyond the curtain made of beads separating the kitchen from the living room, gazing curiously at the two guests in uniforms. We sat many hours on the living room's floor, covered with carpets and cushions, and talked to them. With time, conversation became easier; we learned to mix words from all the languages we knew. We talked about the war, the hope that there would be a Jewish state, and what was the same and what was different in our traditions. That night, a brave bond was forged between us and this wonderful family, despite the differences in our costumes and different practices.[31]

The same family helped Azrieli desert the army. They dressed him up as a peasant (*fallah*), told him to pretend he was deaf and mute, and gave him three silver coins to help him on the road to Palestine. Azrieli wrote: "When parting, all the family gathered around me and I remembered a similar separation in Makov [Poland, his city of birth] three years before. Although we had known each other for only three days, we hugged and kissed as family."[32]

Everything in Azrieli's descriptions indicates strangeness: the different prayer styles, the different language, the different family traditions, and the gender relations. And yet, closeness, appreciation, and warmth override the East/West binary. For the Jewish family, it was a way to help fellow Jews from a position of power and as a sign of their religiosity. For the two refugees from Poland, the Kurdish Jewish family—with the food they offered, with their sense of security in Khanaqin, and with their excessive generosity—offered a paradise of sorts. They felt they had become part of this family.

The feeling of ease and comfort Jewish soldiers felt in northern Iraq is seen in paintings and drawings they made, especially the works of

Edward Henryk Herzbaum (later Hartry; born on 6 October 1920 in Vienna, Austria). His pencil drawings from Khanaqin and Habaniyya do not focus on the exotic, on unusual objects or peoples, or on other features we often identify with Orientalist paintings. Rather, they focus on the beauty of nature, on animals, and on sketches of people he met. These works of art do not mirror a fear of hostility but rather celebrate the nature in which they were produced, with its mountains, blue skies, and magnificent scenery.

The understanding of the meaning of being Jewish changed in northern Iraq as a result of the interactions with Polish Jews. Coming to know Ashkenazi Jews who had escaped Poland and feeling their pain did something to the community. However, in this context, unlike the situation that would develop in Israel, both Ashkenazi and Iraqi Jews could help one another. The Iraqi Jews offered Polish Jews family warmth, hospitality, kindness, and (at least in one case) financial help. The Jewish soldiers offered Iraqi Jews a sense of pride, as Jews who were associated with British imperial power. While some of the Polish Jews did want to migrate to Palestine, northern Iraqi Jews, the urban ones in particular, did not share this desire but were willing to help others who did.

**Figure 6.2.** Watercolor landscape of a wooded grove, by Edward Henryk Herzbaum. *Courtesy:* United States Holocaust Memorial Museum.

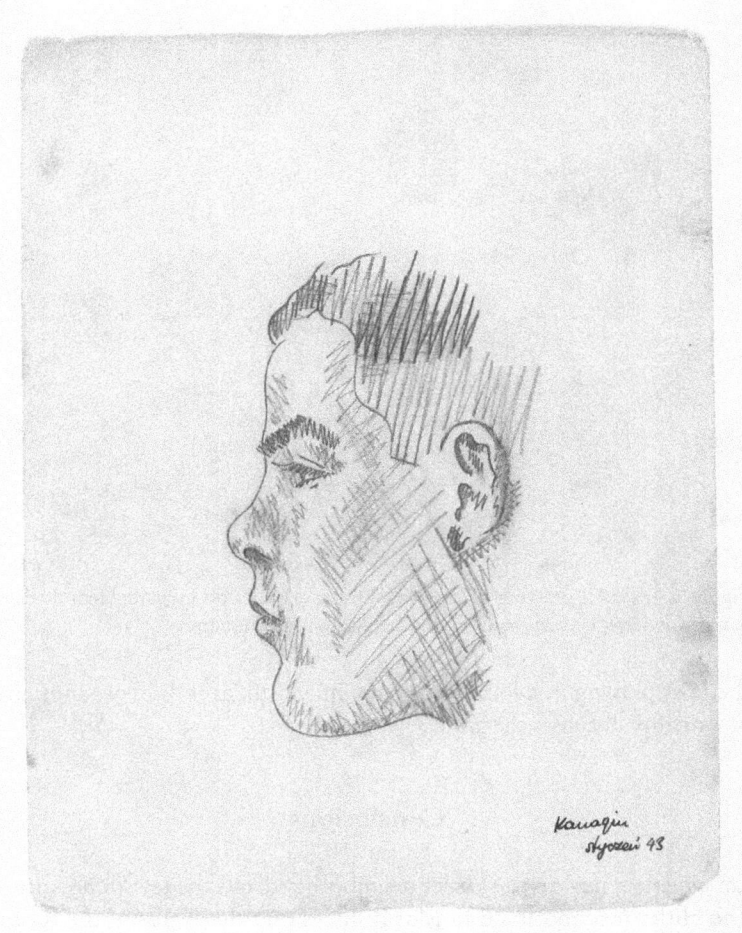

**Figure 6.3.** Pencil portrait of a young man, by Edward Henryk Herzbaum. *Courtesy:* United States Holocaust Memorial Museum.

The help they could offer their Jewish brethren originated from their location in Iraq, as well as from wealth and a sense of security they enjoyed after the crushing of the Kaylani coup and the booming of Jewish business in northern Iraq as a result of providing services to the British. Moreover, it also originated from a deep sense of humanity and from the realization that something horrendous was happening in Europe, an evil they could not fully comprehend. This evil deeply moved and saddened

**Figure 6.4.** Pencil drawing of a young Dorcas gazelle, by Edward Henryk Herzbaum. *Courtesy:* United States Holocaust Memorial Museum.

the Jews praying in a local synagogue in Mosul, as it did Jews in houses of worship all across the globe.

## Conclusions

Let us return now to the Hitler neighborhood and the Jewish prostitute. The Hitler neighborhood in Mosul shows that the events of the Rashid 'Ali al-Kaylani revolt in Iraq, as horrible as they were, did not destroy Jewish life in nothern Iraq. Despite the wide support for Kaylani and his regime in Mosul, attempts at extortion, and mob violence, the ethnic diversity of the north enabled the Jews to pit groups against one another and maintain some sense of security in extremely difficult times. Northern Iraqi Jews learned from these experiences that they had some partners and some people whom they could trust, be they local administrators, imams, muftis, tribal leaders, or friendly neighbors. Above all, the Jews of northern Iraq lived among Kurds, Assyrians, Turkmens, and other minorities, whose own troubles and uncertain relationships with the Arab Iraqi state, seemed at times equal to, and at other times far graver than, the difficulties the Jewish community faced. For the Jews of Mosul in particular, the real way to challenge Hitler, and to flaunt Jewish continuity amid global persecution of Jews, was to build a new neighborhood in Mosul and celebrate their economic success.

As for the prostitute, although silent (we hear her voice only through the voice of her soldier/client) and relegated to the utmost margins of society, she, too, could recognize symbols of a shared religion within the oppressive system of power and gender in which she was forced to live. She, like the Jews of northern Iraq, sensed some connection between her and the Jewish soldier. Indeed, in northern Iraq, despite immense cultural differences, the arrival of the Polish Jewish soldiers signified a moment in which very different Jewish communities came together to assist one another and a period when new notions of Jewish solidarity came into being. Not that the encounter between these two Jews, the prostitute and the solider, changed anything in power relations in either Baghdad or Europe, but for a split second, the small mezuzah joined these two persons, whom, I suppose, never imagined they would ever be together in a Baghdadi brothel. The mezuzah, then, made them realize they had something in common, something that they, and we, as historians of this period, are still trying to unpack.

**Orit Bashkin** is Professor of modern Arab history in the Department of Near Eastern Languages and Civilizations at the University of Chicago. Her publications include twenty-five chapters and articles on the history of Arabs and Jews in Iraq, on Iraqi history, and on Arabic literature. She coedited the book *Sculpturing Culture in Egypt* (in Hebrew, 1999) with Israel Gershoni and Liat Kozma. She is the author of *The Other Iraq: Pluralism and Culture in Hashemite Iraq* (Stanford University Press, 2009) *New Babylonians: A History of Jews in Modern Iraq* (2012) and *Impossible Exodus: Iraqi Jews in Israel* (Stanford University Press, 2017).

## Notes

1. Testimony of Yaqov Zimerman, quoted in Sha'ul Sehayek, *Parasha 'aluma: Korot mifgasham shel alfey hayyalim yehudim polanim 'im yehudim be-'Iraq uve-Iran ba-shanim 1942–1943* (Tel Aviv, 2003), 143–145.
2. Ezra Laniado, *Yehudey Mosul mi-galut Shomron 'ad mivtza' 'Ezra u-Nehemyah* (Tirat-Karmel, Israel, 1981), 121.

3. On Zionism in Iraq, see Haim Cohen, *Ha-Pe'ilut ha-tzionit be-'Iraq* (Jerusalem, 1969); Esther Me'ir-Glitsenshtain, *Zionism in an Arab Country: Jews in Iraq in the 1940s* (London, 2004); Mordechai Bibi, *Ha-Mahteret ha-tzionit ha-halutzit be-Iraq*, 4 vols. (Jerusalem, 1988).
4. In 1919, Iraqi Jews numbered 87,488 in a population of 2.8 million: 50,000 lived in Baghdad, and 14,000 in the north. By the end of 1949, a British account estimated the number of Jews at 180,000: 90,000 lived in Baghdad, 30,000 lived in other towns, and 60,000 were listed as rural Jews. An AIU school official reported that the number of Jews in the vilayet of Mosul was 15,000 in the early twentieth century: Mosul had 3,500 Jews; Kirkuk, 2,800; Zacho, 2,400; Irbil, 1,800; and Sulimaniya, 1,500. Kirkuk had a famous Jewish community, with important rabbis since the eighteenth century; in 1888, the city had 1,200 Jews; the number rose to 1,500 in 1931. Jews living in villages lived in Muslim villages or in villages that were exclusively populated by Jews. Halabja had about 400 Jews (in 1930). The National Archives (hereinafter, TNA), London, AIR 23/806, Appendix A, "The Jews of Iraq," 9 July 1934; TNA, FO 371/75183, Sir Henry Mack (British Embassy Baghdad) to Clement Attlee (FO), 12 December 1949; Orit Bashkin, "Jews in an Imperial Pocket: Northern Iraqi Jews and the British Mandate," in *The Routledge Handbook of the History of the Middle East Mandates*, ed. Cyrus Schayegh and Andrew Arsan (New York, 2015), 379-383; Avraham Ben Ya'aqov, *Kehilot yehudey Kurdistan: Be-tzeruf shirim u-piyyutim* (Jerusalem, 1961), esp. 93, 113, 115, 120; Mordechai Zaken, *Jewish Subjects and Their Tribal Chieftains in Kurdistan: A Study in Survival* (Leiden, 2007); Erich Brauer, *The Jews of Kurdistan* (Detroit, 1993); Haya Gavish, *Hayinu tzionim, Kehilat Zacho be-Kurdistan: Sipur u-mismakh* (Jerusalem, 2004).
5. On Pan-Arab ideology in Iraq and its relation to the nation's ethnic and religious communities and to Fascist and Nazi ideologies, see Peter Wien, *Iraqi Arab Nationalism: Authoritarian, Totalitarian, and Pro-Fascist Inclinations, 1932–1941* (New York, 2006); Ernest C. Dawn, "The Formation of Pan-Arab Ideology in the Inter-War Years," *International Journal of Middle East Studies* 20, no. 1 (1988); Sami Zubaida, "The Fragments Imagine the Nation: The Case of Iraq," in "Nationalism and the Colonial Legacy in the Middle East and the Central Asia," ed. Juan R. I. Cole and Deniz Kandiyoti, special issue, *International Journal of Middle East Studies* 34, no. 2 (2002): 205–215; Michael Eppel, *The Palestine Conflict in the History of Modern Iraq: The Dynamics of Involvement, 1928–1948* (London, 1994); Michael Eppel, "The Elite, the Effendiyya, and the Growth of Nationalism and Pan-Arabism in Hashemite Iraq, 1921–1958," *International Journal of Middle East Studies* 30, no. 2 (1998): 227–250.
6. Reeva S. Simon, "The Teaching of History in Iraq before the Rashid 'Ali Coup of 1941," *Middle East Studies* 22, no. 1 (1986): 43.
7. Orit Bashkin, *New Babylonians: A History of Jews in Modern Iraq* (Stanford, CA, 2012), 112; Mohammad A. Tarbush, *The Role of the Military in Politics: A Case Study of Iraq to 1941* (London, 1982); Walid M. S. Hamdi, *Rashid Ali al-Gailani and the Nationalist Movement in Iraq 1939–1941: A Political and Military Study of the British Campaign in Iraq and the National Revolution of May 1941* (London, 1987). For the role of the revolt within the larger context

of German activities in the Middle East, see Francis R. Nicosia, *Nazi Germany and the Arab World* (New York, 2015), chap. 5.
8. Bashkin, *New Babylonians*, 112–125; Hayyim J. Cohen, "The Anti-Jewish Farhud in Baghdad, 1941," *Middle East Studies* 3, no. 1 (1966): 2–17; Elie Kedourie, "The Sack of Basra and the Farhud in Baghdad," in *Arabic Political Memoirs and Other Studies* (London, 1974), 283–314; Tuvia Arazi, Mordechai Bibi, Shalom Darwish, Rahamim Gabbai, Ezra Haddad, David Pattal, and Ethan Shemesh eds., *Yehudey 'Iraq tahat ha-shilton ha-'aravi, parashat me'ora'ot Baghdad be-rishon bu-ba-sheni be-juni 1941* (Jerusalem, 1960); Shemu'el Moreh and Zvi Yehuda, eds., *Sin'at yehudim u-pra'ot be-'Iraq* (Or-Yehudah, Israel, 1992); Avrahm Twena, *Golim u-ge'ulim, Helek sesh: Me'ora'ot hagg ha-shavu'ot, juni 1941* (Ramla, Israel, 1979).
9. TNA, FO 371/27070, 16 May 1941, from K. Cornwallis (Baghdad) to Foreign Office (London); TNA FO 371/27071, 21 May 1941, from K. Cornwallis (Baghdad) to Foreign Office (London); Laniado, *Yehudey Mosul*, 119–120. On the fears of pro-German spies in Mosul after the revolt, see letter from Enzo Sereni to Shaul Avigur-Meirov, 19 August 1942, reprinted and annotated in Bibi, *Mahteret*, 1:103; Ya'aqov Tzemah, "Eymey Qasim Maqsud be-Mosul," doc. no. 37, printed in Moreh and Yehuda, *Sin'at yehudim*, 311–312.
10. TNA, FO 624/23 11 February 1941, from Iraqi Ministry of Internal Affairs to Captain Holt; account by Shalom Rashba on Kirkuk and Mosul, 15 August 1942, reprinted in Bibi, *Mahteret*, 1:96–99; Twena, *Golim u-ge'ulim*, 77–85; Zaken, *Jewish Subjects*, 303–312.
11. Zaken, *Jewish Subjects*, 303–30f4.
12. Ya'aqov Tzemah, doc. 37, in Moreh and Yehuda, *Sin'at yehudim*, 312. All translations in this chapter are my own unless otherwise indicated.
13. Zaken, *Jewish Subjects*, 307–309.
14. Twena, *Golim u-ge'ulim*, 84–85; testimony of Tzemah, doc. 37, quoted in Moreh and Yehuda, *Sin'at Yehudim*, 311–313; account by Shalom Rashba on Kirkuk and Mosul, 15 August 1942, reprinted in Bibi, *Mahteret*, 1:96–99; Zaken, *Jewish Subjects*, 304–405; Laniado, *Yehudey Mosul*, 120–121.
15. Twena, *Golim u-ge'ulim*, 84–85; testimony of Tzemah, doc. 37, quoted in Moreh and Yehuda, *Sin'at yehudim*, 311–313; account by Shalom Rashba on Kirkuk and Mosul, 15 August 1942, reprinted in Bibi, *Mahteret*, 1:96–99; Zaken, *Jewish Subjects*, 304–309; Laniado, *Yehudey Mosul*, 120–121.
16. Twena, *Golim u-ge'ulim*, 84–85.
17. Shoshana Arbeli Almozlino, *Me-Ha-Mahteret be-Bavel le-memshelt Israel* (Tel Aviv, 1998), 20.
18. Laniado, *Yehudey Mosul*, 111.
19. Account by Shalom Rashba on Kirkuk and Mosul, 15 August 1942, reprinted in Bibi, *Mahteret*, 1:97–100.
20. Ibid. 1:100–101.
21. On Turkey's position toward Nazism and Fascism, see the very pro-Turkish account in Stanford J. Shaw, *Turkey and the Holocaust: Turkey's Role in Rescuing Turkish and European Jewry From Nazi Persecution, 1933–1945* (New York, 1995). For a more critical review of Turkish politics, see Corry Guttstadt, *Turkey, the Jews, and the Holocaust* (New York, 2013).

22. Narrated by Weizmann Haim, recorded by Chaya Gavish, and printed in Herzl Yona, *Kehilat yehudey Irbil, Sippura shel ha-kehila ha-yehudit ve ha mehteret ha-halutzit be-Irbil, Iraq ba-me'a ha-'esrim* (Amutat moreshet yahadut Irbil, 2008), 178; full version: Chaya Gavish, "'Iyun be-sipur yeshu'at yehudey irbil be-me'ora'ot Rashid 'Ali," in *Kocho shel Sipur*, ed. Chaya Bar Yizhak and Irit Pintel Ginsburg (Haifa, 2007), 261–266.
23. Narrated by Menashe Sho'en, recorded by Chaya Gavish, and printed in Yona, *Kehilat yehudey Irbil*, 179; Gavish, "Iyun be-Sipur," 261–266.
24. Yona, *Kehilat yehudey Irbil*, 180–184.
25. Israel Gutman, "Jews in General Anders Army in the Soviet Union," *Yad Vashem Studies* 12 (1977): 231–333; Sehayek, *Parasha 'aluma*, 23–32.
26. On accounts of some of the soldiers who joined the Anders Army, see http://www.yadvashem.org and enter the search term, "Anders Army."
27. Sehayek, *Parasha 'aluma*, 68–150; Laniado, *Yehudey Mosul*, 121–122; David Azrieli, *Tza'ad ehad lefanim* (Jerusalem, 1999), 70–84; Shemesh Yavin, *Mi-Mizrah shemesh, Korot mishpaha u-kehila* (Tel Aviv, 1996), 44–59; David Ben Baruch, *Khanaqin ve-ha-kehila ha-yehudit, Volume 3: Me-Tzeva Andres ve-'ad sha'ar ha-'aliya* (Tel Aviv, 2002).
28. Ibid.
29. Ibid.
30. Pinhas Rosengarten, *Miyomano shel rav tzva'i: Be-heil ha-korpus ha-Polani ha-sheni ba-tzava 'al-shem Anders Wladyslaw bi-shnot Milhemet ha-olam ha-shniya, 1939-1941-1947* (Jerusalem, 1997).
31. Azrieli, *Tza'ad ehad lefanim*, 81–82.
32. Ibid.

# Bibliography

## Archival Source

TNA, FO: The National Archives, United Kingdom, Foreign Office

## Published Sources

Almozlino, Shoshana Arbeli. *Me-Ha-Mahteret be-Bavel le-memshelt Israel*. Tel Aviv, 1998.

Arazi, Tuvia, Mordechai Bibi, Shalom Darwish, Rahamim Gabbai, Ezra Haddad, David Pattal and Ethan Shemesh, eds. *Yehudey 'Iraq tahat ha-shilton ha-'aravi, parashat me'ora'ot Baghdad be-rishon bu-ba-sheni be-juni 1941*. Jerusalem, 1960.

Azrieli, David. *Tza'ad ehad lefanim*. Jerusalem, 1999.

Bashkin, Orit. "Jews in an Imperial Pocket: Northern Iraqi Jews and the British Mandate." In *The Routledge Handbook of the History of the Middle East Mandates*, edited by Cyrus Schayegh and Andrew Arsan, 370–383. New York, 2015.

Bashkin, Orit. *New Babylonians: A History of Jews in Modern Iraq*. Stanford, CA, 2012.

Ben Baruch, David. *Khanaqin ve-ha-kehila ha-yehudit, Volume 3: Me-Tzeva Andres ve-'ad Sha'ar ha-'aliya.* Tel Aviv, 2002.

Ben Ya'aqov, Avraham. *Kehilot yehudey Kurdistan: Be-tzeruf shirim u-piyyutim.* Jerusalem, 1961.

Bibi, Mordechai. *Ha-Mahteret ha-Tzionit ha-halutzit be-'Iraq.* 4 vols. Jerusalem, 1988.

Brauer, Erich. *The Jews of Kurdistan.* Detroit, 1993.

Cohen, Haim. *Ha-Pe'ilut ha-tzionit be-'Iraq.* Jerusalem, 1969.

Cohen, Hayyim J. "The Anti-Jewish Farhud in Baghdad, 1941." *Middle East Studies* 3, no. 1 (1966): 2–17.

Dawn, Ernest C. "The Formation of Pan-Arab Ideology in the Inter-War Years." *International Journal of Middle East Studies* 20, no. 1 (1988): 67–91.

Eppel, Michael. "The Elite, the Effendiyya, and the Growth of Nationalism and Pan-Arabism in Hashemite Iraq, 1921–1958." *International Journal of Middle East Studies* 30, no. 2 (1998): 227–250.

———. *The Palestine Conflict in the History of Modern Iraq: The Dynamics of Involvement, 1928–1948.* London, 1994.

Gavish, Haya. *Hayinu tzionim, Kehilat Zacho be-Kurdistan: Sipur u-mismakh.* Jerusalem, 2004.

Gutman, Israel. "Jews in General Anders' Army in the Soviet Union." *Yad Vashem Studies* 12 (1977): 231–333. http://www.yadvashem.org/odot_pdf/Microsoft%20Word%20-%206217.pdf.

Guttstadt, Corry. *Turkey, the Jews, and the Holocaust.* Translated by Kathleen M. Dell'Orto, Sabine Bartel, and Michelle Miles. New York, 2013.

Hamdi, Walid M. S. *Rashid Ali al-Gailani and the Nationalist Movement in Iraq 1939–1941: A Political and Military Study of the British Campaign in Iraq and the National Revolution of May 1941.* London, 1987.

Kedourie, Elie. "The Sack of Basra and the Farhud in Baghdad." In *Arabic Political Memoirs and Other Studies,* 283–314. London, 1974, 283–314.

Laniado, Ezra. *Yehudey Mosul mi-galut Shomron 'ad mivtza' 'Ezra u-Nehemyah.* Tirat-Karmel, Israel, 1981.

Me'ir-Glitsenshtain, Esther. *Zionism in an Arab Country: Jews in Iraq in the 1940s.* London, 2004.

Moreh, Shemu'el, and Zvi Yehuda, eds. *Sin'at yehudim u-pra'ot be-'Iraq.* Or-Yehudah, Israel, 1992. English Version: Shmuel Moreh and Zvi Yehuda (eds), *Al-Farhud: The 1941 Pogrom in Iraq.* Vidal Sassoon International Center for the Study of Antisemitism. Jerusalem: Hebrew University Magnes Press, 2010.

Nicosia, Francis R. *Nazi Germany and the Arab World.* New York, 2015.

Rosengarten, Pinhas. *Miyomano shel rav tzva'i: Be-heil ha-korpus ha-polani ha-sheni ba-tzava 'al-shem Anders Wladyslaw bi-shnot milhemet ha-olam ha-shniya, 1939-1941-1947.* Jerusalem, 1997.

Sehayek, Sha'ul. *Parasha 'aluma: Korot mifgasham shel alfey hayyalim yehudim polanim 'im yehudim be-'Iraq uve-iran ba-shanim 1942–1943.* Tel Aviv, 2003.

Shaw, Stanford J. *Turkey and the Holocaust: Turkey's Role in Rescuing Turkish and European Jewry From Nazi Persecution, 1933–1945.* New York, 1995.

Simon, Reeva S. "The Teaching of History in Iraq before the Rashid 'Ali Coup of 1941." *Middle East Studies* 22, no. 1 (1986): 37–51.

Tarbush, Mohammad A. *The Role of the Military in Politics: A Case Study of Iraq to 1941.* London, 1982.

Twena, Avrahm. *Golim u-ge'ulim, Helek sesh: Me'ora'ot hagg ha-shavu'ot, juni 1941.* Ramla, Israel, 1979.

Wien, Peter. *Iraqi Arab Nationalism: Authoritarian, Totalitarian, and Pro-Fascist Inclinations, 1932–1941.* New York, 2006.

Yavin, Shemesh. *Mi-Mizrah shemesh, Korot mishpaha u-kehila.* Tel Aviv, 1996.

Yona, Herzl. *Kehilat yehudey Irbil, Sippura shel ha-kehila ha-yehudit ve ha mehteret ha-halutzit be-Irbil, Iraq ba-me'a ha-'esrim,* Amutat moreshet yahadut Irbil, 2008.

Zaken, Mordechai. *Jewish Subjects and Their Tribal Chieftains in Kurdistan: A Study in Survival.* Leiden, 2007.

Zubaida, Sami. "The Fragments Imagine the Nation: The Case of Iraq." In "Nationalism and the Colonial Legacy in the Middle East and Central Asia," edited by Juan R. I. Cole and Deniz Kandiyoti. Special issue, *International Journal of Middle East Studies* 34, no. 2 (2002): 205–215.

*Chapter 7*

# PHILO-SEPHARDISM, ANTI-SEMITISM, AND ARAB NATIONALISM

Muslims and Jews in the Spanish Protectorate of Morocco during the Third Reich

*Daniel J. Schroeter*

SITUATED AT THE FARTHEST NORTHWEST corner of Africa, the Spanish Protectorate of Morocco occupied a unique position in the Arab world during the period of the Third Reich. Yet, it was not only because of Morocco's strategic location at the Strait of Gibraltar, a crossroads of competing powers and a potential bridgehead for territorial ambitions in Africa, the Mediterranean, or even as has been argued, to the United States.[1] The Spanish zone in particular was an important stage in which the various ideological tendencies, political movements, and conflicts that shook the Muslim and Arab world in the 1930s were acted out: Fascism and Nazism, colonialism, Arab and Pan-Arab nationalisms, anti-Semitism, and the Zionist-Arab struggle in Palestine. Arguably, in no other territory in the Middle East and North Africa was the collision of these intersecting and clashing movements put into such sharp focus; yet scholars have largely neglected Spanish Morocco and Tangier during the period of the Third Reich, except as a zone of strategic interest and espionage.[2]

Spanish rule in Morocco was in some ways not much different from French and British colonialism elsewhere in the Muslim and Arab world, and it experienced some of the same dilemmas that the other colonial powers faced in the 1930s. Like the French, maintaining the strength of its colonial holdings in North Africa was of primary importance to Spain, amid concerns of nationalist stirrings, as well as the pro-

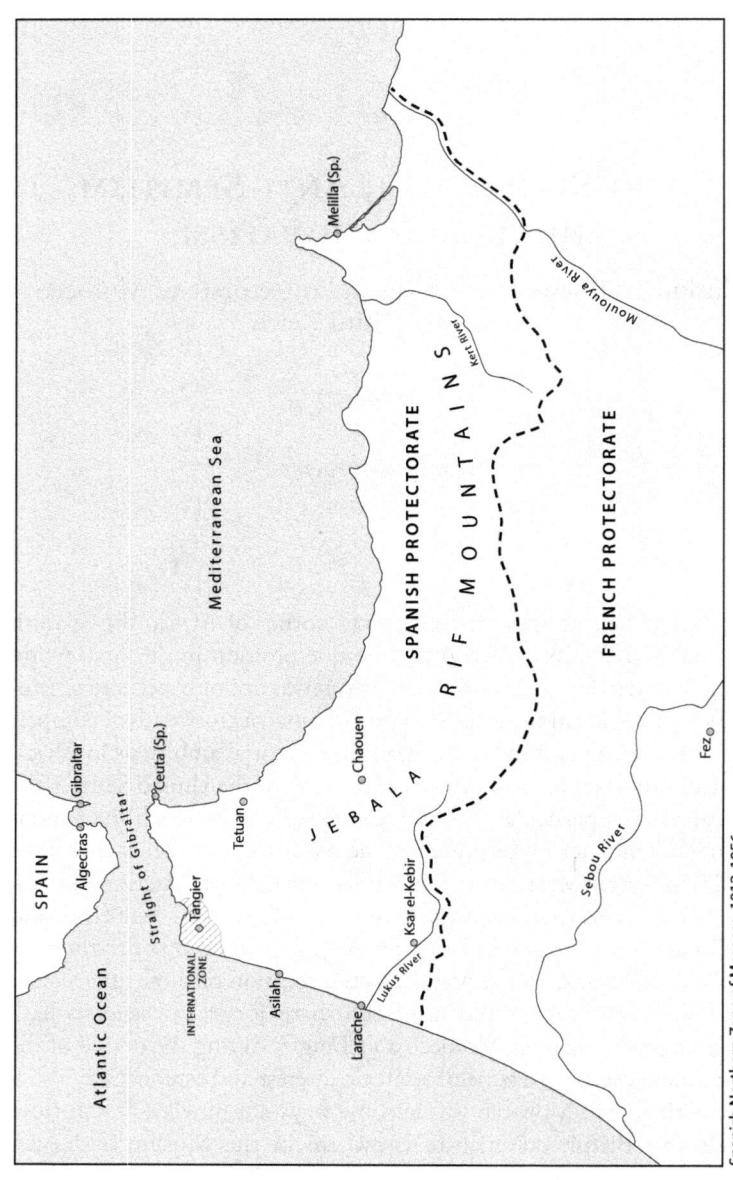

Map 7.1. Map of the Spanish Protectorate in Morocco during World War II. Courtesy of Gregory T. Woolston, Cartographer.

paganda and financial support given to Arab nationalists by the Nazis. Yet, Spanish rule in Morocco was greatly overshadowed by the much more powerful French Protectorate, an even greater obstacle to Spain's imperial ambitions than the incipient Moroccan nationalist movement that in the 1930s had not yet declared its aim of independence. Spain's frustrated status as a weak imperial power, subordinate to its archrival France, shaped its vacillating colonial policy toward its Muslim and Jewish populations, its relationship to Nazi Germany, and its official "neutrality" during the Third Reich.

## Spanish Imperialism in Morocco

"The loss of the last remnant of our great American colonial empire in 1898," wrote the Spanish historian and colonial officer Tomás García Figueras in a book published in 1944, "brought back to the forefront the Moroccan question in Spanish foreign action."[3] By the end of the nineteenth century, Spain had lost all of its American colonies and the Philippines, at the same time that Britain and France were expanding their vast empires in Africa and Asia. For this reason, gaining a foothold in Morocco was a very high priority for Spain. In earlier centuries, Spain's imperial ambitions in the Mediterranean had led to the seizure of territories in North Africa. However, by the end of the eighteenth century, Spain controlled only two enclaves, the towns of Melilla and Ceuta on the Moroccan Mediterranean coast, which remain today as Spanish possessions in the twenty-first century. Spain gained the relatively small colony of Equatorial Guinea in the late eighteenth century but was overshadowed by the colonization of West Africa by the British and French in the nineteenth century. Thus, Spain sought to expand across the Strait of Gibraltar to Morocco and the Western Sahara, regions closer to home that could help restore its stature in the international arena.

The prelude to the Spanish protectorate was its aggressive war against Morocco in 1859 and 1860. The Spanish occupation of the northern Moroccan city of Tetuan ended with its withdrawal in 1862, after Spain and Morocco were pressured, especially by the British, to reach a settlement, under which Morocco agreed to pay major indemnities that bankrupted the Moroccan state (the *makhzan*).[4] Spain's only acquisition in the nineteenth century was on the coast of the Western Sahara in 1885, a rather desolate desert territory, and Spanish settlement there was limited.[5]

Morocco remained independent until 1912. The French and British contest for remaining territories in Africa since the 1880s led to an agreement in 1904 to partition between them separate zones of interest, in which the French were to gain a free hand in Morocco. The British, however, were still reluctant to have its major rival, France, adjacent to Gibraltar, which they considered a crucial stronghold for British interests in the Mediterranean, and they pressured the French to grant Spain a zone of influence in northern Morocco surrounding its enclaves of Ceuta and Melilla. One final player in the imperialist scramble for Morocco was Germany. An emerging power and a latecomer to imperialism that had acquired several territories in sub-Saharan Africa, Germany had been rapidly expanding its commercial interests in Morocco. It was infuriated by the French-Spanish agreement for dividing Morocco but was unable to prevent its partition between France and Spain in 1912.[6]

As the weaker power in these imperialist schemes, Spain played little part in the decisions about the partition of Morocco made by Great Britain and France, which determined its position. Spain's zone in Morocco, considerably smaller than the French Protectorate, was subordinate to the French and dependent on the British, who had an interest in establishing a check on French power and who supported the creation of the international zone of Tangier that came into being in 1923. Though dominated by the much larger French Protectorate—foreign affairs according to the treaty remained in the hands of the French resident general—the Spanish Protectorate authorities, headed by the Spanish High Commissioner, had full powers to administer the northern zone. Morocco was in theory considered a sovereign country, under the rule of the sultan who resided in the French zone, represented in the Spanish zone by his appointed deputy (*khalifa*), a member of the Alawid dynasty that had ruled Morocco since the seventeenth century. The *khalifa,* Mulay El Hassan Ben el Mehdi, like the sultan in the French zone, promulgated decrees (*dahirs*), which were initiated by the Spanish administration in Tetuan, the capital of the Spanish Protectorate. In Tangier, the sultan's sovereignty was represented by a deputy (*mendoub*) in the office known as the *Mendoubia*. While Moroccan sovereignty was maintained in theory to legitimize colonial rule, the French and Spanish exercised real control over the country, conferring little more than symbolic power to the Alawid "sharifian" (meaning its rulers were descended from the Prophet Muhammad) dynasty.[7]

Despite the power vested in the Spanish High Commissioner, Spain had little control over the countryside, and from 1921 to 1926, fought a bloody battle against a resistance movement, led by Abd al-Karim al-Khattabi in the northern Rif Mountains, who wanted to reestablish Moroccan sovereignty.[8] After the Spanish suffered a humiliating defeat, they joined forces with the French, ultimately to defeat Abd al-Karim in 1926. It was in conducting the war in Morocco that Franco rose through the military ranks, in charge of the *regulares,* the Moroccan colonial soldiers. While in Spain, the initial defeat of the Spanish led to General Miguel Primo de Rivera's coup d'état in 1923, a military dictatorship in Spain (1923–1930), and, in turn, the collapse of the Spanish monarchy and the establishment of the second republic in 1931. Franco, and most of the senior officers who revolted against the Republic in 1936 were veterans of the colonial war in Morocco—the *Africanistas,* as they were called. It was a military rebellion in Morocco in July 1936 that precipitated the Spanish Civil War. Arriving from the Canary Islands, Franco took control of the Spanish Army of Africa, the "Moroccan Army Corps," and the Spanish Nationalists took immediate control of the protectorate. They quickly executed officers loyal to the Republic and began a reign of repression and terror. From Morocco, with numerous native troops and the support of both Hitler and Mussolini, the Nationalists launched their attack against the Republic on the mainland. The intensive recruitment of Moroccan volunteers helped sustain the revolt on the mainland, ultimately leading to the Nationalists' victory. Spain's history, therefore, was closely bound up in its colonial venture in Morocco, and its imperial interests there shaped its conduct and policies.[9] Against this background of Spanish colonialism in Morocco, Spain's policies toward Jews and Muslims in the 1930s and during World War II can be understood.

## Philo-Sephardites and Sephardic Hispanophiles

Since the nineteenth century, Jews in northern Morocco had begun to construct a national identity connected to their ancestral homeland, especially from the time of Spain's occupation of Tetuan and the region in 1860. The connection of Jews to the modern nation-state of Spain was strengthened after the establishment of the Spanish Protectorate in Morocco in 1912. In northern Morocco, where large numbers of Iberian Jews had settled centuries earlier, many had maintained their Judeo-Spanish (the Haketía dialect), which was becoming transformed into modern Spanish.[10]

The embrace of the Spanish nation by Moroccan Jews was also a result of the rediscovery by Spain of its Jewish brethren of the "Spanish race." It had its origins in the encounter of Spanish troops with the Spanish-speaking Jews, the descendants of the exiles of 1492, during the Hispano-Moroccan War of 1859 and 1860. With their language skills, they served as useful intermediaries for the Spanish and were instrumental in provisioning the Spanish army. The philo-Sephardi movement that developed in the late nineteenth century reflected Spanish imperialist interests, in which ambitions in Morocco played a central part. Liberal politicians, writers, and intellectuals, who believed Spain's economic and racial decline was a consequence of the Inquisition and the expulsion of the Jews, advocated that reconciliation with the Spanish-speaking Jews through commercial and cultural ties with the Sephardi Mediterranean communities would help Spain recover its former greatness, improve its economy, and revive the "Spanish race." Philo-Sephardism looked to the period of *convivencia* in medieval Spain, the mythical golden age of coexistence between Christians, Muslims, and Jews. The Sephardi community in Morocco, as a branch of the "Spanish race," could serve to legitimize Spanish rule.[11]

After the establishment of the Spanish protectorate, Morocco became in a sense the stage on which this *convivencia* could be performed. Despite the anti-Semitism of many colonialists—who often considered both Jews and Muslims as primitive and blamed Jews for aiding Muslims against Catholic Spain at the time of the *Reconquista* or for financing Abd al-Karim against the Spanish—philo-Sephardism was used by the colonial lobby and the Protectorate authorities, and ultimately by the Franco regime during World War II, to advance Spain's interests in Morocco. Philo-Sephardism, however, was distinct from philo-Semitism. It often operated in conjunction with anti-Semitism, since Ashkenazim were characterized as part of "international Jewry," in negative contrast to Sephardim.[12]

This strategy that favored Sephardi Jews in Morocco was also predicated on the belief that France had used Jewish elites to their advantage in expanding their own empire, especially through the Alliance Israélite Universelle and its network of schools throughout the Mediterranean region, and that embracing the Sephardim by championing the *convivencia* would serve Spanish imperialist aims in Morocco at the expense of their chief rivals, the French.[13] In the 1920s, Francisco Franco himself wrote paternalistically about Moroccan Jews as "the traditional brotherhood of this race,"[14] believing that the Spanish-speaking Sephardim, who controlled much of Moroccan trade, would be useful for Spanish colonial expansion.[15] Sephardi Jews, thus, could be used as a counterfoil to French interests in Morocco.

Though there were undoubtedly some fervent believers in reconciliation with the Jews, many Spaniards saw philo-Sephardism merely as a useful instrument. Franco and the Nationalists, against the background of the Civil War, railed against the "Jewish-Bolshevik-Masonic conspiracy" and often praised the anti-Jewish Nazi legislation, the path to which they proudly argued had been paved by Ferdinand and Isabel in the fifteenth century. The racial distinction that favored Sephardim over Ashkenazim in philo-Sephardi discourse disappears in the rhetoric of the Spanish Nationalists, which blamed Spain's decay on the racial mixing of converted Jews and Spaniards, exposing the political expediency of the claim for defending Spanish Jews during World War II.[16]

## Nazi and Fascist Influence in Morocco

From the very beginning of the Third Reich, the Nazis sought to expand their influence in the Middle East and North Africa and to recruit Muslim support for Germany by positioning themselves as allies of Muslims against the French, the British and the Jews.[17] In 1936, Berlin's interest in Muslim affairs grew, as ties were forged with Muslim communities and leaders.[18]

Morocco was also a target for Nazi propaganda, strategically important for expanding German interests in the western Mediterranean.[19] The Spanish Protectorate in particular was the Achilles' heel of French and British interests in the western Mediterranean, as Spain's rivalry with the French and territorial ambitions in the Maghrib could be used for German imperial expansion. Indeed, with the more active and open activities of Nazi agents allowed into the Spanish zone, the French were concerned about Spain ceding its rights to the protectorate to Germany.[20] The Spanish zone became an important base of operations for German propaganda and for disseminating tracts inciting Muslims against the Jews.[21]

The growth of nationalism and pan-Arabism in the Middle East and North Africa, simultaneous to the rise of National Socialism in Germany, presented the Nazis with an opportunity.[22] In Morocco, the so-called Berber *Dahir* of 1930, a decree promulgated by the French with the aim of separating Berbers from Arabs by removing the former from the jurisdiction of the *sharia,* spurred the growth of the nationalist movement, and mobilized protests throughout the Muslim world.[23] While protests against the Berber *Dahir* caused the French to retreat from its new policy, the Berber *Dahir* became an important symbol for the nationalists and was marked annually by protests in Morocco. The Lebanese leader of the pan-Arab movement, Shakib Arslan, who had established ties with Moroccan nationalists in the 1920s, was particularly active in denouncing the French in defense of Moroccan Muslims, and the Berber *Dahir* was an occasion for launching an international campaign.[24] The French protectorate authorities became increasingly alarmed about the growth of the nationalist movement and the challenge it posed to their position of authority in Morocco.

Fearful of an impending war with Germany and Nazi ambitions in North Africa, the French closely monitored German activities and were especially concerned about possible German support and funding for the nationalist leaders.[25] These reports included not only known German sympathizers in the Spanish Protectorate, but also leading figures in the French zone, such as Allal El Fassi, the future leader of the independence movement.[26] The Moroccan nationalists also posed a threat to the Spanish Protectorate. However, since the primary target of their protest was France, the Spanish authorities were less hesitant in allowing political activities in the northern zone, as well as German support of the nationalists, if only to weaken the French position in Morocco and strengthen their own. As a French-German war appeared to be imminent to many observers, Spain was positioning itself for expanding its dominion in Morocco. While German agents also operated within the French zone, they were given a freer hand in the Spanish Protectorate and were better able to operate in the international zone of Tangier. The German special services in Spain and the embassy in Madrid also served as a conduit for spreading German influence and anti-French propaganda in Morocco.[27] Ceuta, which was administered separately from the Spanish Protectorate, also became a center for Nazi propaganda in Morocco.[28]

Tetuan and Larache, the two major cities of the Spanish protectorate, and the international zone of Tangier, were the most important centers of Nazi propaganda and activities in Morocco. Larache had a sizable German population with commercial ties to Hamburg and air service with Berlin. German consuls in both Larache and Tetuan facilitated Nazi propaganda and espionage. The German consul and forwarding agent in Larache, Reinschausen, channeled funds in support of Nazi propaganda. "Tetuan," wrote the French vice-consul of Larache in a report on German activities in the Spanish zone, was "incontestably one of the nerve centers of the Muslim world because of its educated bourgeoisie." The German consuls of Tetuan and Larache facilitated liaisons between Arab nationalists and Nazis and helped disseminate nationalist and anti-French propaganda into the French zone.[29] German merchants and longtime residents in Morocco, despite the many Jewish agents who had worked for German commercial firms, often became active supporters of Nazi interests and sought to spread anti-Semitic propaganda among the native Muslim population. One of the key players was the longtime and Arabic-speaking German resident in Morocco, Adolf Langenheim. A German spy and merchant with agents throughout Morocco, he became the party chief of the National Socialists in Tetuan and maintained ties with the Moroccan nationalists.[30] Yet reports were contradictory about the impact of anti-Semitic propaganda on the Muslim population as whole, with most observers emphasizing that its influence was negligible outside some of the nationalist circles that had ties with the Nazis.

The French monitoring of Nazi-inspired Judeophobia among Muslims was based not on a principled opposition to anti-Semitism but on how it was instrumentalized by Germany in support of the nationalists. Reports about nationalists receiving financial support from the Germans were frequent. It was claimed in 1935 that funds were left with Shakib Arslan, who then forwarded them to allies in Tetuan, who, in turn, redistributed them to nationalists in the French zone, including, among others, Mohamed Naciri and his brother Mekki Naciri, Mohammed Hassan Ouezzani, and Allal El Fassi. As evidence of the credibility of the information, the report added that El Fassi had "just acquired a house in Fez worth 96,000 francs."[31] It was also reported that the "Nationalist Bloc" in Salé sent a copy of its plan of reforms to Hitler via the German consulate in Tetuan.[32] While some of the reports may have been based on false rumors, or as a deliberate effort to exaggerate or spread misinformation in order to discredit the nationalists by connecting them to the Nazis, they did reflect the anxiety France had about the growing influence of Germany and in its ability to destabilize French imperial control in Morocco.

In the early 1930s, the leading figure among the nationalists in northern Morocco was Abdeselam Bennouna from Tetuan. Like some of the other Arab nationalists from Morocco and elsewhere in the Middle East, Bennouna had ties with the Germans and in 1934 went to Berlin.³³ He was a strong supporter of Shakib Arslan, whom he hosted in Tetuan in 1930, and through the latter's advice, sent his son to study at the University of Nablus in Palestine; other Tetuanis also went to study in Palestine or at Al-Azhar University in Cairo. Tetuan became a hub for nationalist activities, where the Arab press from the Middle East, which was banned in the French zone, could circulate. Another key figure was Abdelkhalek Torrès, who founded the first Arabic language nationalist weekly, *al-Hayat*, in 1934 and became the dominant figure in the movement following the death of Bennouna in 1935. Moroccan Arab nationalists became increasingly engaged in Pan-Islamic causes, with ties to Arslan and Hajj Amin al-Husayni. Solidarity with Palestinian Muslims was one of the driving issues in the 1930s, a factor that sometimes shaped the attitudes of Moroccan nationalists toward Jews more generally and made them susceptible to Nazi anti-Semitic propaganda, which linked its anti-British and anti-French strategy to support for Arab nationalists.³⁴

Some Moroccan nationalists rejected Nazi influence and anti-Semitism as racist and against their own interests, and a few called for Muslim-Jewish entente.³⁵ But the intensification of conflict in Palestine, and the continued association made by Muslims of Jews with the French colonial regime, militated against Muslim-Jewish entente. In the Spanish zone of Morocco, additional factors worked against the idea of Muslims and Jews uniting against racism and anti-Semitism. Nazi influence and German support for the Moroccan nationalists grew after the Francoists seized control of the Spanish Protectorate. The Francoist rebels quickly turned their attention to enlisting the Moroccan nationalists. Torrès broadcasted speeches from Seville in support of the Spanish Nationalists, while Franco officially recognized his leadership of the National Reform Party (Hizb al-Islah al-Watani) to demonstrate his support for Moroccans.³⁶ Fervently anti-Semitic, the Spanish Nationalists divisively encouraged Moroccan nationalists to adopt an anti-French and anti-Jewish stance, while allowing Nazi influence to expand.

The Spanish zone became the most important hub for Moroccan nationalists after the French protectorate authorities took action against the movement. Resident-General Charles Noguès clamped down on the nationalists and their movement (Kutlat al-Amal al-Watani, the National Action Block, or Comité d'Action Marocaine), in 1936 and 1937. The Residency banned the movement, arresting and exiling a number of its leaders.³⁷ The arrest of Allal El Fassi and Mohamed Hassan Ouezzani and the repression of the nationalist movement by the French sparked demonstrations in the Spanish zone, where some of the nationalists found refuge. With both Italian and German support for the nationalists and the collusion of the Spanish authorities, the Muslim nationalists in Tetuan published anti-French propaganda and disseminated Arabic pamphlets, sometimes translations of Nazi anti-Semitic tracts, to the population in both the Spanish and French zones.[38] Some of the nationalist leaders went to Germany, Rome, or, at the invitation of the Germans, Madrid to advance their cause. The French claimed that one of the leaders, Brahim El Ouezzani, was "in the service of Germany and Italy" and seeking German intervention in Morocco. It was reported in May 1938 that Torrès received five thousand pesetas in aid from the Italian consul in Tetuan on the anniversary of the Berber *Dahir*.[39]

The political climate in the Spanish Protectorate with the Francoists in control was conducive to the growth of anti-Semitic nationalist discourse. This included two of the leading nationalist figures who had taken refuge in Tetuan from the repressive measures of the French administration in 1936 and 1937: Mekki Naciri, founder of the Party of Moroccan Unity (al-Wahda al-Wataniya) and Brahim El Ouazzani, who established an Office of Nationalist Defense and a weekly, *Difa'a*.[40]

Spain's willingness to allow Moroccan nationalists to operate within its zone, even if it did not officially support the nationalist cause, was a way to expand its influence by weakening France's position. It was an arrangement of convenience, for Spain's ultimate aim in Morocco, no less than the French, was to strengthen its imperial interests. The Nazis were representing themselves as friends of Islam and enemies of the colonial power, another reason that compelled the Spanish to offer tacit support to Moroccan nationalists and present themselves as different from the French. Franco represented himself as the enemy of atheism and the protector of Islam, claiming that Spain was the country that best understood Muslims and that the Spanish protectorate was more prosperous than the rest of Morocco. Not wanting to alienate the Moroccan nationalists, yet recognizing that they could also pose a threat to Spanish colonial rule, the Fascist government pursued a policy of cooptation and compromise, allowing nationalist political parties to exist and exploiting their division, especially between Torrès, leader of the National Reform Party, and Naciri, head of the Party of Moroccan Unity.[41]

Moroccan nationalists joined Spanish Fascists in their opposition both to the French and the Jews, and expressed sympathy for Germany in order to gain support for their cause.[42] The growing Nazi influence in Spanish Morocco among the Muslim nationalists was alarming, but even more threatening to the Jews was the infusion of Nazi and Fascist anti-Semitic propaganda among Spanish settlers and soldiers, who castigated the Jews as communists and for supporting the Spanish Republic, or even instigating the Civil War. Indeed, soon after the Nationalist takeover of northern Morocco in 1936, scores of Jews were shot or executed. Jews were terrorized by Falangists, who led an anti-Jewish campaign of boycotting businesses, expropriating property, and violence.[43]

The Spanish administration under High Commissioner Juan Beigbeder imposed fines on those accused of hostility to the Francoist regime, including members of the Jewish community. Jews were concentrated in commerce, seen as a good source of income, and therefore liable to expropriation under the pretext of their support for the Republicans. The tables were turned from the previous period, when Jews even enjoyed some favoritism at the hands of the authorities, a factor that may have contributed to Muslim resentment toward them. The Spanish Nationalists were now enlisting Muslim Moroccan soldiers in their cause, offering inducements of autonomy that hinted at eventual independence, and encouraging Moroccan nationalists as well.[44] The heavy recruitment of Muslims to the Spanish Nationalist cause also incited hostility toward and sporadic violence against Moroccan Jews. Discriminatory measures were taken by the Protectorate authorities against the Jews in an effort to gain Muslim sympathy. For example, the authorities forced Jews to lower rents on their property by 35 percent, or exacted payment on the Jews of Tetuan on the occasion of the 'Id al-Adha for enlisted Muslims to purchase sheep used in the sacrifice.[45]

Some in the Spanish administration in Morocco disapproved of the anti-Jewish violence. One of the key figures in shaping Spanish colonial policy in Morocco, Colonel Tomás García Figueras, who was in charge of the region of Larache, strenuously objected to the anti-Semitic campaign. García Figueras was a prolific writer and historian of Morocco, an advocate of *convivencia* who believed that the Spanish colonialist cause could be well served by promoting the advancement of Moroccan natives and forging their common identity with Spain. García Figueras is an interesting case, since he reflected all the contradictions of Spain's policy toward the Jews. A Germanophile, Francoist, Sephardiphile, Francophobe, and anti-Semite, Garcia Figueras believed that Spain had failed to counteract French influence via the Jews and that Moroccan Jews could be instrumental in promoting Spanish colonial interests.[46]

The Nationalists also tempered their treatment of the Jews because of the bad press that resulted from the anti-Semitic attacks. They were concerned that this would influence greater international support for the Republican government and detrimentally affect relations with Britain, still an important player in Morocco. Indeed, Beigbeder himself sought to present Spain in a good light, insisting that there was no Jewish problem in Spain evidenced by the harmonious relationship between Catholics, Jews, and Muslims in Spanish Morocco. Perhaps even more importantly, Franco relied on the financial backing of the Moroccan Jews and Jewish money, from both the Hassan Bank of Tangier and the community of Tetuan, which helped to finance the Nationalists in the Civil War. Jacob Benmaman, a community leader and the agent of the Hassan Bank in Tetuan, collaborated with Beigbeder in financing the Nationalist rebellion.[47]

Jews were undoubtedly also concerned about their precarious position amid the growing anti-Jewish sentiment and the favoritism shown to the Muslim population, and some sought to demonstrate their loyalty to Spain. While there were Jews in Morocco who supported the Republicans—although to a much lesser extent than the Nationalists frequently claimed—many were anxious to maintain their status in the Spanish Protectorate and remain in good favor with the authorities. The Spanish government ironically awarded Jewish community leaders of Tetuan and Melilla the Order of Isabella the Catholic. In an expression of loyalty to Spain, Jewish leaders in the Spanish protectorate organized a public celebration of Franco's victory in the Civil War and sent a delegation to Madrid, where they met with Beigbeder, who had become the new foreign minister, to pledge their loyalty to Franco.[48]

With the end of the Civil War in March 1939 and the outbreak of World War II later that year, the Germans accelerated their efforts to destabilize French rule from the Spanish zone and Tangier through the Moroccan nationalist leaders. The French intercepted in late 1939 anti-French nationalist tracts in Arabic distributed across the border into the neighboring districts of the French zone, which they claimed were inspired by the Germans and emanated from Moroccan nationalists in Tetuan. The pamphlet spoke about how the Muslim population was enslaved by the French infidels, who are Jews, invoking also the fear of the subordination of Muslims by English Jews in Palestine.[49] Brahim El Ouazzani and Abdelkhalek Torrès, among other nationalist leaders, were actively disseminating nationalist literature in the French zone through a network of their agents. French intelligence reported that the German consul in Tetuan, Herbert Richter, and Langenheim had conferred responsibility on Torrès for spreading German propaganda among the

Muslim population.[50] In April 1940, a "Muslim Racist Association" was allegedly founded in the Spanish zone under the leadership of Torrès at the instigation of the Italians and Germans but under a nationalist facade. The French protectorate authorities were alarmed and sent around a circular to the *contrôleurs civils* and military through the French zone to determine if this had caused a revival of anti-Semitism in their districts. The response seems to have been that it had no impact.[51]

Despite the officially neutral position of Spain in the war, the French complained that the Spanish authorities were allowing German propaganda and the collusion of the Moroccan nationalists with the Nazis go unchecked.[52] Beigbeder was a liaison between the German consul in Tetuan (Richter) and Moroccan nationalist leaders.[53] French intelligence even reported that through some Spanish officials, seven million pesetas were deposited with the *khalifa*, in order to involve all of the nationalist parties in spreading anti-French propaganda.[54] In early 1940, the Germans began to recruit Muslim volunteer soldiers to go to Germany allegedly with the collusion of the Spanish. The French reported on the double game being played by the Spanish authorities: while overtly friendly with France, they were also declaring that the French are with the Jews, the worst enemies of Nationalist Spain.[55]

## Vichy in Morocco

The fall of France in June 1940 and the establishment of Vichy rule in the French colonies put to test all of the contradictions of Spain's colonial policy in Morocco under the Nationalist regime of Franco. While the French administration and political structures in Morocco stayed intact, the resident general and the Protectorate authorities now became a part of the French collaborationist government. Repressive measures were adopted against communists, freemasons, and Jews, the same declared enemies of the Francoist regime.

Charles Noguès, the resident general during the Vichy period in Morocco, had been appointed by the Popular Front government in 1936. Despite his military credentials, his commitment to the French empire and settler privilege, and the firm action he took against the Moroccan nationalists, Noguès was little liked by much of the European settler community (the *colons*), who associated him with the socialist Popular Front government. Noguès's efforts to restore the colonial tradition created by the first Resident-General, Hubert Lyautey, with its espoused respect for native customs and traditions, and his effort to forge close ties with the young sultan, Mohammed Ben Youssef, were unpopular among many of the *colons*.[56]

Anti-Semitism among the French *colons* in Morocco had been growing in the 1930s, although was more restrained than in Algeria, where anti-Semitic agitation and violence among the settler population had intensified in the 1920s and 1930s.[57] In contrast to Algeria, where Jews became French citizens en masse by the Crémieux Decree of 1870, a constant source of friction and a challenge to European privilege, the French in Morocco maintained the status of Jews as "indigenous." This precluded them from obtaining French citizenship, therefore limiting their access to European colonial society. But settler antipathy toward the Jews, about a quarter million in the French zone, as well as their perceived advancement in Morocco, was growing in the 1930s. After the election of the Popular Front government in France in 1936, with its Jewish socialist premier, Léon Blum, settler anti-Semitism became more palpable in Morocco.[58]

A significant portion of the European settler population applauded the Nazi-inspired anti-Jewish measures adopted by the Vichy government in Morocco. The colonial authorities in the French zone began implementing the anti-Jewish laws of metropolitan France (the Statut des Juifs of 1940), and following the creation of the *Commissariat général aux questions juives* (CGQJ) in 1941, an even more severe Statute for the Jews was issued. As a protectorate, legislation was implemented through the guise of consultation with the sultan and officially promulgated by *dahir* (royal decree). The anti-Jewish *dahirs* excluded Jews from a wide range of professions and positions in the commercial and public sectors, and a numerus clausus was imposed, restricting the number of Jews in public schools and in liberal professions. Jews were ordered to submit to a census, where they were required to declare their place of residence, civil and family status, profession, and property. Jewish companies and businesses were to be closed. The purpose of these measures was the eventual expropriation of Jewish property—the "Aryanization," as it was called, of the Jewish economy.[59]

The anti-Jewish *dahirs* in most respects replicated the Metropolitan *Statut des Juifs* and were applied to both Moroccan and non-Moroccan Jews resident in Morocco. However, a significant distinction was made regarding Moroccan Jews in allowing them to continue to practice traditional artisanal activities and retail trade. Despite the ideological commitment to the Aryanization of the economy, Vichy conceded that this goal needed to be balanced by maintaining the economic strength of the French empire that could be jeopardized if the traditional economy were undermined. At the local level, Noguès and many in his administration were less zealous about implementing the anti-Jewish Statute than were the metropolitan Vichy authorities; they were more concerned about maintaining order and stability of governance than the ideological aims of Vichy's National Revolution. Consequently, the residency granted exemptions or delays to individuals in applying the law, or stalling tactics in promulgating metropolitan laws in Morocco. The efforts to attenuate the impact of the laws, however, were limited by the zealousness with which Vichy and the CGQJ sought to have the *Statut des Juifs* fully implemented and closely monitored the Residency's enforcement of the restrictions and regulations.[60]

Franco's government shared many of the ideological goals of Vichy's National Revolution and often spoke approvingly of the Nazis' anti-Jewish laws. But the anti-Jewish *dahirs* were not applied in the Spanish protectorate. Despite the Fascist ideological anti-Semitism that had had no use in differentiating Sephardi from international Jewry, philo-Sephardism was revived as an instrument of undermining France's position in Morocco.

## Jewish Policy in the Spanish Protectorate during Vichy

The defeat of France offered Spain the prospect of taking over French Morocco, which it had long coveted. Spain proposed to Hitler that it seize all of Morocco and expand its territories in Northwest Africa. Yet Germany had its own strategic interests in the region and was suspicious of Franco. Ultimately, Vichy-Nazi collaboration precluded the possibility of Spain fulfilling its expansionist aims, since it ensured the continuation of French rule in Morocco. Without the military support that would come from an alliance with Germany, Spain had little hope of dislodging the French from Morocco. "Neutrality" was Spain's best option for strengthening its position in Morocco during the war.[61]

"¡Qué alegría de España en Tánger y de Tánger en España!" (What a joy to see Spain in Tangier and Tangier in Spain!).[62] On 14 June 1940, a week before the fall of France and the German-French armistice, Spain occupied the international zone of Tangier, under the pretext of ensuring the international zone's neutrality, for the International Control Commission (ICC) was composed of a French chief with representatives of Great Britain, Holland, Italy, Spain, and Portugal. "Until June of 1940," wrote García Figueras, "the travesty of the international regime of Tangier continued to exist for the benefit of France and against National Spain."[63] The "liberation" of Tangier, was a well-calculated move by Spain, knowing that none of the European powers—and above all France, which was in the dominant position in Tangier—was in a position to block what was regarded as a flagrant violation of the treaty agreements and international law. In November 1940, the ICC and the other international institutions were closed, and in March 1941, the office representing the Sharifian government, the *Mendoubia,* was suppressed, the premises provided to Germany for reopening a consulate that had been banned from the international zone of Tangier. The *khalifa* "triumphantly" entered Tangier, symbolically making the city a part of the Spanish protectorate.[64] The annexation of Tangier and the suppression of the *Mendoubia* dramatically underscored France's weakness (and Germany's strength) by removing the sultan's representative, who was by proxy France's instrument of authority that legitimized French domination in the international zone that was still considered under the sovereignty of the Moroccan sultan.

About twelve thousand to fourteen thousand Jews lived in the city of Tangier, which included about two thousand refugees, mainly from Central and Eastern Europe. With about another fifteen thousand already living in the Spanish Protectorate, this almost doubled the Jewish population living under Spanish rule in Morocco. For the first time since 1492, a substantial Jewish population lived under Spanish rule, most of whom resided in Morocco. The number of Jews residing in mainland Spain was about four thousand, with perhaps another two thousand refugees since 1936, many being stateless Jews and Polish nationals. After Tangier was incorporated into the Spanish protectorate, Spain was reluctant to allow entry to any more Jewish refugees. Spain took control of Tangier's Jewish community institutions, and the protectorate authorities now appointed formerly elected leaders of the Jewish council.[65]

Because of Spain's neutrality during World War II, its Moroccan colony seemed like a relatively safe haven for Jews, compared to the French Protectorate where Jews were at much greater risk. Spain seized upon the tribulations the Jews faced under Vichy rule in the French zone as an opportunity. Critical of the anti-Jewish measures, the Spanish authorities assured the Moroccan Jewish population of their good disposition toward its "brothers of the Sephardi race," launching again its philo-Sephardi policy.[66] The official Spanish Nationalist press criticized

France's anti-Jewish measures, highlighting that in Fez and Meknes, the Jews sought the protection of the *makhzan,* while many fled to America and to the Spanish zone, especially to Tangier.[67]

The emphasis on the protection of both Spain and the *makhzan* for the Jews, in the face of the French anti-Jewish policy, could serve to displace the dominant position of France in the Moroccan protectorate. The sultan and ruler of the dynasty, Mohammed Ben Youssef, was the sovereign of all three zones, represented in the Spanish zone by the *khalifa,* and in Tangier by the *mendoub.* The figurehead sultan, under the control of the French, legitimized French claims of influence over all of Morocco and the subordinate role of the Spanish. Yet the sultan had rubberstamped, as he was obligated to do, the anti-Jewish *dahirs.* Spain's effort to elevate the sovereignty of the *khalifa* and its suppression of the *mendoub* in Tangier, sought to reverse the preponderant position of France over the Sharifian *makhzan* administration by giving credit to the *makhzan* for protecting the Jews while ignoring the sultan who was also cultivating his image of protector of the Jews to assert his role as national leader.[68] The Jewish question thus gave the Spanish another way to undermine the legitimacy of French rule in Morocco, by emphasizing its defense of the Jews in all of Morocco while Jews were turning to the *makhzan* for protection from the French.

The Spanish renewal of a philo-Sephardi policy by repudiating the anti-Jewish legislation in the French zone was counterbalanced by pressures from the Nazis to implement anti-Jewish laws as the French had done in Morocco and by the continued tacit support of Moroccan nationalists. However, during Vichy rule, the Spanish position with regard to the anticolonial actions of the Moroccan nationalists was more ambivalent, since colonial Vichy was implementing Nazi-instigated policies.

Anti-Semitism was echoed in some Moroccan nationalist publications in the northern zone during the Vichy period, although it was arguably not central to their ideology. Whatever antipathy the Moroccan nationalist leaders in the Spanish zone may have had toward the Jews, what is certain is that anti-Semitism was used as an instrument of anti-French protest and as a strategy to curry favor with the Germans. Torrès published an article in *al-Huriyya* when the second Jewish statute *dahir* was issued in 1941, claiming that the *dahir* was "purely a French act . . . willy-nilly to put an end to the actions of Jews in its country." Torrès disapproved of the exceptions made for Jews who rendered service or fought for France (rather than Morocco), which he claimed enabled Jews to escape the consequences of the legislation, and denounced how the French had allowed the evils of Jewish influence to grow. The law, Torrès argued, was a long-needed first step to restrain Jewish activities, but he contended it did not go far enough.[69]

Torrès's attitude is also reflected in a report from the consul of France in Larache, who writes of the favorable reception of the Muslim population in Larache and El-Ksar to the anti-Jewish legislation in the French zone. The nationalists, however, reacted by showing their sympathy for Germany by spreading rumors that the measures were only taken because they were imposed on France and Morocco by the Third Reich, not out of belief. The pro-German position of the Arab nationalists in the Spanish zone of Morocco was used not only against the French Protectorate but also as a means to put pressure on the Spanish authorities in Morocco who had revived, at least ostensibly, their philo-Sephardi policy.

The Moroccan nationalists therefore brought out the conundrum in Spain's Jewish policy and indirectly put pressure on the Spanish authorities. Ultimately, for Spain, support for Sephardi Jews, partly motivated by exaggerated notions of Jewish money and power, was seen as an even more powerful weapon to undermine French interests in Morocco.

Spain sought ways to utilize politically the growing disenchantment of Jews with France and economically by the prospect of rich Moroccan Jews, whose wealth risked expropriation, to move to the Spanish zone, where they could be granted Spanish citizenship. Spanish High Commissioner Luis Orgaz Yoldi wrote to the Spanish Ministry of Foreign Affairs in October of 1941 about the protests produced by the French Jewish statute:

> Would it not be a good opportunity to exploit this situation in the neighboring protectorate, which could be of such great political and economic importance for us, by taking advantage of the forced flight of Jewish capital and its influx to our Protectorate, where the Jews are seeking refuge, and where they would feel secure, at least for now? Moreover, it should not be forgotten that as a consequence of the often mentioned statute, the Jews now in essence consider France their enemy and also the Muslims of the neighboring zone, it seems, are not happy with the restrictions that they are currently enduring.[70]

The Spanish authorities devised various strategies for "protecting" Sephardi Jews. For example, the French consul in Tangier wrote to

Noguès in 1941 that Spain had offered Spanish passports to "ex-French protégés" residing in the Spanish zone. Many Moroccan Jews, as protégés of foreign powers, had enjoyed extraterritorial rights under the jurisdiction of foreign states in the precolonial period. This system of "protection" (or capitulations) was abolished when the protectorate was established, and only the British and the Americans refused to accept the annulment of the capitulations. This meant that former French protégés were henceforth considered Moroccan subjects.

The French consul thus pointed out that Spain's intention was to take in as Spanish protégés all the Jews of Tangier, "particularly," as he sardonically remarked, "those who possess a certain fortune." This initiative, wrote the consul, "was inspired by certain Jews seeking to escape the measures against them by the Protectorate, encouraged by the fact that the American and British consulates were inciting their Jewish protégés not to comply with the requirements of the Jewish statute."[71]

The Spanish also turned their attention to their protégés in the French Protectorate who were now to be subjected to the same anti-Jewish laws affecting all foreigners. Spain invited Jews living in the French zone to apply for Spanish nationality, causing some alarm among French authorities. Naturalization of Sephardi Jews as an instrument of policy was not new to this period but had legal precedence. Philo-Sephardism, accompanied with the idea that Jews wielded considerable economic power, had already in 1924 led to a royal decree, which granted full citizenship to anyone of Spanish origin who had been protégés under the regime of Capitulations in the former Ottoman Empire, understanding that this referred primarily to Jews. It was made quite explicit that this did not require settling in Spain. The decree was to remain in effect until the end of 1930.[72] While only a limited number of Jews, mainly from the Balkans, were able to take advantage of the decree, the precedent was important and played out in very complicated ways in World War II. While later cast as a humanitarian gesture, Spain's claim over Sephardi Jews in Europe was more about acquiring their properties than about repatriating them to Spain. Morocco, however, was a different story. During World War II, Sephardic Jews with Spanish nationality acquired because of the 1924 decree who sought refuge in Spain were liable to be deported to North Africa.[73]

In May 1942, reporting on the application in Morocco of the anti-Jewish laws of metropolitan France, the French Residency wrote about the "abusive campaign of naturalizations" led by the Spanish government.

The current wish of Madrid, motivated by a concern that is easy to detect, is for us to accept that Moroccan Jews, the majority descended from former emigrants of Castile, are Spanish subjects. The consulates of Spain in Morocco are encouraged to pursue a policy of attraction among these communities who settled here centuries ago and are currently in the French zone. The Statute for the Jews in Morocco makes their propaganda so much more effective that Spain, distinguishing between "national Jews" and "international Jewry," reminds us at every moment that the former are cherished as Spaniards of pure race.[74]

The French protectorate authorities and the *makhzan* refused to recognize these naturalizations, considered them an abuse of the law, and expressed the hope that in the future Jews might see the advantages of remaining Moroccan subjects over becoming naturalized Spaniards.

Indeed, the French could claim the illegality of Spain's actions by virtue of an article in the 1880 Treaty of Madrid that came to define Moroccan citizenship, which stipulated:

Every Moroccan subject naturalized abroad who shall return to Morocco must after a period of residence equal in time to that which was legally necessary to obtain naturalization, choose between his complete submission to the laws of the Empire and the obligation to leave Morocco, unless it be proven that the foreign naturalization was obtained with the consent of the Moroccan government.[75]

The Treaty of Madrid was the outcome of a meeting between the European powers and Morocco, with the goal of curing the abuse of the system of consular protection. While intended not as a nationality law but rather to limit the possibility of Jews obtaining foreign nationality abroad and returning to Morocco with their newly acquired status as "foreigners," the principle of "perpetual allegiance" established in the article became the basis of the legal concept of citizenship during the Protectorate. Indeed, it became the legal justification for exclusion of Jews from acquiring French citizenship and for maintaining the vast majority of Jews as indigenous subjects of the sultan.

Yet this policy clashed with Spain's laws of citizenship, under which the Spanish claimed that Jews born in their zone in Morocco were Spanish. But the French claimed that the sultan considered them Moroccan by the principle of *jure sanguinis,* based on their origins, and that they lost their status as Spanish when they left the Spanish zone.[76] For those Jews whom Spain regarded as their nationals in the French Protectorate, discrimination against them challenged Spanish sovereignty and was detrimental to Spanish prestige. The French advanced the argument that, in any event, if they were considered Spaniards, the metropolitan Jewish statute would be applied even in Morocco, which, they asserted, was more severe than the separate Jewish *dahir* that was adopted for Moroccan Jews.

As discussed above, the main difference between Moroccan and non-Moroccan Jews in the anti-Jewish *dahir* was the stipulation that allowed Moroccan Jews to engage in artisanal activities and retail trade. Subsequent regulations that applied to Moroccan Jews, such as not requiring them to declare their property unless it exceeded a value of fifty thousand francs, may have made it advantageous to be a Moroccan subject over non-Moroccan nationality, as High Commissioner Orgaz observed in 1941.[77] There was probably a sense that greater allowances for exemptions and delays in the removal of Jews from professions were applied to Moroccans. Perhaps this was also hinting at the fact that the *makhzan* were more restrained in implementing the laws on Moroccan Jews, an image the Residency was anxious to project in order to deflect criticism from the metropolitan Vichy authorities for their own laxity in carrying out parts of the anti-Jewish measures.[78]

Yet Spain was adamant about protecting its nationals in French Morocco and continued to issue certificates and passports, which the French refused to recognize. Protests of the Spanish Ministry of Foreign Affairs to the Vichy government were to no avail. In light of the official persecution of Jews in France, the Vichy government was undisturbed by Spanish threats of retaliation against Jews of French origin living in the area of Tangier.[79]

Furthermore, the French would not yield to the demand that Spanish nationals be exempt from the census and declaration of properties. The question of Jewish property, as was the case for Spanish intervention on behalf of Sephardi Jews in Europe, was one of the major, if not the most important, concerns with regard to Spain's intervention on behalf of Jews in Morocco, a point often observed by the French authorities. While it seems that the Spanish nationals residing in the Spanish zone would not be required to declare their property in the French zone, the same was not the case for Spanish Jews in the French protectorate who were subject to the same laws that affected all foreign Jews. A Jew from Tangier, in a letter to the French Consul General, highlighted this fact, as he remarked to his compatriots living in the French zone "that in the glorious Spain of the Caudillo Franco, there are not two classes of Spaniards."[80] Yet Spain's efforts to protect those it considered Spanish nationals in the French zone were in vain; both Vichy and the French Residency refused to yield with respect to foreign Jews. At the very least, they could present Spaniards as trustees for expropriated Jewish property, *administrateurs provisoires.*

The vehemently anti-Semitic and pro-Nazi Spanish ambassador to Vichy, José Félix de Lequerica, in fact, boasted about Spain being the only country that the Vichy government allowed to have their own nationals, rather than French citizens, serve as "trustees" for Jewish property. Other countries with "democratic tendencies" that declared Jews as "ordinary citizens completely disregarding their religion," failed in their "arrogant request" behind which was the purpose of defending "international Jewry" and criticizing the anti-Jewish measures of the French government.[81] Vichy thus requested from the Spanish for both France and the North African colonies that they submit lists of potential Spanish *administrateurs provisoires*. In Morocco, Spanish consular authorities in the French zone from Rabat, Casablanca, Fez, Marrakesh, and Oujda submitted lists of potential Spanish Christian trustees so that the CGQJ could choose in each case while French settler applicants were applying to become trustees of Jewish property and businesses.[82] But the metropolitan law of 22 July 1941 to place Jewish property under non-Jewish trustees remained "under consideration" by the French Residency in Morocco and was never adopted before the Allied landing in North Africa in November 1942.[83]

Ironically, after the Allied landings and the abrogation of the anti-Jewish laws, the Spanish press denounced that the Jews in North Africa were recovering their rights.[84] At the same time, as the tide was now turning in the war, Franco began to proclaim how Spain had endeavored to protect Jews. In Morocco, now under Allied control, there was no longer any particular advantage to Spain continuing to offer special assistance to Sephardi Jews in the French zone. Its main concern regarding the treatment of Moroccan Jews was in cultivating its humanitarian image because of the negative view in the world of Franco's Fascist dictatorship that had seized power with the help of Nazi Germany and Fascist Italy and continued to be closely associated with Nazi Germany during World War II despite its neutrality. Indeed, the World Jewish Congress (WJC) was monitoring the situation of the Jews under Spanish rule in Morocco, and the protectorate authorities were anxious to demonstrate that Jews were well treated.[85]

At the same time, Spain sought to placate the Muslim population and the Moroccan nationalist movement that was now calling for independence. The Germans also took advantage of the neutrality of the Spanish Protectorate, not occupied by the Allies, to center their propaganda activities, which could then be disseminated to the French zone of Morocco and to Algeria.[86] While the Spanish authorities may well have sympathized with the German anti-French position and were also positioning themselves vis-à-vis the Moroccan nationalists, Spain's imperial position was weak. With Germany's imminent defeat, the most Spain could hope for was a return to the status quo through the support of the Allied powers, and Spain was indeed forced by the Allies to withdraw from Tangier at the end of the war, as its international administration was restored. In the years following the war, Franco came to terms with the inevitability of decolonization, and, hoping to gain friends in the Arab world, he came to accept that Spain would leave Morocco together with the French.[87]

What remained essential for Franco's efforts to gain acceptance in the international community was the image of Spain's benevolent Jewish policy during World War II. In an assessment of the achievements of the Spanish protectorate in Morocco, García Figueras pointed out how Spain refused to follow the French in implementing the racist anti-Semitic laws, praised Franco for giving refuge in Tangier to the persecuted Jews of Europe, and asserted that "no other peoples had shown such noble generosity."[88] Spain sought to demonstrate that it exercised its influence to save Jews by sheltering Jewish refugees and intervening to protect the Sephardim.

Yet Spain's record of helping Jews, even Sephardi Jews, during World War II can at best be described as ambivalent. Despite the popular image of the benevolent actions of Franco for the Jews during the war, economic interests, not humanitarianism, motivated Spain's policy regarding its Sephardi Jewish nationals. Spain was most concerned about the confiscation of Sephardi properties in Vichy France, French Morocco, and countries under German occupation, which would deprive Spain of huge assets of which Spain should be the beneficiary. Since Spain was not a hostile power, and Spanish law did not make racial distinctions, argued the chargé d'affaires of the Spanish Embassy in Paris, it should be able to extend its protection to its Jewish nationals on condition that they contribute economically to the country.[89] The Spanish Ministry of Foreign Affairs instructed its diplomatic agents that they should not intervene and that Jewish citizens should submit to the anti-Jewish measures; they should declare their property in a special registry, and declare and give proof of their Spanish nationality so their interests as Spanish citizens could be defended.[90]

As the situation became increasingly dire for Jews in Europe under Nazi occupation and deportations to the death camps accelerated, Germany issued a series of ultimatums to allow the repatriation of Jews to neutral and Nazi-allied countries within three months beginning in late December 1942 to early January 1943. Spain dragged its feet and then only allowed a limited number out of concern for its image among the Allies as the tides were turning in the war. Franco was opposed to Jewish immigration to Spain; even Sephardi Jews with Spanish nationality were refused permanent residency. Morocco, however, was another matter, and it even proposed to the Germans in 1941 to allow emigration of Sephardi Jews from occupied Europe to Morocco, a scheme that Germany rejected.[91]

Spain not only opposed "repatriating" Sephardi Jews but also imposed restrictions on issuing Spanish transit visas to Jewish refugees, including those with Spanish passports. The destination of an estimated twenty thousand to thirty-five thousand Jews who managed, either legally or illegally, to pass through the borders of Spain, was Portugal, where many sought passage across the Atlantic.[92] To the extent that Spain allowed transit of Jews through Spain—motivated in part by its image abroad, especially after the Allies were gaining ground in Europe—the Madrid government was adamant that Spain would not be their final destination. In 1943 and 1944, most of the refugees were transferred to other countries; many were sent to Fedala in French Morocco and to other camps in North Africa.[93]

When preparations for a special war emergency conference of the WJC in New York were underway for May 1944, inquiries were made by WJC leadership about the situation in Spanish Morocco. There was an interest in having a delegation from the Spanish zone.[94] Instructions were given to the prospective delegate named by the Tetuan community, Salomon Israel, on how to represent Spain: the Spanish Protectorate of Morocco is scrupulous in its respect for Jewish customs and practices; it pursued a policy of protecting Sephardim abroad; those in concentration camps were allowed to move to Spain and thousands of Jewish refugees were offered asylum in the Iberian mainland, while many were allowed transit in the Spanish zone of Morocco for going to the Americas; among the refugees were many famed individuals in the sciences, arts, and humanities.[95]

The conference to be held in Atlantic City was delayed until November 1944, and efforts were renewed to have representation from the Jewish Community of Tetuan. The president and secretary of the Jewish Community Council of Tetuan, Jacob M. Benmaman and Moises A. Hassan, wrote to the WJC with regret that Spanish Morocco would not be able to send delegates to the conference because of difficulties of transport. The WJC responded that it would be regretful if they could not attend and requested a report on the conditions of Jews in Spanish Morocco. Benmaman and Hassan again apologized that they were unable to send a delegation because of problems of transport and the need for the leadership to remain in Morocco to deal with the problems the community was facing, but they would be present spiritually. Benmaman and Hassan, both backers of Franco in the Civil War, praised High Commissioner Orgaz for allowing entry to five hundred Jewish children, refugees from Hungary. The Jewish Community Council instead submitted a report, dated September 1944, in response to the WJC's questionnaire on conditions in Spanish Morocco.[96]

It is not clear, however, if Orgaz had in fact given permission for a delegation to attend the conference. The Spanish Ministry of Foreign Affairs mused that if the High Commissioner were not to authorize

El jalifa de la Zona del Protectorado de España en Marruecos y el alto comisario, general Orgaz, en el acto de Sidi Alf (Septiembre de 1936)

**Figure 7.1.** Photograph of Moroccan Khalifa Mulay El Hassan Ben el Mehdi with Spanish High Commissioner Luis Orgaz Yoldi, 1936. *Source:* Tomás García Figueras, *Marruecos (la acción, de España en el norte de Africa)* (Madrid, 1944).

a delegation, it would put Spain in a bad light but ruminated that attendance would also come with risks. So the delegates needed to be vetted by the High Commissioner. There could potentially be resolutions hostile to totalitarian systems and against Spanish interests, so the delegation needed to abstain from critical or hostile attitudes toward any countries in the war, emphasizing instead Spain's humanitarian position toward the Jews in total contrast to other countries, either occupied or at war.[97] In the end, however, no delegates from Spanish Morocco were at the war emergency conference. The Spanish government was, in any event, able to cultivate good ties with the WJC, especially with the head of its political committee, Maurice Perlzweig, who was sent a list of measures taken by Spain to rescue persecuted Jews, the basis on which Spain was represented favorably at the conference. The result was a resolution of the conference that thanked Spain, together with the Vatican and the governments of Switzerland and Sweden, for their rescue efforts on behalf of the persecuted Jews of Europe under German domination.[98] The narrative of humanitarian actions toward the Jews that Spain promoted was largely accepted in Jewish organizations, thus creating the myth of Franco's benevolence during World War II.

## Conclusion

In June 2015, the Spanish parliament passed a long-anticipated bill that extended the right to descendants of Jews expelled from Spain in the fifteenth century to apply for Spanish citizenship to rectify the injustice of five hundred years ago.[99] The initiative to offer citizenship to Moroccan Jews was greeted with outrage for only recognizing the injustice done to Jews in total disregard of Muslims. For descendants of the Moriscos (Muslims who were forced to convert to Christianity in Spain and subsequently expelled in the first two decades of the sixteenth century, many of whom settled in Morocco), the privileging of the Sephardim smacked of a double standard.[100] When the law went into effect in October 2015, 4,302 Sephardi Jews were granted Spanish citizenship. The criteria established by the 2015 law made the naturalization process difficult, and it was clear in any event that most Jews of Spanish descent, real or imagined, were not going to apply. Most who have applied are Israelis seeking dual citizenship with a European country but are unlikely to settle in Spain.[101]

Much of the press took the announcement of the legislation at face value, a bill that sought to redress the wrongs committed by Spain five centuries ago, but without investigating the legal precedent in Spain's Jewish policy in Morocco during the Holocaust and, even earlier, in the royal decree of 1924. While circumstances are obviously different in 2015, compared to the period of the Third Reich, the recent bill echoes some of the same contradictions of Spain's "philo-Sephardi" position during World War II, a policy based on expediency, racial hierarchies, and colonialism. In the postcolonial present, the number of Jews in Spain, many of Moroccan descent, has climbed only to about twelve thousand, while its Muslim population is more than a million and rapidly growing, which is part of Spain's often forgotten colonial legacy in Morocco. Though some legislators criticized the obstacles placed in the way of naturalization, it is likely that few imagined or desired any kind of large-scale Jewish settlement in Spain.

Whatever historical injustice that some legislators believed the law redresses, the illusory hope of attracting large-scale Jewish investment in Spain on the one hand and "investing" in the symbolic capital of the *convivencia,* representing Spain as a land of tolerance, on the other seems to be a more plausible explanation for the revival of the policy. In this sense, it bears a striking resemblance to Franco's philo-Sephardi policy during World War II: of attracting Jewish capital rather than Jews and presenting an image of a tolerant and humanitarian country. If the intent of Spain's policy during World War II was to mask the oppressive Fascist dictatorship, based in part on colonial exploitation in Morocco, its present policy is also a response to its postcolonial anxieties of Moroccan migrants in Spain. The 2015 law of naturalization for Sephardi Jews, a law that ignores the same right to descendants of Muslims expelled from Spain, might serve as a mask of the intolerance toward its large and growing Muslim population, considered by many to be unwanted guests.

**Daniel J. Schroeter** is the Amos S. Deinard Memorial Chair in Jewish History at the University of Minnesota. His books include *The Sultan's Jew: Morocco and the Sephardi World* (2002) and *Merchants of Essaouira: Urban Society and Imperialism in Southwestern Morocco, 1844–1886* (1988), both translated in Arabic and published in Morocco. He is co-editor of *Jewish Culture and Society in North Africa* (2011) and an editor and contributor to the *Encyclopedia of the Jews in the Islamic World* (2010). He was the 2014–2015 Ina Levine Scholar-in-Residence at the

Mandel Center for Advanced Holocaust Studies of the United States Holocaust Memorial Museum and is currently working on a book with Aomar Boum on Morocco and the Holocaust.

## Notes

Research for this article was made possible thanks to my tenure as Ina Levine Invitational Scholar at the Jack, Joseph and Morton Mandel Center for Advanced Holocaust Studies, United States Holocaust Memorial Museum (USHMM).

1. Norman J. W. Goda, *Tomorrow the World: Hitler, Northwest Africa, and the Path toward America* (College Station, TX, 1998), 16–17.
2. An exception to this general neglect of studying the Spanish Protectorate in the context of the Third Reich is Isabelle Rohr, *The Spanish Right and the Jews, 1898–1945* (Brighton, 2007).
3. Tomás García Figueras, *Marruecos: La acción de España en el Norte de África*, 3rd ed. (Madrid, 1944), 99. All translations in this chapter are my own unless otherwise indicated.
4. Germain Ayache, *Etudes d'histoire marocaine* (Rabat, 1979), 97–109; María Rosa de Madariaga, *Marruecos ese gran desconocido: Breve Historia del protecorado español* (Madrid, 2013), 38–39, 53–54, 58–59; Susan Gilson Miller, *A History of Modern Morocco* (New York, 2013), 24–27.
5. On Spanish colonization in the Western Sahara, see Tony Hodges, "The Western Sahara File," *Third World Quarterly* 6, no. 1 (1984).
6. Madariaga, *Marruecos*, 61–69. For a general survey of the politics that led to the colonial division of Morocco, see C. R. Pennell, *Morocco since 1830: A History* (New York, 2000).
7. Madariaga, *Marruecos,* 88–90; Pennell, *Morocco,* 166–174. On Tangier, see Graham H. Stuart, *The International City of Tangier* (Stanford, CA, 1955).
8. C. R. Pennell, *A Country with a Government and a Flag: The Rif War in Morocco, 1921–1926* (Wisbech, 1986); Madariaga, *Marruecos,* 129–170.
9. Sebastian Balfour, *Deadly Embrace: Morocco and the Road to the Spanish Civil War* (Oxford, 2002); Shannon E. Fleming, "Spanish Morocco and the Alzamiento Nacional, 1936–1939: The Military, Economic and Political Mobilization of a Protectorate," *Journal of Contemporary History* 18, no. 1 (1983); Stanley G. Payne, *The Franco Regime, 1936–1975* (Madison, WI, 1987), 70–75; Madariaga, *Marruecos,* 142–150, 161–163, 169–170, 257–275, 325–335.
10. Rohr, *Spanish Right,* 12–13, 19–25.
11. Ibid., 19–25; Bernd Rother, *Franco y el Holocausto* (Madrid, 2005), 33–39. For an extensive study on philo-Sephardism, and its connection to Morocco, see Michal Rose Friedman, "Recovering Jewish Spain: Politics, Historiography and Institutionalization of the Jewish Past in Spain (1845–1935)," PhD diss., Columbia University, 2012.
12. Rohr, *Spanish Right,* 19–25.
13. Ibid., 17–18, 21–24.

14. Rother, *Franco*, 54.
15. Rohr, *Spanish Right*, 68.
16. Ibid., 65–96.
17. A recent study focusing on Nazi relations with Muslims and the Islamic world during World War II states that Berlin showed little interest in the Muslim population of the Middle East and North Africa, satisfied that the region was "justly under European imperial rule," and that this only changed as a result of German military involvement in the Maghrib. See David Motadel, *Islam and Nazi Germany's War* (Cambridge, MA, 2014), 74–75. Yet, another study asserts that even before World War II, Hitler was interested in imperial expansion in the Maghrib and Africa, inspired by Mussolini's actions in Libya and East Africa, which served as a model for German colonial ambitions. See Patrick Bernhard, "Borrowing from Mussolini: Nazi Germany's Colonial Aspirations in the Shadow of Italian Expansionism," *Journal of Imperial and Commonwealth History* 41, no. 4 (2013). Efforts to undermine French and British influence through courting Arab and Pan-Arab nationalists were well underway in the 1930s, as the case for Morocco suggests.
18. Bibliothèque Nationale du Royaume du Maroc, Rabat (hereinafter BNR), C 390, in United States Holocaust Memorial Museum Collections Division, Archives Branch (herineafter USHMM), RG-81.0024M, 4 December 1936, Note sur l'action allemande au Maroc français et les moyens de coordonnner l'action de nos differents services d'information.
19. In 1934, the French intelligence reports received "information from a good source" that a "Popular League for Germanism in Morocco" was founded in Germany with the aim of propaganda among the Muslim population. BNR, C 390 in USHMM, RG-81.0024M, Rabat, 8 September 1934
20. BNR, C 390 in USHMM, RG-81.0024M, 20 September 1934, Contrôleur Civil of Petitjean (Sidi Kacem).
21. Mohammed Kenbib, *Juifs et musulmans au Maroc, 1859–1948* (Rabat, 1994), 529–530.
22. Already in 1934, the French were alarmed about information on German funding of the nationalist movement in North Africa. BNR, C 390 in USHMM, RG-81.0024M, 5 November 1934.
23. The Berber *Dahir* of 1930 was in fact the culmination of efforts by the French administration to separate Berbers from the beginning of the Protectorate through a process of invention and reform of Berber customary law. See Adam Guerin, "Racial Myth, Colonial Reform and the Invention of Customary Law in Morocco, 1912–1930," *Journal of North African Studies* 16, no. 3 (2011); Gilles Lafuente, *La politique berbère de la France et le nationalisme marocain* (Paris, 1999).
24. Lafuente, *La politique berbère*, 227–240; Raja Adal, "Constructing Transnational Islam: The East-West Network of Shakib Arslan," in *Intellectuals in the Modern Islamic World*, ed. Stéphane A. Dudoignon, Komatsu Hisao, and Kosugi Yasushi (London, 2006), 197–202.
25. The resident general circulated a secret memo to the contrôleurs civils and generals throughout Morocco to monitor German propaganda. BNR, C 390 in USHMM, RG-81.0024M, Rabat, 22 November 1934, J. Helleu.

26. BNR, C 390 in USHMM, RG-81.0024M, 19 June 1935, Contrôleur Civil of Petit Jean (Sidi Kacem).
27. BNR, C 390 in USHMM, RG-81.0024M, 5 November 1935.
28. BNR, C 390 in USHMM, RG-81.0024M, 4 December 1936, Note sur l'action allemande au Maroc français et les moyens de coordonnner l'action de nos differents services d'information.
29. BNR, C 390 in USHMM, RG-81.0024M, 11 December 1934, vice-consul of France in Larache.
30. Secret report on German activities in Morocco in BNR, C 392, RG-81.0027, 5 November 1936. Rohr, *Spanish Right*, 86. Membership in Nazi party cells abroad was strictly limited to German nationals.
31. BNR, C 390 in USHMM, RG-81.0024M, 10 April 1935, Direction des Services de Sécurité du Maroc. Reports also in 1937 of Torres and Bennouna channeling money to Allal al-Fassi. BNR, C392 in USHMM, RG-81.0026, 11 October 1937.
32. BNR, C 390 in USHMM, RG-81.0024M, Rabat, 30 April 1935, Contrôleur Civil Peyssonnel.
33. BNR, C 390 in USHMM, RG-81.0024M. On the Moroccan nationalist figures who made the "pilgrimage" to Berlin during the Third Reich, see Jamaâ Baïda, "Le Maroc et la propaganda du IIIème Reich," *Hespéris-Tamuda* 28 (1990): 92–93, 99–100.
34. Madariaga, *Marruecos*, 218–231. On the connection between Moroccan nationalists and the Pan-Islamic movement and on the Palestine issue and its repercussions on Muslim-Jewish relations in Morocco, see Kenbib, *Juifs et Musulman*, 524–529.
35. Mohammed al-Kholti invited Jews to reject Zionism and join common cause with Muslims to defend their Moroccan homeland. Some Muslims in Algeria supported Jews in establishing branches of the *Ligue internationale contre l'antisémitisme* (LICA) to combat racism and anti-Semitism. See Aomar Boum "Partners against Anti-Semitism: Muslims and Jews Respond to Nazism in French North African Colonies, 1936–1940," *Journal of North African Studies* 19, no. 4 (2014): 554–570.
36. Balfour, *Deadly Embrace*, 273–274.
37. John P. Halstead, *Rebirth of a Nation: The Origins and Rise of Moroccan Nationalism, 1912–1944* (Cambridge, MA, 1969), 243–250; Mostafa Bouaziz, *Aux origines de la koutla démocratique* (Casablanca, 1997), 56–57.
38. Kenbib, *Juifs et musulmans*, 572–573; BNR, C 391 in USHMM, RG-81.0023M, 24 March 1937.
39. BNR, C 391 in USHMM, RG-81.0023M, 29 May 1938.
40. Kenbib, *Juifs et Musulmans*, 574–575.
41. Madariaga, *Marruecos*, 291–299; Kenbib, *Juifs et Musulmans*, 569–570, 573–575.
42. Mokhtar El Harras, "La presse écrite et l'image de l'Allemagne dans la 'zone nord' du Maroc, 1934–1945," in *Marocains et allemands: La perception de l'autre*, ed. Abdelwahed Bendaoud and Mohamed Berriane, (Rabat, 1995), 21–36.
43. Rohr, *Spanish Right*, 84–85. Rohr refers to the worst excesses taking place in Ceuta and Melilla. Quite possibly, this was because of the somewhat more fa-

vorable attitude toward the Jews of the military officers in charge of the Spanish Protectorate.
44. Balfour, *Deadly Embrace*, 272–276; Goda, *Tomorrow the World*, 55–56.
45. Rohr, *Spanish Right*, 86. The author refers to the feast of *korban*.
46. On Figueras, see Madariaga, *Marruecos*, 283, 307, 338; Rohr, *Spanish Right*, 87, 103–104.
47. Rohr, *Spanish Right*, 88–89, 99; Madariaga, *Marruecos*, 278–279.
48. USHMM, 1996.a.0329, Selected Records from the Foreign Ministry of Spain. Rome, 15 July 1939, José de Yanguas, report from the Spanish Embassy in Italy on an article in the newspaper, "Regime Fascista," based on an article in the Heraldo de Aragón, which criticizes the Jews for celebrating a victory which had liberated the country from the grips of "Jewish Bolshevism"; Rohr, *Spanish Right*, 103.
49. BNR, C 391 in USHMM, RG-81.0023M, 2 November 1939, Noguès to French foreign minister. Noguès is forwarding tracts discovered on 2 October in French with Arabic translation.
50. BNR, C 391 in USHMM, RG-81.0023M, Rabat, 10 February 1940. On expansion of German propaganda efforts, see Baïda, "Le Maroc et la propaganda," 97–98.
51. BNR C 392 in USHMM, RG-81.0026M, Tangier, 8 May 1940; Rabat, 30 April 1940.
52. BNR, C 391 in USHMM, RG-81.0023M, 26 September 1939.
53. Goda, *Tomorrow the World*, 56.
54. BNR, C 391 in USHMM, RG-81.0023M, Casablanca, 12 September 1939.
55. BNR, C 391 in USHMM, RG-81.0023M, 3 October 1939. Among the Arab recruits in Germany were a number of Moroccans. Baïda, "Le Maroc et la propagande," 92.
56. On Noguès, see William A. Hoisington Jr., *The Casablanca Connection: French Colonial Policy, 1936–1943* (Chapel Hill, NC, 1984).
57. Michel Abitbol, "Waiting for Vichy: Europeans and Jews in North Africa on the Eve of World War II," *Yad Vashem Studies* 14 (1981); Sophie B. Roberts, "Anti-Semitism and Municipal Government in Interwar French Colonial Algeria," *Journal of North African Studies* 17, no. 5 (2012); Joshua Cole, "Constantine before the Riots of August 1934: Civil Status, Anti-Semitism, and the Politics of Assimilation in Interwar French Algeria," *Journal of North African Studies* 17, no. 5 (2012).
58. Abitbol, "Waiting for Vichy," 154–155; Michel Abitbol, *The Jews of North Africa during the Second World War* (Detroit, 1989), 35–36.
59. Abitbol, *Jews of North Africa*, 62–74; Michael M. Laskier, "Between Vichy Antisemitism and German Harassment: The Jews of North Africa during the Early 1940s," *Modern Judaism* 11, no. 3 (1991); Daniel J. Schroeter, "Vichy in Morocco: The Residency, Mohammed V, and His Indigenous Jewish Subjects," in *Colonialism and the Jews*, ed. Ethan B. Katz, Lisa Moses Leff, and Maud S. Mandel (Bloomington, IN, 2017), 219-221.
60. Schroeter, "Vichy in Morocco," 221-231.
61. Francis R. Nicosia, *Nazi Germany and the Arab World* (New York, 2015), 142–144; Payne, *Franco Regime*, 268–273; Payne, *Franco and Hitler: Spain,*

*Germany, and World War II* (New Haven, CT, 2008), 64–86; Goda, *Tomorrow the World*, 113–164.
62. Enrique Arquès, *El Momento de España en Marruecos* (Madrid, 1943), 126.
63. Figueras, *Marruecos,* 347.
64. Ibid., 347–348; Payne, *Franco and Hitler: Spain, Germany and World War II* (New Haven, CT, 2008), 131; Goda, *Tomorrow the World*, 57–58, 128–132; National Archives and Records Administration (hereinafter NARA), RG 59, General Records of the Department of State, Box 5760. 30 December 1940, Tangier, White, enclosing a memorandum of El-Khazen on "Spanish moves in the three zones of Morocco" and a report on the suppression of the *mendoub,* 20 March 1941, Wallace Murray.
65. Rohr, *Spanish Right,* 103–106.
66. Kenbib, *Juifs et Musulmans,* 618–621.
67. Ministère des Affaires Étrangères (hereinafter MAE)-Paris, AD, Vichy-Maroc, vol. 18, carton 6, dossier 1, in USHMM, RG-43.006M, reel 1, Madrid, 15 December 1941, Communiqué on "La question juive au Maroc d'après la propaganda espagnole," from the French embassy in Spain to Darlan.
68. Schroeter, "Vichy in Morocco," 239-241.
69. Translation of an article in *Al-Ḥurriya,* sent on 25 August 1941 in MAE-Paris, AD, Vichy-Maroc, vol. 15, in USHMM, RG-43.006M, reel 1, vol. 18. Torrès, unlike his rival Naciri and some of the nationalists in Tetuan who deployed racist discourse, was still interested in maintaining entente between Muslims and Jews, and seems here to be "playing the German card." Kenbib, *Juifs et Musulmans,* 575, 614–615. No anti-Jewish diatribes are found in Torrès's collected writings and speeches, though the question of Palestine does come up occasionally. 'Abd al-Khāliq al-Ṭurrīs, *Min turāth al-Ṭurrīs* (Rabat, n.d.).
70. USHMM, 1996a.0329. This document is reprinted in full, in English translation, in Appendix H.
71. BNR, D 667 in USHMM, RG-81.0012M, 1 October 1941.
72. Antonio Marquina Barrio and Gloria Inés Ospino, *España y los judíos en el siglo XX: La acción exterior* (Madrid, 1987), 41–79; Rother, *Franco,* 43–51.
73. USHMM, 1996a.0329. Vichy, 16 September 1942, Lequerica, with enclosed letter in translation from the French government.
74. BNR, D 667 in USHMM, RG-81.0012M, Rabat, 9 May 1942.
75. Cited in Leland L. Bowie, "An Aspect of Muslim-Jewish Relations in Late Nineteenth-Century Morocco: A European Diplomatic View," *International Journal of Middle East Studies* 7, no. 1 (1976): 5.
76. USHMM, 1996.a.0329, Report on the Jews (1942?)
77. USHMM, 1996.a.0329, 25 October 1941, Orgaz to the Minister of Foreign Affairs, Madrid.
78. Schroeter, "Vichy in Morocco," 227–231.
79. Haim Avni, *Spain, the Jews, and Franco* (Philadelphia, 1982), 89–90; Rohr, *Spanish Right,* 120.
80. BNR, D 667 in USHMM, RG-81.0012M, 1 October 1941, with letter from Cohen Ohana attached.
81. USHMM, 1996a.0329, Vichy, 16 March 1942.

82. USHMM, RG-36-002M. Spanish Diplomatic and Consular Correspondence, reel 4, note verbale, Vichy 31 October 1942, Ministère des Affaires Etrangères; 7 November 1942, Consulate-General of Spain, Rabat. See also Schroeter, "Vichy in Morocco," 83.
83. MAE-Nantes, Protectorat Maroc, Direction de l'Interieur, 1MA/250, article 1, in USHMM, RG-43.154, 17 June 1943, "Note sur la question juive au Maroc." See also Schroeter, "Vichy in Morocco," 230.
84. Rohr, *Spanish Right*, 131.
85. An inquiry was made by Easterman, the political secretary of the World Jewish Congress to the Spanish ambassador in London on reports on anti-Jewish demonstrations in Tangier, asking what steps the Spanish authorities were taking. USHMM, 1996.a.0329, 13 September 1943 and 20 December 1943.
86. Nicosia, *Nazi Germany and the Arab World*, 236–237. On the increased German propaganda in North Africa after the allied landings, see Charles-Robert Ageron, "Les populations du Maghreb face à la propagande allemande," *Revue d'Histoire de la Deuxième Guerre Mondiale* 29, no. 114 (1979): 28–39.
87. María Rosa de Madariaga, "Confrontation in the Spanish Zone (1945–56): Franco, the Nationalists, and the Post-War Politics of Decolonisation," *Journal of North African Studies* 19, no. 4 (2014).
88. Tomás García Figueras, *España y su protectorado en Marruecos, 1912–1956* (Madrid, 1957), 184.
89. USHMM, 1996a.0329. Paris, 7 December 1940, Mario de Pinies. As proposed by the minister-counselor, chargé d'affaires of the Spanish embassy, Embassy of Spain in Paris.
90. Avni, *Spain, the Jews, and Franco*, 84–85.
91. Rother, *Franco*, 195–238; Payne, *Franco and Hitler*, 222–228.
92. Avni, *Spain, the Jews and Franco*, 72–79; Rother, *Franco*, 158. Rohr, *Spanish Right*, 138–153.
93. Rother, *Franco*, 291–349, Payne, *Franco and Hitler*, 225–228.
94. The WJC came to be regarded by Spain as "the recognized body of world Jewry" and the "favored interlocutor on the matters regarding Jewish refugees." Rohr, *Spanish Right*, 132–133.
95. USHMM, 1996.a.0329, Madrid, 17 March 1944; Rother, *Franco*, 387.
96. The World Jewish Congress New York Office Records, H255, file 2 in USHMM, 67.014M, reel 257, Tetuan, 21 April 1944, Benmaman and Hassan to Leon Kubowitzki; 23 June 1944, Arieh Tartekower and Baruch Zuckerman; 7 September 1944, Benmaman and Hassan to WJC.
97. USHMM, 1996.a.0329, 12 November 1944, Report of the Ministry of Foreign Relations.
98. Rother, *Franco*, 387–397; "World Jewish Congress $10,000,000 Drive No Challenge to Other Groups, Leaders Say," *Jewish Telegraphic Agency*, 3 December 1944.
99. Raphael Minder, "Spain Approves Citizenship Path for Sephardic Jews," *New York Times*, 11 June 2015.
100. Gil Shefler, "Spanish Muslims, or Moriscos, Seek Parity with Jews Expelled from Spain," *Washington Post*, 5 June 2014.

101. Lisa Goldman, "Spain's Offer of Citizenship to Sephardim Raises Questions," *Al Jazeera America*, 17 June 2015; Shira Rubin, "Five Centuries after It Kicked Them Out, Spain Welcomes Back Sephardic Jews," *New Republic*, 20 May 2015; Alan Clendenning, "Spain Grants Citizenship to 4,300 with Sephardic Jew Roots," *Associated Press*, 2 October 2015.

# Bibliography
## Archival Sources

Archivo General de la Administración del Ministerio de Cultura, Madrid. United States Holocaust Memorial Museum (USHMM), Washington, DC., RG-36.
Bibliothèque Nationale du Royaume du Maroc, Rabat. USHMM, RG-81.
Foreign Ministry of Spain, selected records. USHMM, 1996.a.0329.
Ministère des Affaires Étrangères, France. USHMM, RG-43.
National Archives and Records Administration, College Park, MD.
World Jewish Congress New York Office Records. USHMM, 67.014M.

## Published Sources

Abitbol, Michel. *The Jews of North Africa during the Second World War*. Detroit, 1989.
———. "Waiting for Vichy: Europeans and Jews in North Africa on the Eve of World War II." *Yad Vashem Studies* 14 (1981): 139–166.
Adal, Raja. "Constructing Transnational Islam: The East-West Network of Shakib Arslan." In *Intellectuals in the Modern Islamic World*, edited by Stéphane A. Dudoignon, Komatsu Hisao, and Kosugi Yasushi, 176–210. London, 2006.
Ageron, Charles-Robert. "Les populations du Maghreb face à la propagande allemande." *Revue d'Histoire de la Deuxième Guerre Mondiale* 29, no. 114 (1979): 1–39.
Arquès, Enrique. *El Momento de España en Marruecos*. Madrid, 1943.
Avni, Haim. *Spain, the Jews, and Franco*. Philadelphia, 1982.
Ayache, Germain. *Etudes d'histoire marocaine*. Rabat, 1979.
Baïda, Jamaâ. "Le Maroc et la propaganda du IIIème Reich." *Hespéris-Tamuda* 28 (1990): 91–106.
Balfour, Sebastian. *Deadly Embrace: Morocco and the Road to the Spanish Civil War*. Oxford, 2002.
Barrio, Antonio Marquina, and Gloria Inés Ospino. *España y los judíos en el siglo XX: La acción exterior*. Madrid, 1987.
Bernhard, Patrick. "Borrowing from Mussolini: Nazi Germany's Colonial Aspirations in the Shadow of Italian Expansionism." *Journal of Imperial and Commonwealth History* 41, no. 4 (2013): 617–643.
Bouaziz, Mostafa. *Aux origines de la koutla democratique*. Casablanca, 1997.
Boum, Aomar. "Partners against Anti-Semitism: Muslims and Jews Respond to Nazism in French North African Colonies, 1936–1940." *Journal of North African Studies* 19, no. 4 (2014): 554–570.

Bowie, Leland L. "An Aspect of Muslim-Jewish Relations in Late Nineteenth-Century Morocco: A European Diplomatic View." *International Journal of Middle East Studies* 7, no. 1 (1976): 3–19.

Cole, Joshua. "Constantine before the Riots of August 1934: Civil Status, Anti-Semitism, and the Politics of Assimilation in Interwar French Algeria." *Journal of North African Studies* 17, no. 5 (2012): 839–861.

El Harras, Mokhtar. "La presse écrite et l'image de l'Allemagne dans la 'zone nord' du Maroc, 1934–1945." In *Marocains et allemands: La perception de l'autre*, edited by Abdelwahed Bendaoud and Mohamed Berriane, 21–36. Rabat, 1995.

Figueras, Tomás García. *España y su protectorado en Marruecos, 1912–1956*. Madrid, 1957.

——. *Marruecos: La acción de España en el Norte de África*. 3rd ed. Madrid, 1944.

Fleming, Shannon E. "Spanish Morocco and the Alzamiento Nacional, 1936–1939: The Military, Economic and Political Mobilization of a Protectorate." *Journal of Contemporary History* 18, no. 1 (1983): 27–42.

Friedman, Michal Rose. "Recovering Jewish Spain: Politics, Historiography and Institutionalization of the Jewish Past in Spain (1845–1935)." PhD dissertation. Columbia University, 2012.

Goda, Norman J. W. *Tomorrow the World: Hitler, Northwest Africa, and the Path toward America*. College Station, TX, 1998.

Guerin, Adam. "Racial Myth, Colonial Reform and the Invention of Customary Law in Morocco, 1912–1930." *Journal of North African Studies* 16, no. 3 (2011): 361–380.

Halstead, John P. *Rebirth of a Nation: The Origins and Rise of Moroccan Nationalism, 1912–1944*. Cambridge, MA, 1969.

Hodges, Tony. "The Western Sahara File," *Third World Quarterly* 6, no. 1 (1984): 74–116.

Hoisington, William A., Jr. *The Casablanca Connection: French Colonial Policy, 1936–1943*. Chapel Hill, NC, 1984.

Kenbib, Mohammed. *Juifs et musulmans au Maroc, 1859–1948*. Rabat, 1994.

Lafuente, Gilles. *La politique berbère de la France et le nationalisme marocain*. Paris, 1999.

Laskier, Michael M. "Between Vichy Antisemitism and German Harassment: The Jews of North Africa during the Early 1940s." *Modern Judaism* 11, no. 3 (1991): 348–355.

Madariaga, María Rosa de. "Confrontation in the Spanish Zone (1945–56): Franco, the Nationalists, and the Post-War Politics of Decolonisation." *Journal of North African Studies* 19, no. 4 (2014): 490–500.

——. *Marruecos ese gran desconocido: Breve historia del protecorado español*. Madrid, 2013.

*Marruecos: La acción de España en el Norte de África*, 3rd ed. Madrid, 1944.

Miller, Susan Gilson. *A History of Modern Morocco*. New York, 2013.

Motadel, David. *Islam and Nazi Germany's War*. Cambridge, MA, 2014.

Nicosia, Francis R. *Nazi Germany and the Arab World*. New York, 2015.

Payne, Stanley G. *Franco and Hitler: Spain, Germany, and World War II*. New Haven, CT, 2008.

——. *The Franco Regime, 1936–1975*. Madison, WI, 1987.

Pennell, C. R. *A Country with a Government and a Flag: The Rif War in Morocco, 1921–1926.* Wisbech, 1986.

———. *Morocco since 1830: A History.* New York, 2000.

Roberts, Sophie B. "Anti-Semitism and Municipal Government in Interwar French Colonial Algeria." *Journal of North African Studies* 17, no. 5 (2012): 821–837.

Rohr, Isabelle. *The Spanish Right and the Jews, 1898–1945.* Brighton, 2007.

Rother, Bernd. *Franco y el Holocausto.* Translated by Leticia Artiles Gracia. Madrid, 2005.

Schroeter, Daniel J. "Vichy in Morocco: The Residency, Mohammed V, and His Indigenous Jewish Subjects." In *Colonialism and the Jews,* ed. Ethan B. Katz, Lisa Moses Leff, and Maud S. Mandel, 215–250. Bloomington, IN, 2017.

Stuart, Graham H. *The International City of Tangier.* Stanford, CA, 1955.

Ṭurrīs, ʿAbd al-Khāliq al-. *Min turāth al-Ṭurrīs.* Rabat, n.d.

# Appendices

## Appendix A
### "The Jewish Question"

Article by Hüseyin Cahit Yalçın, in the Turkish Newspaper
*Yeni Sabah*,[1] 24 January 1939

We currently face a major Jewish question that the world is busy with. A mishandled minor matter has recently brought attention to this issue in our country.[2] Although the incident and the concerns that it generated have been immediately addressed, it would be appropriate to say a few words about this global issue.

First, regarding Jews who are Turkish citizens, we can guarantee that they should have no concerns. The political rights of the Jews who have been peacefully living and working in Turkey for centuries are recognized by the constitution. The Turkish constitution makes no distinction among citizens based on race or religion. All citizens have the right and responsibility of working together as equals and with absolute freedom of conscience for the benefit of the motherland. Although the Republic's government considers the single-party rule as the most favorable form of government for the interests of the country, it has been hesitant to enforce it in a very strict manner. In fact, the Republic has been tolerant enough to even allow in the parliament Jewish representatives who are not members of the Republican People's Party.

All schools are open to the Jewish citizens of Turkey. They can work in any job that they want. They can be appointed as government employees. They can travel to every corner of the country. They can publish newspapers. In sum, they can live in the country just like the Muslim and Turkish majority.

These words are not promises; they are not wishes; nor are they future goals. They constitute the reality of our present day in that if there existed no worldwide Jewish question or if this issue had not generated certain qualms, it would have been unnecessary to mention them here.

There is also absolutely no chance that the rights and responsibilities granted by the constitution to all citizens regardless of race or religion might be altered in the future. I have the authorization to guarantee this in the clearest language possible. I am not stating it as my personal opinion. I say it with a certainty of having noted the opinions and considerations of the highest state authorities in Ankara [the capital of Turkey].

With regard to Jews who are foreign citizens: Since there exists no hostility toward Jews in Turkey, we consider the Jewish question from strictly a humanitarian perspective. The fact that the professors we invited from Europe to our universities include individuals of the Jewish race is proof that our borders have not been closed to the Jewish race in a hostile manner. These professors' regard of our land as their second home and their dedication to the development of our youth and the country's sciences have generated feelings of gratitude among us for their highest character and earnestness.

If necessary, Turkey may come again to the aid of the scientists and people of technology in the same fashion, regardless of any consideration of race. However, the question of opening our borders to all Jewish peoples who have been or will shortly be deported from other countries is an entirely different one. Turkey's economic and social circumstances might prevent the country from allowing Jewish masses in its lands. Thus, although the suffering of the Jewish people in Europe has generated sympathy among us for their struggles, this feeling does not lead to accepting Jewish immigrants in Turkey.

Why do some European countries not want Jews? Those who tend to explain historical developments by economic factors only will certainly try to rationalize the hostility towards Jews by numbers and statistics. I have no doubt, however, that what has been happening in Europe is related to a subconscious hostility related to a two-thousand-year-old bigotry.

I am also sure that, although some European leaders may not personally subscribe to this bigotry, they nevertheless seek the survival of their nations by sacrificing the Jews to the greed and ravenousness of the masses, and they explain this choice by inventing scientific and moral excuses. Economic considerations may appear to justify the appropriation of Jewish wealth and property or the replacement of Jewish workers and professionals with non-Jewish ones. But in reality, the hostility shown to the Jewish people represents a perversion of humanity's major moral and ethical principles. The Turks' devotion to virtues of justice and loyalty, their humane and moral nature, would prevent them from associating with these types of actions.

*Source:* Yalçın, Hüseyin Cahit. "Yahudi Meselesi." *Yeni Sabah,* 24 January 1939, from the personal collection of Corry Guttstadt. Translated from the Turkish by Boğaç Ergene.

# Appendix B

## German–Turkish Non-Aggression Pact Signed at Ankara, 18 June 1941

The German Reich and the Turkish Republic, desiring to place their relations on a basis of mutual trust and sincere friendship, have agreed, without prejudice to existing obligations of the two countries, to conclude a treaty. For that purpose, the following Plenipotentiaries have been appointed:

By the German Reich Chancellor:
Herr Franz von Papen, Ambassador Extraordinary and Plenipotentiary of the German Reich,
By the President of the Turkish Republic:
His Excellency M. Şükrü Saraçoğlu, Deputy from İzmir, Minister of Foreign Affairs,

who, having communicated to each other their full powers, found to be in good and due form, have agreed as follows:

### Article 1

The German Reich and the Turkish Republic undertake mutually to respect the integrity and inviolability of their territories, and not to take measures of any sort aimed directly or indirectly against the other contracting party.

### Article 2

The German Reich and the Turkish Republic undertake in the future to consult with one another in a friendly spirit on all questions affecting their common interests in order to reach an understanding regarding the treatment of such questions.

### Article 3

This treaty shall enter into force on the day of its signing and shall remain in force from that date for a period of ten years; the contracting parties will consult with one another at the appropriate time about an extension of the Treaty.

The Treaty shall be ratified and the instruments of ratification shall be exchanged as soon as possible in Berlin.

Done in duplicate in the German and Turkish languages, the two texts being equally authentic.

Ankara, 18 June 1941

                            Franz von Papen      Ş. Saraçoğlu

*Source*: Documents on German Foreign Policy (DGFP) 1918–1945: Series D, Vol. XII, No. 648 (Washington, DC, 1962), 1051.

## Appendix C

## "Immigration to the United States is Best!! The Supporters of Immigration to Palestine Are Few!!"

Article in the Palestinian Newspaper *Filastin*, 15 July 1938

Évian, 14 July—The sessions of the international conference are coming to an end after the subcommittees heard the representatives of the countries and the Jewish organizations and others, who are concerned with the issue of the Jewish refugees.

A vast amount of "comments" circulated during the conference whose source is [Norman] Bentwich, former attorney general in Palestine, who represented the non-Zionist Jewish leaders in England, such as Lord Herbert Samuel and others. His concern was to convince the representatives of the American countries to accept the highest possible number of Jewish refugees.

No one invokes the name of Palestine or the sending of some of the refugees there except the Jewish Agency's representatives and the emissaries of Dr. Chaim Weizmann, and they hardly number four persons. But the representatives of the other Jewish associations are interested in transferring the refugees to safe countries willing to permanently absorb them, without agitating them with the movements and developments. Their first preference is the United States, and then the colonies of France and England, and then the Latin American commonwealth. The reason for their choice of the American commonwealth is the existence of vast opportunities that can benefit the Jewish refugees and enable them to take advantage of the countries, which suit their spirit and the nature of their businesses.

The important question that the conference tackled was the issue of funds. The Jews have already declared that they are bankrupt, and the countries are confused about who would guarantee the loan [fund] that they intend to create. This international loan will be wasted in vain if it would be designated for the displacement and resettlement works and it would not be possible to recover it. If the money collected for the Jews in America and in other places will be used, Zionism will rise up against this and try to obstruct the conference and offset its understandings on this matter, because the Zionist leaders are firmly convinced that they need to prepare a great amount of millions of dollars for the partition plan in Palestine.

It is understood that the clouds that loomed over the sky of the conference dissipated, and the conference could not escape from dealing with the immigration of some of the refugees to Palestine when the countries' delegations and the Jewish organizations exposed their desire on this aspect.

But the danger of the conference for the Palestine issue and the immigration of Jews there still exists, because the period between the end of the conference and its reconvening next 3 August is enough for the submission of a schedule with names of the countries to which a number of refugees would be sent, and undoubtedly, the Zionists will try to push the name of Palestine among those countries.

*Source: Filastin,* 15 July 1938. Translated from the Arabic by Esther Webman.

# APPENDIX D

## "The Policy of Force and Violence in the World"

Article in the Egyptian Newspaper *Al-Ahram*, 15 November 1938

**New principles undermine the bases of human society's order.**
**The persecution of the Jews in Germany and England's position.**
The reader finds in the news from Germany today new evidence that pity and compassion have no effect on souls, and that the world does not recognize any law but the law of force and any plan but the plan of violence.

This situation threatens to return humanity to the remotest barbaric eras, and to destroy the bases of modern life even if its consequences remain confined to the political and economic spheres. It will adapt and exceed its boundaries and affect the weak souls, which are impressed by success regardless of its kind and reason, and the fragile personal and national principles and values that cannot endure the storms of life.

All those who are still seeking their way to the future, and those who lost their hope because of the events and surrendered to despair, and the unfortunate who rush to disastrous adventures, and those whose lives became filled with fears and doubts and stand confused not sure what to do. All those and others like them consider these lessons, practically imposed by the dictatorial governments on humanity, as lessons that they should necessarily follow and act upon in life. If it will be impressed on the people's minds that force is above the law and nations and individuals can achieve what they want by the force of the gun or the cannon, which fate awaits humanity and what future is in store for it?

If these principles become universal and force dominates the achievement of goals of individuals and nations, life will become a heavy burden for humanity, worthless and ugly. We walk now in the curves of the streets under police protection and we run to them if any incident happens to us. Who would guarantee that it will always be possible to find the police in places of refuge, if the principle of force and violence will penetrate the souls? This is an awful situation for individuals and all the more so for nations.

The victory that the principle of force gained in recent months eliminated all the moral achievements that humanity achieved until now. The religions, enjoining good and forbidding evil, teach people that their duty is to respect the weak and protect his right and that the greatest victory of man is the victory of containing his impulses and desires. The new principles attempt now to destroy them [religions] and disrupt their teachings and prove by the day that these teachings are worthless and insignificant, and the victory over the soul should be preceded by a victory over the other and the suffocating of the weak wherever he is.

No doubt that the incidents presumably now taking place in Germany are unfortunately a new step in the path of these new detrimental principles. It is even more regrettable that no country or nation in the world possesses an effective voice and an effective word to speak on behalf of humanity, since we live now in an era that we can repeat to everyone what Jesus Christ said: "let he who is without sin cast the first stone."

England is the most suited country to raise this voice in view of its history and glorious deeds in the service of humanity. But it barely broadcast yesterday that it is determined to raise its voice in defense of the Jews, and Germany preceded it, warning "take care first of Palestine's Arabs."

The Germans say that Germany is their country and they are entitled to reject whomever they do not want, and that the fine imposed on the Jews – one billion Marks, are the funds taken by them from the Germans themselves. As for Palestine, the English want to bring in other inhabitants, and to fight those natives who do not share their opinion, and they impose on the peaceful inhabitants fines which are, when compared, much heavier than a billion Marks, considering the poverty of those who are expected to pay them.

Thus, it is not easy for England after the incidents in Palestine to advise Germany to behave like it in justice, fairness, and compassion. If it could promote this, its voice could be the loudest voice that Germany hears, and hundreds of thousands of innocent people would have been saved from persecution, considering the good relations, the strengthened ties between the two countries after the Munich meeting, and Germany's zeal to preserve England's friendship and the gains that it is expected to earn from it.

As to the other countries, it is not assumed that their intervention would have any instrumental effect in improving the situation of the Jews in Germany, either because these countries are hostile to Germany like Russia, or compete with it like France, or support it like Italy, or accused of being under Jewish influence like America. Recommendations from all these countries are not expected to lead to the result that one recommendation offered by England to Germany now could accomplish.

*Source: Al-Ahram,* 15 November 1938. Translated from the Arabic by Esther Webman.

# Appendix E

## Memorandum on the Arab Question by the Director of the Political Department of the German Foreign Office, 7 March 1941

Berlin, 7 March 1941

A memorandum on the Arab question is herewith submitted in accordance with instructions.

The memorandum of Minister Grobba,[3] of 18 February, together with the sealed letter of the Grand Mufti to the Führer is submitted again at this time.

Reference is made to the report on Greater Arabia and the situation in Syria by Minister von Hentig.[4] Use has been made of the conclusions of that report in the present memorandum.

Herewith submitted to the Foreign Minister through the State Secretary.[5]

Woermann[6]

[Enclosure]

Berlin, 7 March 1941.
Pol. VII 123 g. Rs.

### MEMORANDUM ON THE ARAB QUESTION

The instruction was that a proposal be drawn up for the further handling of the Arab question, especially on how this problem is to be handled with reference to our aim of achieving England's defeat. *A summary of the proposals will be found at the end of this memorandum.*

(I) *Delimitation of the Arab Area*

Consideration of the Arab question, for the purposes of the present memorandum, will be limited to the following countries: Saudi Arabia, Yemen, Iraq, the British sphere of influence in the Arabian peninsula and the mandated territories of Palestine, Transjordan, Syria, and Lebanon.

The Arab sphere includes also Egypt and the Anglo-Egyptian Sudan. These countries, however, have been considered here only as required in the context. A map is attached as annex.

Annex 2 contains the population figures for these countries as also the number of Arabs in the most important North African territories, which also are not being considered here.

A complex system of treaties exists among the Arab states and between them and Turkey and Afghanistan, as shown in Annex 3. Friend and foe in the Arab world are intermingled in a motley pattern. For this reason alone, it cannot be expected that anything will remain secret.

The Islamic idea (Holy War) is impracticable under the present grouping of powers. Arab nationality and Islam are not identical. The Arabs to be brought into our plans are fighting not for religious, but for political, aims. The questions touching Islam, however, must be dealt with tactfully.

(II) *The Significance of the Arab Area*
Seen in the context of the war with England, the Arab area holds a position of great strategic significance. The Arab area, which includes the Suez Canal, one of the most important English sea routes, forms a land bridge between Africa and India. Vast numbers of troops and war material have been shipped in the east-west direction to Egypt, and war material to Turkey and probably also to Greece through Iraq, Transjordan, and Palestine. There is a possibility that now, with British troops released in North Africa, a movement in the opposite direction will also take place: Palestine and Transjordan as possible jump-off points for an English thrust toward Syria, or through Syria in the event of an intervention in Turkey. Reports about English intentions in this respect are increasing.

These territories are of special importance for the air routes of the British Empire.

Essential for Britain's conduct of the war are finally the oil fields of Mosul with the pipeline to the Mediterranean; for particulars, see Annex 4, with special map.

(III) *Possibilities for Action in the Arab Area*
A *decisive* blow to the British Empire could be delivered in this area only through operations against Egypt and/or military occupation of the Arabian land bridge.

An appraisal of the operational possibilities, including those of the Luftwaffe, is not the subject of this memorandum. This is a problem, however, that deserves our greatest attention. We may reasonably proceed from the assumption that this area lies beyond the effective range of the Axis Powers *at the present time* – except with respect to the Luftwaffe. This situation will not change as long as Turkey remains neutral.

The remaining opportunities for action in the Arab area have for the time being no decisive bearing on our aim of crushing England. This does not mean, however, that these opportunities should not be exploited in every manner.

The leadership in the Arab question is claimed by Egypt, as well as by King Ibn Saud and Iraq. While certain contacts with Egypt still exist, the country is at the moment more or less out of the picture in this connection, as far as we are concerned. Rather, our potential partners are King Ibn Saud and the Iraq Government.

In addition to these, the *Grand Mufti* of Jerusalem,[7] who is now living in Baghdad, occupies a recognized if not entirely unchallenged position of leadership among the Arabs. At least he enjoys recognition as a front. Information on his person will be found in Annex 5. Liaison with him is maintained through his secretary who has several times been in Berlin and Rome, and is now in Berlin. The main thread of the all-Arabian question should be spun in this way.

A sealed letter from the Grand Mufti to the Führer, which the secretary left here, is being separately submitted. It will not be necessary to grant to the Grand Mufti the monopoly of the all-Arabian questions, which he is seeking to obtain. Rather, it is desirable to keep on maintaining other contacts such as with Ibn Saud and directly with the Iraq Government, or the contacts again started in Syria by Minister von Hentig; these latter of course only insofar as they do not involve us in a conflict with the Grand Mufti.

Specifically, the following possibilities may be taken under consideration apart from any military action:

(1) *Propaganda*
Propaganda will be conducted mainly by radio broadcasts in the Arabic language, the exertion of influence on Arab newspapers and periodicals, the cultivation of personal relations with individual Arabs, etc. The machinery for this is [available] (see Annex 6), and efforts for improving it are continuing.

Additionally, something conspicuous needs to be done from time to time, such as the dispatch of Minister von Hentig to Syria.

The reception of Ibn Saud's representative, Khalid al Hud, by the Führer had a telling effect.

(2) *Sabotage and Uprisings*
In the area referred to, the Arabs can be of value to us to a limited extent by carrying out acts of sabotage and uprisings. The Grand Mufti and his men are to some extent already active in this respect. Further organizing activities in this regard would be primarily a matter for the Abwehr. So far, in compliance with the wishes of the Foreign Minister, it has refrained from action for the most part, especially out of consideration for Italy. Greater latitude of action in this respect, also with a view to improving the intelligence system, is essential in the interest of the struggle against England. The Italian Government could be informed of this in quite general terms, without any details being disclosed, so as to ensure secrecy. Acts of sabotage could be carried out in Egypt, Transjordan, Palestine, and against the English installations in Iraq. Uprisings would at this time be of some purpose only in Palestine and Transjordan, but not in the other countries, including Syria and Lebanon.

Admiral Canaris[8] has requested that activities along these lines be authorized in writing.

(3) *Political Declaration for Greater Arabia*
The Arabs have pointed out time and again that they are ready to enter a relentless struggle against England, but that they would have to know what goals they were fighting for. They consequently seek a declaration stating that Germany and Italy promise them the full independence of a future Greater Arab empire on a federative basis. They have indicated that such a declaration would be the essential prerequisite for an open struggle against England. The declaration that we issued earlier over the radio and in the press, and also in writing (Annex 7), is too vague, as had been emphatically stated here by the Grand Mufti's secretary and as we also have learned through the Italian Minister in Baghdad. The scope of the Arab wishes in this regard is indicated by the proposal that the Grand Mufti's secretary has presented to Minister Grobba (Annex 8).

Purely from the standpoint of German interests, there could be no objection to such a political declaration. Given the Arabs' dislike of the English and of the Italians, it would certainly be easy for us to attain a position of influence in a Greater Arab empire. To be sure, there is no uniform opinion regarding the question whether the Arabs are sufficiently mature for such a form of state, however. The weakness of such a state would lie in the absence of the possibility for self-defense. This problem need not, however, stand in the way of giving them such a declaration now. The difficulties, rather, arise from considerations relating to other powers.

(a) Considerations for Italy
We are aware that the Italian Government is pursuing plans of its own in the Near East; for achieving these, broad guarantees of full independence and federation of the Arab states are undesirable. In dealing with us the Italian Government has therefore been very reserved on the Arab question until a short time ago. Recently there has been a certain relaxation of this attitude; it has kept us better informed than before, as for example, by referring to the Grand Mufti's secretary, who first came to Rome, to us in Berlin. The cautious attitude of the Italian Government is indicated by the draft of a declaration, handed in by the Italian chargé d'affaires here in February, which is so tortuous that it would be preferable to have it dropped (Annex 9).

A decision should be made whether an open discussion should be entered into with the Italian Government, to have it define its objectives in the Arab area. The moment for this, however, does not seem to have arrived as yet.

(b) Considerations for France?
A declaration issued at this time favoring a Greater Arabia would, because of Syria, be contrary to our general policy of not including the French colonial empire, at the present time, among the subjects under discussion. As it is, it has already been necessary to depart from this principle because of our Japanese policy. Such a policy could have the result that the already strong de Gaulle movement in Syria might bring about an open defection to the de Gaulle camp; the necessary support in this matter could be supplied by the English in Palestine and Transjordan. Even France herself and other parts of her colonial empire might in this way be driven further toward de Gaulle and England.

Ambassador Abetz,[9] who was consulted on this point, has stated his view of the subject, as indicated in Annex 10; in this connection he correctly calls attention to the terms of the Armistice Agreement.

As regards France, this question is of more than mere tactical significance at the moment. Underlying it is also the question whether French influence in Syria is to continue at all.

These questions, too, are not yet ripe for discussion.

(c) Considerations for Turkey?
Ambassador von Papen[10] has repeatedly spoken in favor of discussions with the Turks on Arab questions. For practical purposes, this would

mean among other things that Turkey could be promised a portion of Syria under certain conditions.

It remains to be decided whether this consideration should be included in our calculations at the present time.

(d) Considerations for the Soviet Union?
The question to be decided would be whether, e.g., as regards Iraq, our Arab policy must take account of the Soviet Union (diversion of Soviet aspirations toward the south).

When all these factors are taken into account, it appears to be difficult in any case to issue a declaration in favor of a Greater Arab federation, which is based on an accord with Italy and goes substantially beyond our former declaration. Some kind of reaction to the wishes expressed by the Grand Mufti and to his letter addressed to the Führer, which could be given to the Grand Mufti's secretary to take along, would however be desirable (see draft, Annex 11).

In any event, it will always be safe to repeat in talks with the Arabs that the victory of the Axis Powers is certain, that Germany has no territorial ambitions in this area, and that we are linked with the Arabs by being opponents of their English oppressors; that we share their views on the Jewish question and that the Arabs can always be sure of our support within practical limits whenever they themselves take up the struggle against England.

(4) *Assistance by Arms and Ammunition*
In the present circumstances, such assistance should be considered mainly with regard to Iraq. Smaller shipment of arms, e.g., to Palestine, could easily be effected as part of the task assigned to the Abwehr.

The Iraq army, according to the information available, consists of four or five fully equipped divisions and one good constabulary division.

The Iraq Government has approached us, Italy, and Japan with the request for arms and ammunition. The question will have to be considered first of all from the point of view of German capabilities for delivery. The Iraqis want, immediately,

400 light machine guns with ammunition,
50 light tanks,
10 antiaircraft batteries with ammunition and instruments,
high explosives,
antitank material, including machines,
100,000 gas masks,

and, in addition, equipment for a full division. This matter has been the subject of discussions between the specialist of the Economic Policy Department and the OKW;[11] details of this are found in Annex 12. According to it, neither captured English arms nor arms from German Army stocks may in any substantial quantities be released without the Führer's authorization. It will not be necessary to seek such an authorization, however, until the question of a route for the transport of the material has been definitely settled. Since the route through the Soviet Union must be ruled out, there is no route except through Turkey. Today, Turkey would surely refuse transit of shipments to Iraq. But since Turkey permits transit of arms shipments to Iran and Afghanistan, the question is now being studied of whether it might not be possible, under some camouflage, to add such shipments to those going to Iran. This matter, too, has been dealt with in Annex 12. This could not be accomplished, however, without the cooperation of either the Iranian or the Afghan Government. A suitable middleman would be the Afghan Minister of Economics, Abdul Majid, who is here now and who can be regarded as reliable.

The Japanese Government has so far shown great reserve with regard to Iraq's wishes to obtain assistance in arms. The discussions have been suspended since the reorganization of the Iraq Government. The objective of Japanese deliveries of arms should be actively pursued through Ambassador Oshima.

(5) *Financial Support*
This is to be taken under consideration with respect to Iraq and the Grand Mufti.

(a) Iraq would like to obtain financial support in the form of easy credit terms in connection with the arms deliveries. This request could be granted if arms transactions should come about.
(b) Iraq also wants a pledge of financial support in the event that she should enter the struggle against England. A general statement on this point could be issued even at this time.
(c) The Grand Mufti has repeatedly asked for financial support for his own plans, especially for sabotage and uprisings in Palestine and Transjordan. The Foreign Minister agreed in principle to such financial support some time ago, making it, however, contingent on Italy's concurrence. Consulted on this matter, the Italian Government replied at the time that it was already supplying the Grand

Mufti with so much money that it did not feel that any additional support was necessary. It is characteristic of the increasing relaxation of the Italian attitude toward us in the Arab question, that recently the Italian chargé d'affaires brought up the subject again on his own accord, informing us in accordance with instructions that the Italian Government had no longer any objection to any support given by Germany, but merely wished that it be kept informed in the same fashion as it had kept us informed of the financial assistance which it had extended. The Grand Mufti's secretary has mentioned a required amount of £20,000 a month, to be supplied in equal shares by us and by Italy. A support in such an amount appears to be unnecessary at this time. It is therefore suggested that for the time being the Grand Mufti receive the equivalent of 100,000 Reichsmarks through the suitable channels and in the appropriate ways.

(6) *Inducing Iraq to Enter the War*
In conversations that were held between the Italian chargé d'affaires in Baghdad and General Dallah Hudin, in the presence of the then Minister President Gaylani[12] in January 1941, the latter laid down specific political conditions for Iraq's open resistance to England, namely:

The political declaration, dealt with above;
Formation of a national government in Syria;
Neutrality on the part of Turkey and Iran, to be guaranteed by the Axis Powers.

Our position on the political declaration has been stated above. Formation of a national government in Syria, the Italian Government also agrees, would not be in accord with the present situation. No guarantee can be assumed regarding the attitude of Turkey and Iran.

Given the present situation and the facility for English troops to be moved by sea, by way of Basra, and over the Arabian land bridge from Egypt, open resistance by Iraq against England could have only a brief success, and in the final outcome, in the view of the Italian Government too, lead to a success that would strengthen English prestige.

In these circumstances, it must be our policy to keep Iraq's confidence in us alive through the measures discussed above, so that Iraq will strike when the over-all military and political situation makes such action desirable.

If the moment should arrive that our own troops are on the Arabian land bridge or if the moment of England's collapse is near, Iraq could still render valuable services to us, e.g., by sudden destruction of the British airfields and communications in Iraq, annihilation of British troops in transit, and, if circumstances permit, by a thrust in the direction of Transjordan and Palestine.

(7) *Syria*
In accordance with the proposals of Minister von Hentig, a German delegation to the Italian Armistice Commission in Syria should be established, to be headed by Minister von Hentig (formally perhaps in his military capacity of Major in the reserves).

Removal of de Gaulle followers in key positions from Syria.

(IV) *Summary of the Proposals*
(1) With respect to Italy, that country's claim to predominance in the Arab area is not affected, but Germany will take greater initiative, making due allowance for Italian sensibilities. A change to that effect is already under way.
(2) Expansion of propaganda activities.
(3) Authorizing the Abwehr to develop its intelligence system in the Arab area, to undertake acts of sabotage, and instigate uprisings in Palestine and Transjordan.
(4) Further examination of the possibilities of a political declaration, jointly with the Italian government. A declaration in favor of a Greater Arab federation taking full account of the wishes of the Arabs is impracticable at this time out of consideration for Italy and other powers.

A friendly interim reply to the Grand Mufti's secretary, in conformity with Annex 11, perhaps with reference to the Grand Mufti's letter to the Führer, which should, however, not be answered by the Führer himself.
(5) Further following up of the matter of support by means of arms and ammunition. If necessary, a decision of the Führer may be requested, once the question is sufficiently clarified.

Authorization for the Economic Policy Department to discuss the matter with the Afghan Minister of Economics, Abdul Majid. Ambassador Oshima is to pursue further the matter of Japanese arms deliveries.
(6) Financial support according to the proposals, especially immediate payment of the equivalent of 100,000 Reichsmarks to the Grand Mufti.

(7) Iraq's open rebellion against England should not be actively promoted until the moment is conducive of success. Meanwhile the will to resist must be kept alive.
(8) Establishment of a German delegation with the Italian Armistice Commission in Syria.
(9) Démarches with the French Government, in accord with the Italian Government, regarding the removal from Syria of officials and officers friendly to de Gaulle.

WOERMANN

*Source:* Documents on German Foreign Policy (DGFP) 1918–1945: Series D, Vol. 12, No. 133 (Washington, DC, 1962), 234–243.

## APPENDIX F

### Telegram from German Foreign Minister Joachim von Ribbentrop on Axis Policy and Arab Independence, 20 July 1941

Telegram

Special Train Westfalen, 20 July 1941   3:10 AM
Arrival,         20 July 1941   3:20 AM

*No. 684*

> To the Minister's Office Berlin
> For the Deputy State Secretary

I am asking that everyone in the Foreign Office who works on propaganda regarding the Arab Question be advised of the following instructions:

Our respect for French rule in Syria has forced us in the past to be restrained regarding the question of support for Arab demands for political freedom and independence. With the collapse of French resistance against England in Syria, the reason for this restraint no longer exists. Therefore, from this point on in the handling of propaganda in the Arab Question, I am instructing you to unequivocally support the Arab wish for the attainment of complete independence. This propaganda must be promoted under the rallying cry "The Axis is fighting for the Freedom of the Arabs." For this we will have to secure the appropriate Italian agreement.

Ribbentrop

*Source:* Zentrum Moderner Orient (ZMO), Berlin: 1.26 (5). Translated from the German by Francis R. Nicosia.

## Appendix G

### The High Commissioner of Spain in Morocco [Luis Orgaz] to His Excellency, the Minister of Foreign Affairs [Ramón Serrano Súñer], Madrid, 25 October 1941

Subject: Policy to follow related to Spanish Jews residing in the French Zone
From: The High Commissioner of Spain in Morocco—Diplomatic Secretariat
To: His Excellency the Minister of Foreign Affairs, Madrid

Dear Sir,

Since the implementation of the Jewish Statute in the neighboring [French] Protectorate, with the prohibitions and restrictions decreed against Jewish persons, activities, and interests, the Jews have begun to create, openly and in writing, tacitly and stealthily, an atmosphere of protest and hostility toward the conduct of the French against them, which they consider arbitrary, inspired by Nazi policy guidelines adopted by the Germans.

For this reason, the atmosphere in the neighboring Protectorate against the French and their intervening authorities has become unbearable, above all, because of the behavior of the Resident General of France in Morocco. Knowing the infinite resources the Jews can draw from to diminish or annul in part the effects of the Statute (e.g., sending messages and gifts to the Sultan and his relatives to gain favors), the French government of Morocco had to give the Statute a new interpretation, with the agreement of the French government, to whom General Noguès had to appeal, in an attempt to calm, in part, the concerns and worries of the Jews resident there.

Thus, new procedures were established for applying the Statute based on the distinction established between Moroccan and foreign naturalized Jews.

In the first case, although declarations must still be made about the family situation, civil status, and profession, Moroccan Jews now do not have to declare their possessions if the total value does not exceed fifty thousand francs. Furthermore, in cases when it does exceed that amount, all that is needed is a simple declaration of the general nature, condition, and overall value of real estate and personal property; and values of accounts and deposits in banks. Otherwise, Moroccans are also exempt from declaring personal property, belongings, and jewelry.

In the second case, that is when the Jews are considered foreigners, they have to submit to all the regulations stipulated in the Statute.

This varying treatment that the Jews are now subjected to, whether or not they are Moroccans, has caused them and their respective consular representatives in the neighboring Protectorate to protest vigorously, but until now the French have apparently only been ignored by the objections of the English who have threatened to adopt the same measures against the French subjects.

Regardless of the Statute, there are Jews who are American and English subjects and protégés (from the Capitulatory Regime), and a few Italians and Portuguese along with numerous Spaniards whose nationalities are not recognized by the French unless proven that the interested parties acquired their nationalities with the approval of the Sharifian Government, conforming to the stipulation in the Madrid Convention of 1880.

This is the case of the Jews born in Spain and their direct descendants who became naturalized in our country, having ignored such Sharifian authorization. This has caused a lot of confusion among our Consuls in the French Zone, who are hard-pressed to know how to handle the situation. On the one hand, according to the instructions they received from our Ministry, they have to defend them. On the other hand, they cannot oppose the French for applying the Jewish Statute to those who they consider foreigners, in which case the latter are humiliated and perhaps ultimately deprived of all their possessions, in an indirect way, as has been reported by our Consul General in Rabat.

What is there we can do about this very serious situation that the Spanish Jews find themselves in?

Would it not be a good opportunity to exploit this situation in the neighboring protectorate, which could be of such great political and economic importance for us, by taking advantage of the forced flight of Jewish capital and its influx to our Protectorate, where the Jews are seeking refuge, and where they would feel secure, at least for now?

Moreover, it should not be forgotten that as a consequence of the application of the often mentioned Statute, the Jews now in essence consider France their enemy and also the Muslims of the neighboring zone, it seems, are not happy with the restrictions that they are currently enduring.

In addition, we all know that the conduct of the Resident General toward our subjects and naturalized citizens is nothing new; it already was imposed by the policy of the Popular Front at the start of our last war of liberation. Before then, the French had never investigated nor questioned the validity of the documents that as Spaniards quite a few Jews and Muslims possess, having acquired our nationality for one of the aforementioned reasons.

The repercussions produced by this situation, as can also be seen in the attached copy of a secret report received from the French Zone, and the circumstance of the clearly defined position that the accredited foreign consular representatives in the French Zone have already taken on this subject, have obliged me to inform your excellency in detail about what is happening so that, if deemed opportune, Your Excellency can order that this important question be examined and definitively resolved by the department under your honorable charge, which will enable this High Commissariat, as well as for the consular representatives of the neighboring Protectorate, to know where they stand in a precise and certain manner.

May God be with you, Your Excellency,
Luis Orgaz

*Source:* United States Holocaust Memorial Museum (USHMM): Selected Records from the Archive of the Foreign Ministry of Spain, 1996.a.0329. Translated from the Spanish by Daniel Schroeter, drawn from a November 1996 rough translation by the late Elli Carroll, a survivor-volunteer at the USHMM.

# Appendix H

## Ambassador of France in Spain [François Piétri] to Mr. Admiral of the Fleet, Minister Secretary of State for Foreign Affairs [François Darlan], 15 December 1941

Embassy of France in Spain
Directorate of Political and Commercial Affairs

> Madrid, 15 December 1941.
> Communiqué to the Sub-Directorate for Europe
> Ambassador of France in Spain [François Piétri]
> to Mr. Admiral of the Fleet, Minister Secretary of State for Foreign Affairs [François Darlan]

As the Embassy has already indicated, Spain, in order to support its African ambitions, sometimes boosts Moroccan self-esteem, professing to be the country best qualified to understand the Islamic peoples and thus able to ensure their evolution in the direction of greater national freedom. Such undertakings are not without danger. The tolerance, even encouragement, in which certain notorious agitators are the beneficiaries in the Spanish zone, is a manifestation of this policy.

Even more interestingly, it has been observed that for a while Spain has directed similar propaganda at the Jewish population apparently with the purpose of securing economic collaboration. The weekly revue "Mundo," which the official [news] agency EFE controls, published in its 7 December issue, an article in which the essential ideas certainly reflect those of the government of Madrid and the High Commissioner of Tetuán.

This article purports to demonstrate: (1) that "Morocco did not wait for the recent French legislation, with regard to the Jews, to take the necessary measures; (2) that these measures were much more flexible in their application and more humane in the details."

On this point, the anonymous author contrasts the new attitude of France with "the Moroccan tradition that never considered the Jewish problem as having the character of racial struggle and always advocated the use of the Hebraic element of the population as a complement to its national activity per se, while keeping them in a system where they could cause no harm.

He added, with obvious satisfaction, that in Fez and Meknes, the Jews have sought the protection of the Makhzan authorities according to the ancient custom of the "Zouagha"[13] and that many others have fled to America as well as *to the Spanish zone, particularly to Tangier, bringing with them their capital and jewels*. He concludes with the tendentious observation, the only one in this article, which breaks, to some extent, with these terms: "The Jews are now the object of persecution and vexations by officials who had formerly supported and favored them. The Muslims show indifference to this human inconsistency, and feel no sympathy for these innovations. Their policy towards them had been clearer, more just, and definitely more sincere."

In fact, the policy of Spain, and especially the military administration, as defined by "Mundo," has always been to make use of Moroccan Jews, by necessity to flatter them without being dominated by them. Colonel Beigbeder[14] formerly said to one of my staff that during his command in Tetuán there had always been a particular Jewish secretary, placed on an equal footing with the Muslim secretary. He explained "this extreme tolerance" of Spain by invoking the multiplicity of African and Asiatic races that have contributed to forming the Spanish nation and, particularly, the contribution of Jewish blood, which, by conversions, has left deep ethnic traces in many regions of the Iberian Peninsula.

Nevertheless, the maneuvering that is evident in the article of "Mundo" should be monitored closely.

*Source:* USHMM: RG-43.006, Selected Records from the Ministère des Affaires Etrangères, 1939–1945. Translated from the French by Daniel Schroeter.

## Appendix I

### Letter from Amin al-Husayni and Raschid Ali al-Gailani to the German Foreign Minister Joachim von Ribbentrop, 28 April 1942

To the Reichminister of Foreign Affairs,
Herrn Joachim von Ribbentrop
Berlin                                            Rome, 28 April 1942

Herr Reichsminister!

In our conversations with you we have conveyed the trust of the Arab people in the Axis powers and in their high goals, and we have expressed the national goals of the Arab lands of the Near East that are currently suffering under English oppression. We have declared the readiness of the Arab people to join in the struggle against our common enemies until final victory.

We ask now the German government to declare its readiness to guarantee to the Arab lands currently suffering under British oppression all possible support in their struggle for liberation, to recognize the sovereignty and independence of the Arab lands of the Near East currently suffering under English oppression and their unity if the participating states so desire, as well as to agree to the elimination of the Jewish National Home in Palestine.

We are in agreement that the text and the content of this letter must be kept secret, until this can be changed by mutual agreement.

Please accept, Herr Reichsminister, the assurance of our highest regards.

Amin al-Husayni
Raschid Ali al-Gailani

*Source:* Gerhard Höpp, ed. *Mufti-Papiere: Briefe, Memoranden, Reden und Aufrufe Amin al-Husaynis aus dem Exil, 1940–1945.* Berlin, 2004. pp. 39–40. Translated from the German by Francis R. Nicosia.

# Appendix J

## Memorandum from Amin al-Husayni to an Unknown Recipient, 20 October 1943[15]

Memorandum                            Berlin, 20 October 1943
To: [?]

Muslims are the true friends of Germany, and in a German victory they see their own victory. For Germany, there are no truer friends than these four hundred million Muslims, who are recognized as brave fighters. Although victory is the first goal for this connection, we must bring together all of the elements of cooperation, and above all those that include victory as a necessity of life. We see that the allies are trying everything, despite their large populations, to pull other peoples into the struggle on their side. But we also see that Japan, the ally of Germany, is pursuing a policy of helping the peoples of East Asia, and are working together with countries such as China, Burma, and the Philippines both politically and militarily. Furthermore, Japan has issued a declaration for the liberation of India and favors a similar declaration for the liberation of the Islamic and Arab world. Japan supports the creation of an Indian army that will fight by its side.

The connections between Germany and the Arab-Islamic world are so clear that they need not be mentioned here. These connections are in a common struggle against common enemies (Jews, the English, and the Bolsheviks) for common goals. Since the beginning of the war, I have worked for real cooperation, and have endeavored to expand the basis of this cooperation, and I hope that the German government is also prepared, in a friendly manner, to pursue our common goals of victory for Germany and its allies, and the establishment of freedom for the Arab-Islamic peoples.

Therefore, I would like to remind Your Excellency of the following important points:

1) I consider the establishment of a German Office for Islamic-Arab Affairs to be very important, and I have already suggested this many times to the Ministry of Foreign Affairs. This Office must be directed by important civil servants who are familiar with the large areas that constitute the Islamic-Arab lands. They will then be able to work together on all questions with the Arab-Islamic

Missions, and advise on possible ways to expand cooperation. I wish to emphasize that leaving this matter to a very small number of clerks, even assuming their strong efforts, cannot be successful. The result is that many questions of cooperation remain unresolved. I had already made this suggestion when Ambassador Prüfer directed the Islamic-Arab department, and since his departure the need to establish such an Office has become more pressing. This Office could achieve much success with good and lasting cooperation, such as, for example, the creation of a large unit of Muslim and Arab volunteers in Europe for the struggle against the common enemy in Europe.

(1) It could work on the creation of an Islamic army consisting of Muslims from North Africa who are living in France, and Muslims from the Balkans and from Soviet Russia who would fight alongside German troops. Furthermore, it could win over more volunteers than before from among prisoners currently in custody if the right propagandists and speakers are sent to these prison camps and to the Muslin units in order to influence them for a more active cooperation with Germany.

(2) The best expression of the cooperation between Germany and the Arabs and Muslims would be a declaration from the German government about the future of Muslims in general and the Arab states and their freedom in particular, and that the Reich government recognizes the independence of the Arab lands and agrees to the abolition of the Jewish National Home in Palestine. We have always sought this declaration, and we still call for it, especially since Italy has surrendered.

We hope that the declaration for the independence of the Arab-Islamic states will be given as soon as possible, for such a declaration would also bring with it the suppression of enemy propaganda and effectively counter enemy efforts to pull one Arab state after another into the war against Germany.

(3) One could summon an Islamic-Arab Congress as the best proof for the cooperation of Arabs and Muslims with Germany. In this regard, official declarations from the Reich government would result in a very large echo.

(4) Propaganda from Germany to the Muslims in general, and to the Arabs in particular, requires better direction. We are ready for active cooperation in the improvement of the Islamic-Arab propaganda so that it achieves the best results for both sides.

(5) Moreover, I request that the responsible German authorities support me in the building of a secret radio station for Islamic-Arab propaganda. This station will work independently under my direction for our common purpose.

These are the important foundations and suggestions for the desired cooperation between us and the German government. I hope that they will be accepted and put into practice by the responsible German authorities so that no aspect of the cooperation will be diminished, and that all of our efforts on the side of the German government to achieve victory together, of which we are certain, are realized, if each performs its duty and if the relevant elements are given the opportunity to participate in the struggle.

*Source:* Gerhard Höpp, ed. *Mufti-Papiere: Briefe, Memoranden, Reden und Aufrufe Amin al-Husaynis aus dem Exil, 1940–1945.* Berlin, 2004. pp. 187–189. Translated from the German by Francis R. Nicosia.

## Appendix K

### Letter from Amin al-Husayni to German Foreign Minister Joachim von Ribbentrop, Regarding the Movement of Jews to Palestine, 25 July 1944

Berlin, 25 July 1944

To His Excellency
The Reich Minister for Foreign Affairs
*Berlin*

Excellency!

Earlier I drew the attention of Your Excellency to the ongoing attempts of the Jews to emigrate from Europe and to reach Palestine, and begged Your Excellency to undertake all necessary steps to prevent the Jews from emigrating. Also, with regard to the plan to exchange Egyptians living in Germany for Palestinian Germans, I sent a letter to Your Excellency on 5 June 1944 begging that Jews be excluded from this endeavor. However, I have learned that in spite of this, Jews left for Palestine on 2 July 1944, and I fear that additional transports of Jews from Germany and from France will be sent to Palestine and exchanged for Palestinian Germans.

On the part of the Germans, this exchange would encourage the Balkan states to expel their Jews to Palestine. Furthermore, this step would render the statement of Your Excellency of 2 November 1943 that "the destruction of the so-called Jewish National Home in Palestine is an unchangeable component of the policy of the Greater German Reich" unfathomable for Arabs and Muslims and would awaken in them deep feelings of disappointment.

Therefore, I beg Your Excellency to do what is necessary to prevent the emigration of Jews to Palestine, and thereby offer a new and practical example of the policy of an allied and friendly Germany to the Arab nation.

Permit me to extend to you my highest esteem.

Yours,
[Amin al-Husayni]

*Source:* Gerhard Höpp, ed. *Mufti-Papiere: Briefe, Memoranden, Reden und Aufrufe Amin al-Husaynis aus dem Exil, 1940–1945.* Berlin, 2004. p. 215. Translated from the German by Francis R. Nicosia.

# Notes

1. The author, Hüseyin Cahit Yalçın, was also the editor of the newspaper and a member of the parliament. He was close to the leadership of the ruling Republican People's Party. Thus, his opinions can be considered representative of Turkish official position on the "Jewish question." He was also known to subscribe to anti-German opinions. The reader should note in the editorial the reference to Turkey's admission of Jewish university professors, an incident Corry Guttstadt discusses in her chapter in this volume.
2. This may be related to Turkish government's intention to expel many Jewish families of Austrian origin back to their countries, which caused major consternation among the Jews of Turkey. Subsequently, the government changed its position. We thank Corry Guttstadt for this information.
3. Fritz Grobba, Middle East specialist, German diplomat, and ambassador to Iraq from 1932 to 1939.
4. Werner-Otto von Hentig, Middle East specialist, director of the Department of the Near East in the German Foreign Office from 1937 to 1939.
5. Ernst von Weizsäcker, State Secretary in the German Foreign Office from 1938 to 1943.
6. Ernst Woermann, Under State Secretary in the German Foreign Office from 1938 to 1943.
7. The Grand Mufti of Jerusalem, Haj Amin al-Husayni.
8. Admiral Wilhelm Canaris, chief of the Office of Foreign Intelligence and Counterintelligence of the German army (OKW) from 1935 to 1944.
9. Otto Abetz, representative of the German Foreign Office to the German military commander in France, and German ambassador to the French government in Vichy from 1940 to 1942.
10. Franz von Papen, German ambassador to Turkey from 1939 to 1944.
11. OKW (Oberkommando der Wehrmacht): High Command of the German Army.
12. Rashid Ali al-Gaylani, Iraqi Prime Minister 1940 to 1941, leader of a coup d'etat government in Iraq from 3 April to 3 June 1941.
13. A Berber tribe, probably referring to the custom of animal sacrifice when invoking the protection of the authorities.
14. Juan Beigbeder y Atienza was High Commissioner of the Spanish Protectorate from 1937 to 1939.
15. The recipient of this memorandum is unknown. Amin al-Husayni, the Mufti of Jerusalem in exile in Berlin beginning in November 1941, had previously sent similar policy memoranda and requests to Adolf Hitler, to Reich Minister for Foreign Affairs Joachim von Ribbentrop, and to the State Secretary in the Foreign Ministry, Ernst von Weizsäcker.

# INDEX

NOTE: page numbers with an *f* are figures

## A
Abd al-Karim, al-Khattabi, 183
'Abd al-Nasir, Jamal, 83
Abyssinia (Ethiopia), 93
academic exile (in Turkey), 57
Achcar, Gilbert, 4, 7, 28
'Aflaq, Mishal, 132
*afyal jahannam* [hell], 94
al-*Ahram*, 106, 107, 110. See also Egypt; formation of Hitler's government (January 30, 1933), 107–8; "The Policy of Force and Violence in the World," 223–25
*al-Ahrar*, 136
*Akbaba*, 52*f*, 53*f*
"Allegations on the Persecution of the Jews" (*maza'im idtihad al-yahud*), 111
Alliance Israélite Universelle (AIU), 158, 184
Allied invasion of France (1943), 14
*al-nizam al-Naz al-jadid* [new Nazi order], 92
Anders, Władysław, 165
Anders' Army, 165, 166*f*
Anglo-Egyptian Treaty of Alliance (1936), 79
Anglo-French Mandate states, 1922, 10*f*
Anglo-Iraqi Treaty of 1930, 157
Ankara, Turkey, 42. See also Turkey
anti-Arab arguments, 30
anti-Black racism, United States, 34, 35
anti-communism, 51, 52
anti-intellectualism, 51

anti-Jewish policies in Germany, 135
anti-Jewish riots (Turkey), 54–55
anti-Nazism, 77; cartoon in *Ruz al-Yusuf*, 78*f*; in Northern Iraq, 163
anti-Palestinian arguments, 30
anti-Semitism, 2, 6, 32; *Akbaba*, 52*f*, 53*f*; European, 23; French *colons* in Morocco, 193; Jews in Turkey, 49–54; *Millî İnkilâp*, 50, 51*f*; in Morocco, 179; new, 27; in Northern Iraq, 154; stereotypes, 54; Turkey's stance toward, 48–49
anti-Zionist conflicts, 120
anti-Zionist prejudice, 31
al 'Aqqad, 'Abbas Mahmud, 5, 81, 86–92
April 1, 1933 boycott, 109–12
Arab-German relations, 11
Arab-Israeli conflict, 24
Arab nationalism in Morocco, 179
Arab Nationalist Party (al-Hizb Al-Qawmi Al- 'Arabi), 141
Arab question, memorandum on the, 226–35
Arab renaissance movement *(al-nahda)*, 130
Arabs, 3; anti-Jewish hatred among, 29; Germany's policies toward, 8–15; helping Jews (in Northern Iraq), 155; reactions to Nazism (and the Holocaust), 23–41
*The Arabs and the Holocaust: The Arab- Israeli War of Narratives* (Achcar), 28
Arab world, unification of, 140–44
Arab-Zionist/Arab-Israeli conflict, 23
Aramaic, dialects of, 155
Arendt, Hannah, 32

## A

Armenian genocide, 29
Arslan, Shakib, 186, 187, 188
Aryan master race, 78, 92, 94
Ashkenasi, Abraham, 33
Ashkenazi Jews, 165, 167
Atay, Falih Rıfkı, 48, 49
Atilhan, Cevat Rıfat, 44, 50
Atsız, Nihal, 44
axiological neutrality, 27
Axis policy, 3, 8–15; Joachim von Ribbentrop telegram, 236
*Ayın Tarihi* (History of the month), 64
Al-Azhar University (Cairo, Egypt), 188
Azrieli, David, 168, 169

## B

Baghdad, Iraq, 153, 155
Balfour, Arthur James, 25
Balfour Declaration, 111
Barazani, Suleiman, 158
Barutçu, Faik A., 46
Bashkin, Orit, 6, 7
Basra, Iraq, 155
Beigbeder, Juan, 190, 191, 192
Beinin, Joel, 80
Belge, Burhan, 45
Benmaman, Jacob, 191, 204
Bennouna, Abdeselam, 187
Bentwich, Norman, 221
Berber *Dahir* of 1930, 182, 185, 186, 189
Bergen-Belsen, concentration camp at, 65
Berkes, Niyazi, 66
bestial power *[al-quwwa al-hayawaniyya]*, 90
Blum, Léon, 193
book burning of May 10, 1933, 112–13
Boran, Behice, 66
Boratav, Pertev, 66
Bourdieu, Pierre, 27
boycotts of Jews in Thrace, 54
British Eighth Army, 165
Bush, George W., 36

## C

Çakmak, Fevzi, 50
Cesaire, Aime, 32
Chaplin, Charlie, 48
Christianity: Gospel of Matthew, 28; in Lebanon, 134; in Syria, 137
Christians: in Northern Iraq, 155; in Turkey, 56
Churchill, Winston, 8, 9, 10, 90
Citizen, Speak Turkish *(Vatandaş Türkçe Konuş)*, 49
citizenship, revocation of (Jews in Turkey), 62
Cohen, Mark, 29
Cold War, 24
colonialism, 179; Middle East states post WWI, 105; philo-sephardism, 184
*Commissariat général aux questions juives* (CGQJ), 193
communism, 51, 52, 129
concentration camps, 43, 65
conspiracy theories, 51
coup *[inqilab]*, 109
Crémieux Decree of 1870, 193
Cumhuriyet Halk Partisi (Republican People's Party—CHP), 43
Cüppers, Martin, 3
Czechoslovakia, 46; break up of, 13; German conquest of, 47f

## D

*al-Dabbur,* 137
*dahir,* 200
Darlan, François, 240–41
Darwin, Charles, 131
Dawn *(Tan),* 53
de Lequerica, José Félix, 201
democracies, 86, 91
demon, Hitler portrayed as, 81
de-Nazification programs, 86
denial, Holocaust, 4, 29, 31
Denmark, German conquest of, 47f
deputy *(khalifa),* 182
*Der Angriff,* 43
de Rivera, Miguel Primo, 183

*Der Stürmer*, 50, 51*f*
dictated peace *(Diktat)*, 129
*Discourse on Colonialism* (Cesaire), 32
discrimination: against Muslims in Europe, 134; National Socialism, 137
District Governor *(qaim maqam)*, 159

## E

Effendi, Mula, 164
Egger, Vernon, 80
Egypt, 5, 8; April 1, 1933 boycott, 109–12; book burning in Germany of May 10, 1933, 112–13; Évian Conference (1938), 114–17; Fascism in, 80; formation of Hitler's first government (January 30, 1933), 107–8; Free Officers Movement (July 1952), 107; al-Hakim, Tawfiq, 82–86; intellectuals confronting Nazism, 77–104; international allies in, 128; Jewish Defense League, 110; July revolution (1952), 83; Kristallnacht, 117–20; negativity toward Hitler in Parliament, 81; Nuremberg Race Laws, 113; persecution of Jews in Germany (public discourse), 105–27; pro-Nazi groups in, 79; struggle for independence, 106; sympathies for Nazism, 79; al-Zayyat, Ahmad Hasan, 93–97; al 'Aqqad, 'Abbas Mahmud, 86–92
Egyptian Medical Association, 112
Einstein, Albert, 83, 136
elephants of hell *[afyal jahannam]*, 94
England, 46
eradication, Nazi policies of, 4
Ergene, Boğaç, 37
Ethiopia (Abyssinia), 93
ethnic cleansing, 24, 30
ethnocentrism, 28

Europe, 1; anti-Jewish hatred among Arabs, 29; anti-Semitism, 6, 23; discrimination against Muslims in, 134; Fascism in, 145; Nazism in, 145
European-controlled states of North Africa, 1914, 9*f*
European Islamic conference (1955), 134
Évian Conference (1938), 58, 114–17
*The Evolution of Nations [Nushu al-umam]*, 138
extremists *[mutatarrifin]*, 109

## F

Falangists, 190
*Farhud*, 157, 162, 164
Fascism, 2, 33, 44, 93, 129, 179; anti-Fascism, 77; crimes committed by leaders of, 84; in Egypt, 80; in Europe, 145; in Morocco, 185–92; in Northern Iraq, 154; in Turkey, 66
el Fassi, Allal, 186
Faysal II (King), 158
Fertile Crescent, 10, 12, 14
*Filastin*, 106, 107, 111, 114, 116. *See also* Palestine; formation of first Hitler's government (January 30, 1933), 107–8; "Immigration to the United States is Best!! The Supporters of Immigration to Palestine Are Few!!," 221–22
final solution, 1
forced labor service (Turkey), 55–57
France, 46; Allied invasion of (1943), 14; anti-Jewish legislation in Morocco, 196; colonialism, 179 (*See also* colonialism); Franco-Syrian Treaty of Independence, 141; Germany's victory over (1940), 13; mandate rule (Nazism in Lebanon and Syria), 128–52; Middle East state post–WWI, 105; in Morocco, 182; reactions to Nazism, 23

Franco, Francisco, 184, 201, 204
Franco-Syrian Treaty of Independence, 141
Free Officers Movement (July 1952), 107
French *colons* in Morocco, 193
French Republic, 129
Freud, Sigmund, 83

**G**

al-Gailani, Raschid Ali, 14, 47, 157, 161–163, 242
García Figueras, Tomás, 181, 190, 195
Gavish, Haya, 163
Gaza Strip, 36
Gazi (King), 160
genocide, 23. *See also* Holocaust; Armenian, 29; Turkey's response to, 42
Gensicke, Klaus, 3, 33
German Ministry of Education, 112
German National Socialism, 2, 4
German–Turkish Non-Aggression Pact (1941), 219–20
Germany, 1, 8; alliance with Italy, 45; anti-Jewish policies in, 135; anti-Semitism, 48 (*See also* anti-Semitism); collective identity of, 132; deportation of Turkish Jews, 63; formation of Hitler's first government (January 30, 1933), 107–8; history of, 87; Hitler's rise to power, 77; in Morocco, 182; persecution of Jews (1930s), 92; policies toward Arabs, 14; post–World War I, 13; ultimatum on repatriation, 63–64; victory over France (1940), 13; Weimar, 11
Gershoni, Israel, 5
Goebbels, Joseph, 111, 119
Gospel of Matthew, 28
Great Britain, 14; British bases in Iraq, 166; colonialism, 179 (*See also* colonialism); Évian Conference (1938), 114, 115; Jewish National Home, 9; Middle East state post–WWI, 105; in Morocco, 182; White Paper (1939), 106, 118
*The Great Dictator*, 48
Greco-Turkish War of 1919–1922, 45
Grossman, David, 34
Grynszpan, Herschel, 117, 118
Guttstadt, Corry, 6, 7
gypsies, 135

**H**

*Haaretz*, 108
Haim Barlas, 59
Haketíía dialect, 183
al-Hakim, Tawfiq, 5, 81, 82–86; attitude toward Nazi Germany, 82
Hakko, Vitali, 55
Halk Evleri (People's Houses), 54
Hashemite dynasty, 35
Hassan, Moises A., 204
Hassan Bank, 191
*Heimschaffung* (return them home), 63
Herf, Jeffrey, 2, 3
Herzbaum, Edward Henryk, 170, 170*f*, 171*f*, 172*f*
*Himari Qala Li* (My donkey told me), 84
Hispano-Moroccan War of 1859 and 1860, 184
History of the Month *(Ayın Tarihi)*, 64
*Hitlar fi al-Mizan* (Hitler in the balance), 87, 89, 91
Hitler, Adolf, 1, 8, 43; Allied invasion of France (1944), 14; appointment as Reich Chancellor, 131; April 1, 1933 anti-Jewish boycott, 109–12; death of father, 87, 88; education performance, 88; Egyptian intellectuals confronting, 77–104; as embodiment of Western imperialism, 78; as a false prophet, 85; formation of

## Index

first government (January 30, 1933), 107–8; *Mein Kampf,* 50, 84, 87, 91, 92, 94, 95, 112, 141; negativity toward in Egyptian Parliament, 81; personality of, 89; as pre-monotheistic (*"jahili"*) infidel, 85; psychological studies of, 89; reestablishing Germany's glory, 131; rise to power, 129; takeover of power, 135
Hitlerian Nazism *(al-naziyya al-Hitlariyya),* 93
*Hitler in the Balance* (Hitlar fi al-Mizan), 87, 89, 91
Hitlerism, 90
Hitler Youth, 133
al-Hizb Al-Qawmi Al-'Arabi (Arab Nationalist Party), 141
Holland, German conquest of, 47*f*
Holocaust, 1; Arab reactions to, 23–41; denial, 4, 29, 31; reaction in Turkey, 67; Turkish responses to, 42–76
Holocaust Studies, 30
human races, 138
*al-Huriyya,* 196
al-Husayni, Amin, 30, 242, 243–45, 246

### I

immigration: Évian Conference (1938), 114–17; Jews (into Turkey), 57; prevention of (Jews into Turkey), 64–65
"Immigration to the United States is Best!! The Supporters of Immigration to Palestine Are Few!!," 221–22
imperialism, 78, 79; Spanish in Morocco, 181–83
independence, struggle for, 106
India, 9
industrialization, 130
İnönü, İsmet, 44
*inqilab* [coup], 109
International Control Commission (ICC), 194, 195

Iran, 2, 166
Iraq, 2; Anglo-French Mandate states, 1922, 10*f*; Baghdad, 153, 155; Basra, 155; British bases in, 166; collaboration between Jews and Kurds, 156; Faysal II (King), 158; influence of Nazism in, 156; international allies in, 128; Jewish community in northern, 153–78; Jewish solidarity in, 165–72; Kirkurk, 161, 168; map of, 154*f*; Mosul, 158 (*See* Mosul, Iraq (Jewish community in)); Rashid 'Ali al-Gailani Revolt, 155–65
'Isa Daud 'Isa, 107
Islam: history of, 29; Jews under the protection of, 160
Islamic Republic of Iran, 25
Islamism, 105
Islamophobia, 35
Israel: Arab-Israeli conflict, 24; nuclear bomb, 26
Istanbul, Turkey, 54
Italian Fascism, 44, 129
Italy, German alliance with, 45

### J

*jahiliyya* (pre-Islamic era), 98
Japan, 34
Jewish Defense League, Egypt, 110
Jewish National Home, 9, 11, 12, 13, 14
Jewish Studies, 30
Jews, 1. *See also* anti-Semitism; allies in Northern Iraq, 159; anti-Jewish riots (Turkey), 54–55; April 1, 1933 anti-Jewish boycott in Germany, 109–12; Ashkenazi, 165; book burning of May 10, 1933, 112–13; collaboration with Kurds, 156; conscription of non-Muslims (in Turkey), 55–57; consequences of population policies (Turkey), 62–63; crimes committed against in Northern Iraq, 154; customs of in Northern Iraq, 167;

end of Jewish immigration to Palestine, 106; Évian Conference (1938), 114–17; fear of leaving home (in Northern Iraq), 158; formation of Hitler's first government (January 30, 1933), 107–8; German ultimatum on repatriation (Turkey), 63–64; Jewish solidarity in Northern Iraq, 165–72; killed during the *Farhud,* 164; Kristallnacht, 117–20; leaving Turkey, 50; in Morocco, 179–215; Mosul, Iraq (Jewish community in), 153–78; National Socialist policies toward, 135; Nazi policies of eradication, 4; in Northern Iraq, 155; number of Turkish Jews killed (World War II), 65; Nuremberg Race Laws, 113; in Palestine, 3; Nazi persecution of (Egypt, Palestine pubic discourse of), 105–27; persecution of (Germany and England's position on), 223–25; persecution of (Germany, 1930s), 92; German policies toward (Turkey, 1933–1945), 42–76; policies in Morocco, 194–205; prevention of immigration (Turkey), 64–65; under the protection of Islam, 160; Rashid 'Ali al-Gailani Revolt, 155–65; repatriation of (Spain), 203; reports of German hatred of, 136; revocation of citizenship (Turkey), 62; Spain's policies toward, 183; transit refugees, 59–61; in Turkey, 49–54; Turkish refugee policies, 57–59; Turkish Jews under Nazi persecution, 61–62
jokes, anti-Jewish, 137
July revolution (1952), 83
*jure sanguinis,* 199

## K
*Karikatür,* 47*f*
Kemalism, 129, 131
Kemalist project of Turkification, 49
*khalifa* (deputy), 182
Khuri, Raif, 5, 138, 144–45
Kirkurk, Iraq, 161, 168
Kristallnacht, 117–20
Küntzel, Matthias, 33
Kurds, 28, 31; collaboration with Jews, 156; helping Jews (in Northern Iraq), 155; in Northern Iraq, 155

## L
*La Bourse Egyptiene,* 118*f*
Lammen, Henri, 140
Larache, Morocco, 186, 187, 197
*La Syrie: Precis Historique* (Lammen), 140
League of Nations, 135
Lebanon, 7, 14, 36; Anglo-French Mandate states, 1922, 10*f*; Christianity in, 134; Khuri, Raif, 144–45; nationalism, 134–37; Nazism in, 128–52; rethinking society, 130–34
letters, Amin al-Husayni, 246
liberalism, 86; Turkish journalists, 44
Lockman, Zachary, 80
Lyautey, Hubert, 192

## M
*Ma'alim al-wa'i al-qawmi [Signposts of National Consciousness],* 144
*Majallat al-Mu'allimun w-al-Mu'allimat,* 132, 133
*makhzan,* 196, 199
Mallmann, Klaus-Michael, 3
Mandatory Palestine, 161
Mann, Thomas, 83
maps: Anglo-French Mandate states, 1922, 10*f*; European-controlled states of North Africa, 1914, 9*f*; Iraq, 154*f*; Morocco during World War II, 180*f*
Maronite Christians, 138
Marxism, 25
Maximalists, 33

*maza'im idtihad al-yahud* ("Allegations on the Persecution of the Jews"), 11
el Mehdi, Mulay El Hassan Ben, 204*f*
*Mein Kampf* (Hitler), 50, 84, 87, 91, 92, 94, 95, 112, 141
memorandums: on the Arab question, 226–35; al-Husayni, Amin, 242, 243–45
*Mendoubia*, 195
Metropolitan *Statut des Juifs*, 193
Middle East: pro-Nazism in, 79; states (colonialism post WWI), 105
Middle East and North Africa (MENA), 1, 2, 7, 8
*Millî İnkilâp*, 50, 51*f*
*Millî Şef*, 44
*Milliyet*, 43, 44
minorities, discrimination against in Europe, 134–37
modernization, end of Ottoman Empire and, 130
Morocco, 6, 179–215; Fascism in, 185–92; Jewish policy in, 194–205; Larache, 186, 187, 197; map of (during World War II), 180*f*; Muslims in, 206; nationalism in, 187; Nazism in, 185–92; philo-sephardism, 183–85; rejection of Nazism, 188; Spanish imperialism in, 181–83; Tetuan, 186, 187; Vichy period in, 192–94
Mosul, Iraq (Jewish community in), 153–78; British bombs in, 158
*al-Mudhik al-Mubki*, 137
Musa, Salama, 80
Muslim Racist Association, 192
Muslims, 1, 3, 9; discrimination against in Europe, 134; in Morocco, 179–215, 206; recruitment by Spanish Nationalists, 190; Spain's policies toward, 183; Varlık Vergisi (wealth tax), 55–57
Mussolini, Benito, 45, 84, 93
*mutatarrifin* [extremists], 109
My donkey told me *(Himari Qala Li)*, 84

**N**
Naciri, Mekki, 187, 189
Naciri, Mohamed, 187
Nafi, Basheer, 128
*al-nahda* (Arab renaissance movement), 130
Nahhas, Mustafa, 109*f*
al-Naqib, Ra'uf, 160
narratives: Arab-Israeli conflict, 24; Arab reactions to Nazism (and the Holocaust), 23–41
National Bloc, 134
nationalism, 67; growth of in Middle East, 185; Jews in Turkey, 49–54; Khuri, Raif, 144–45; Lebanon, 134–37; in Morocco, 179, 187; Pan-Arab, 156, 160, 163; Rabbath, Edmond, 140–44; revival of traditions, 133; Sa'ada, Antun, 132, 137–40; Syria, 134–37; Zurayq, Constantin, 140–44
National Reform Party, 189
national revolution (Turkey), 44
National Socialism, 44, 94–5, 129, 130, 131, 185; discrimination, 137; hatred of Jews, 53; against Jewish influences, 136; policies toward Jews, 135; *see also* Nazism
Nazi dictatorship *(al-tughyan al-nazi)*, 96
Nazi project, 78
Nazis, 2, 8. *See also* Germany; neutrality of Turkey, 45–48; policies of eradication, 4; Turkey's reaction to seizure of power, 43–44; Turkish Jews under Nazi persecution, 61–62
Nazism, 7, 94, 179; anti-Nazism, 77; anti-Semitism, 32; April 1, 1933 boycott, 109–12; Arab reactions to, 23–41; Egyptian intellectuals confronting, 77–104; in Europe, 145; formation of

first government (January 30, 1933), 107–8; influence of Nazism in, 156; Kristallnacht, 117–20; in Lebanon, 128–52; in Morocco, 185–92; rejection of (in Morocco), 188; in Syria, 128–52; *see also* National Socialism
*al-naziyya al-Hitlariyya* (Hitlerian Nazism), 93
neutrality of Turkey, 45–48
new anti-Semitism, 27
New Deal (United States), 129. *See also* Roosevelt, Franklin D.
New Historians, 34
new Nazi order [*al-nizam al-Naz al-jadid*], 92
News, Arabs and Kurds helping Jews (in Northern Iraq), 155
Nicosia, Francis, 37
noble message (Zurayq), 143
Noguès, Charles, 188, 189, 192, 194
Nordbruch, Götz, 5, 7
North Africa, 2, 12, 99; deportation to, 198; European-controlled states of, 1914, 9f; French colonialism in, 179
Northern Iraq, 153–78. *See also* Iraq; anti-Nazism in, 163; collaboration between Jews and Kurds, 156; crimes committed against Jews in, 154; customs of Jews in, 167; Jewish allies in, 159; Jewish solidarity in, 165–72; pro-Nazism in, 163; Rashid 'Ali al-Gailani Revolt, 155–65; World War II in, 153
Norway, German conquest of, 47f
Nuremberg Race Laws, 113
*Nushu al-umam [The Evolution of Nations]*, 138
al-Nusuli, Muhyi al Din, 133
al-Nusuli, Munir, 133

**O**

oil fields and refineries in Iraq, guarding, 165

Orgaz Yoldi, Luis, 197, 200, 204, 204f, 237–39
*The Origins of Totalitarianism* (Arendt), 32
Ottoman Empire, 8, 198; after breakup of, 129, 130
El Ouezzani, Brahim, 189, 191

**P**

Palestine, 5, 8; Anglo-French Mandate states, 1922, 10f; anti-Zionist conflicts, 120; April 1, 1933 anti-Jewish boycott in Germany, 109–12; book burning in Germany of May 10, 1933, 112–13; end of Jewish immigration to, 106; ethnic cleansing, 24; Évian Conference (1938), 114–17; formation of Hitler's first government (January 30, 1933), 107–8; "Immigration to the United States is Best!! The Supporters of Immigration to Palestine Are Few!!," 221–22; international allies in, 128; Jewish National Home, 11, 12, 13, 14; Jews in, 3; Kristallnacht, 117–20; liberation of, 26; Nuremberg Race Laws, 113; persecution of Jews (public discourse), 105–27; protest against Jewish immigration, 115; Arabs as second-class citizens, 26; struggle for independence, 106
Palestine Liberation Organization (PLO), 26
Palestine Symphony Orchestra, 109f
Pan-Arab nationalism, 156, 160, 163
Papen, Franz von, 48, 219–220
Party of Moroccan Unity, 189
Pasha, Kemalettin Sami, 43
Peel Commission (1937), 105, 114
People's Houses (Halk Evleri), 54
Perlzweig, Maurice, 205
Persian Gulf, 2
philo-sephardism, 179, 183–85, 198, 200

Piétri, François, 240–41
Poland, 13, 46; Anders' Army, 165, 166f; German attack on, 59; German conquest of, 47f; reactions to Nazism, 23; Warsaw Ghetto Uprising (1943), 168
policies: anti-Jewish policies in Germany, 135; consequences of population policies (Turkey), 62–63; Jewish policy in Morocco, 194–205; Jewish refugees (Turkey), 57–59; Joachim von Ribbentrop telegram (Axis policy), 236; toward Jews (Spain), 183; toward Jews (Turkey, 1933–1945), 42–76
"The Policy of Force and Violence in the World," 223–25
Polish II Corps (*see also* Anders Army), 165, 166f
pre-Islamic era *(jahiliyya)*, 98
prejudice, anti-Zionist, 31
pre-monotheistic (*"jahili"*) infidel, Hitler as, 85
pro-Nazism: in Egypt, 79; in Northern Iraq, 154, 163
property, Jewish in Morocco, 201
*The Protocols of the Elders of Zion*, 110
province *(wilayat)*, 159
psychological studies of Hitler, 89

## Q

*al-Qabas*, 131, 134
qaim maqam (District Governor), 159
Qajar Iran, 8
Qassab, Daniel, 164
*al-quwwa al-hayawaniyya* [bestial power], 90

## R

Rabbath, Edmond, 5, 132, 138, 140–44
Rashba, Shalom, 161
Rashid 'Ali al-Gailani Revolt, 155–65, 171; consequences of, 158
Rath, Ernst vom, 117

Ravensbrück, concentration camp at, 65
*Realpolitik,* 128
refugees: policies (Turkey), 57–59; transit, 59–61
Reich Chancellor (Hitler's appointment as), 131
The reign of darkness *(Sultan al-Zalam),* 82
repatriation, 63, 64; of Jews (Spain), 203
Republican People's Party (Cumhuriyet Halk Partisi—CHP), 43
Resolution 181, 35, 36
return them home *(Heimschaffung),* 63
Revisionist-Zionists, 33
Ribbentrop, Joachim von, 95, 96, 236, 242, 246, 247
Richter, Herbert, 191
riots, anti-Jewish (Turkey), 54–55
*al-Risala,* 82, 93. See also al-Zayyat, Ahmad Hasan
Rodinson, Maxime, 31
Rommel, Erwin, 99
Roosevelt, Franklin D., 114
Rosenberg, Alfred, 115
Rosengarten, Pinhas, 168
Rothschild, Walter, 25
al-Rumi, Ibrahim, 160
Russia, 9
*Ruz al-Yusuf,* 78f

## S

Sa'ada, Antun, 5, 132, 137–40
al-Sabunji, Mustafa, 160
al-Sadat, Anwar, 83
safe haven, Turkey as, 43
Said, Edward, 26
al-Sa'id, Nuri, 157
Samuel, Herbert, 221
Sarper, Selim, 48
Satan, Hitler portrayed as, 81
*al-saytara al-'alamiyya* [world domination], 90
Schellenberg, Walter, 56

## Index

schizophrenia, 89
Schroeter, Daniel, 6, 7
secularism in Syria, 137
*Selma*, 35
September 11, 2001, 36
Sha'ul, Habib Saleh, 160
Shoah, 24. *See also* Holocaust
Sidqi, Bakir, 157
*Signposts of National Consciousness [Ma'alim al-wa'i al-qawmi]*, 144
Simon, Reeva, 156
Six-Day War of June 1967, 26
Socialism, 44
Solel Boneh, 161
solidarity (Jews) in Northern Iraq, 165–72
Soviet Union, 14. *See also* Russia
Spain: imperialism in Morocco, 181–83; neutrality of during World War II, 195; philo-sephardism, 198, 200; policies towards Jews and Muslims, 183; repatriation of Jews, 203; rule of Morocco, 179, 181 (*See also* Morocco)
Spanish Civil War, 183
Spanish Nationalists, 190
Special Construction Unit–Palestine, 161
SS *Drottningholm*, 65
Stahmer, Friedrich, 10
*Stampa*, 116
stereotypes, anti-Semitism, 54
Sterling, Eleonore, 33
*Struma*, 60
*Sultan al-Zalam* (The reign of darkness), 82
Súñer, Ramón Serrano, 237–39
Syria, 2, 7, 14, 28; Anglo-French Mandate states, 1922, 10*f*; Christianity in, 137; Khuri, Raif, 144–45; nationalism, 134–37; Nazism in, 128–52; Rabbath, Edmond, 140–44; rethinking society, 130–34; Sa'ada, Antun, 137–40; secularism in, 137; Zurayq, Constantin, 140–44

Syrian Nationalist Party (Al-Hizb Al-Suri Al-Qawmi), 138, 139, 140. *See also* Sa'ada, Antun

## T

Tali, İbrahim, 54, 55
*Tan* (Dawn), 53
Tangier, 179, 182
*Tanin*, 66
Taqla, Bishara, 107
Taqla, Salim, 107
taxes, wealth (Varlık Vergisi), 55–57, 66
Tetuan, Morocco, 186, 187
"The Jewish Question" (Yalçın), 216–18
Third Reich, 11. *See also* Hitler, Adolf; Nazism; Morocco during, 179–215, 197
Thrace, Turkey, 54–55
Torrès, Abdelkhalek, 188, 191, 196, 197
transit refugees, 59–61
Transjordan, Anglo-French Mandate states, 1922, 10*f*
treaties: Anglo-Egyptian Treaty of Alliance (1936), 79; Anglo-Iraqi Treaty of (1930), 157; neutrality of Turkey, 46; Treaty of Madrid (1880), 199; Versailles Treaty (1919), 12, 45
*al-tughyan al-nazi* (Nazi dictatorship), 96
Turkey, 1, 7, 11; after World War II, 65–66; anti-Jewish riots, 54–55; Christians in, 56; conscription of non-Muslims, 55–57; consequences of population policies, 62–63; Fascism in, 66; German–Turkish Non-Aggression Pact (1941), 219–20; German ultimatum on repatriation, 63–64; Holocaust in, 67; Jewish refugee policies, 57–59; Jews in, 49–54; Kemalism, 129, 131; national revolution, 44; neutrality of, 12, 45–48; prevention of

Jewish immigration, 64–65; reactions to Nazi seizure of power, 43–44; responses to Holocaust, 42–76; revocation of citizenship (Jews), 62; as a safe haven, 43; stance toward anti-Semitism, 48–49; "The Jewish Question" (Yalçın), 216–18; transit refugees, 59–61; Turkish Jews under Nazi persecution, 61–62; in World War II, 42
Turkification, Kemalist project of, 49
Turkish Ministry of Foreign Affairs, 57
Tzemah, Sasson, 159

## U
*Ulus*, 43, 45
*umma* (people), 139
unification of the Arab World, 140–44
United Kingdom (UK), 35
United Nations, 24
United States, 14, 24; anti-Black racism, 34, 35; New Deal, 129
urbanization, 130

## V
Varlık Vergisi (wealth tax), 55–57, 66
*Vatan*, 48
*Vatandaş Türkçe Konuş* (Citizen, Speak Turkish), 49
Versailles Treaty (1919), 12, 45
Vichy period in Morocco, 192–94; Jewish policy in, 194–205; Vichy-Nazi collaboration, 194
*Volk*, 131, 132, 134, 156

## W
*Al-waʻi al-qawmi* (Zurayq), 141
war on terrorism, 36
Warsaw Ghetto Uprising (1943), 168

wealth tax (*Varlık Vergisi*), 55–57, 66
Weber, Max, 27
Webman, Esther, 7
Weimar Germany, 11
Weizmann, Chaim, 119
White Paper (1939), Great Britain, 106, 118
*wilayat* (province), 159
Winterton (Lord), 114
*Workers on the Nile: Nationalism, Communism, Islam, and the Egyptian Working Class 1882–1954* (Beinin/Lockman), 80
world domination *[al-saytara al-ʻalamiyya]*, 90
World Jewish Congress (WJC), 201, 203, 204, 205
World War I, 5, 25; Germany post, 13; Middle East states (colonialism), 105
World War II, 1, 3, 8, 11, 25; Egypt during, 80; Egyptian intellectuals confronting Nazism, 77–104; map of Iraq during, 154f; map of Morocco during, 180f; in Northern Iraq, 153; Spain (neutrality of during), 195; Spanish Jews during, 185; Turkey after, 65–66; Turkey in, 42
World Zionist Organization (WZO), 119

## Y
Yalçın, Hüseyin Cahit, 48, 53, 216–18
Yalman, Ahmet Emin, 48, 52
*Yeni Sabah*, 48, 53, 216–18
Yochai, Shimon Bar, 164
Youssef, Mohammed Ben, 193, 196

## Z
al-Zayyat, Ahmad Hasan, 5, 93–97
Zionism, 25, 26, 31, 105, 137
Zurayq, Constantin, 5, 138, 140–44, 142f

www.ingramcontent.com/pod-product-compliance
Lightning Source LLC
Chambersburg PA
CBHW070914030426
42336CB00014BA/2418